VERBAL BEHAVIOR AND POLITICS

DORIS A. GRABER

Verbal Behavior and Politics

UNIVERSITY OF ILLINOIS PRESS
Urbana   Chicago   London

LIBRARY OF CONGRESS CATALOGING IN PUBLICATION DATA

Graber, Doris Appel, 1923–
  Verbal behavior and politics.

  Bibliography: p.
  Includes index.
  1. Communication in politics. I. Title.
HM258.G677   301.5'92'0141   75-25830
ISBN 0–252–00262–8

To My Mother
AND THE MEMORY OF
My Father and Sister

Acknowledgments

Authors usually want to give credit to all those whose efforts or sacrifices bear directly on the writing of their books. In this spirit, I thank the members of my family for graciously accepting my long hours of communion with the typewriter which kept me from joining in their activities. I wish to express appreciation to the Graduate College of the University of Illinois at Chicago Circle; the appointment which it granted me as a post-doctoral fellow in 1971 released me from part of my regular teaching activities so that I could engage in research for this book. I am grateful for the expert secretarial services which I received from various members of the staff of the political science department at the University of Illinois at Chicago Circle. For able help with proofreading and indexing, thanks go to Jack and Susan Graber.

The manuscript has benefited in substance and style from the suggestions of those who read parts or the whole, including the readers whose identity is hidden behind the collective label of "consultants for the University of Illinois Press." The contributions of Paul J. Hiniker, my friend and colleague at UICC, have been particularly outstanding. He carefully critiqued each chapter, giving me the benefit of his keen insights into the processes of political communication and his profound knowledge of the scattered literature of the field. The footnotes throughout the text which acknowledge his suggestions are but a small indication of the stimulating impact which he has had on my thinking about this book.

John Donne reminded us many centuries ago that "No man is an Iland, intire of itselfe; every man is a peece of the Continent, a part of the maine." I gratefully acknowledge vast intellectual debts to my fellow scholars who have recorded, described, and analyzed man's verbal behavior throughout the ages. With them, I wish to share the credit which accrues to social scientists for their contributions to advancing human knowledge and welfare through the study of verbal processes. With them, I bear the burden of blame which falls on all of us for the shortcomings in our work, and for the many pressing questions which social scientists have not even begun to answer about the verbal symbols which dominate our lives.

Preface

Politics is by definition a social activity which involves interaction among people, through various forms of communication, to make and enforce rules for their social systems. Much of this communication takes the form of the spoken or written word. Though verbal interchange is indispensable to modern politics, the study of verbal behavior has been neglected. As Benjamin Whorf remarked decades ago, "Natural man, whether simpleton or scientist, knows no more of the linguistic forces that bear upon him than the savage knows of gravitational forces."[1]

Aside from the study of rhetoric by early Greek political philosophers, political science has neglected linguistic studies more than other social sciences. Psychologists and sociologists concentrate on verbal behavior in psycholinguistics and sociolinguistics. Philosophers deal with "ordinary language philosophies which make inferences about mind, morals, nature, and God from the use of language."[2] However, there is as yet no disciplinary subfield of political linguistics which focuses on verbal behavior as an important aspect of politics. Minor areas of concentration purport to teach how to use language effectively to formulate political viewpoints and to persuade, but they rarely delve beneath the practical aspects of political persuasion to underlying principles, and they do not cover verbal behavior in its broader aspects.

This book is intended to fill a small part of that knowledge gap. Through description and analysis of verbal behavior studies pertaining to politics, the book seeks to show how and why knowledge of verbal behavior is important to an understanding of politics. This endeavor calls for a discussion of the functions which verbal behavior performs in the conduct of politics, the manner in which those functions are performed under various circumstances, and the consequences of verbal behavior, including the inferences which may be drawn from it.[3]

1. Benjamin Lee Whorf, *Language, Thought and Reality: Selected Writings of Benjamin Lee Whorf*, ed. John B. Carroll (Cambridge: MIT Press, 1956), p. 251.

2. Vere C. Chappell, ed., *Ordinary Language* (Englewood Cliffs, N.J.: Prentice-Hall, 1964).

3. This book deals primarily with the part of language study known as pragmatics, rather than semantics and syntactics. Pragmatics "directs its attention to the investigation of language as human activity, not only its specific cognitive uses, but also its emotional, volitional, and other essentially private psychological effects. Pragmatics also concerns itself with the action, circumstances of the action, and outcomes which obtain on the occasion of linguistic use" (A. James Gregor, *An*

It also involves an examination of alternative verbalizations which were available but not used, and discussion of the differences which their use might have made. Such speculations are worth making because verbal behavior, more than most other behaviors, allows the speaker a wide array of choices for coping with the exigencies of a particular political task. If one knows the options from which the ultimate choice was made, one may gain important insights into the decision-making process.

At present, most verbal choices of substance and form of expression are made and judged intuitively. There is little theory to guide the speaker or analyst in predicting the probable consequences of alternative verbalizations. Choices and analyses would be improved if verbal theories and their applications were more fully developed. Development of pre-theories and theories is one of the most pressing tasks of studies dealing with verbal behavior.[4] This book therefore not only describes various forms of verbal behavior and their consequences; it also surveys theories and techniques which have been developed for the analysis and measurement of verbal behavior.

The first two chapters deal with the major political functions of verbal behavior, and with problems of constructing and deciphering political messages. The next two chapters contain a general discussion of various political effects of verbal formulations, also scrutinizing important inferences to be drawn from verbal data. Then comes a fifth chapter examining the philosophies underlying several techniques for measuring verbal outputs. It presents an overview, rather than detailed techniques, of various quantitative and qualitative methods now used to study verbal behavior.

Part Two analyzes verbal behavior in selected political settings; each has been chosen because of its intrinsic political importance and because it illustrates a different facet of verbal behavior. Chapter 6 shows how the mass media contribute to conceptual environments which shape the agenda for political life. Chapter 7 treats the verbal behavior of political elites, indicating why and how it is significant. Chapters 8 and 9 focus on verbal behavior as an interaction process in different types of political settings. The importance of settings is noted, and the political consequences of interactions in particular settings are deline-

Introduction to Metapolitics [New York: Free Press, 1971], p. 44). Semantics, by contrast, deals with the rules concerning the meaning of symbols, and syntactics with the rules governing the grammatical relation of words to each other.

4. See Harold D. Lasswell, Daniel Lerner, and Ithiel de Sola Pool, *The Comparative Study of Symbols* (Stanford: Stanford University Press, 1952), p. 64.

ated. Chapter 10 deals with an especially powerful tool of verbal behavior, the condensation symbol. This magical verbal concoction can activate a whole host of feelings, evaluations, and cognitions which may inspire political action. A brief epilogue presents a glance backward over the intellectual territory traveled thus far, and forward to the challenges which face students of verbal behavior in politics in their search for new substantive knowledge, theories, and research tools.

Obviously, many aspects of verbal behavior have not received extensive treatment in this book; others have been omitted altogether. In making decisions about inclusion or exclusion of topics, two questions were asked: How significant is this aspect for political outcomes? How well has it been covered by other studies? For example, the decision to exclude voice attributes from extended treatment was made on the grounds that they are relatively insignificant — much verbal output receives its widest exposure through indirect transmissions, written or paraphrased by the media. Furthermore, in gatherings of professional politicians, voice attributes are often consciously discounted or overshadowed by other considerations.

The decision to focus on the message aspects of verbal behavior rather than on senders, receivers, or message environment followed from the second criterion. Although the literature is not extensive, psychological, sociological, and rhetorical studies have given a great deal more prominence to message senders, their audiences, and their environments than to the nature of the message.[5] Certain types of verbal activity were adjudged to be so well covered by other studies that they could be omitted from this book. These include deliberate manipulative behavior, such as propaganda, political campaigning, public relations work, and the rhetorics developed for them.[6] Availability of other studies also led to the exclusion of analyses of communication networks which trace the flow of verbal communications and the consequences of verbal flow patterns.[7] The vast area of language varieties

5. Neglect of message studies pervades the social sciences. For instance, in "Ideology as a Cultural System," Clifford Geertz complains that ideologies are rarely studied as symbol systems. See David Apter, ed., *Ideology and Discontent* (New York: Free Press, 1964), pp. 47–76.

6. Brief studies with extensive bibliographies are: Terence H. Qualter, *Propaganda and Psychological Warfare* (New York: Random House, 1965); Dan Nimmo, *The Political Persuaders: The Techniques of Modern Election Campaigns* (Englewood Cliffs, N.J.: Prentice-Hall, 1970); and Stanley Kelley, Jr., *Professional Public Relations and Political Power* (Baltimore: Johns Hopkins University Press, 1966).

7. Examples are Karl W. Deutsch, *The Nerves of Government: Models of Politi-*

among and within nations as bases for national and subnational cohesion or conflict has likewise been omitted. Although this is not usually the primary focus of social science studies, it has been touched upon in a number of works which deal with the politics of individual countries, regions, or the international system.[8]

No broad theory of verbal behavior undergirds this book; ". . . there is as yet no good theory of symbolic communication by which to predict how given values, attitudes, or ideologies will be expressed in manifest symbols. . . . There is almost no theory of language which predicts the specific words one will emit in the course of expressing the contents of his thoughts."[9] However, there are a number of middle-level theories derived from analysis of specific verbal behavior situations. Many of these are borrowed partly or wholly from psychological and sociological research; theories which involve the prediction of future political behaviors from regularities of past verbal output are one example.[10] This volume uses such theories in its appraisal of various forms of verbal behavior and verbal behavior studies.[11] Nonetheless, far too many of the observations about verbal behavior presented in this book remain intellectual orphans in search of their theoretical parentage.

Fortunately, the prospects for rapid development of empirical studies and theories of verbal behavior seem brighter than ever. The new social science techniques which use computers and various mathematical operations have made it possible to study large samples of verbal output more systematically, making it easier to discern patterns of verbal behavior and test hypotheses on large bodies of data. One would hope that such additional studies will be neither "the piling up of sterile information . . . nor monuments of worship of whatever facts

cal Communication and Control (New York: Free Press, 1966) and Nationalism and Social Communication (New York: Wiley, 1953); also Richard R. Fagen, Politics and Communication (Boston: Little, Brown, 1966).

8. See for example Rupert Emerson, From Empire to Nation (Boston: Beacon Press, 1960). Charles F. Gallagher, "Language, Culture, and Ideology: The Arab World," in Kalman H. Silvert, Expectant Peoples: Nationalism and Development (New York: Vintage, 1967), pp. 199–231.

9. Lasswell, Lerner, and Pool, Comparative Study of Symbols, p. 49. The fact that this more than twenty-year-old observation is still valid documents the painfully slow growth of theory in this field.

10. Examples would be predictions of hostile international behavior, predictions of judicial decision-making, or predictions of leadership style. See pp. 70–72, 78–88, below.

11. Lasswell warns against confusing theories about ideas with theories about symbols (Comparative Study of Symbols, p. 65). Since this book deals with the significance of verbalization of ideas, as well as with the significance of symbols, it has been difficult to heed this warning consistently.

and practices exist." [12] Rather, with skill and luck, these data can help us discover how verbal behavior can bring about some of the political and social advances which we have captured in words and dreams, but which elude us in reality.

12. Karl W. Deutsch, "On Political Theory and Political Action," *American Political Science Review*, 65 (1971), 19.

Contents

PART ONE

General Characteristics of Verbal Behavior

1 Importance of Verbal Behavior in Politics

> Words *do* have a magical effect — but not in the way that the magicians supposed, and not on the objects they were trying to influence. Words are magical in the way they affect the minds of those who use them. "A mere matter of words," we say contemptuously, forgetting that words have power to mold men's thinking, to canalize their feeling, to direct their willing and acting. Conduct and character are largely determined by the nature of the words we currently use to discuss ourselves and the world around us.
> — Aldous Huxley, "Words and Their Meanings" [1]

What is verbal behavior in politics? Most simply, when A formulates a verbal message and transmits it to B, that is verbal behavior. A has both consciously and subconsciously selected ideas for verbalization. He has more or less deliberately chosen the words with which he wishes to express them. Word choice may have been guided by a desire to evoke predetermined cognitive, evaluative, and affective responses from the receivers of the message. When verbal behavior occurs in a context which has political significance, it falls within the purview of this study.

Since zillions of words are emitted each day in political settings, the focus of any book dealing with verbal behavior in politics must be selective. "Political significance" must be construed narrowly; here it refers to those verbal stimuli which contain political messages which reach or affect large numbers of people — the outputs of the mass media which convey information about politics; political messages by significant actors in politics, such as high-level public officials; or verbal transactions in an open or closed political meeting, such as a session of the UN General Assembly or a meeting of a congressional committee.

WORDS AND THE SOCIAL ORDER

"Verbal behavior in politics" conjures up visions of cigar-chomping politicians. Politics is obviously fueled by word power. Politicians use

1. In Max Black, ed., *The Importance of Language* (Englewood Cliffs, N.J.: Prentice-Hall, 1962), pp. 1–2.

words to report and exhort, to bargain and persuade, to threaten and conciliate.[2] They talk to their constituents, negotiate privately, argue in public assemblies and committees, and give orders which are to be transformed into further orders or physical action.

Politicians are judged in part by their verbal skills. Do they know what to say and what not to say at a particular time? Do they know how to couch their arguments in the most persuasive form? Great care is required in selecting the most effective verbal approaches for each occasion. If a politician wants public support for integrated schools, he must know the language cues which will appeal to his potential backers; talking about the justice of racial balance may be futile, but an appeal stressing economic arguments — saving money — may work. Knowing which appeal works best, and putting it in its most persuasive form, can bring success instead of failure. In fact, the choice of proper language is often such a delicate task that it is left to professionals in the art of verbal formulation.

However, verbal communications by politicians are only a small part of the verbal behavior which shapes politics. Even in the age of television, the bulk of the average person's politically relevant information comes from verbal descriptions of events, rather than from direct experience. We have "more contact with the phantasy of words than the reality of things."[3] Aside from pictures, verbal descriptions (primarily written ones) are the only source through which one can know events which have occurred in the past or visualize occurrences in the future. We view the world through semantically colored glasses. Kenneth Burke asks poignantly, ". . . can we bring ourselves to realize . . . just how overwhelmingly much of what we mean by 'reality' has been built up for us through nothing but our symbol system? Take away our books, what little do we know about history, biography, even something so 'down to earth' as the relative position of seas and continents? What is our 'reality' for today . . . but all this clutter of symbols about the past combined with whatever things we know mainly through maps, magazines, newspapers, and the like about the pres-

2. Lee C. McDonald, "Myth, Politics and Political Science," *Western Political Quarterly*, 22 (1969), 150.
3. Charles E. Osgood, "Conservative Words and Radical Sentences in the Semantics of International Politics," in Gilbert Abcarian and John W. Soule, eds., *Social Psychology and Political Behavior: Problems and Prospects* (Columbus, Ohio: Charles E. Merrill, 1971), p. 103. Also see the seventh chapter in Toshiki Izutsu, *Language and Magic* (Tokyo: Institute of Philological Studies, 1956), which discusses the power of words to evoke vicarious sense experiences.

ent? . . ." He concludes, "And however important to us is the tiny sliver of reality each of us has experienced first hand, the whole over-all 'picture' is but a construct of our symbol systems."[4]

Moreover, for much of our verbal reality there is no natural counter-part, or "empirical referent," as philosophers would phrase it. A moun-tain can be seen and experienced, even if it is not named; "law" or "communism" cannot.[5] An understanding of politics depends heavily on verbal symbols which lack extraverbal reality; when we characterize a country as a "democracy" or a "dictatorship," we are presenting ver-bal images of relationships which have no reality beyond the verbal. Language permits us to generalize, to organize wide ranges of experi-ence, and to communicate them to others without bringing about physi-cal and spatial changes in the world around us.

Sometimes natural counterparts for our words may have existed but disappeared beyond retrieval. Past experiences by which present po-litical action is informed and guided are prime examples. As Kenneth Boulding points out, ". . . nations are the creation of their historians — it is the image of the past that gives rise both to the image of the pres-ent and the future."[6] The word pictures of the past are then combined with verbally mediated knowledge of the present to fashion notions of current reality. We see the world primarily through the words of others. Once word-based images are formed, they serve as molds for the flow of subsequent direct and indirect experiences. As Walter Lipp-mann observed long ago, "For the most part we do not first see and then define, we define first and then see."[7] The outcome often is a mul-tiplicity of perceptions springing from the same stimulus.

". . . by naming and classifying the features of our environment, new modes of behavior as well as possibilities of manipulating that en-vironment, are brought into existence."[8] Facts as well as fictions be-

4. Kenneth Burke, *Language as Symbolic Action* (Berkeley: University of Cali-fornia Press, 1966), p. 5.

5. For a discussion of the ways in which language permits abstract reasoning, see O. Hobart Mowrer, "The Psychologist Looks at Language," in Arthur W. Staats, *Human Learning: Studies Extending Conditioning Principles to Complex Behavior* (New York: Holt, Rinehart and Winston, 1964), pp. 176ff.; and A. James Gregor, *An Introduction to Metapolitics* (New York: Free Press, 1971), pp. 53ff.

6. Kenneth Boulding, *The Image: Knowledge in Life and Society* (Ann Arbor: University of Michigan Press, 1956), p. 114.

7. Walter Lippmann, *Public Opinion* (New York: Free Press, 1965), p. 81.

8. Alfred R. Lindesmith and Anselm L. Strauss, *Social Psychology*, 3rd ed. (New York: Holt, Rinehart and Winston, 1968), p. 43. Also see J. G. A. Pocock, *Politics, Language and Time* (New York: Atheneum, 1971), pp. 3–41.

come the basis for social action. "This makes words creative in the truest sense. They create situations which are no longer there, or which have never existed, and people behave as if they were real." [9] In our day, many a new nation in search of a proud past to undergird a bright future has created verbal history from the flimsiest evidence. National leaders do so knowing full well that it is common practice to "recall and construct pasts 'useful' to the creation of legitimations for actions at present." [10]

Words not only provide man with a vision of the past, present, and future; they also are essential to create human societies. "Speech is the great medium through which human cooperation is brought about. It is the means by which the diverse activities of men are coordinated and correlated with each other for the attainment of common and reciprocal ends. Men do not speak simply to relieve their feelings or to air their views, but to awaken a response in their fellows and to influence their attitudes and acts." [11]

Society depends on the ability of the members of social groups to communicate with each other through mutually comprehensible symbols and to agree to social structures and actions. It normally rests on shared values derived from verbally mediated mental processes such as making comparisons, developing abstractions, and deducing consequences. Since communication of ideas, perceptions, and values among humans occurs primarily through written or spoken words, especially in complex societies, it is probably no exaggeration to claim that modern societies could not exist without mutually comprehensible ver-

9. Bernard Berelson and Gary F. Steiner, in *Human Behavior: An Inventory of Scientific Findings* (New York: Harcourt, Brace & World, 1964), pp. 664–665, point out that men find it hard to face the conflicts and threats of the real world. Language helps them to manipulate their environment, making it less threatening and more tolerable. "The word can be applied to fit occasions more easily than the occasion modified to fit the word. In the end, as well as in the beginning, is the word. . . . man lives not only with the reality that confronts him but with the reality he makes."

10. Hugh Dalziel Duncan, *Symbols in Society* (New York: Oxford University Press, 1968), p. 131.

11. Grace A. De Laguna, quoted in Julius Laffal, *Pathological and Normal Language* (New York: Atherton Press, 1965), p. 26. For a discussion of the psychological processes through which meaning is transferred or released, see Mowrer, "The Psychologist Looks at Language," pp. 176–191. Whether words transfer meaning to a listener or release meaning in him is immaterial to our discussion of the effects of verbal behavior.

bal symbols.[12] "Verbal statements are thus, in a very real sense, the connective tissue without which civilization is impossible."[13]

Words have the power to join society and lead to cooperation; conversely, they can also bring about conflict and antagonistic action. Conflict can arise through the transfer of shared meanings which makes it clear that interests or viewpoints differ, or as a result of misunderstandings of verbal messages which cloud the existence of shared interests and of means for reaching agreement. Some students of political conflict claim that most conflicts spring from diverging patterns of understanding, rather than from actual conflicts of interest.[14]

One can argue that ideas, rather than words, are powerful. But like an unfired bullet, an idea not couched in words and broadcast to a receptive audience has latent power only. Once dispatched, its impact may depend almost entirely on the verbal configuration selected for it. When we talk about the fearful power of words of men such as Adolf Hitler or Mao Tse-tung, we mean just that. Without verbalization in a rhetorically appealing manner, the ideas contained in their words would never have become a powerful political force. As the social anthropologist Bronislaw Malinowski states, "The great leaders such as Hitler or Mussolini have achieved their influence primarily by the power of speech, coupled with the power of action which is always given to those who know how to raise the prejudices and the passions of the mob."[15]

Most physical acts which affect the political life of society are likewise initiated by verbal behavior and strongly dependent on the meanings assigned to words.[16] The Japanese attack on Pearl Harbor was

12. "Social groupings depend on and are pervaded by complex symbolic processes" (quoted in Lindesmith and Strauss, *Social Psychology*, p. 7). "Social order cannot exist without integrative symbols" (quoted in Duncan, *Symbols in Society*, p. 131). " 'He talks like us' is equivalent to saying 'He is one of us' " (quoted in Edward Sapir, *Culture, Language and Personality: Selected Essays*, ed. David G. Mandelbaum [Berkeley: University of California Press, 1962], p. 17).

13. Ithiel de Sola Pool, *Symbols of Democracy* (Stanford: Stanford University Press, 1952), p. iv.

14. See, for example, Edmund Glenn, Robert H. Johnson, Paul R. Kimmel, and Bryant Wedge, "A Cognitive Interaction Model to Analyze Culture Conflict in International Relations," *Journal of Conflict Resolution*, 14 (1970), 41. For differential perceptions of the Vietnam war, see Ralph K. White, *Nobody Wanted War: Misperceptions in Vietnam and Other Wars* (Garden City, N.Y.: Doubleday, 1968).

15. Bronislaw Malinowski, "The Language of Magic," in Black, *The Importance of Language*, p. 79.

16. See Ch. 3.

planned verbally, with contingencies for specific strikes spelled out in words. How these words were interpreted and translated into commands for physical action determined the course of the initial phases of the war. Even attitudes which determine physical action are created primarily through verbal cues. The political candidate who is able to infuse a meeting of his campaign workers with a sense of pride and mission may find that they will double and triple their campaign activities. Many potentially physical actions never move beyond the verbal stage; for example, a presidential warning that troops will be used to man railroads in case of a threatened railroad strike may avert that strike without moving a single soldier or even issuing orders to move troops.[17]

POLITICAL ANALYSIS OF VERBAL BEHAVIOR

Despite its great political significance, man's verbal behavior has received relatively little attention in political analysis. Justification for the neglect rests on three lines of reasoning. First, there is the contention that verbal descriptions of reality are of secondary importance. It is reality which matters, rather than its verbal images, so political scientists ought to study situations and relationships as they actually exist, rather than analyzing their verbal shadows. Second, suggestions that the verbal output of political leaders and elites merits close attention are rejected on the grounds that politicians dissimulate, obfuscate, and lie. The third contention is that even if verbal output can indicate political reality and political perceptions, it is not the most reliable indicator. Perceptions, beliefs, or future actions cannot be reliably inferred from words; therefore other approaches to the study of politics are much more valuable.

Verbal versus Empirical Reality

All three contentions are vulnerable. To discount the importance of verbal pictures of reality is to ignore the fact that much of reality can be known only through such pictures. Like the average citizen, the social scientist finds it impossible to tap sources other than verbal images for much of the reality which he seeks to study. This may be

17. Robert C. North, "Research Pluralism and the International Elephant," *International Studies Quarterly*, 11 (1967), 407, envisions a mediated stimulus-response model of international relations in which either S or R may be wholly verbal.

an uncomfortable notion, "much like peering over the edge of things into an ultimate abyss"; it may explain why man, "the symbol-using animal . . . clings to a kind of naive verbal realism that refuses to realize the full extent of the role played by symbolicity in his notions of reality."[18] Even when facts and figures are available, such as a body count of casualties in a battle, it is important to know verbal descriptions. If newspaper reports of the battle understate the casualties and make defeat appear to be a victory, they may have significant political consequences, quite aside from the consequences springing from the actual loss of lives.

For most occurrences there may then be two or even three types of realities, each important in its own way. There is the reality of the objective world, if one concedes that things can exist even though they are not perceived. There is the reality of the symbolic world, where things exist as verbal and other symbols abstracted from reality, or developed imaginatively. And there is the reality of the perceptual world, where objective and symbolic stimuli are combined with the observer's previous perceptions into a new perceptual image. Each of these realities is important in its own way; and each can serve as a social stimulus. Phenomena which exist only in symbols or in the imagination can stimulate thought and action nonetheless, at least as much as their physically verifiable counterparts can.

Verbal images of reality deserve to be studied in their own right. Their concordance with objective reality and even with perceptual reality is merely one of many aspects involved with their study.[19] For instance, when anti-Castro Cubans with American support landed at the Bay of Pigs in the spring of 1961, it was important to know what had really occurred, but it was also important to know how the situation was verbally described by Fidel Castro and John F. Kennedy, and by the mass media in Cuba, the United States, and elsewhere. The verbal pictures of the affair painted in the UN Security Council may well have determined the actions of that body and the views of its members. The body was confronted with a series of conflicting versions

18. Burke, *Language as Symbolic Action*, p. 5.

19. Ernst Cassirer argues that it is the function of language to symbolize reality, rather than copy it. The copying stage is "mimetic"; there is meaning only in the analogical or symbolic stage. Philosophers such as Burke and Whitehead have pioneered in examining symbol structure as something other than reality representation. Quoted in Wilbur M. Urban, "Cassirer's Philosophy of Language," in Paul A. Schilpp, ed., *The Philosophy of Ernst Cassirer* (Evanston, Ill.: Library of Living Philosophers, 1949), VI, p. 416. Also see Ernst Cassirer, *Language and Myth* (New York: Harper, 1946), pp. 28–31.

of reality from which members constructed their own views of the situation. Each version, in turn, had a reality of its own in making some sort of impact on the assembled audience.[20]

Realization that the world of verbal images has a life of its own, quite aside from the situations it seeks to describe, has led to the concept of language as "Zwischenwelt." This concept means that the images of the world created through language constitute an intermediate world between man and reality.[21] The conformance of this verbal world with the world it seeks to picture varies; at best, every assertion about the "objective" world involves the distortion which springs from interpretation, mediated by perceptual and mental mechanisms in the speaker.[22] If the speaker is familiar with the object he describes, conformance of object and world reality tends to be closer than if the reality described is remote from the speaker's experience.

Linguists have also noted the difficulty of communicating cross-culturally about the real world when a verbal world of equivalent symbols is lacking. The meaning of "compromise" often cannot be conveyed because a number of languages lack a word for the concept; the nearest equivalent may be "surrender."[23] Likewise, when UN Security Council debates were analyzed in their various translations, it was evident that each language version was creating a different reality for its audience. The Russian version of one particular debate gave the impression that the speakers had expressed universal principles, while the English version seemed to indicate that principles applicable only to the case at hand were discussed, and the French version presented an intermediate impression. Idiosyncrasies of the respective languages, rather than poor translations, explained the differences in image; however, the consequence was that each audience was exposed to and responded to a different Zwischenwelt, with little chance of ever sharing the same image of reality.[24] The limits of each experiential world coincided with the limits of its language system.[25]

20. Also see Ole R. Holsti, "The Value of International Tension Measurement," *Journal of Conflict Resolution*, 7 (1963), 608.

21. See Laffal, *Pathological and Normal Language*, p. 10. Linguists who share this view include Leo Weisgerber, Walther von Wartburg, Rudolf Hallig, and Benjamin Lee Whorf.

22. Gregor, *Introduction to Metapolitics*, p. 54.

23. Lindesmith and Strauss, *Social Psychology*, p. 132.

24. Edmund S. Glenn, "Meaning and Behavior: Communication and Culture," *Journal of Communication*, 16 (1966), 249.

25. The controversy over the degree to which language is predetermined by its linguistic structure and by social factors of communication is well outlined by Hansfried Kellner, "On the Sociolinguistic Perspective of the Communicative Situ-

There are obvious intergenerational gaps in verbal worlds. Today "semantic maps of the real world become outmoded more and more quickly," [26] yet most older people change their existing maps only slowly, if at all, while the young internalize the new maps. Most political decisions are made by "men whose maps were outlined at least thirty years ago." As a result, "the language gap threatens to become an abyss." [27]

Lies, Half-Truths, and Other Reality Distortions

What about the second charge — that politicians' words are unworthy of attention because they are intended to hide reality and perceptions, rather than to disclose them? While it has a sound basis, this argument must not be carried to extremes. In the first place, many verbal images are close representations of the reality they depict, and of the speakers' perceptions. They are useful for analyzing existing situations and perceptions, and for predicting future events. "Indeed, the round of daily life is inextricably dependent upon the assumption that what people *say* they will do corresponds closely with what in fact they *will* do." [28] While hypocrisy is common, it remains the exception rather than the rule. Half-truths and lies are told more often than puritans would like, but far less often than most cynics claim. The reasons are simple: it is difficult to lie successfully in open, competitive societies, and it frequently does more harm than good. The politician whose pronouncements have been studied and exposed as a constant

ation," *Social Research*, 37 (1970), 72–73. For further readings, see the sources cited in Kellner's long footnote 5; also Harry Hoijer, ed., *Language in Culture* (Chicago: University of Chicago Press, 1954), pp. 47–81, 93–95, 225–239; Alfred G. Smith, ed., *Communication and Culture: Readings in the Codes of Human Interaction* (New York: Holt, Rinehart and Winston, 1966), pp. 490–491, 509; Benjamin Lee Whorf, *Language, Thought and Reality: Selected Writings of Benjamin Lee Whorf*, ed. John B. Carroll (Cambridge: MIT Press, 1956), pp. 26–34; Friedrich Waismann, "The Resources of Language," in Black, *The Importance of Language*, pp. 107–120, and Joyce O. Hertzler, *A Sociology of Language* (New York: Random House, 1965), pp. 119–130, which contains a brief history of the Sapir-Whorf hypothesis. Kellner rules out linguistic instrumentalism, which views language as merely a tool for expressing experiences and thoughts, and not as a shaper of these thoughts. He also rules out linguistic determinism (best expressed in the Sapir-Whorf hypothesis), which holds that experience of reality is largely dependent upon the language of a given society. I share Kellner's belief that "language functions so as to filter and mediate cognitive processes; it does not casually determine them" ("On the Sociolinguistic Perspective," p. 76). Language thus predisposes to certain interpretations, even though it does not make them inevitable.

26. Osgood, "Conservative Words and Radical Sentences," p. 103.
27. *Ibid.*
28. Pool, *Symbols of Democracy*, p. iv.

stream of half-truths and lies will find that he loses prestige and public appeal, as well as credibility.[29] In a moralistic society, he may also lose self-respect. The Watergate tragedy of the Nixon administration provides a sorry list of prominent political figures whose political efficacy vanished when exposure of lying destroyed their credibility.

When credibility is lacking, it becomes more difficult to communicate and negotiate, because the other side will not believe verbal pledges unless they are accompanied by supporting evidence. In international politics, for instance, many an armistice agreement or treaty has floundered because the credibility of the negotiators was questioned and nonverbal evidence of good faith was difficult to obtain.[30] In American electoral politics, when high political offices are at stake, a lie unmasked may seriously impair a candidate's chances for election. Given such dangers, blatant trifling with the truth remains the exception rather than the rule in many significant areas of political life. Half-truths and evasions are more common, but by no means ubiquitous.

However, there are numerous aspects of political discourse which represent exceptions to the general rule. Many of these involve occasions where communication has become heavily ritualized and the expected must be said, regardless of its truth or accuracy. It is well accepted, for instance, that American politicians competing for a variety of political offices will often make exaggerated or even false claims; such claims are considered part of the ritual of campaigning. Like other ritualistic expressions, campaign statements are not generally viewed by politicians and their public audiences as expressions to be judged by rigorous criteria of truth or falsity.[31] They therefore do

29. On the political importance of a reputation for truthfulness, see Robert Jervis, *The Logic of Images in International Relations* (Princeton: Princeton University Press, 1970), pp. 78–84; and Daniel Lerner, "Strategy of Truth: Symbol and Act in World Propaganda," in Lyman Bryson, Louis Finkelstein, R. M. MacIver, and Richard McKeon, eds., *Symbols and Values: An Initial Study* (New York: Harper, 1954), p. 372.

30. Deterrence theorists like Herman Kahn, *On Escalation: Metaphors and Scenarios* (New York: Praeger, 1965), pp. 57–58, and Thomas C. Schelling, *Arms and Influence* (New Haven: Yale University Press, 1966), ch. 2, point to the necessity of keeping one's word. However, in some cultures there is little expectation that the written word is binding. See the discussion of Oriental views of written commitments in Robert T. Oliver, *Leadership in 20th Century Asia: The Rhetorical Principles and Practice of the Leaders of China, Korea, and India from Sun Yat-sen to Jawaharlal Nehru* (University Park: Pennsylvania State University Press, 1966), pp. 38–40.

31. Ritual language has been called "noncognitive" because it is not primarily intended to convey information. See Gregor, *Introduction to Metapolitics*, pp. 316ff. It has also been called "phatic" communication, intended to convey moods or serve a social purpose, rather than conveying information.

relatively little harm to the politician's credibility, just as the myriad "white lies" of social politeness do not discredit the average person. The danger of credibility impairment arises only when lying and misrepresentation are extended into political interactions where veracity is traditionally expected. However, the boundary between the spheres where truth is expected and those where tampering is acceptable is fluid and uncertain, depending on cultural differences and the interrelationships among communicators. The verbal skirmishes about whether or not boundaries have been overstepped have been numerous and heated.[32]

In some areas of politics, verbal interaction may be conducted simultaneously on ritualistic and realistic levels. An interesting example is presented by the Vietnam peace negotiations in Paris, which extended from 1968 to 1973. Much ritualistic sparring took place in the formal sessions, with the parties taking the positions presumably expected by their constituencies. But the diplomatic negotiators did not take these verbal encounters too seriously — they met simultaneously in secret sessions to exchange their real views.

Much of what is often branded as lies represents truth from a different vantage point. Discrepancies in truth perceptions arise from the fact that reality perception varies with the perceiver's characteristics and experiences.[33] When politician X claims that a cut in taxes is sound economics, and politician Y deems this a deliberate lie, Y may be unable or unwilling to understand the rationale behind his opponent's claim. Analysis of the verbal justification offered by X might provide him with valuable clues about X's perceptions of the economic situation and the effects of the proposed tax cut.

Even if X's view of the economic situation is distorted and his appraisal of the consequences of a tax cut is totally at odds with actuality, his pronouncements should be known and studied for their political significance. If they reveal his perceptions, they may shed light on the political thinking and action which can be expected of him in the future.[34] His statements may win or lose him political followers at a

32. For a discussion of criteria on which expectations of truth or deception can be based, see Erving Goffman, *Strategic Interaction* (Philadelphia: University of Pennsylvania Press, 1970), pp. 126–132. For a perspective on differences in cultural requirements for truthfulness, see Paul J. Hiniker, "Chinese Reactions to Forced Compliance: Dissonance Reduction or National Character?" *Journal of Social Psychology*, 77 (1969), 174–175, and sources cited there.

33. Alden E. Lind, "Perceptions and Political Bargaining," APSA paper (1969), p. 20.

34. See Nazli Choucri, "The Perceptual Base of Non-Alignment," *Journal of Conflict Resolution*, 13 (1969), 57. Choucri calls verbalizations "objective in-

crucial time; they may influence economic conditions as people prepare for the eventuality of a tax cut. Regardless of truth or falsity, language has important effects on the cognitions, emotions, and evaluations of audiences who are exposed to a given communication.

In the international arena, frequent violations of alliances and treaty commitments are often cited as evidence that words deserve to be ignored because they often do not square with actions. But just as a high incidence of crime does not prove that a society's written laws are pointless, so the fact that many treaties are broken does not mean that they are meaningless. As long as most treaty provisions are observed most of the time, the ability of verbal commitments to shape action must be recognized.[35] In the case of international treaties, the widely accepted rule of *rebus sic stantibus* (as long as things remain as they are) gives legal sanction to many breaches of treaties. Nations can escape treaty obligations when conditions have changed so materially that performance endangers vital national interests. In domestic interactions, by contrast, such rules are rarely applied and most contractual commitments are deemed fully binding.

Even if statements are known to be deceptive or slanted, they are still worthy of study. For instance, if a politician falsely denies that he has promised to work for the retention of a military base, the denial may indicate that he has reasons for concealing his promise. Politically significant inferences may be possible. There may be inferences about the character of the deceiving politician, or inferences about his perception of the situation. As one team of investigators put it, "Language, however, deceives the deceiver; it cannot be stripped bare of its complex relation to a total flow of subjectivity. Within limits, it remains an unwilling 'mirror of the soul.'"[36]

Like differential perceptions, lies may be believed by politically sig-

dices of perceptual orientations." The extent to which verbal behavior is an index of mental life, or merely a conditioned response which reflects previous reinforcements in response to verbal output, remains a subject of debate among scholars. A brief review of the views of B. F. Skinner, Noam Chomsky, and other participants in the intellectual battle can be found in W. C. Holz and N. H. Azrin, "Conditioning Human Verbal Behavior," in Werner K. Honig, ed., *Operant Behavior: Areas of Research and Application* (New York: Appleton-Century-Crofts, 1966), pp. 790–826.

35. Lerner, "Strategy of Truth," pp. 371–372, points out that despite frequent discrepancies between words and actions, "between words and deeds there exists a systemic relationship, which enables us to understand either better if we examine both together. . . . Our words and deeds inform on each other."

36. Satish K. Arora and Harold D. Lasswell, *Political Communication: The Public Language of Political Elites in India and the United States* (New York: Holt, Rinehart and Winston, 1968), p. 2.

nificant audiences. In politics, most data on which pronouncements rest cannot be verified by listeners, so it is extremely difficult to separate truth from untruth. Riots have erupted on the basis of spurious information. When the false news spread that a hair of the prophet Muhammad had been defiled by Hindus, thousands of people died in orgies of revenge and counter-revenge in Pakistan in the early days of that nation. By the time the lie was unmasked, it was impossible to undo the political consequences, or even to destroy the belief that the defilement had taken place. Such events are graphic proof that the political analyst cannot afford to disregard verbal output, even when he knows it to be a perversion of the truth.

The Comparative Soundness of Verbal Data

The third contention, that verbal behavior is a less reliable indicator of political events than other data, also rests on shaky foundations. "Hard" nonverbal data share many of the weaknesses of "soft" verbal data. There are many opportunities to lie by manipulating physical objects and transactions; to use a crude example, in wartime it is common to construct dummy weapons to deceive enemies. During World War II, Volkswagens disguised as tanks and wooden floats dressed up as battleships fooled generals and caused them to alter their strategies. The flow of gold has been manipulated by governments and speculators to deceive market observers. At other times, what seemed like massive programs have turned out to be only token efforts. A much-touted public housing scheme may cease after the building of a few units; in retrospect, it may still be impossible to discover how predictions of the program's scope based on early activities could have been more accurate.___

Even when deception or the projection of future events is not involved, appraisal of hard data is still an onerous task. When troops are massed along a border, it may be extremely difficult for the observer to judge whether the mobilizing country intends to attack a neighbor, is engaged in a defensive maneuver, or is merely exercising its armed forces. When Premier Khrushchev put missiles into Cuba, it was impossible to tell whether the reason was a concern for Cuba's security or Russian security, endangered by a widening missile gap, or whether it was the first step in aggression against the United States, or a maneuver to force the dismantling of U.S. bases in Turkey. Likewise, flights by U.S. reconnaissance planes over East Germany could be interpreted as accidental straying, as a deliberate spying mission to discover Soviet capabilities, or as attempts to locate sites for future missile targets.[37] Taken by themselves, actions often do not suggest the guidelines by which they ought to be interpreted. These guidelines are supplied by the interpretation of contextual criteria, which generally involves verbalized processes such as abstracting, categorizing, and stating of alternative interpretations.[38]

These examples should make it clear that neither hard nor soft data are free from ambiguity. Most social science data need corroborating evidence to clarify their import within a given societal context.[39] This corroboration may spring from the observer's familiarity with the societal context, which permits him to put the data into proper perspective, or it may come from the use of other ancillary data which support the findings to which the initial data point. For instance, if an expressed threat of military attack is coupled with the massing of troops and with historical and military evidence that a country is willing and able to mount and sustain an attack, the combination of data may permit the conclusion that an attack is probable. The verbal data may have provided the initial clue which led to further data gathering, or they may have been the final piece of evidence in an analysis initially based on military intelligence about troop movements. It is true that "uncritical reliance upon analysis of 'symbol flow' to interpret attitudes, opinion, or probable future behavior is . . . an extraordinarily risky business," but "it would be equally dangerous to assume that verbal statements . . . have no scientific value in social analysis, prognosis, and prediction."[40]

IMPORTANT AREAS OF VERBAL BEHAVIOR

Thus far I have argued that man's verbal environment is politically significant and that verbal data deserve study by social scientists, despite some shortcomings which these data share with other social science data. Now to note the significance of the specific areas of verbal behavior analyzed in this book. Three major areas of verbal be-

37. Jeremy J. Stone, *Strategic Persuasion: Arms Limitations through Dialogue* (New York: Columbia University Press, 1967), p. 50.

38. Several relevant examples from the Quemoy crisis of 1958 are cited by Charles A. McClelland, "Action Structures and Communication in Two International Crises: Quemoy and Berlin," *Background*, 7 (1964) 207ff.

39. For more details, see Herbert C. Kelman, "Social-Psychological Approaches to the Study of International Relations: Definition of Scope," in Herbert Kelman, ed., *International Behavior* (New York: Holt, Rinehart and Winston 1965), p. 22.

40. Pool, *Symbols of Democracy*, pp. iii–iv.

havior hitherto neglected by scholars have been chosen to receive attention. The significance of one of these areas — study of the verbal environment in which societies operate — has already been delineated in the opening sections of this chapter. Most political experiences involve verbal activities and verbally created images of reality; more than any other kinds of stimuli, verbal stimuli shape political life.

The second area — study of individual political actors' perceptions and perceptual projections — has also been partly outlined. Few would question the importance of knowing how influential political actors perceive the political scene. Expressed perceptions may become blueprints for action for their subordinates and followers; moreover, most information about prospective actions, as well as the motivations and reasoning processes which underlie the activities of political actors, comes to us through their words. Actions and visual clues, such as observations of facial expressions which may register anger, disgust, fear, or joy, may provide additional information. But most information about the perceptions, reasoning, and actions of political figures comes from oral or written communications, either in the form of explicit statements or as language cues from which perceptions and reasoning processes can be inferred. Adolf Hitler's hectoring of the French during the signing of a peace treaty in World War II left no doubts that he viewed German-French interaction as a master-slave relationship, even though these terms were never explicitly mentioned.

As noted before, these verbal data are imperfect clues to perceptions. Political actors may intentionally or unintentionally misstate their perceptions and reasoning; inferences may be ambiguous or difficult to discern. Even careful attempts to overcome these difficulties by examining numerous expressions by the same actor and searching for corroborating evidence may reduce but not eliminate the problem. Despite these difficulties, verbal data still are the most prolific source of information about perceptions. Moreover, as already discussed, where information about perceptions is deliberately distorted and that fact can be established, the nature of the manipulation may yield important information about the political actors' motives and perceptions.

The third area — study of verbal interactions in political transactions — has been barely touched upon thus far. Verbal communication among political actors is an interactive process; the message sent by A becomes a stimulus for responses by B and C. Various aspects of the stimulus, many of them under the control of the sender, determine the nature of the responses. A one-word epithet ("liar!") hurled at a political opponent during a negotiating session may terminate potentially successful negotiations. What is said and how it is said thus are crucial forces which shape decision-making. Besides explaining political events, examination of verbal interaction processes may lead to the discovery of certain cause-effect regularities which may permit theory construction and formulation of rules for successful political interaction.

One major aspect of the study of verbal interactions in political bodies is the creation of verbal settings. Aside from its specific messages, verbal interchange may create a mood of anger or goodwill. It may, through the choice of agenda or initial arguments, set boundaries to what will and will not be discussed. It may identify and freeze individuals into positions which they might not have chosen had the pressures of verbal interaction been absent. A study of these types of consequences of verbal behavior forms an important part of the analysis of verbal interactions.

Numerous dimensions of verbal behavior are worthy of analysis for their political relevance. It is possible to distinguish an analysis of the subject matter of the verbal output — what was said — from an analysis of the manner of verbalization — how it was said. Each of these categories is investigated in this book. Consideration of subject matter will focus mainly on subject selection, sometimes called the "gate-keeping" function, rather than on a description of subject matter. What subjects are selected for presentation in various political contexts, what effects spring from this selection, and what inferences can be made from the selection process? For instance, if mass media dwell on candidates' personalities and neglect their stands on issues, how does this affect election results, and what does it tell us about the media's perception of their clientele? Basically, this is a question about categories of verbal settings, as distinguished from a question about the nature of a particular setting. In the approach to verbal behavior analysis chosen for this book, it is more useful to know that the mass media put heavy emphasis on the violent aspects of rioting in American cities in 1967 than to have records of the precise stories which were printed or broadcast.

In any situation, the things that could be said are almost without limit. What is actually said, and left unsaid, defines the situation in which political action takes place. Both of these aspects of choice will be examined. As Charles Osgood points out, "Things that are semantically coded are sharpened in thinking . . . things that are not so coded are blurred in thinking." The "antiquated semantics of power politics" keeps people thinking of mutual security pacts, alliances, and similar ventures; a semantic shift away from power politics might focus attention on more constructive policies instead.[41]

Various factors contribute to the manner of verbalization. The mode of transmission is significant; words come to us in various written forms, in face-to-face encounters in small or large groups, over the telephone, through a television set, or over the radio. Choice of words, sentence structure, and sequence of arguments are important.[42] In oral communication, voice quality and speech mannerisms shape the impact of verbal output. When visual cues are added, as in direct and film encounters, these in turn modify the impact of the verbal output. This book is only peripherally concerned with these and related matters of setting and style, concentrating instead on the logical and semantic processes reflected in the manner of presentation. How are ideas conceptualized and linked in verbal presentations? What does conceptualization tell us about the speaker's reasoning processes, knowledge, perceptions, and values? How does verbal conceptualization affect the verbal environment which is created? Traditionally, political studies have dealt with expressed demands, rather than with the reasoning matrix in which they were verbally embedded. This study seeks to redress that imbalance.

It is extremely important in understanding political perceptions and verbal environments to know what ideas are linked verbally, implying relationships in causes or effects. One can learn a great deal about political perceptions and likely policies and actions of a political leader and his constituents by knowing how he verbally justifies the creation of more jobs for blacks. The leader may ask for the jobs on moral grounds, claiming that society is obliged to aid every man in securing a job. Or he may appeal to a sense of guilt by alleging that white racism has deprived his constituents of the right to jobs which would otherwise have gone to them. He may appeal to theories of racial differences in abilities, finding blacks inherently less capable of obtaining and holding jobs and therefore in need of more help than others. Economic motivation is yet another pitch; the leader may argue that black unemployment hurts the entire community, and that therefore it is economically beneficial for everyone if more jobs are made

41. Osgood, "Conservative Words and Radical Sentences," p. 105.

42. The argument whether substance or mode is more significant has been joined by such eminent social scientists as Max Weber and Sigmund Freud. Weber, in discussing the Chinese literati, argued that mode determined substance and vice versa; Freud believed that the meaning of a dream must be judged as much by its form as by its content. Cited in Duncan, *Symbols in Society*, p. 5.

available for blacks. The manner in which the demand for jobs is phrased reveals significant differences in conceptualization of politics.

The choice of a particular conceptualization may be dictated by the politician's beliefs, or by strategy considerations. Often there is a series of strategy options, each satisfying a different combination of goals and needs. In the example of a plea for jobs, the optimum outcome may hinge on astute calculations about the type of conceptualization that will have the greatest appeal to groups who control available jobs. Regardless of the reasons which favor the choice of one conceptualization, rather than its alternatives, the choice itself may be crucial for the impact of the message and for the verbal environment that it creates.

In addition to paying attention to verbalization choices and linkage processes, this volume examines important political aspects of verbal settings. Chapters 8 and 9 analyze the impacts of different settings — a public political assembly and a smaller bargaining group — on verbal output. Chapter 7 deals primarily with verbal output that becomes significant because the message-senders are responsible for conducting major political affairs. Their political roles lend weight to their pronouncements, with important political consequences.

One may well conclude a chapter on the importance of verbal interaction with a brief reminder of the stress which many social scientists place on the importance of a well-functioning communications system. Political malfunctions within and among nations have been blamed on communication breakdowns. As Hugh Duncan asserts, albeit too categorically, "Disrelationships are not *reflected* in communication; they *originate* in communication. If we cannot create forms for communication over new problems or adjust traditional forms to new conditions of community life, there can be no consensus, and thus no common action." [43]

SUMMARY

The average citizen in a complex modern society perceives most of the world vicariously through the words of others. Verbal messages, rather than direct experiences, purport to tell him what is, has been, and will be. They supply him with reasons and values. They inform him about the attitudes and reasoning processes of political leaders, and about

43. *Ibid.*, p. 130. Also see the examples in George N. Gordon, *The Languages of Communication: A Logical and Psychological Examination* (New York: Hastings House, 1969), p. 33.

the consequences of verbal interactions among political leaders. Even when empirical reality can be directly observed and experienced, it must be analyzed and categorized in terms of verbally formed concepts, based on past experiences which have been largely acquired through words.

Verbal behavior makes human social existence possible and determines how human communities conduct their public business. The political fate of millions is decided by what political elites say or fail to say in the conduct of politics. The elites' verbalized descriptions of past, present, and future political reality, along with their explanation of causality and interrelationships, form the conceptual settings into which political contests are cast. These verbal settings influence political outcomes and may even predetermine them.

Study of verbal data has been impeded by charges that they are seriously flawed. However, the debilitating effects of these flaws have been exaggerated; most shortcomings of verbal data as tools for interpreting the political world and forecasting political behavior are common to all social science data and can be ameliorated through appropriate research techniques. The shortcomings should therefore be viewed as hurdles, rather than as insurmountable barriers to analysis of verbal behavior.

Even the frequency and import of problems such as outright lying and other forms of verbal distortion common in politics have often been overstated. Message-interpretation techniques help in assessing the probability of distortion and in unraveling truth from falsehood. Verbal behavior which does not correspond to phenomena in the empirical world, or to the communicator's actual perceptions or deeds, still provides important political information about the verbal Zwischenwelt. Moreover, lies, half-truths, and intentional or unintentional deceptions and misinformation often constitute powerful political stimuli which must be appraised quite aside from their correspondence to truth.

Since scholars of politics agree that effective verbal communications are essential for political success at all societal levels, it seems imperative to perfect and pursue verbal behavior analysis. In particular, attention needs to be focused on neglected areas such as the verbal environments in which societies operate, the substance and reasoning matrix of perceptions verbalized by political actors, and verbal interaction processes among political elites and their audiences.

2   Construction of Political Messages

> Human beings do not live in the objective world alone, nor alone in the world of social activity as ordinarily understood, but are very much at the mercy of the particular language which has become the medium of expression for their society. It is quite an illusion to imagine that one adjusts to reality essentially without the use of language and that language is merely an incidental means of solving specific problems of communication or reflection. The fact of the matter is that the "real world" is to a large extent unconsciously built up on the language habits of the group. . . . We see and hear and otherwise experience very largely as we do because the language habits of our community predispose certain choices of interpretation.
> — Edward Sapir [1]

The Building Blocks of Political Language

Referential Symbols

The nature and consequences of verbal behavior depend substantially on the manner in which messages are encoded into verbal form.[2] Therefore, some basic elements of message construction must be considered. Senders of verbal messages, political or other, have the option of couching their messages in referential or instrumental verbal symbols. When referential symbols are used, the message carries its meaning in a given cultural setting through the culturally shared denotation of the words in their syntactical context. The message means precisely what the words state. "The Democratic candidate won the gubernatorial election in Illinois in 1972" conveys a readily understood message to an average American audience. The syntax indicates the interrelation of the words in the sentence. The denotations — dictionary meanings — of such words as "Democratic," "candidate," "election,"

---

1. Edward Sapir, *Culture, Language and Personality: Selected Essays*, ed. David G. Mandelbaum (Berkeley: University of California Press, 1962), p. 69.

2. William J. Paisley, "Studying 'Style' as Deviation from Encoding Norms," in George Gerbner, ed., *The Analysis of Communication Content* (New York: John Wiley, 1969), p. 134, defines "encoding" as "any activity in which a person selects elements from a symbol system and arranges them in a pattern spread over time, or space, or both. Most but not all encoding behavior is further characterized by purposefulness in creating one pattern instead of others. . . ." A message, as used in this book, is a combination of verbal symbols intended to convey a distinct meaning to a selected audience.

and "1972" are readily understood because these words are "steeped in the historic experiences of concrete communities."[3] The audience does not have to read between the lines for meaning.

Slight changes in wording or message composition can lead to significant variations in impact, even when the substance of the message remains unchanged. For instance, in place of the initial message one could also say, "In 1972 the people of Illinois elected a Democratic governor," or "A Democrat was elected governor in 1972." The second message might give the impression that the emphasis was on the public's influence on the election, while the third amounts to a restatement of the first in a less formal and stilted way. This change would make the third message more readily comprehensible to unsophisticated audiences who might not bother to decipher the first. While impact would vary, cognitive aspects of the message would remain the same: the listener would be informed about the party which captured the governor's office in 1972.

It is not easy to compose unambiguous messages from referential symbols with clear denotations. The intricacies and ambiguities of language rank high among the manifold reasons for difficulty; ordinary language lacks the precision of mathematics, where given symbols have uniform meanings for all who know the language. An anecdote about the problems encountered by a group of linguists who tried to speak unambiguously to an English-Russian translating machine illustrates the point. The scientists gave what they deemed a perfectly clear referential message to the machine: "The spirit is willing but the flesh is weak." When the Russian "equivalent" was re-translated into English, it told the red-faced scientists: "The liquor is good but the meat is lousy."[4]

Instrumental Symbols

There are also many messages whose meaning is not manifest from analysis of the dictionary definitions of the words of the message. When this occurs, we speak of the use of "instrumental symbols." Besides carrying manifest meanings, these symbols are instrumental in evok-

3. Lee C. McDonald, "Myth, Politics and Political Science," *Western Political Quarterly*, 22 (1969), 150. The meanings of words depend solely on agreement or convention; see Hugh Dalziel Duncan, *Symbols in Society* (New York: Oxford University Press, 1968), p. 6.

4. Joyce O. Hertzler, *A Sociology of Language* (New York: Random House, 1965), pp. 112–115, 131. Also see J. R. Pierce, *Symbols, Signals and Noise* (New York: Harper and Row, 1961).

ing latent meanings — meanings not readily apparent from the denotations of the words. Understanding of the latent meanings usually requires insight into the context in which the verbalization has occurred. For instance, an assertion that the party which captures the votes for president in a given state always captures the governorship as well may be parried by the statement, "A Democrat was elected governor in Illinois in 1972." In that case, the latent meaning of the statement would be that the assertion about congruence of presidential and gubernatorial votes is wrong. A party split occurred in Illinois in 1972. The message would be instrumental in conveying this meaning, and its manifest meaning would tend to be ignored.

Besides carrying latent substantive information, an instrumental statement (and many referential statements as well) may also carry attitudinal messages which are not apparent from the wording. A terse message may indicate anger or other stress; a prolix message may convey a desire to please or inability to condense a situation to its essentials. Tone, pitch, timbre, inflection, and rhythm in oral messages may convey a variety of meanings, sometimes almost independently of the verbal symbols which are used. ". . . in a speech, an orator tries to convince as much by the warmth, attractiveness, and persuasiveness of his voice as by the purely logical implications of what he states."[5] Abraham Moles calls this esthetic information, to be distinguished from the semantic information conveyed by messages. Semantic information, carried by the words of the message, has a structured, articulable, presumably universal logic. Esthetic information, by contrast, is transmitted by the message as a whole and may carry meanings apparent only to people who share a common repertoire of knowledge.[6]

Social relationships can also be expressed instrumentally. Speeches by autocratic politicians tend to interpose psychological distance between the speaker and the audience; the terms of self-reference become impersonal, lengthy, and stereotyped. By contrast, democratic speakers usually reach out for common speech and person-to-person phrases.[7] In fact, linguist Edward Sapir makes the sweeping claim that "one of the really important functions of language is to be constantly declaring to society the psychological place held by all of its members."[8]

5. Abraham Moles, *Information Theory and Esthetic Perception* (Urbana: University of Illinois Press, 1968), p. 133. Also see Toshiki Izutsu, *Language and Magic* (Tokyo: Institute of Philological Studies, 1956), pp. 42–43.

6. Moles, *Information Theory*, pp. 129–133.

7. Harold D. Lasswell, Nathan Leites et al., eds., *The Language of Politics: Studies in Quantitative Semantics* (Cambridge: MIT Press, 1965), p. 123.

8. Sapir, *Culture, Language and Personality*, p. 20.

Instrumental meanings are even more difficult to convey than referential meanings because of the amorphous nature of instrumental symbols. The referential symbol, by definition, operates as a stimulus of known dimensions; one needs only to calculate its effect on a given audience. The instrumental symbol is composed of dimensions whose meanings must be determined through estimating or observing contextual clues. Since meanings are implicit, rather than explicit, they are more likely to be missed or misconstrued by the target audience.[9]

To use a few simple examples: it may have been quite obvious to American diplomats in 1970 that President Nixon's effusive praise of the hospitality of the city of Madrid was a veiled indication of his unwillingness to praise dictator Franco. But did this message get across to the Spaniards? Did it get across to those Americans who criticized the President for visiting a dictatorial country and broadcasting such glowing reports? When a diplomat declines to accept an official invitation, claiming prior commitments or illness, is he stating the facts, or is he merely using a polite form for declining an invitation he does not care to accept?

Since instrumental messages present great encoding and decoding difficulties, why are they used? The examples just given supply one answer. A polite guest does not openly insult his actual or prospective host; as long as President Nixon considered it advisable to visit Spain, he had to consort with Franco. Yet political necessities at home and in other anti-Spanish countries demanded that he should indicate that his visit was not an approval of the dictator's policy. Hence the instrumental approach was used to convey this message. It left no trail of tell-tale words of slight for the leader; in fact, such intentions might readily be denied. At the same time, the message was understood perfectly by at least some of the audiences to whom it was addressed. Diplomatic language fills the same need, maintaining "an atmosphere of calm, while enabling statesmen to convey serious warnings to each other which will not be misunderstood."[10]

Tactical considerations may make the instrumental approach advisable or inevitable.[11] A country seeking American foreign aid funds may

9. "Target audience" is used to distinguish the audience for which a message is intended from unintended audiences who may happen to be listening. If these unintended audiences differ in nature from the target audience, their understanding of the message and reaction to it may be quite different.

10. Harold Nicolson, *Diplomacy*, 3rd ed. (London: Oxford University Press, 1963), p. 123.

11. For additional details, see Robert Jervis, *The Logic of Images in International Relations* (Princeton: Princeton University Press, 1970), ch. 5.

not wish to make an outright request, fearing that an outright request might be resented and might be embarrassing to its own government if refused. It may therefore prefer to discuss American foreign aid policy in other countries, in hopes that this will convey its own desire for aid to a perceptive American official. To use another example, in 1949 the Soviet Union indicated its willingness to lift the Berlin blockade through a series of subtle hints and omissions scattered through seemingly routine Communist pronouncements.[12] The hints were so subtle that the United States decided to seek confirmation of Russian intentions through informal conversations between ambassadors Philip Jessup and Jacob Malik at the United Nations.

Connotational Meanings

Most messages have connotational meanings in addition to their referential and instrumental meanings. They carry a variety of specific cognitive, emotional, and evaluative meanings for different audiences and individuals. Since these meanings are far less universally shared, they often are not well known or understood; indeed, they tend to vary not only from audience to audience, but also from time to time and place to place. The denotation or referential meaning is what the message means generally to audiences when symbols have a standardized empirical referent. The connotation is what the message means to a particular individual or group at the particular time when it is placed into the context of personal or group predispositions and experiences. Symbols are related to other symbols in a manner which is unique for each audience and not necessarily inherent in the denotation of the message. Connotations determine personal reactions to the concepts elicited by the message.

Connotational meanings may be elicited by the message-sender intentionally, or he may be aware of their existence, or they may be stimulated to his pleasant or unpleasant surprise.[13] The message that "in 1972 the people of Illinois elected a Democratic governor" may elicit a triumphant feeling from Democrats and a feeling of defeat from Republicans. Stress on "the people of Illinois" may cause audiences to think that the speaker demands their acceptance of the result because it was sanctioned by the populace. Omission of this phrase

12. W. Phillips Davison, *The Berlin Blockade: A Study of Cold War Politics* (Princeton: Princeton University Press, 1958), pp. 254ff.

13. John G. Pocock, "Political Ideas as Historical Events," APSA paper (1970), p. 9.

might imply to some audiences that the election was rigged and did not carry popular approval.

A political message-sender must be aware of the connotations which messages are apt to carry to the audiences which he addresses, if he wishes to control the meanings which his messages convey. He may deliberately phrase messages so that their connotations (especially emotional and evaluative ones) help him in influencing people. Stirring up of emotions is particularly important because it arouses the receiver to respond to a stimulus.[14] However, as with instrumental symbols, effective control over connotative meanings is difficult because these meanings are not standardized and are readily influenced by a wide variety of conditions which may be difficult to foresee or manipulate.

ENCODING PROBLEMS

Given available verbal tools, how does the sender of a political message create verbal stimuli to elicit desired responses? He does this by combining words in particular patterns which transform them into mediators of meanings. The first problem is to decide what meanings to convey or avoid, then to select from a plentiful but by no means unlimited vocabulary words and word combinations which referentially or instrumentally carry the desired cognitive, affective, and evaluative meanings. These words are couched in one of a variety of possible grammatical constructions, again with the same goal in mind. When possible, the effect of the message is monitored. The feedback can be used to analyze message deficiencies and rectify them through supplementary messages or in future encodings.

Sometimes silence rather than verbal expression is chosen to convey meaning. Omission of certain statements from official communiqués may indicate that the subject matter is not important, or that it is deemed too controversial for a verbal formulation. Societally unacceptable reasons for action may be shrouded in silence, providing mute testimony to social conventions. For instance, during the Mideast debates in the United Nations, religious differences have seldom been cited as cause for conflict, despite wide agreement that religious antipathies created much friction.[15] On the other hand, silence in the face of controversial governmental action may be construed by officials and public audiences as a tacit endorsement of these actions.

14. Izutsu, *Language and Magic*, p. 85.
15. Doris A. Graber, "Conflict Images: An Assessment of the Middle East Debates in the United Nations," *Journal of Politics*, 32 (1970), 366.

During the initial selection process, the verbal and physical context in which the encoding takes place becomes the paramount criterion for choice. One gropes for the right formulation for the particular time, place, situation, and audience, aware of the warning that "no word ever has exactly the same meaning twice." "Any utterance is made in a multi-dimensional matrix . . . [it does not] exist in only one dimension at a time"; rather, "learned memories, symbols, habits, operating preferences, and facilities" of the audience affect its meaning.[16] One dreads the adverse consequences that may ensue when a message encoded as a private communication or for a specific audience is disclosed to an unintended group of receivers.

Appraisal of Audience Characteristics

Appraisal of the characteristics of the intended audience is particularly important in message formulation. Four audience factors are generally considered in message encoding.[17] The first is response hierarchy, which refers to the fact that certain stimulus words are apt to elicit certain responses. The message-sender asks himself what the likely response of his audience will be, based on past experience. In the process, he must be aware of the fact that many of the most common words in social usage have diverse and often clashing interpretations. "Democracy" has substantially different meanings for people raised in the Soviet Union and those raised in the United States; even within each country different population groups define the essential elements of democracy in a wide variety of ways, some of them contradictory. When gauging likely responses, the message-sender must be aware of these different definitions of the concept.

The second factor relates to the needs, conflicts, and psychic structures of members of the audience. A suspicious audience may require verbal stimuli quite different from those used with an audience that trusts the message-sender and the actors involved in the situation under discussion. An appeal for racial integration would have to be couched in different phrases when addressed to members of a white suprema-

16. The quotes are from S. I. Hayakawa, *Language in Thought and Action* (New York: Harcourt, Brace, 1949), p. 60; Pocock, "Political Ideas," p. 8; and Karl W. Deutsch, *Nationalism and Social Communication* (New York: Wiley, 1953), p. 70.

17. Julius Laffal, *Pathological and Normal Language* (New York: Atherton Press, 1965), p. 12. Also see Erving Goffman, *Strategic Interaction* (Philadelphia: University of Pennsylvania Press, 1970), pp. 12–13, which discusses the process of empathizing with an audience as part of the encoding procedures.

cist audience or a group of black nationalist leaders. A street mob requires different verbiage than a United Nations assembly.

The third factor relates to the credibility demands of the particular situation; what can be said credibly will be heavily determined by what has occurred and how it has been described. An example from World War II comes to mind: American military propagandists, trying to get German troops to defect, described the treatment which military prisoners were likely to receive. Appeals included a description of a typical breakfast menu in prisons camp as consisting of fruit, eggs, and coffee, along with bread and cereal. Even though the description was accurate, it was not credible to Germans, given their experience with stringent food rationing during the war and their indoctrination about the rigors of prison life. To make it credible, a far more general analysis of food supplies available to Americans would have been required; even then it might have been impossible to convey the message.

Finally, intrusive coincidental stimuli must be considered; these are the physical conditions under which a message is received which may intrude themselves on the response. During the domestic crisis precipitated by the assassination of President Kennedy, certain foreign affairs messages reaching President Johnson were interpreted as heralding possible foreign attacks on the United States. Had these messages arrived at a calmer time, it is unlikely that they would have been interpreted in such a calamitous vein. Often the coincidence of a number of messages must be considered in anticipating their meaning. A strongly worded request for Israel to abstain from raids in Egypt on penalty of adverse action may be interpreted as threatening a complete withdrawal of American help, if it comes in the context of many messages of annoyance; it may be interpreted merely as a mild warning if it comes in the context of many messages of support.

When making these calculations about the anticipated impact of a message, a sender uses what has been called "psychologics" or "feel" in addition to logic.[18] Through psychologics, most readily learned through sharing a socio-political culture, a sender knows intuitively what types of words, structures, and appeals work best with various audiences at particular times. Vice-President Agnew knew how to talk to middle-brow America, even though he was off the mark for the liberal-intellectual fringe. When Agnew talked about "effete intellectual snobs," middle-brow Americans were grateful because he had formu-

18. George N. Gordon, *The Languages of Communication: A Logical and Psychological Examination* (New York: Hastings House, 1969), p. 32.

lated widespread yet vaguely articulated political sentiments into a crisp, appealing phrase.

Different cultures, subcultures, and social classes have unique linguistic codes, key values, and symbols. Use of the appropriate language style, values, and symbols stirs a strong response. "The key symbols make people feel at home. They are the most reliable basis for public appeals. They accomplish the public's psychological softening or hardening before the real purpose of the message is achieved." [19] Key symbols representing idealized values such as equality, national honor, or self-determination are especially useful in preparing audiences psychologically for a message. However, knowledge of other values is also important.

A few studies of government attempts to elicit public action have tried to determine which appeals work best. A study of Kate Smith's highly successful bond drive during World War II showed that it was devoid of any economic self-interest appeals. By contrast, analysis of family planning communications has shown that appeals to the financial self-interest of the couple and their children work well in modernized societies; in traditional societies, appeals to the general welfare of the local society have the greatest effect.[20] Failure to use appropriate appeals for particular audiences may cause failure to communicate effectively.

The fact that certain types of verbalizations are preferable does not mean that only one form of encoding is suitable. Different combinations of verbal stimuli can elicit equally desirable responses; the personality of the message-sender as he interacts with his audience and his adeptness in handling various language styles may determine which style and form is best for him. [21] Winston Churchill could attain his political goals by inspiring his audiences with ringing phrases. Franklin Roosevelt could achieve his purposes by soothing audiences with

19. Quote from Karin Dovring, *Road of Propaganda: The Semantics of Biased Communications* (New York: Philosophical Library, 1959), p. 45. On class-based linguistic codes, see Claus Mueller, *The Politics of Communication: A Study in the Political Sociology of Language, Socialization, and Legitimation* (New York: Oxford University Press, 1973), pp. 14–15, 45–85.

20. Elihu Katz, Michael Gurevitch, Brenda Danet, and Tsiyona Peled, "Petitions and Prayers: A Method for the Content Analysis of Persuasive Appeals," *Social Forces*, 47 (1969), 459–460.

21. For relevant laboratory experiments involving verbal conditioning, see Joel Greenspoon, "Verbal Conditioning and Clinical Psychology," in Arthur R. Bachrach, ed., *Experimental Foundations of Clinical Psychology* (New York: Basic Books, 1962), pp. 518–549.

reassuring fireside chats. Adolf Hitler could arouse Germans by using blustering verbal assaults. And Huey Long could charm American Southerners with colloquial pronunciation and deliberate flouting of grammatical rules.

Encoding Failures

Sometimes the encoding process is unsuccessful: the message which seems appropriate or clear to the sender is inept or unclear to the receiver. It may be encumbered with unexpected connotations or intrusive coincidences which distort the intended meaning, despite the most expert care in composing the message. For example, even when various alliance agreements among Western powers are carefully drafted, the partners have often disagreed about their meanings. The formal SEATO commitments were variously construed by Pakistan, the United States, Britain, and France. The United States argued that the agreement's terms bound SEATO members to join in common defense against Chinese aggression; however, Pakistan contended that the alliance was not directed against China, and Britain and France also differed with the United States about the meaning of the agreement in relation to military action in Vietnam. The NATO alliance has likewise been plagued by problems of finding language which clearly elicits concerted action among the parties.[22]

An intentional lack of clarity permits alliance partners to adopt different interpretations; such language is used when conclusion of a formal agreement seems desirable but it is impossible, for a variety of reasons, to concur on all essential points. The need for external support by diverse interest groups also may make ambiguity advisable. However, in many instances ambiguity is unintentional and undesirable. It reflects encoding difficulties, pure and simple. Whether or not a particular case involves deliberate or unintended ambiguity is often argued heatedly by politicians and scholars.

Misunderstood messages can be particularly tragic when political units are in conflict. Many of the shocking excesses in military activities, including civilian massacres, can be partly blamed on faulty en-

22. Franklin B. Weinstein, "The Concept of Commitment in International Relations, *Journal of Conflict Resolution*, 13 (1969), 39–40. The difficulties of encoding and decoding international agreements are discussed fully in Myres S. McDougal, Harold D. Lasswell, and James C. Miller, *The Interpretation of Agreements and World Public Order* (New Haven: Yale University Press, 1967), esp. pp. 3–35. For a discussion of conceptual frameworks of interpretation, see David N. Weisstub, "Conceptual Foundations of the Interpretation of Agreements," *World Politics*, 22 (1970), 255–268.

coding of messages which were subsequently misconstrued. Conflict may continue or escalate because the parties are unable to communicate settlement terms to each other, even though a basis for agreement may exist. In fact, some conflict theorists believe that most conflicts arise from misunderstood messages and persist because verbal messages fail to convey their intended meanings.[23]

One disastrous communication failure occurred during the Korean War. The United States wanted to inform its Chinese antagonists that it intended to unite Korea by force, but that it did not intend to spread the conflict beyond Korea's borders. On several occasions this message, encoded in a variety of verbal forms, was presented to the United Nations in hopes that Chinese leaders would be pacified by this information. But the verbal efforts in the United Nations came to naught. Apparently neither the denotative nor the instrumental meanings transmitted by the messages had been made sufficiently clear, credible, or politically acceptable to convince the Chinese leaders that their protective strike across the Yalu River was unnecessary.[24]

Similarly, in World War I, peace feelers by the Central Powers and by the Allies may never have been made clear enough to be grasped by the opposing side. In World War II the bombing of Hiroshima and Nagasaki might have been prevented if the Japanese response to the Potsdam Declaration had been worded less ambiguously. Instead, the doubtful meaning of a single word, "Mokusatsu," led to an excessively hostile interpretation of the message.[25] The Japanese news agency Domei reported that the Japanese cabinet would "ignore" the Potsdam surrender ultimatum. The cabinet's intended meaning had been that it would "withhold comment," pending its decision. "The proper implication was that the Cabinet had the matter under serious positive consideration."[26]

23. For strong arguments along these lines, see Erich Fromm, *May Man Prevail?* (Garden City, N.Y.: Doubleday, 1961).

24. Allen S. Whiting, *China Crosses the Yalu: The Decision to Enter the Korean War* (New York: Macmillan, 1960), p. 168. Whiting concludes: "Inadequate communication, or the failure to convey accurately to an opponent one's intentions and one's responses, played a pivotal role between August and October 1950 in precipitating war between CPV and U.N. forces." For a discussion of the use of indexes to lend credibility to verbal signs, see Jervis, *Logic of Images*, pp. 26–65, 174–224.

25. George H. Quester, "Wars Prolonged by Misunderstood Signals," *Annals of the American Academy of Political and Social Science*, 392 (1970), 33. Also see Paul Kecskemeti, *Strategic Surrender* (Palo Alto: Stanford University Press, 1958), pp. 155–211.

26. Weston LaBarre, *The Human Animal* (Chicago: University of Chicago Press, 1954), p. 171.

DECODING PROBLEMS

Decoding is subject to the same difficulties as encoding. First, the audience must determine the denotational, instrumental, and connotational meanings of the message, given the particular time, place, and situation. We have already noted the difficulty of finding the right words and phrases to convey intended meanings, even when the sender knows his audience well. Encoding skills must be matched by equally complex and sophisticated decoding skills. Even the best-formulated message may miss its mark if the decoding audience is unable to decipher it accurately.

Decoding of instrumental messages can be particularly difficult, for cues can be missed or misconstrued; furthermore, an audience may ascribe instrumental meanings to a message which was not intended to carry such meanings. A statement about the poor performance of a public official who happens to be a woman or a member of a minority group may be misinterpreted as a deliberate attack on women or minorities. When political messages touch upon politically sensitive matters, such as sex and race discrimination, it may be almost impossible to convey criticisms without risking faulty decoding.

The decoding process becomes both more and less complicated when it involves face-to-face communication.[27] It is less complicated because errors in decoding can often be readily detected by the message-sender through instantaneous feedback. The encoder can then alter his encoding strategies on the spot. In non-face-to-face situations, the process is much slower and more cumbersome; if no feedback is transmitted, misunderstanding may pass unnoticed. When feedback is delayed and decisions have been made on the basis of the original decoding, revisions may be difficult.

The increased complexity in decoding arises from the fact that additional verbal and nonverbal cues must be interpreted in face-to-face communication. How does one interpret a political foe's categorical statement that he will fight for leadership of the party until the bitter end, when his voice is tremulous and his face shows signs of grave strain? What meaning does one place on a statement when the speaker's tone seems mocking, or when knowing glances are exchanged among fellow negotiators as they present their terms to the opposing team? Additional cues which may contradict the ordinary meanings of the words uttered make decoding all the more difficult.

27. In "indirect" communication, messages pass from the initial sender through one or more intermediary encoders before finally reaching the receiver.

If encoding is not tailored to the background and experience of the audience, decoding may be impossible. If a primitive village receives a message stating that a water source should be abandoned because it has a very high bacterial count, the villagers are not very likely to understand or react properly. Even if they learn the meaning of "bacterial count," they are not likely to understand its implications. The message must be recoded into simple terminology of sickness and health, reinforced by reference to the forces which the villagers deem responsible for these matters.

Poor decoding performance is sometimes linked to preconceived appraisals of the situations described in messages. During World War II, American intelligence officials cracked the Japanese Code and intercepted messages which dealt with the forthcoming attack on Pearl Harbor; however, the content of these messages was misinterpreted because top-ranking officials had already determined that the Japanese were not going to attack the United States. Such " 'self-evident' beliefs are involved in most intelligence failures." [28]

A combination of clumsy encoding and unperceptive or deliberately distorted decoding is often responsible for damaging interpretations of brief messages or phrases. Many a politician has come to grief because a poorly phrased remark has been decoded by his enemies in a politically harmful manner. Often during campaigns "a slip of the tongue is inflated to a major statement of policy." [29] During his pre-presidential campaign in 1968, Governor Romney of Michigan told reporters that he had been "brainwashed" by military and diplomatic officials after a visit to Vietnam. He meant to imply that the wealth of information received from officials in Vietnam had persuaded him that their appraisal of the Vietnam situation was correct. After he returned home and reflected further, he had second thoughts about the validity of the official views presented to him. The media and a media-aroused public pounced on the word "brainwashed." It was argued, with devastating results, that a man who could be so easily "brainwashed" was not presidential timber. [30]

Vice-presidential candidate Agnew alienated many voters with his 1968 remark that if one had seen one slum, one had seen them all. This was interpreted as a callous slighting of problems of urban poverty and

28. Joseph de Rivera, *The Psychological Dimensions of Foreign Policy* (Columbus, Ohio: Charles E. Merrill, 1968), pp. 21, 55.

29. Theodore White, *The Making of the President, 1968* (New York: Atheneum, 1969), p. 66.

30. *Ibid.*, pp. 67–69.

deprivation, even though a friendly listener might have decoded the phrase to mean that slum conditions were equally appalling in all urban slums. Senator Goldwater's feeble showing in the presidential election of 1964 was attributed partly to inept verbalizing. His statement that extremism in defense of liberty was no vice (by which he meant to convey the idea that he would zealously guard public liberties) was decoded as the announcement of witch hunts directed against Leftist opponents.

Several possible meanings have been readily apparent in the examples used so far. In many other instances meanings may be obscure. Decoding then involves the additional task of calculating the message-sender's intent on the basis of the message's denotations and possible connotations. In making these calculations, a broad variety of factors needs to be examined. ". . . words and sentences are interpreted with the aid of information about their context, i.e., about the speaker's past history, his motives, his present circumstances, and his relation to the audience. . . ."[31] For instance, statements of the leaders of North Vietnam and the National Liberation Front were examined with great care during the Vietnam war "for new or possibly even hidden meaning. Hanoi's use of the words 'unconditional' or 'definitive' or 'permanent' in their latest reference to a halt in our bombing is noted with great interest by both government and lay analysts. A change from 'could' to 'will' in a speech by the North Vietnamese Foreign Minister was the occasion for memoranda, editorials, orations and intense diplomatic activity."[32] Messages from sources which are important to the audience for a variety of reasons are likely to receive the most careful consideration.

Principles of message interpretation vary widely when message context is in flux. Joseph de Rivera tells the story of the American ambassador to Korea who had requested additional military supplies.[33] His request was turned down because the military situation seemed stable to higher authorities. Shortly thereafter the ambassador sent a message warning of the imminent outbreak of hostilities in Korea. In the context

31. Duncan MacRae, Jr., "Scientific Communication, Ethical Argument, and Public Policy," *American Political Science Review*, 65 (1971), 40. For a general discussion of decoding problems and emphasis on testing message validity, see Lee Thayer, *Communication and Communication Systems in Organization, Management and Interpersonal Relations* (Homewood, Ill.: Richard D. Irwin, 1968), pp. 166–171.

32. Chester L. Cooper, "The Complexities of Negotiation," *Foreign Affairs*, 46 (1967), 458.

33. de Rivera, *Psychological Dimensions*, p. 19.

of his previous request, it was discounted as a high-pressure maneuver to induce his superiors to heed future requests for military supplies. Without the context created by the initial message, the second message would probably have been given much more serious attention. The incident illustrates that message receivers tend to decode messages in ways that require minimal reorganization of their perceptual matrices. Once assumptions have been made about an actor's motivation, subsequent interpretations of his messages are usually cast into the assumed conceptual molds.

If audiences and message-senders know each other intimately, meanings already shared may not be made explicit. Statements may be brief, even cryptic and unintelligible to outsiders. In peer groups, communication often proceeds with minimal verbalization because the members are attuned to each other's verbal cues. In the broader political arena, people who share ideologies find encoding and decoding of messages infinitely easier than do people whose basic world-views differ. In fact, ideologies have been likened to language in that they furnish a set of basic perceptual categories which prescribe the meanings to be assigned to words. People who share ideologies thus share a political language.

When message-senders anticipate decoding difficulties among their audiences due to a lack of common experiences, they often limit themselves to standard forms and clichés, hoping that the audience knows the accepted meaning of such language or can readily discover it. In certain types of social relations where accurate understanding is extremely important, stylized languages have been created; in scientific interchange, diplomacy, and law, stylized messages and signs have clearly specified meanings which eliminate idiosyncratic interpretations. An "unfriendly act" in diplomacy is much more than a slight, for the country which labels another's actions as "unfriendly" is likely to resort to hostile countermeasures. Likewise, if a country specifies the time by which a reply must be given to a complaint, this is deemed an ultimatum with potentially grave consequences, and not merely a tactic to speed up negotiations.[34]

Even when stylized language is used, misunderstandings still are common. The tomes of interpretations of laws, contracts, treaties, and scientific theories are eloquent testimony to the difficulties of unambiguous communication. Moreover, when certain words (such as "separate but equal" in racial treatment) have been interpreted in one way

34. Nicolson, *Diplomacy*, p. 123.

during a particular period of history, later changes in social conditions may cast the words into a different cultural context which leads to different interpretations.[35]

Besides appraising the content and meaning of a message, a decoder often must judge the affective quality of the message. He may consider it friendly, terse, or hostile; or he may say that the message-sender had high praise, or faint praise, or moderate praise for a certain institution or policy. Generally speaking, these types of appraisals are made through comparisons of messages or comparisons of actual with anticipated output. They are therefore relative at best, and prone to great imprecision.

Decoding problems are particularly difficult when languages must be translated across vast cultural gaps. ". . . each language is a complex unique system, whose structural and stylistic elements cannot be reproduced with complete exactitude of form, meaning and intent in any other language. . . . The difficulties are greatest between entirely unrelated languages — for example, the notorious difficulties of translating Chinese, Bantu, Vietnamese, or Hopi into American English."[36] Different languages often lack parallel parts of speech. Metaphors, images, and idiomatic expressions may be difficult to interpret. When Premier Khrushchev, using a Russian idiom, told an American audience "we will bury you," translators could not agree whether this should be interpreted as "we will outlive you" or "we will destroy you."[37]

The biggest barriers to effective decoding are cultural and experiential differences which tend to be heightened by language diversity. Such barriers can be partially overcome through frequent communication and conscious attempts to transcend cultural boundaries — among members of multi-national assemblies, like the United Nations, after a prolonged period of exposure to each other; or among diplomats, mass media personnel, and business people who have lived in a foreign culture area for a long time. But even at best, such people's decoding abilities lag behind those of native speakers who possess equal verbal skills.

A final decoding problem concerns connotational meanings assigned

35. Also see Daniel Lerner, "Strategy of Truth: Symbol and Act in World Propaganda," in Lyman Bryson, Louis Finkelstein, R. M. MacIver, and Richard McKeon, eds., *Symbols and Values: An Initial Study* (New York: Harper, 1954), p. 379.

36. Hertzler, *Sociology of Language*, pp. 128–129.

37. Jack Sawyer and Harold Guetzkow, "Bargaining and Negotiations in International Relations," in Herbert Kelman, ed., *International Behavior* (New York: Holt, Rinehart and Winston, 1965), p. 479.

to messages. Decoders need to distinguish connotational meanings which they have added to the message but which the sender did not intend, or even anticipate, from connotational meanings intentionally conveyed through the message. Often it is nearly impossible to establish intent. If a message seems frightening or hostile, was this intended, or does it spring from the receiver's paranoid fears? If the message is reassuring and friendly to the receiver, was it meant to be so, or is he an eternal optimist? There may be no firm answer, even after careful examination of the message context.

ENCODING AND DECODING CHAINS — MULTIPLE DECODERS

Problems in encoding and decoding are magnified in political communication because so many messages pass through numerous encoders and decoders using a variety of encoding media. Each link in the chain may introduce variations into the original message;[38] in the process, the message may become so altered that it no longer serves the encoders' intended purpose. Conversely, the decoder, uncertain what changes have been made in the message during its transmission, may find it difficult to construe the sender's intended meaning.

A statement by Prime Minister Gandhi about relations between India and Pakistan may pass through an encoding and decoding chain which involves the prime minister, a member of her cabinet, a reporter from the *Times of India*, a rewrite man at the *Times*, a *Times* editor, a United Press International reporter stationed in New Delhi, a series of professional employees at the *New York Times*, and a press analyst at the White House. The message, as transmitted to an American president, might thus have traveled through nearly a dozen human transmission points via face-to-face contact, written messages, telephone, radio, and television. Encoding and decoding at each successive transmission point presents an opportunity for misinterpretation. The final message may become seriously distorted.

Decoding is even more difficult when the initial message involves description and interpretation of a physical event, rather than conveyance of a verbal construct. The initial verbal encoding involves a rigorous selection and elimination process by which only a limited number

38. Marshall McLuhan's famous aphorism "the medium is the message" indicates the impact which links in the encoding chain may have. For a discussion of distortions arising from multiple links in transmission chains, see Gordon Allport and Leo J. Postman, "The Basic Psychology of Rumor," *Transactions of the New York Academy of Sciences*, 8, II (1945), 61–82.

of the phenomena involved in the situation are described, usually in abbreviated form. Generally the level of abstraction is so high that decoding audiences find it difficult or impossible to reconstruct the full reality from the verbal description. Since more detail is lost with each successive decoding and encoding, the meaning conveyed by the final decoding may be no more than a shadow of the picture which the original encoder attempted to evoke.

Additional complications arise from the fact that distortions and blurring which spring from the encoding process may be systematic. In many cases, particularly when the mass media transmit messages, they tend to "accentuate the unusual, bizarre, controversial, violent, and unexpected." [39] Other systematic distortions may spring from ideological convictions. A Marxist reporter describing riots in Polish cities may encode these events in a manner which differs substantially from a report by his non-Marxist counterpart. When sender and receiver are in direct contact, the receiver can take the sender's idiosyncrasies into consideration, but when the message is transmitted through a series of unknown encoders and decoders, these distorting influences often become obscure.

Yet another factor contributes to distortion where the encoding and decoding chain lies within a bureaucratic organization. "Uncertainty absorption," described by James March and Herbert Simon in the analyses of communication within bureaucratic organizations,[40] refers to this phenomenon; within large organizations, personnel at various levels know or imagine the organization's accepted interpretation of events. As messages are decoded and encoded along the hierarchical chain, they are summarized and interpreted to accord with the interpretations which presumably have been accepted by the organization. Summaries and interpretations are passed along without the original evidence. If these interpretations conform to prevailing views within the organization, uncertainty is reduced. For instance, if the prevailing view in the State Department's China section is that the Chinese are going to intervene in an ongoing war in Vietnam, then messages from China which could be interpreted as supporting this idea are reported in ways that corroborate the official assumption. Messages which contradict the idea may be discounted or not passed up the chain at all. The resulting picture reinforces preconceived notions, rather than cre-

39. Morton Deutsch, "A Psychological Basis for Peace," in Quincy Wright, *Preventing World War III* (New York: Simon and Schuster, 1962), p. 375.
40. James March and Herbert Simon, *Organizations* (New York: John Wiley, 1958), pp. 161–169.

ating a picture based on full and accurate decoding of the intended message.

The chains described so far can be visualized as composed of connecting links, where messages originating from a single source (an individual or group) are passed on to a single audience via intermediate steps which also involve single-sender, single-receiver transmission. Of course, this oversimplifies the realities of many forms of political communication; messages dealing with identical or related situations are often transmitted by a variety of sources addressing the same audience. The audience then must decide which messages to decode and how to resolve differences in meaning among them, especially if several are jointly considered. This multiplicity of verbal stimuli regarding the same subject may introduce additional difficulties and uncertainties into the decoding process. Encoders sometimes try to reduce confusion by including in their messages comments about the interrelation and acceptability of competing messages; they may attempt to monopolize audience attention so that other messages will be ignored. Depending on the circumstances this may help, or it may further confuse the decoders.

An equally serious difficulty springs from the fact that a single message in one verbal form may have to be addressed to a variety of audiences with different decoding proclivities. The sender may know who these various audiences are, or chance may determine the matter. Messages addressed to the United Nations General Assembly illustrate the first contingency; with representatives from more than a hundred nations in attendance, no single message can hope to reach all these audiences effectively. The encoder must strive for a message which will suit those nations with whose reactions he is most concerned, without doing major damage to his relations with the remaining countries. For instance, an American statement commenting on the United Nations' condemnation of South Africa for its racial segregation policies would have to steer a course which avoids both the anti-apartheid feeling among nonwhite nations, and the ire of nations closely allied to South Africa. The result may be a highly ambiguous message which all audiences find difficult to decode.

The encoder of the American message would face a further problem: statements addressed to the United Nations are disseminated to audiences all over the world. Some of these are anticipated and familiar, such as black leaders in the United States. Others might be unpredictable. The speaker might not be able to predict which countries will receive his message via the mass media, or the types of audiences which it will reach. If his message reaches an African country at a time when insurgent groups are contemplating invasion of a colonial territory, it might have an inciting or inhibiting effect on these insurgents. Since message-senders cannot plan for all such contingencies while encoding, the possibility of touching off unforeseen adverse consequences is always a frightening prospect.

SUMMARY

A given political message can generally be conveyed through a wide variety of verbal formulations. Messages can be encoded in referential form, so that meanings correspond to dictionary definitions; they can also be encoded in instrumental form, so that all or part of the information conveyed by the message must be inferred from the message's form, context, and paralinguistic features. Both forms of encoding require identification of appropriate combinations of ideas and the application of semantic skills.

If perfect clarity is desired, a message should convey only the information which the sender intended to convey, and it should elicit only the response which he sought to obtain. The inherent ambiguities of everyday language, along with deliberate attempts to keep meanings ambiguous, make achievement of these goals rare. Difficulties in encoding and decoding are worsened by the instrumental codings often dictated by political convenience and necessity. Connotational meanings present a further obstacle to adequate coding and decoding because they depend on individual life experiences and social settings where variety, rather than uniformity, is the rule. Skillfully conveyed referential and instrumental meanings often lead to shared understandings, but the connotations which messages carry for individuals or groups are rarely shared completely.

Encoding or decoding of messages entails evaluations of various aspects of the social and psychological settings in which message-senders and receivers operate. Important factors include the needs and psychic states of senders and receivers, their encoding and decoding capacities, their basic values, and the key symbols which stir these values. The effects of reciprocal interactions between message-senders and their audiences also must be examined and evaluated. When message transmission must surmount linguistic, cultural, and experiential barriers, judgment of background factors becomes exceedingly arduous.

Despite careful preparation, many messages are misunderstood or receive multiple interpretations, often with politically disastrous consequences. Prejudices or limited comprehension capabilities may be responsible; an audience may be so strongly predisposed to a specific interpretation that it can accept no other meaning, or it may be exposed to a message which was not intended for it and was not adapted to its needs. Such a message is very likely to be construed improperly.

Deliberate misinterpretation of messages is also common when this seems advantageous to one of the parties to the message transaction. Deliberate ambiguity may be used to cloud issues or to permit diverse interpretations when political conditions so require. In areas of politics such as public law and diplomacy, where the need for accurate message transmission is particularly acute, stylized language forms have been adopted with set meanings for specified phrases. Even these attempts to surmount interpretation difficulties have not been notably successful.

The organizational chains through which messages travel may introduce systematic message distortions which obscure the intended meanings. These distortions often spring from attempts to tailor incoming information to presumed needs of an organization, from efforts to make messages conform to prejudgments or ideological patterns, and from the necessity to trim down the flow of messages. When the nature of such systematic distortions is not fully known, or when their presence is not even suspected, it becomes impossible to make allowances for them during decoding.

3 Functions and Effects of Verbal Behavior

Language is at once a commonplace and a great puzzlement. It is the principal vehicle of communication, an indispensable mnemonic aid in the collection, storage, and retrieval of information and a superlative creative tool — and yet it is a treacherous source of confusion and error as well. We employ language to tender *knowledge claims* as well as produce their warrant. We report, opine, and predict — and we describe, deduct, induct, and explain. We employ language to *express* and *persuade.* We exult, lament, expostulate, approve, disapprove, thank, and congratulate — we recommend, propose, petition, reprove, evoke, invoke, and exhort. We employ language to *perform.* We admit, inquire, proclaim, declare, command, request, confess, and promise.

— A. James Gregor, *Metapolitics* [1]

Throughout history man has sensed the power of words.[2] "The Word" has been presented in most of the great religions as the essence of wisdom and the source of creation. Folklore ascribed magical power to it. Legal lore still insists that a broken oath begets divine punishment.[3] Savants have said that "the pen is mightier than the sword." Nursery wisdom has countered this aphorism with "Sticks and stones can break my bones, but words can never hurt me"; however, the nursery sages are patently wrong. Verbal messages obviously can be instruments of change which may produce widespread anguish, anger, or joy.

What major political functions does verbal activity perform? The first chapter presented an overview of the more general significance of verbal activitity, noting the important effect which language has on human society by providing, through a complex communication system, the very means of forming large and small social bodies. Language also supplies the means for creating and transmitting extensive knowledge among the members of societies. It creates, reinforces, or changes atti-

1. A. James Gregor, *An Introduction to Metapolitics* (New York: Free Press, 1971), p. 77.
2. Joyce O. Hertzler, *A Sociology of Language* (New York: Random House, 1965), pp. 269ff.; Toshiki Izutsu, *Language and Magic* (Tokyo: Institute of Philological Studies, 1956), esp. introductory chapters.
3. Izutsu, *Language and Magic*, p. 38.

tudes, often by using various tools of verbal persuasion. Furthermore, language provides clues to the perceptions of political actors which can be used to guide political decision-making. The second chapter discussed a number of significant political consequences of the encoding and decoding processes by which messages are cast into particular verbal forms. Chapter 4 will deal with inferences drawn from verbal behavior. Inasmuch as inferences do become bases for action, they constitute "effects" of verbal behavior.

Since the breadth of functions and effects has already been demonstrated, we shall not attempt to cover all possible types in this chapter. Rather, we shall concentrate on eight politically significant functions of verbal behavior occurring in a wide variety of settings. These settings may range from tête-à-têtes to weighty pronouncements submitted to a global audience. The eight functions are: attracting attention to political situations; creating political linkages and definitions; creating and maintaining reality sleeves; making political commitments; producing policy-relevant moods; stimulating nonverbal action; using words as action; and using words as symbolic rewards.[4]

Underlying the choice and sequence of presentation of these eight functions and the effects which their performance produces is a communications model which has been widely used by sociologists to study the effects of communication on the modernization process.[5] The model categorizes and arrays the performance of verbal functions according to their contributions to the spread and subsequent adoption of new ideas by social groups. Since adoption of modern ideas and of their attendant action patterns is the ultimate goal, the model rates adoption as the most significant effect. Other effects are arrayed in descending order of significance, according to their usual occurrence during the adoption process. This process begins with awareness, when an audience takes notice of a new idea. Next comes the information stage, when the audience learns more about the innovation, usually through verbal messages which link new knowledge to past experiences. Evaluation follows; the audience relates the idea to its own perceptions and objective conditions and then rates it within its hier-

---

4. The concept of "reality sleeves" has been adapted from Erving Goffman's essay on "Fun and Games" in *Encounters: Two Studies in the Sociology of Interaction* (Indianapolis: Bobbs-Merrill, 1961), p. 81.

5. See Everett M. Rogers and F. Floyd Shoemaker, *Communication of Innovations: A Cross-Cultural Approach* (New York: Free Press, 1971); and Joe M. Bohlen, "Research Needed on Adoption Models," in Wilbur Schramm and Donald F. Roberts, eds., *The Process and Effects of Mass Communication* (Urbana: University of Illinois Press, 1971), pp. 798–815.

archies of values. Trial and adoption may then culminate the process. (The stages are not necessarily separate and sequential.)

Using a similar model, our study of functions and performance effects begins with three types of verbal behavior that involve making audiences aware of and knowledgeable about certain political conditions to the exclusion of others. Next follows discussion of three types of functions and performance effects which are related to success or failure in adoption of the political message; verbal commands intended to instigate political action are included. The final two types of functions and performance effects which are examined involve the use of verbal stimuli as surrogates for political action, rather than as intervening stimuli which lead to action. By analogy to the communications-modernization model, when words amount to actions, this should be the culminating effect. However, the ultimate consequences of verbal behavior are not always most profound when words amount to actions; directing the attention of an individual to knowledge which he has not yet recognized as politically relevant may have far more profound political consequences than commitments or promises or threats.

THE ATTENTION AROUSAL FUNCTION

It is useful to picture individuals, groups, and entire societies as living in verbal environments shaped by the particular ideas and symbols which are verbally brought to their attention. Anatol Rapoport has put this in ecological terms:

> Just as all living organisms live in certain specialized environments to which they adapt and which completely determine their lives, so do human beings live, to a significant extent, in an ocean of words. . . . We secrete words into the environment around us just as we secrete carbon dioxide and, in doing so, we create an invisible semantic environment of words which is part of our existence in quite as important ways as the physical environment. The content of verbal output does not merely passively reflect the complex social, political, and economic reality of the human race; it interacts with it as well. As our semantic environment incorporates the verbal outputs secreted into it, it becomes both enriched and polluted, and these changes are largely responsible for the course of human history.[6]

Verbal symbols, says Weston LaBarre, "carve out of total reality the organically chosen aspects of it to which the organism elects to attend,

6. Anatol Rapoport, "A System-Theoretic View of Content Analysis," in George Gerbner, The Analysis of Communication Content (New York: John Wiley, 1969), p. 36.

to the calmly outrageous ignoring of all the rest of that which is." [7] Words, deliberately or unwittingly selected by political actors, define the arenas of political action by calling attention to some matters and neglecting others. Politics varies depending on what information political actors choose to put into words and transmit, and what they elect to leave unexpressed and unpublicized. Hence, as Harold Lasswell notes, "we must describe the fluctuating focus of collective attention if we are to trace the connection between environment and response." [8]

The pages of past and current political history brim with examples. If one compares the images of the American Revolution as pictured in British and American textbooks, or the story of the Civil War as detailed in history books sold respectively in the North and South, or the sequence of events which led to World War I as depicted by the actors in various participating countries, one observes the diverse collections of facts which are selected for attention, and one is struck even more by the totally different images conveyed by these models of reality. Given the near-universal practice of selecting items which put one's own nation into a far more favorable light than the adversary, it is small wonder that nations generally feel righteous about and seek to perpetuate their own policies while remaining hostile to the policies of others. [9]

In the 1950's, when civil rights became a major focus of verbal attention, many people's perceptions of American political reality changed. [10] Scores of political situations which involved discrimination were suddenly brought to public awareness, even though these situations had existed for decades. Inferior educational facilities in schools for black children, underrepresentation of blacks on voter registration lists, greater infant mortality rates among black babies, and lower average incomes among black workers than among their white counterparts suddenly became hot political issues. History books were rewritten to emphasize facts which had heretofore been ignored. By contrast, other

7. Weston LaBarre, *The Human Animal* (Chicago: University of Chicago Press, 1954), p. 173.

8. Harold D. Lasswell, *The Analysis of Political Behavior: An Empirical Approach* (Hamden, Conn.: Archon Books, 1966), p. 299. The Hoover Institute World Attention surveys undertaken by Lasswell and associates were designed to discover the areas to which certain mass media were paying attention.

9. A discussion of the different images which spring from dissimilar information bases is presented in William Buchanan and Hadley Cantril, *How Nations See Each Other* (Urbana: University of Illinois Press, 1953).

10. The chicken-egg puzzle is pertinent here, of course. A movement may require a certain degree of power or influence before it can force itself to verbal attention. However, as will be discussed below, verbal attention bestowed even for capricious reasons may endow a weak movement with power.

significant social conditions which did not come to public knowledge because no one put them into verbal form have lost much of their potency as stimuli for political action. The suppression of other minority groups, a newly invented electoral scheme, or a massacre of enemy civilians in a far-off land does not influence the course of politics unless verbalized in the right places.

Bringing matters to verbal attention may make political mountains out of molehills. Much of the anti-Communist hysteria of the McCarthy era was due to the verbal emphasis which public figures and the mass media placed on the Communist "threat"; likewise, extensive discussion of the implications of the minor psychiatric care which Senator Eagleton had received led to his removal from the 1972 vice-presidential ticket, dramatizing an otherwise negligible political issue into a major political debacle.

In the international arena, Edmund Stillman warned in 1969 that talk of Soviet naval influence in the Mediterranean had become a self-fulfilling prophecy. "Rhetoric about the new Soviet Mediterranean venture . . . has pretty well given the Soviets . . . an effective presence, for diplomatic purposes at least, in a region where, in fact, they are weak. . . . Alas, we are helping them, by our cries of alarm over what is very nearly a toy flotilla. . . ."[11]

When an event has been chosen for verbal attention, political consequences may be strongly affected by the emphasis or deemphasis accorded to it. During the 1948-49 Berlin crisis, for instance, Western policy-makers and media minimized hostile activities in the Berlin area. This contributed to an atmosphere of calm and unconcern in the West. By contrast, Communist sources dwelt on hostile actions and their possible dire consequences, stirring up anxiety and concern among their audiences.[12] In the days preceding the Japanese attack at Pearl Harbor, American military officials discussed at length the possibility of a Japanese attack at various points in Southeast Asia. Little verbal attention was devoted to the possibility of attack on Hawaii; hence precautionary measures for Hawaii were neglected. A redressing of the verbal balance, even without basic changes in appraisal of the likelihood of a Pearl Harbor attack, might have altered strategic preparations.[13]

Since capturing the limelight is essential for the growth of viable

11. Edmund Stillman, "Perpetual Crisis," *World View*, 12 (1969), 10–11.
12. Oran R. Young, *The Politics of Force: Bargaining during International Crises* (Princeton: Princeton University Press, 1968), pp. 396–398.
13. K. J. Holsti, *International Politics: A Framework for Analysis*, 2nd ed. (Englewood Cliffs, N.J.: Prentice-Hall, 1972), p. 361.

political movements and for resolution of many political issues, attempts to get attention are a vital maneuver in politics. The political movement which gets its ideas before the public, which can command the airways and printed media and can gain a wide audience for its verbal pleas, has taken a giant step toward acquiring political significance. In fact, political power of a group or leader is often measured by its ability to transmit its messages to large audiences, as well as to influential political receivers. In periods of social change, particularly during revolutions, leaders of the new and old orders invariably try to capture or control major communication channels so that they can transmit certain political information and suppress or counteract conflicting information.

Establishing Political Linkages and Definitions

Facts and concepts which have been selected for political attention are usually placed into some kind of verbal context which affects their meaning and hence their impact. The chance to set this context for an audience — to define the situation verbally by imaginatively combining and recombining the data of politics — permits the politician to encourage others to view the world from his perspective and act accordingly. He creates distinct perceptual and conceptual worlds — hypothetical patterns of reality [14] — which may confine his audience's mental horizons, thereby changing the course of history. It is the province of politics to make linkages and seek their wide acceptance through "spreading the word"; "indeed, most major political conflicts within any policy areas may be seen as the attempt by partisans to attach the available legitimacy symbols to the policies they advocate and to sever the relationship between these symbols and the policies of their opponents." [15]

14. The phrase is from Lasswell, *Analysis of Political Behavior*, p. 127. Linkages, if they are believed, have important consequences, regardless of their accuracy. National Socialist and Communist attempts in Germany to create new linkages through reinterpretation of old terms, and through new stock phrases, are described in Claus Mueller, *The Politics of Communication: A Study in the Political Sociology of Language, Socialization, and Legitimation* (New York: Oxford University Press, 1973), pp. 24–42. The structuring of consensus through verbal manipulation is discussed on pp. 92–94.

15. Richard M. Merelman, "Learning and Legitimacy," *American Political Science Review*, 60 (1966), 553. Daniel J. Boorstin, *The Image: A Guide to Pseudo-Events in America* (New York: Harper, 1964), p. 187, calls political images "public portraits" in which the original is "successfully synthesized, doctored, repaired, refurbished, and improved."

Three types of linkages are particularly common and effective. *Causal linkages* identify one or several of various possible causes as responsible for a particular event; the nature of the alleged cause then determines the appropriate reaction to the event. *Conceptual linkages* place people or events into familiar conceptual categories, along with other people or events for which positive or negative evaluations already exist. *Analogic linkages* are similar to conceptual linkages — but instead of placing events into general conceptual categories, they liken the structure of events to particular previous structures of events or personages which, although substantially different in most respects, nonetheless present striking similarities. In either case, the linkages tie the linked concepts to particular courses of action. A series of examples may clarify the distinctions.

Causal Linkages

During the 1890's the United States was plagued by a great deal of domestic unrest. "Nativist nationalism offered two easy verbal solutions to the painful dilemma of a changed and unstable America. By blaming disunity on the evil influence of new immigrants, it absolved from blame and protected from criticism the more basic contradictions in the economic and social system. If immigrants were the root of the trouble, the solution was comparatively simple: keep them out." [16] Immigrants became convenient verbal scapegoats, described as "unassimilable, revolutionary, and inherently inferior." [17] It does not require much imagination to detect similar causal linkages in the political rhetoric of twentieth-century America. In each case, the widely verbalized and accepted causal linkage led to specific policy recommendations.

Since most receivers of political messages happily accept mono-causal and mono-conceptual explanations, politicians are strongly tempted to debase the verbal currency; thus demagogues are born and mass followings manufactured. Once policy responses have been established to cope with specific "causes" of political difficulty, the acceptance of a given causal linkage will bring forth an almost automatic response. "When a stimulus is of a kind that has been experienced repeatedly in the past, the response will ordinarily be quite routinized.

16. Marilyn Blatt Young, *The Rhetoric of Empire: American China Policy, 1895–1901* (Cambridge: Harvard University Press, 1968), p. 4.

17. *Ibid.* See Gregor, *Introduction to Metapolitics*, pp. 283ff., for a discussion of the dynamic effects of normative terms.

The stimulus will evoke . . . a well-structured definition of the situation that will include a repertory of response programs, and programs for selecting an appropriate specific response from the repertory." [18]

Political parties and factions usually compete for support by peddling different allegations about causal linkages. Spiraling inflation can be blamed on faulty economic policies of the party in power, on predatory labor leaders, or on international economic conditions. When a local bridge has been dynamited, it can be labeled the work of a "maniac," the deed of "criminal elements in our city linked to local politicians," or part of a "Communist conspiracy" financed from abroad. Public reactions and suggested remedies will vary widely, depending on which cause is verbally linked to the deed.

A linkage of worldwide current significance is the explanation of political and economic underdevelopment. Third World leaders have claimed that the backwardness of their countries has been caused by European colonialist exploitation which prevented socio-economic development; [19] this causal linkage suggests that termination of political control by colonial powers would allow retarded development to take place. The explanation absolves the people of the underdeveloped areas of responsibility for their backwardness and leads them to expectations of instant development following independence. The history of post-independence events in many Third World countries is ample testimony to the fact that the causal linkages and inferences drawn from them were vastly oversimplified. Grave disenchantment and political unrest have frequently resulted.

Other causal linkages have been no more felicitous in their consequences. During much of the colonial period Western countries contended that underdevelopment was due to intellectual and psychological deficiencies of subject peoples, to the scarcity of technical skills among them, to the nature of physical resources, or to geographic and climatic conditions. These explanations largely removed from Western powers the blame for the lack of economic and political progress. Moreover, most of the causes cited for backwardness (physical and population resources, climate and geography) were unchangeable, thus sealing the fate of these regions. [20]

18. James March and Herbert Simon, *Organizations* (New York: John Wiley, 1958), pp. 139–140.

19. Kenneth W. Grundy, "African Explanations of Underdevelopment: The Theoretical Basis for Political Action," *Review of Politics*, 28 (1966), 62–63.

20. *Ibid.*, pp. 74–75.

Conceptual Linkages

A message may channel political action in different directions, depending on the conceptual linkages which have been created in verbal pictures. The linkages act as intervening variables between the message and the policy response. For instance, successful verbal linkage of police action against the Black Panther party with the concept of "genocide" has made the police, rather than the Panthers, the focus of adverse political reaction. Had the activities against the Black Panthers been firmly linked to the concept of legitimate police security operations against a violent group, the political future of the Panthers and of police officials involved would have been quite different. The conceptualization of "genocide" on the one hand and "legitimate police action" on the other served as intervening variables between the action of shooting members of the party and the social behavior required in response to the action.[21]

Consider the consequences of linking American action in Vietnam to the domino theory. This theory implies that Communist victory in one country is part of a series of inevitably linked events which will ultimately touch all of Southeast Asia, and may even reach America's shores. Acquiescence in the first take-over will automatically initiate subsequent take-overs, making resistance to the first take-over imperative.[22] A related fateful conceptual linkage has been perennial political talk about America's "vital stake" in Asia. "Tragically, definitions of the precise nature of America's vital interest in Asia have been rare, yet the idea that this country has a major role to play there remains fixed in the foreign policy of the United States."[23]

Conceptual linkages need not be elaborate; simple semantic linkages may do the trick. Thus Arab perception of the non-Arab world may be strongly affected by the conceptual distinction between *dar-al-Islam* and *dar-al-Harb*. One refers to the "domain of Islam," the other to the "domain of war" which covers all territory beyond the domain of Islam.[24] Semantically rooted conceptual distinctions between in-groups

21. Conceptual linkages as intervening variables are discussed in James N. Rosenau, "Foreign Policy as Adaptive Behavior: Some Preliminary Notes for a Theoretical Model," *Comparative Politics*, 2 (1970), 383. Also see J. G. A. Pocock, *Politics, Language and Time* (New York: Atheneum, 1971), pp. 26–29.

22. Rosenau, "Foreign Policy as Adaptive Behavior," p. 382.

23. Young, *Rhetoric of Empire*, p. 230.

24. Richard H. Pfaff, "The Function of Arab Nationalism," *Comparative Politics*, 2 (1970), 153.

and out-groups in politics and religion, common in many cultures, may partly explain the great hostility shown to out-groups throughout the world.

Conceptual linkages may become self-fulfilling prophecies. When a social situation is defined and verbalized in terms of conflict theory, conflict may be produced where none existed before.[25] Continued use of Cold War terminology became a conceptual prison which prevented people from seeing events in new contexts when world conditions changed over the years. Charles Osgood noted plaintively at the end of the 1960's: "The Cold War is steadily fired by application of its own tired rhetoric, which regularly appeals to the pivotal concepts of GOD and DEVIL for its sustenance — thus being a kind of Holy War."[26]

Analogic Linkages

Examples of analogic linkages are plentiful. When Prime Minister Eden found a close analogy between Hitler's diplomacy and objectives in 1938 and Nasser's behavior in the Middle East in 1956, the course of British policy was set.[27] Britain and France could not tolerate "another Munich" — a concept which embodied the idea of surrender to dictatorship, gullibility of a high order, and extreme moral weakness if not depravity.

Similarly, when President Truman likened the North Korean invasion of South Korea to the German march into Czechoslovakia, the perceptual stage of American politics was set to react to a major international threat. Had he linked the events conceptually to American incursions into Mexico, the policy consequences might have been quite different. Once a country becomes or is about to become enmeshed in war, the war is quite commonly linked to high moral principles. When wars are conceptualized as crusades to "make the world safe for democracy," to "save the world from the infidels," or to "insure justice, honor, and liberty," it becomes difficult to bring peace through compromise. The war must be fought to the finish. By contrast, a war linked to less exalted goals, like gaining a piece of territory or fishing rights, or punish-

25. Hansfried Kellner, "On the Sociolinguistic Perspective of the Communicative Situation," *Social Research*, 37 (1970), 72–73.

26. Charles E. Osgood, "Conservative Words and Radical Sentences in the Semantics of International Politics," in Gilbert Abcarian and John W. Soule, eds., *Social Psychology and Political Behavior: Problems and Prospects* (Columbus, Ohio: Charles E. Merrill, 1971), p. 116. For a wide variety of examples, see John G. Stoessinger, *Nations in Darkness* (New York: Random House, 1971).

27. Holsti, *International Politics*, p. 368.

ing a neighbor for border violations, can often be settled through give-and-take bargaining.

Political ideologies may provide a formal verbal framework for link-ages of all types. The words of the ideology establish "the intellectual framework through which policy makers observe reality. All messages and cues from the external environment are given meaning, or inter-preted, within the categories, predictions, and definitions provided by doctrines comprising the ideology."[28] The ideology thus automatically supplies a series of coordinated causal, conceptual, and analogic link-ages for leaders and followers who can be persuaded to accept it. Sharing these linkages amounts to sharing a common world-view and supporting policies in agreement with the implications of this world-view.

Many people who give lip service to a common ideology may not understand the basic doctrines involved. Nevertheless, they "derive slogans, phrases, or words" from the ideology, which then "become magnified as political symbols and taboos" channeling political action. Words like "imperialist," "capitalist," "colonialist," "Communist," have become effective street slogans even when those who use them to stir up emotional reactions have only the haziest notion of what they mean, conceptually.[29]

THE CREATION OF REALITY SLEEVES

The political linkages discussed thus far create particular perceptions of reality by linking a new event to a familiar cause, concept, or analogy. In the process they create new perceptual realities for receivers who accept the linkages; these new perceptual realities, in turn, are apt to become prisms through which future information is filtered and shaped. Discrepant information is excluded, while potentially com-patible information is adapted to make it consistent with previously accepted ideas, lending support to the overall perceptual structure of the communication receiver.[30] Gradually, a firm conceptual structure is built up which becomes extremely difficult to dislodge. One can then speak of "reality sleeves' — conceptual straitjackets which tightly en-

28. *Ibid.*, p. 266.

29. George I. Blanksten, "Ideology and Nation-Building in the Contemporary World," *International Studies Quarterly*, 2 (1967), 4.

30. For theories of perceptual consistency, see Leon Festinger, *A Theory of Cognitive Dissonance* (Evanston, Ill.: Row, Peterson, 1957) and sources cited there. Also see Joseph T. Klapper, *The Effects of Mass Communication* (New York: Free Press, 1960), p. 96.

close the minds of individuals and groups and prevent them from accepting conflicting perceptions.

It is particularly easy to create reality sleeves in those areas of politics where the average information-receiver lacks direct perceptions, prior knowledge, or facilities or motivations to check new information. This forces him to rely completely on secondary messages, often those of a single message source. Foreign policy provides many examples.[31]

Most people, including professional politicians, have few contacts with other nations; they therefore depend on verbal pictures for most of their mental images concerning other nations. Bryant Wedge presents a fairly typical example of image distortion from a study of Latin American political leaders who visited the United States. These leaders shared misperceptions about widely held social and political values in the United States; their false views could be traced to uncritical acceptance and retention of verbal images adopted many years earlier. "Such images, it appears, persist not only because they have become established as myths or truisms of the national culture, but also because they are sustained and fed by perceptions of new information in ways confirmatory of the image."[32]

The rigidity of perceptual matrices even among members of high-level political elites has been documented in biographies of such public figures as Woodrow Wilson, Adolf Hitler, and John Foster Dulles,[33] none of whom would change his perceptions of the Germans, English, or Russians respectively, even in face of strong evidence contradicting preconceived notions.

Verbal images are often passed on from nation to nation. The Chinese view of international relations during the Korean war apparently was based exclusively on published Russian interpretations of political events; predictably, the Chinese reality, as expressed by Chinese political leaders and mass media, closely paralleled the official expressed Russian reality.[34]

31. For examples see Holsti, *International Politics*, pp. 360–361.

32. Bryant Wedge, "Nationality and Social Perception," *Journal of Communication*, 16 (1966), 274.

33. Alexander and Juliette George, *Woodrow Wilson and Colonel House: A Personality Study* (New York: John Day, 1956); William L. Shirer, *The Rise and Fall of the Third Reich* (Boston: Simon and Schuster, 1960); Ole R. Holsti, "Cognitive Dynamics and Images of the Enemy," in David J. Finlay, Ole R. Holsti, and Richard R. Fagen, eds., *Enemies in Politics* (Chicago: Rand McNally, 1967), pp. 25–96. Also see Joseph de Rivera, *The Psychological Dimensions of Foreign Policy* (Columbus, Ohio: Charles E. Merrill, 1968), p. 21.

34. Allen S. Whiting, *China Crosses the Yalu: The Decision to Enter the Korean War* (New York: Macmillan, 1960), p. 12.

The Effects of Verbal Commitment

In the process of creating reality sleeves for others, political leaders often "create a 'map' of the territory of experience" and commit themselves to its accuracy and to the political course they have charted on it.[35] Since fidelity to one's pronouncements and pledges has been widely regarded as a strong moral obligation, commitments often remain binding even if the map is later found to be inaccurate. The pressure to provide speedy but logically coherent explanations for many political occurrences often forces political leaders to chart maps with undue haste, rendering the effects of commitment particularly dangerous.[36]

The binding effects of commitment spring from a number of sources, in addition to moral considerations. Most obviously, questions of prestige are involved. The politician who changes his pronouncements may be accused of various intellectual shortcomings because his initial statements were incorrect; he may be charged with lack of steadfastness, with dangerous unreliability, or with deliberate attempts to deceive. If an initial pronouncement has received wide public support, it may be particularly difficult to withdraw from it, even if it was incorrect or misunderstood. Joseph de Rivera tells how Senator Vandenberg abandoned his strong isolationism after a speech which was widely interpreted as anti-isolationist had received extensive public acclaim.[37] Though insisting that he had been misquoted, the senator chose to modify his official position in accordance with his statements. Many a politician, buoyed by an applauding audience, has stumbled into a public stance on the strength of casually chosen words. "Men on the accession routes to power are peculiarly susceptible to such self-induced 'brain-washing.'"[38]

Reluctance to abandon a prior verbalization, especially when it was made in public, springs not only from fear of losing prestige, but also from psychological factors. People internalize ideas to which they are publicly committed in order to avoid the mental discomfort that springs from cognitive dissonance; they actually bring their beliefs into accord with their pronouncements because this is easier than repudiating the

35. Hertzler, *Sociology of Language*, p. 28.

36. Raymond A. Bauer, "Problems of Perception and the Relations between the United States and the Soviet Union," *Journal of Conflict Resolution*, 5 (1961), 223–229.

37. de Rivera, *Psychological Dimensions of Foreign Policy*, p. 37. Also see Arthur R. Cohen, *Attitude Change and Social Influence* (New York: Basic Books, 1964), pp. 10–11.

38. Osgood, "Conservative Words and Radical Sentences," pp. 117–118.

pronouncements. The more people are forced to express and defend their beliefs, the firmer the beliefs become. The very act of verbal expression of an idea begets pressures for its perpetuation.[39]

Public expression of ideas may also enhance their "boomerang effects." Political leaders do not necessarily practice what they preach, but the psychological and political pressures for action which ensue from the expectations aroused by the preaching may force decisions which might not have been made otherwise. The political pressures to bring words and deeds into accord can be exceedingly strong. This may explain why ideologues so frequently become political activists.[40]

Verbal commitments have a strongly normative effect for groups as well as for individuals; knowledge of this fact lies behind many conscious and unconscious efforts to have groups publicly proclaim their norms. Pledges of allegiance, voting by show of hands, resolutions of unanimity, recitation of a group's cardinal principles, and repeated public reference to the sanctity of law or the inviolability of certain commitments all serve to make norms more binding.

39. Klapper, *Effects of Mass Communication,* p. 96, notes: "Persons who are required to parrot — and even more, those who are required to supplement — the arguments of a communication with which they initially disagree often tend to accept the arguments." For a review of experimental evidence, see Alfred G. Smith, ed., *Communication and Culture: Readings in the Codes of Human Interaction* (New York: Holt, Rinehart and Winston, 1966), p. 545.

40. The propensity of ideologues to become activists was called to my attention by Paul Hiniker. Further discussion of the restraining force of verbal commitment can be found in Jack W. Brehm and Arthur Cohen, *Explorations in Cognitive Dissonance* (New York: John Wiley, 1962), pp. 8–9, 198–217; James M. Fendrich, "A Study of the Association among Verbal Attitudes, Commitment and Overt Behavior in Different Experimental Situations," *Social Forces,* 45 (1967), 347–349; Doris A. Graber, "Conflict Images: An Assessment of the Middle East Debates in the United Nations," *Journal of Politics,* 32 (1970), 363; and Thomas C. Schelling, *Arms and Influence* (New Haven: Yale University Press, 1966), pp. 52–83. Allan W. Wicker, "Attitudes v. Actions: The Relationship of Verbal and Overt Behavioral Responses to Attitude Objects," *Journal of Social Issues,* 25 (1969), 65, surveys the literature on coincidence of attitudes and actions. Wicker concludes: "It is considerably more likely that attitudes will be unrelated or only slightly related to overt behaviors than that attitudes will be closely related to actions. Product-moment correlation coefficients relating the two kinds of responses are rarely above .30, and often are near zero." It seems doubtful that these findings are applicable to freely expressed attitudes (as contrasted to attitudes elicited during an interview or by a questionnaire) by prominent public figures in a public setting. The forces which Wicker cites as mitigating against attitude-action conformance in the average individual, such as situational factors, expected publicity, and community and personal norms, are likely to push a publicly committed politician into attitude-action conformance. For additional information, see Ulf Himmelstrand, "Verbal Attitudes and Behavior: A Paradigm for the Study of Message Transmission and Transformation," *Public Opinion Quarterly,* 24 (1960), 224–250.

When major resources have been invested in a verbal image reality, it becomes particularly resistant to conceptual changes. The domino theory used by American political leaders to conceptualize the war in Vietnam is a case in point. Once major military and political resources had been expended in pursuit of policies dictated by the domino theory, the United States and its leaders had an ever-growing stake in supporting the initial conceptualization. Competing views of reality were strongly resisted, since they challenged not only the initial conceptualizations, but also the wisdom and usefulness of consequent major military and political activities in Vietnam. Verbal commitment, followed by action, followed by further verbal commitment forged an ever-stronger chain tying the hands and minds of political leaders and followers.[41] The credibility of the verbal commitments had risen in direct proportion to investments made on behalf of the commitments and the costs of default.

THE CREATION OF POLICY-RELEVANT MOODS

Aside from conveying messages and adding interpretations and evaluations, messages can be used to convey or create politically significant psychic states and moods. When West Berliners were told during the Berlin blockade that the whole world was looking up to them, this apparently helped them withstand the rigors of the blockade. President Kennedy's widely publicized announcement that "I am a Berliner" boosted morale tremendously because it made West Berliners feel that they had the moral support of the non-Communist world.

Mussolini, when referring to the glories of the Roman Empire in his speeches, aroused in Italian audiences the feeling of pride in a heroic history. This feeling helped to create a public mood favorable to expansion through military action, so when the dictator deemed the time opportune, he had a willing and eager people at his beck and call for imperialist war.

In his famous fireside chats at the beginning of the Depression, Franklin D. Roosevelt succeeded in creating a mood of confidence in the American public. The mood, readily gauged by such economic indicators as stock market fluctuations, helped to put the nation back on its economic feet. Hitler attempted to create a mood of hatred which would stir the Germans against their neighbors to the east and south;

41. See Robert Jervis, *The Logic of Images in International Relations* (Princeton: Princeton University Press, 1970), chs. 4, 6.

he succeeded well. One could cite many more examples, from Fidel Castro's exhortations to Cubans to Sukarno's *confrontasi* oratory inciting Indonesians to war against Malaysia.

A sample of Churchillian prose, taken from a broadcast describing the Nazi invasion of Russia, represents the genre of mood-creating oratory. Anti-Nazi audiences were chilled by visions of the fiendish German forces advancing on their Russian victims.

> I see advancing . . . in hideous onslaught the Nazi war machine with its clanking, heel-clicking, dandified Prussian officers, its crafty expert agents fresh from the cowing and tying-down of a dozen countries. I see also the dull, drilled, docile, brutish masses of the Hun soldiery plodding on like a swarm of crawling locusts. I see the German bombers and fighters in the sky, still smarting from many a British whipping, delighted to find what they believe is an easier and safer prey.
>
> Behind all this glare, behind all this storm, I see that small group of villainous men who plan, organize and launch this cataract of horrors upon mankind.[42]

Oratory like Churchill's creates the psychological intangibles which condition action. Pride, confidence, trust, love, hate, anxiety, fear, and despair all are vital moods which words can evoke.

The creation of moods is a crucial aspect of political interaction in public assemblies and bargaining groups. The achievements of such groups depend heavily on the good will or hatred, tension or relaxation, fear or hope prevalent in the psychological climate in which they operate. A friendly interchange among group members is usually most conducive to cooperation and achievement of group goals; in fact, verbal interchange *per se* can be soothing, even when no relevant information is transmitted. "Small talk" and cocktail-circuit inanities may smooth the way for successful bargaining.[43] A shouting match or an exchange of barbed insults and accusations is apt to poison the atmosphere, making negotiations difficult. Verbal behavior can be shaped accordingly. When a climate of threats and fear seems more advantageous, as happens when one seeks to discourage negotiations or to cow an opponent into submission, verbal tools are often sufficient. Even when additional signals such as threatening gestures are required to enhance the mood of fear, verbal behavior plays an important part.

The crucial effects of angry rhetoric are exemplified by an event

42. Quoted in Reed Whittemore, "Churchill as Mythmaker," in Thomas P. Brockway, ed., *Language and Politics* (Boston: D. C. Heath, 1965), p. 61.
43. Edward Sapir, *Culture, Language and Personality: Selected Essays*, ed. David G. Mandelbaum (Berkeley: University of California Press, 1962), p. 18.

which occurred during the Truman administration. The American government was prepared to accede to Communist China's admission to the United Nations, but when Chinese negotiators called the American representatives "reactionary butchers" and "imperialists," public and congressional ire rose to such a pitch that the administration felt constrained to continue its opposition to China's UN membership. This American response to the Chinese insults, in turn, convinced the Chinese of American ill will and made them less eager to negotiate conflicts which arose at a later date. "These developments influenced the later interaction between Peking and Washington in the Korean war by reinforcing the xenophobic and aggressive elements in the Chinese and ideological components of the policy." [44]

THE USE OF WORDS TO STIMULATE ACTION

The emphasis thus far has been on the language's functions in creating mental images and states; now the focus will shift more directly to its functions in stimulating action. Words can be used as a direct stimulus to action — in fact, this is their most widespread, basic use in primitive societies and during childhood. [45]

Stimulus language may be in the form of direct commands, exhortations, suggestions, laws, or rules which order people to engage in specified action or to do what is needed to achieve a specific goal. [46] Language stimuli also may operate indirectly. The condemnation of a police force by labeling it as corrupt may be an indirect command to a crowd to destroy that police force's headquarters. "Most of what happens socially . . . is mediated by language, incited and propelled by language, instructed and programmed by language, directed and controlled by language. . . . Right words, appropriate time-tested phrases, and more complexly organized forms of speech — the proper ritual verbalisms — are powerful agents of effective change in social action and interaction." [47]

Words also become a stimulus for action when they set up models or goals which political leaders and followers seek to turn into political reality. Initially these goals are nothing but verbal formulations, often

---

44. Whiting, *China Crosses the Yalu*, p. 12.
45. Izutsu, *Language and Magic*, pp. 52–56.
46. The reverse occurs also; a physical stimulus may elicit a purely verbal response. See Robert C. North, "Research Pluralism and the International Elephant," *International Studies Quarterly*, 11 (1967), 407.
47. Hertzler, *Sociology of Language*, p. 281.

of nonexistent conditions. Politicians then try to make reality conform to these verbally created utopias.

Political power is frequently measured by the ability of political leaders to spur action through their verbal commands. "The indexes of power may be largely verbal (ordering-obeying, proposing-endorsing), and the like. Words are involved in the readjustment of power — in revolutionary agitation, in constitutional innovation."[48] Successful social movements generally begin with a dramatic verbal formulation of grounds of dissatisfaction with existing social arrangements and include plans for restructuring these arrangements, or even for rebuilding the entire society. Leaders rally the faithful through carefully chosen verbal appeals and attack the opposition with fighting words. Victory through revolution, evolution, or electoral majorities requires a variety of verbally instigated physical activities which bring about major changes in the body politic.[49]

The Use of Words as Action

Language alone may bring about changes normally accomplished through nonverbal activities. The nonverbal activities may be held in abeyance as an alternative, should verbal action fail. Action may be purely verbal, with no nonverbal substitutes;[50] conversely, nonverbal action can perform some of the functions of words. The Berlin airlift of 1948-49 declared to the world the West's determination to keep Berlin free from Soviet control.[51] The United States used words in place of actions in Cuba in 1961. The American government could have sent armed forces into Cuba or used airborne explosives to rid the island of Russian missiles; instead, a series of verbal messages — later reinforced by a military alert — accomplished this result. The messages in essence told Cuba and Russia, "If you do not remove the missiles, the United States will use military force to remove them."[52] What was put in the form of a threat might have been put in the form of a stern

48. Harold Lasswell, Nathan Leites et al., eds., *The Language of Politics: Studies in Quantitative Semantics* (Cambridge: MIT Press, 1965), p. 18.

49. Hertzler, *Sociology of Language*, p. 287.

50. Bronislaw Malinowski, *Coral Gardens and Their Magic* (New York: American Book Co., 1935), p. 54, discusses this point.

51. Charles A. McClelland, "Action Structures and Communication in Two International Crises: Quemoy and Berlin," *Background*, 7 (1964), 201–217.

52. For the verbal aspects of the crisis, see Young, *Politics of Force*, pp. 408–411. To prevent influx of additional Russian military supplies into Cuba, a naval blockade was also proclaimed.

demand, a polite plea, or a promise of reward for compliance. In many cases, credible threats, or persuasive promises or pleas can bring about changes which might otherwise require physical action.

The frustrations which arise when words fail to substitute for actions are well captured in statements by Presidents Kennedy and Johnson. Kennedy blasted Premier Khrushchev, saying, "That son of a bitch won't pay any attention to words, he has to see your move." Similarly, Johnson voiced his disappointment during air attacks on North Vietnam in 1965: "I wish it were possible to convince others with words, of what we now find it necessary to say with guns and planes." [53]

Pledges are another common type of verbal action intended to obviate the need for physical action. The Soviet Union's pledge to come to Egypt's defense during the 1956 Suez crisis was intended to deter Western military activities in the area;[54] likewise, Britain's continued formal commitment to the defense of some former colonies constitutes a verbal gesture of deterrence intended to make active military measures unnecessary. Besides having deterrence effects, the Soviet and British verbal alignments also affect political balances by altering or maintaining the influence of the protector nation in the verbally protected country.

The explicit verbal commitments made to anti-Castro Cubans prior to the 1960 Bay of Pigs invasion provide another example of the policy-shaping influence of official pledges. Though the incoming president, John F. Kennedy, opposed American help for the planned invasion of Cuba, he felt that the United States could not break its promises for moral reasons, as well as for the sake of preserving its credibility. Although this consideration was only one factor which made it difficult to stop an already partially effected policy, it was a powerful one.

American promises to protect South Vietnam against its northern enemies are another graphic example. In the moralistic-legalistic vein which has frequently characterized debate about American foreign policy making, American leaders talked about the "sanctity" of such promises and the involvement of "national honor" in keeping the pledged word. In 1967 Secretary of State Rusk warned, "If it should be discovered that the pledge of the United States is meaningless, the structure of peace would crumble and we would be well on our way to a terrible catastrophe." [55] Such arguments make the keeping of prom-

53. Quoted in Schelling, *Arms and Influence*, p. 150.
54. Franklin B. Weinstein, "The Concept of Commitment in International Relations," *Journal of Conflict Resolution*, 13 (1969), 47.
55. Quoted *ibid.*, p. 52. The coordination of words and acts is discussed in

ises compelling. If believed, they lend credibility and force to pledges which might otherwise be discounted as mere words.

Blame and praise are verbal activities that do not necessarily entail the possibility of physical action as a substitute, should the verbal activity fail. Properly wielded, blame and praise can effectively diminish or enhance the power of political units at all levels. Because no physical action is involved, these verbal tools are particularly useful for weak actors. A small country, like Cuba, can lower the prestige of the United States, or even prevent American military forces from entering Cuban soil, merely by verbal assaults casting blame on real or imaginary American actions.

The United States has suffered severe losses in influence and has seen its policy options sharply reduced as a result of verbal criticism. It has shown its sensitivity to criticism by a number of strong reactions, such as the delay in sending an ambassador to India in 1973 after Prime Minister Gandhi had been sharply critical of U.S. policy in Vietnam.[56] The Soviet Union experienced a major decline in prestige and influence in the wake of widespread, virulent criticism of its invasion of Czechoslovakia in 1968.[57] Its verbal justifications, designed to counteract criticism, were unsuccessful. The Union of South Africa has seen its political and commercial influence reduced and its military security impaired as a result of verbal criticism by actors unwilling or unable to use physical action.

In making threats and commitments, effectiveness often depends on the strength of the belief that physical action will really occur if the verbal action is ignored. In blaming, praising, and related verbal tactics, the effects may depend on the target's sensitivity to blame or praise, the message-sender's power and social relationship to the target, and the nature of the activities which occasion blame or praise.[58]

During the Cuban missile crisis, the United States accused Russia of breaking accepted rules of international conduct by deploying missiles to Cuba. It branded Soviet actions as illegitimate and unjustifiable. Considering the hostility between the parties, the firmness of East-West bloc lines, and the high blame-resistance of the Soviet Union, this American verbal tactic probably did little toward modify-

Alexander L. George, David K. Hall, and William E. Simons, *The Limits of Coercive Diplomacy: Laos, Cuba, Vietnam* (Boston: Little, Brown, 1971).

56. State Department spokesmen termed the Gandhi statements "inadmissible" and "unwelcome." *New York Times*, February 8, 1973.

57. Helge Hveem, "'Blame' as International Behavior," *Journal of Peace Research*, 4 (1970), 49.

58. *Ibid.*, p. 52.

ing Russian action. However, it may have influenced the attitudes and actions of spectator countries; since it was an inexpensive weapon, it seemed worth using.

Recent studies in international relations have examined the relationship between verbal maneuvers in international conflict and physical acts of violence to determine the conditions under which each type of action tends to be used. For instance, Charles A. McClelland examined patterns of verbal and physical conflict for a fifty-four-month period prior to July 1, 1970.[59] He counted 7,655 verbal and physical conflict events, most of them involving dramatic incidents like the six-day Arab-Israeli war of 1967 and the Russian intervention in Czechoslovakia in 1968. The data showed a trend toward increase of both physical aggression and verbal assaults, and a decline of defensive statements. McClelland concluded that "the more prevalent the acts of defensive verbal conflict, the less likely the subsequent occurrence of violent physical acts." [60] He warned, however, that this does not necessarily mean that defensive verbal behavior obviates the likelihood of need for physical conflict. Future studies may confirm some international relations scholars' belief that verbal assaults and defenses may, at times, be satisfactory substitutes for the release of tensions which might otherwise lead to war.[61]

The potency of verbal action may depend largely on the skills with which various messages are selected, combined, and presented. When a political caucus meets to select candidates or to determine future action, the participants are properly viewed as combatants in verbal battles over political resources. They are described as parrying thrusts, assembling the big guns, blasting the opposition, or torpedoing its main argument. When a victorious point is scored, it may be acknowledged with "touché," drawn from fencing parlance. Participants and observers understand that victory for candidates and measures may be determined not by their respective merits, as judged by widely shared criteria, but by the proponents' rhetorical skills in saying the right things at the right times to the right audiences.

The use of verbal tactics to affect political outcomes has been studied most carefully in the field of campaigning. Practitioners and students of the art have analyzed audience predispositions, issue salience,

59. Charles A. McClelland, "Verbal and Physical Conflict in the Contemporary International System," APSA paper (1970).

60. *Ibid.*, p. 17.

61. See Hugh Dalziel Duncan, *Symbols in Society* (New York: Oxford University Press, 1968), p. 108.

and manner of presentation to determine the most effective verbal behavior. Practitioners apply this information in their campaigns to affect election outcomes. While the precise contribution of verbal tactics to electoral outcomes remains disputed, most studies acknowledge that significant measurable effects do occur.[62]

Lobbyists use similar methods to call attention to their arguments for and against certain legislative proposals and executive measures. In fact, one of the main social benefits of lobbying lies in the preliminary research done by lobbyists to marshal facts and weave them into effective verbal presentations. Proponents and opponents of various measures often learn their best verbal arguments from lobbyists. When a lobbyist succeeds in pinning the label "poison" on a food additive, he has effectively destroyed the usefulness of the product to the food industry; no further action is ordinarily required.

Verbal action also forms an important part of the work of public agencies. Such action is often designed to gain support for programs among selected lay and professional publics; this requires effective verbal formulation of agency goals and transmission of these to selected audiences. To make presentations expert, the task is frequently delegated to professional public relations staffs. However, government leaders and the public are highly suspicious and fearful that government agencies might stray from informational to propagandistic activities. Propaganda, it is feared, would leave the public helpless to determine truth or falsity of claims. Accordingly, government publicity work has legal restraints intended to limit its persuasive force. Fears that government agencies will tamper with the spontaneity and amateurishness of communication have retarded the systematic application of communications research and its findings to the public relations work of government bodies. The price is diminished communications efficiency.

USE OF WORDS AS SYMBOLIC REWARDS

Verbal activities can be construed as action in still another sense. In many political situations, nonverbal physical action is impossible

62. See Harold Mendelsohn and Irving Crespi, *Polls, Television, and the New Politics* (Scranton, Pa.: Chandler Publishing, 1970), pp. 247–314; Dan Nimmo, *The Political Persuaders: The Techniques of Modern Election Campaigns* (Englewood Cliffs, N.J.: Prentice-Hall, 1970), pp. 111–119; and Ithiel de Sola Pool, Richard Abelson, and Samuel L. Popkin, *Candidates, Issues and Strategies: A Computer Simulation of the 1960 and 1964 Presidential Elections* (Cambridge: MIT Press, 1965).

or undesirable; the demand for action under those circumstances can be satisfied by verbal assurances that no action is needed, by promises of future action, or by a statement that the demands are being considered. These assurances, promises, or acknowledgments serve as symbolic action, satisfying needs and reinforcing allegiances which would ordinarily have required physical action.

A familiar example is the government official who patiently examines a complaint and then announces reassuringly that he will take the matter under advisement. He may even promise that a committee will be appointed to look into the matter. The petitioners' sense of fear or dissatisfaction may be alleviated by the promise, quite aside from any physical action. Sometimes the promise of aid may be nothing but a palliative to the pleading group; the intent to fulfill the promise may be frustrated by inability or incapacity to do so. Or a commission may indeed be appointed, and it may issue a report indicating that the grievances are real and possibly making recommendations for their alleviation. Such reports usually offer another symbolic benefit to claimants, who feel that action has been taken on their behalf. But action has been largely verbal — symbols of prospective deeds, instead of actual deeds.

Token action, such as the elimination of a few blocks of slum housing, coupled with verbal promises of future action, may alleviate strong tensions which are building up. The clearance of a few blocks becomes a reassuring symbol that promises of future action should be believed. The promises serve as a balm for anguished minds, even when no future action occurs.

Likewise, assertions and promises of current and future greatness, or recitals of progress and reform, may be accepted by political groups in lieu of action. If made convincingly by a trusted speaker, no reality basis and no further action may be required to make these groups feel and react as if greatness and progress were a reality. In an age of mass literacy and mass communication, manipulation of the symbolic rather than the material environment is particularly tempting. People no longer need to see and experience to believe. They need merely to hear, or to hear and see a little and then project from the little they see, in order to create a new "reality" which furnishes symbolic gratifications for needs for which material gratifications would otherwise be expected.[63]

63. Murray Edelman, *The Symbolic Uses of Politics* (Urbana: University of Illinois Press, 1964), pp. 22–43.

SUMMARY

Eight major functions of verbal behavior lead to important political effects. Attention arousal and attention focusing determine which politically relevant events and pseudo-events will become widely known and discussed. When politically influential sources focus attention on specific political issues, action on these issues is almost assured. By contrast, issues which are not brought to public attention may die through verbal neglect. The agenda for civic action is formed from those issues which political elites adopt after public attention has been verbally focused on them.

Political actors attempt to create broadly accepted perceptual and conceptual patterns by defining political situations and linking political categories. The resulting perceptual and conceptual patterns set forth alleged causes and effects and suggest evaluations and justifications through conceptual and analogic linkages. They provide criteria for judging what institutions and events are legitimate and desirable or illegitimate and objectionable. Verbal patterns that are widely accepted determine the interpretations which a polity places on the flow of past and current events, and the kinds of predictions, plans, and policies it makes for the future.

Reality sleeves are created as a result of linkages, definitions, and attention-focusing. The reality sleeve acts like a set of blinders which permits political actors to observe only part of the perceptual and conceptual stimuli which surround them; elites and their publics can embed compatible new information while excluding incompatible information. Verbal descriptions, definitions, and linkages also create politically significant psychic states and moods in individuals and groups. High or low morale, pride, anger, or frustration are among psychic states which may generate, sustain, or destroy vital political activities.

The power of words has been belittled by some commentators because words often are not matched by corresponding deeds. Various verbal tactics have evolved which increase the potency of words to compel action. Verbal commitments are one example; their force springs from the notion that it is morally obligatory or politically expedient to abide by publicly expressed positions and implied promises. Besides, abandonment of stated positions is deemed costly because it is apt to entail losses in credibility and prestige which may impair the defaulting parties' political effectiveness. Moral and practical considerations are further reinforced by psychological pressures toward consistency. Widely publicized verbal commitments therefore enhance the probability that the committed actor will perform in accordance with his pronouncements or implied promises.

The relationship between words and actions is even closer when words are used as compelling commands or suggestions, or when they become actions (or symbolic surrogates for action) in themselves. The soldier who claims "superior orders" to justify killing civilians claims exemption from punishment on grounds that verbal commands were irresistible. Accusations which tarnish the reputation of a political entity, formal pledges of support to an allied power, or formal endorsements of a specific policy are verbal behaviors which constitute actions affecting power relationships. When demands for immediate relief of undesirable conditions are satisfied through promises of forthcoming actions, blunted by expressions of sympathy and concern, or met with an offer to formally investigate the situation, the verbal expressions are symbolic surrogates for action. They bestow psychic satisfactions which may restore political quiescence as effectively, or almost as effectively, as if the undesirable conditions had been actually alleviated.

4 Inferences Drawn from Verbal Behavior

All our reasonings concerning matter of fact are founded on a
species of Analogy, which leads us to expect from any cause the same
events which we have observed to result from similar causes. Where
the causes are entirely similar, the analogy is perfect, and the inference, drawn from it, is regarded as certain and conclusive. . . .
But where the objects have not so exact a similarity, the analogy is
less perfect, and the inference is less conclusive; though still it has
some force, in proportion to the degree of similarity and resemblance.
— David Hume, "An Enquiry Concerning Human Understanding,"
   Section IX

Say first, of God above or man below,
What can we reason, but from what we know?
Of Man, what see we but his station here,
From which to reason, or to which refer?
Thro' worlds unnumber'd, tho' the God be known,
'Tis ours to trace him only in our own.
— Alexander Pope, "Essay on Man," Epistle I, Line 17

Words are "epiphenomena which exist on the surface of the social
system."[1] In addition to their manifest and latent meanings, they carry
information about the social environment in which they have been
uttered and received. These assertions imply that a regular stimulus-
response relationship exists between environmental stimuli impinging
on an individual and his verbal and nonverbal responses. If this is
true, then one can infer from a response and knowledge of the respondent the stimuli which probably led to the response.[2]

To "infer," the dictionary says, means "to conclude or decide from
something known or assumed; to derive by reasoning." In verbal inference, the known or assumed generally is the meaning of the symbols which compose the message. From this meaning one derives additional information through logical processes, often with the aid of

1. Hugh Dalziel Duncan, *Symbols in Society* (New York: Oxford University
Press, 1968), p. 6.
2. For a fuller discussion, see B. F. Skinner, *Verbal Behavior* (New York: Apple-
ton-Century-Crofts, 1957), p. 457. Also Charles E. Osgood, "The Representational
Model and Relevant Research Methods," in Ithiel de Sola Pool, ed., *Trends in
Content Analysis* (Urbana: University of Illinois Press, 1959), pp. 36–39.

supplementary information gleaned from the context in which the message was sent.

The possibility of making valid inferences from verbal data is tempting in the many instances when more direct sources of important political information are not readily available. Under wartime conditions, for instance, there may be few clues, other than verbal inferences, about international conditions within an enemy country. If clues exist, verbal inferences may provide confirmation for guesses and suspicions which cannot be otherwise verified. When strikes or riots erupt, statements by the participants prior to and during the crisis may be the only readily available source for insights into the parties' perceptions of grievances and into their assessments of their own and their opponents' strengths and weaknesses. Information which is not explicit may nonetheless become available through processes of inference.

Hazards of Inference-Making

Doubts have frequently been expressed about the accuracy of inferences from verbal behavior, since verbal behavior is so highly susceptible to conscious manipulation. The detection and deciphering of manipulated messages, while difficult, is not an insurmountable problem. As discussed more fully in the fifth chapter, when consideration of situational contexts forms a framework for verbal analysis, the message, true or false, warped or straight, yields clues about the sender and his world. A distinction must be drawn between the inferential process under discussion here and the process of predicting action on the basis of expressed attitudes or intentions. In the latter, the expressed meaning of the message becomes the point of departure. It is compared with subsequent action to check how or whether the stated intent was carried out. The many instances in which expressed intent does not match action have led to doubts about the predictive value of words *per se*, without additional situational data. In the inferential process, the analyst looks beyond the expressed meaning of the message to unintended revelations which the message, analyzed in context, may carry. In fact, the expressed meanings may be of little interest. Inferences that action will conform with the message may be made, but this is only one of a wide variety of uses to which the inference process may be put.

Inferences about relations among complex human behaviors are always risky. The analyst can never be certain that he has included all relevant factors into his calculations. Ole Holsti states categorically that "inferences about the antecedent causes of messages drawn solely from content data cannot be considered self-validating" because of "differences in the ways people may express their feelings, intentions, and other traits . . . it is hazardous indeed to assume, without corroborating evidence from independent, noncontent data, that inferences . . . may be drawn directly from content data." [3]

While substantial, the hazards of inference-making are no greater for verbal than for other forms of behavior, provided that the verbal data are carefully examined in their social context. As B. F. Skinner has pointed out, inferences regarding relations among physical phenomena are equally dependent on a knowledge of, or assumptions about, surrounding circumstances. One cannot account for temperature change in a room without knowing a set of situational factors.[4] The social context which needs to be examined in making inferences from verbal behavior includes an analysis of the situation in which the communication was made and of the characteristics of the actors, including their degrees of commitment to the message which they have sent.[5] As with other social science predictions, faith in verbal inferences is strengthened in direct proportion to the number, variety, and assumed validity of sets of measures, verbal and nonverbal, which support the inference.

Scholars who have compared the accuracy of inferences from verbal behavior with that of inferences from nonverbal behavior have noted comparable degrees of validity. For instance, after making inferences from verbalized perceptions of hostility and nonverbal indexes of hostility, Dina Zinnes concluded that "while differences exist between physical behavior and written expression, these differences are not appreciable." [6] Other investigators have concluded that verbal data permitted accurate inferences about hostility, friendship, frustration, and satisfaction of political actors as readily as did fluctuations in exchange and interest rates, the flow of gold, and prices on the commodity and security markets. ". . . the 'soft' variable derived through content

3. Ole R. Holsti, *Content Analysis for the Social Sciences and Humanities* (Reading, Mass.: Addison Wesley, 1969), p. 32.

4. Skinner, *Verbal Behavior*, p. 457.

5. James M. Fendrich, "A Study of the Association among Verbal Attitudes, Commitment and Overt Behavior in Different Experimental Situations," *Social Forces*, 45 (1967), 347.

6. Dina A. Zinnes, "The Expression and Perception of Hostility in Prewar Crisis, 1914," in J. David Singer, ed., *Quantitative International Politics: Insights and Evidence* (New York: Free Press, 1968), p. 119.

analysis traces a pattern almost identical with that of the 'hard' variables."[7] The risks in making inferences from either type of indicators were similar. During World War II analysts at the Federal Communications Commission developed inferential criteria concerning German communications to the point where post-war checks on the accuracy of wartime inferences showed an 85 percent accuracy rate.[8] Likewise, inferences about the judicial philosophy of Supreme Court justices, drawn from verbal analysis of their opinions, have shown high correlations with inferences drawn from the voting behavior of these judges.[9]

When the inference process becomes suspect because inferences drawn from verbal behavior are later disconfirmed, the suspicion may sometimes be misplaced. Inference failure may be due to the fact that the verbal behavior had consequences which led to a change of policy. For instance, when one country expresses itself in a manner which another interprets as an intention to attack, behavior in response to this inference may lead to precautions or bargaining which may make the attack unwise or unnecessary.

Even if inferences from verbal data are viewed with skepticism, it is still important to understand the assumptions and procedures involved, for they are widely used in politics. Speculations from known words to unknown political conditions are constantly made by political actors, mass media personnel, scholars, and the general public. To predict their inferences and the actions which will be based on them, one must understand the kinds of inferences they are likely to draw from various forms of verbal behavior.

CLUES FOR DRAWING INFERENCES FROM VERBAL DATA

Though widely used in a number of behavioral sciences, inferential procedures remain largely in the nature of an intuitive art, rather than a systematic science. The problem in communications analysis "has its counterparts in many diagnostic fields — for example, clinical psy-

7. Ole R. Holsti, Robert C. North, and Richard A. Brody, "Perception and Action in the 1914 Crisis," *ibid.*, pp. 123–158; Ole R. Holsti and Robert C. North, "Perceptions of Hostility and Economic Variables," in Richard L. Merritt and Stein Rokkan, eds., *Comparing Nations: The Use of Quantitative Data in Cross-National Research* (New Haven: Yale University Press, 1966), pp. 169–190; quote on p. 190.

8. Alexander L. George, *Propaganda Analysis* (Evanston, Ill.: Row, Peterson, 1959), p. 267.

9. Glendon Schubert, "Jackson's Judicial Philosophy: An Exploration in Value Analysis," *American Political Science Review*, 59 (1965), 962.

chology, psychiatry, psychoanalysis, clinical medicine, and the analysis of responses to open-end questions in opinion and attitude surveys. . . . No mechanical or clerical procedure has yet been devised which will replace the skill of the experienced diagnostician." [10] This does not mean, however, that the process is wholly without scientific guidelines.

In a book which describes the procedures used by the Federal Communications Commission to make inferences from German wartime communications, Alexander George outlines the major components of the inferential process within a "logic-of-the-situation" approach. [11] In this approach, a communications analyst familiarizes himself with seemingly relevant aspects of the social system from which the communication originates. Using this inferential model, the analyst postulates choices which political communicators in the system are likely to have faced in coping with problems he presumes they have cognized or sensed. By matching the actual choice of communications to the solution for the presumed problems, the analyst deduces the circumstances which led to the actual choice. The whole process amounts to an effort to unravel the sequence of calculations which went into the original message-encoding process.

The inferential process rests on a number of basic assumptions about human behavior, such as the assumptions that human behavior is generally purposive, that it shows a high degree of regularity in the face of basically unchanged circumstances, and that choices are rational, given limited availability of information and the logic commonly used by the communicator in question. [12] The analyst who makes inferences draws his clues from four types of information. These are: general aspects of the state of the social system in which the message originated; general principles of human behavior presumably operative in the particular social system; knowledge of the behavioral idiosyncrasies of the communicators involved; and idiosyncratic aspects of the particular communication situation. A few examples will illustrate the process.

Situational Context Clues

When the analyst is aware of a situation in which a country is menaced by a neighbor, he may infer that a series of speeches in which

10. George, *Propaganda Analysis*, p. xiii.

11. *Ibid.*, pp. 46–59.

12. See *ibid.*, pp. 112–116, for suggestions of areas of information which are essential for inference-making. Specific ways in which inferences may be drawn from verbal and nonverbal behavior in international politics are outlined by Robert Jervis, *The Logic of Images in International Relations* (Princeton: Princeton University Press, 1970), pp. 28–40.

leaders boast of the country's strength is intended to intimidate the threatening neighbor. Depending on the state of military preparations at the time of the speech, he may also draw inferences about the likelihood of preventive war. If a country does not appear to be threatened, militant speeches by its leaders might lead to inferences about their aggressive intentions, especially when coupled with substantial increases in offensive military capabilities. Likewise, an analyst who knows about charges of financial irregularities in an administrator's office may be able to make certain inferences from the administrator's sudden refusal to discuss his fiscal policies with the media, whereas without such knowledge of the situation, the refusal to talk might be baffling. When the leader of a striking union begins a major verbal campaign to exhort union members to remain on the picket lines, one needs to know at what stage of the strike these exhortations were made before inferring that enthusiasm about the strike is waning among union members.

General Behavioral Context Clues

General knowledge of behavioral responses under various types of conditions, and in various mental states, also may supply clues for inference. Some of these mental states, such as paranoia, cognitive dissonance, or high threat perception, may be revealed by speech behavior. Once the behavior-shaping factors have been identified, likely behavioral responses can be inferred.

For instance, the same speech, given by a paranoid personality and by a leader with more normal mental traits would produce different inferences. On the basis of cognitive dissonance theory, one can predict that highly committed political leaders, whose widely publicized predictions are disconfirmed by events, are likely to increase their efforts to find believers and make the predictions come true, rather than abandoning them.[13]

When verbal behavior reveals a high degree of threat perception by political actors, one can make inferences about the quality of decision-making. Actors under great psychological stress tend to perceive a narrower spectrum of alternatives than unpressured actors; they also tend toward less rational balancing of action commitments and action resources. "As tensions rise and effective communication between par-

13. A relevant political study is Paul J. Hiniker, *Ideological Polarization in Mao's China* (forthcoming). For an interesting case study on the effects of failed religious predictions, see Leon Festinger, H. W. Riecken, and Stanley Schachter, *When Prophecy Fails: A Social and Psychological Study of a Modern Group That Predicted the Destruction of the World* (New York: Harper, 1956).

ties increases in difficulty, stereotyped images not only are relied upon more but tend to become even more simplified and uni-dimensional."[14] Likewise, the scope and tempo of economic development in various societies can be inferred from the amounts of achievement imagery found in their literature during different historical periods.[15]

Idiosyncratic Behavioral Context Clues

Productive clues in inference-making often come from examining past relations between a source's verbal output and other conditions. For instance, in the early years of World War II, Germany's attacks on neighboring countries were generally preceded by a barrage of verbal accusations. The intention to attack was usually denied at the time of the verbal barrage, but from previous sequences one could readily infer that such verbal assaults, emanating from German leaders, were apt to be followed by military invasion.

In the Soviet Union the extent of media coverage of a political actor frequently is an index to his status in the political hierarchy. An actor's rise to power is usually preceded by a rise in the volume of media coverage devoted to him; when he declines, coverage may cease altogether, sometimes well in advance of his fall. Hence one can often predict the imminent rise or fall of a Soviet leader from analysis of mass media coverage. Events in Nikita Khrushchev's rise and decline are a case in point.

During the Indochina war of the 1950's, French official comments about military losses had been relatively calm without any indication of great doubt about ultimate victory. Reactions to the fall of Dienbienphu were quite different. Although the fall of the garrison was a relatively minor blow, official French comments pictured it as a major disaster which meant that the war could not be fought through to victory. By contrasting these comments with earlier verbal responses to military reverses, the American government correctly inferred that France's will to resist had been broken and the withdrawal of French forces from Vietnam was imminent.[16]

14. Ole R. Holsti, "The Value of International Tension Measurement," *Journal of Conflict Resolution*, 7 (1963), 613; also see Dina A. Zinnes, Robert C. North, and Howard E. Koch, Jr., "Capability, Threat and the Outbreak of War," in James N. Rosenau, ed., *International Politics and Foreign Policy* (New York: Free Press, 1969), pp. 469–476.

15. See Richard de Charms and Gerald H. Moeller, "Values Expressed in American Children's Readers: 1900–1950," *Journal of Abnormal and Social Psychology*, 64 (1962), 136–142, and sources cited there.

16. Jervis, *Logic of Images*, pp. 30–31.

Communication Context Clues

Verbal patterns and frequencies may permit inferences about perceptual and situational conditions implied by these features. Most commonly, inferences are made on the basis of the frequency with which various themes are mentioned, based on the contention that high frequency of mention of symbols or concepts indicates that the message-sender places great importance on the message, or at least that the message has high prominence in his thinking. Conversely, lack of mention or infrequent mention is considered evidence of lack of concern.[17]

Inferences based on this theory have proven valid in many communications situations. The frequency with which political concepts are mentioned in the mass media has permitted inferences about which matters are of high or low political concern in a given society.[18] Likewise, when a topic has been mentioned by many different countries in an international assembly or by many different politicians in a national assembly, one can validly infer that it had importance or political utility initially, or would acquire such traits by virtue of frequent discussion. At the very least, one can infer that a cultural value was involved and that the speakers expected to derive benefit by calling attention to it frequently.[19]

In other circumstances these canons of inference have been inapplicable. Frequency and importance may not coincide; a political actor may discuss those things which he thinks others want to hear, although he deems them unimportant. In that case the message may permit inferences about the actor's perception of the foci of interest of his target audience, or about the actor's desire to divert attention from potentially explosive topics. Certain important factors may be so well understood as not to require mention: failure to mention French small arms capacity in the discussions of military potential in World War I did not reveal lack of concern by the parties; rather, all parties were so well aware of this capacity that they deemed it unnecessary to stress it.

The frequency criterion must also be used cautiously in inferring the effects of verbal behavior. It is not necessarily true that those matters which are mentioned most frequently have the greatest impact

17. Jum C. Nunnally, "Individual Differences in Word Usage," in Sheldon Rosenberg, ed., *Directions in Psycholinguistics* (New York: Macmillan, 1965), pp. 208ff.

18. Ithiel de Sola Pool, *The 'Prestige' Papers: A Survey of Their Editorials* (Stanford: Stanford University Press, 1952).

19. Doris A. Graber, "Conflict Images: An Assessment of the Middle East Debates in the United Nations," *Journal of Politics*, 32 (1970), 339–378.

on audiences, for there may be a crest of attention; if matters are talked about too frequently, the crest is reached and interest diminishes. By knowing the background of verbal behavior, one can establish the limits for this crest in various societies. Cuban listeners seem to have a far higher tolerance for Fidel Castro's repetitive oratory than one would expect American audiences to have in a similar situation.

The sheer volume of communication between two parties may provide a clue to their attitudes. Ole Holsti contends that "as the feelings of hostility between two states deepen, the volume of direct communication between them falls and they increasingly use their respective allies as audiences toward which to pour out their feelings of frustration and hostility." [20] So, too, from increased amounts of communications and the use of extraordinary transmission channels one can infer that potential tensions are rising. [21]

The comparison of messages coming from various sources may permit inferences about characteristics of the sources, such as the extent to which they share ideologies or action programs. Comparison of short-wave radio propaganda beamed by Berlin, Rome, and Tokyo to the United States during World War II permitted inferences about propaganda collaboration among the three countries. [22] Such inferences from verbal comparisons have been deemed reliable enough for American courts to admit them as evidence regarding motivation and affiliation of message-senders. Accordingly, the similarity (and often identity) of messages sent by Fascist or Communist organizations in the United States to messages emitted by their foreign prototypes has been accepted by courts as proof of Fascist or Communist tendencies and affiliations. [23]

Many types of perceptions are paired: individuals displaying perception A can be expected to hold perception B as well. Analysis of verbal behavior in United Nations debates on Arab-Israeli tensions showed that 80 percent of the countries which expressed themselves strongly in favor of international law in general terms, also expressed them-

20. Holsti, "Value of International Tension Measurement," p. 612.
21. Ole R. Holsti, "The 1914 Case," *American Political Science Review*, 59 (1965), 369–377.
22. Bernard Berelson and Sebastian de Grazia, "Detecting Collaboration in Propaganda," *Public Opinion Quarterly*, 11 (1947), 244–253.
23. See Karin Dovring, *Road of Propaganda: The Semantics of Biased Communications* (New York: Philosophical Library, 1959), p. 121; Harold D. Lasswell and Nathan Leites, "Propaganda Detection and the Courts," in Harold D. Lasswell, Nathan Leites et al., eds., *The Language of Politics: Studies in Quantitative Semantics* (Cambridge: MIT Press, 1965), pp. 177–178. Examples are cited on pp. 178–226.

selves in favor of opening the Suez canal. Once this covariation had been confirmed, one could deduce respect for international law, or preference for the opening of the Suez canal, from the presence of the corollary expressed attitude.[24]

When word and action correlations have been confirmed for certain actors or situations, the action can be inferred from the word and vice versa. Analysis of speeches given by Adolf Hitler and Franklin Roosevelt prior to World War II showed that Hitler's speeches stressed military strength more than twice as much as Roosevelt's.[25] If a correlation had been established between aggressive action and his speech behavior, future attacks on neighboring countries might have been predicted.

Analysis of the content of the message may permit inferences about the sources of information available to the sender, and about his assumptions, perceptions, beliefs, expectations, goals, and motivations.[26] These inferences may have little or nothing to do with the intent of the message. For example, during the early stages of the 1972 election campaign, President Nixon's message which opposed busing to achieve racial balance permitted inferences about his assumptions regarding black voters, his estimates about public opinion on busing, and his willingness to use national legislative and judicial powers to further integrationist causes. None of these matters was explicitly covered in the speech, but the fact that he broadcast his opposition to busing to the nation at a crucial time, knowing full well that every possible meaning would be extracted from it, conveyed a great deal of inferential grist for the mills of political analysts.

INFERENCE REALMS

There are three areas in which politically useful inferences have often been drawn from verbal behavior. In the first place, inferences about the *antecedents* of a message are common. Antecedents are the conditions existing before or at the time when the message was formulated or sent. When a message is sent to or overheard by a receiver, he may well ask, "What made the sender say that?" The verbal statement becomes a clue.

In the second place, inferences often are made about the *sources*

24. Graber, "Conflict Images," pp. 370–374.
25. Ralph K. White, "Hitler, Roosevelt and the Nature of War Propaganda," *Journal of Abnormal and Social Psychology*, 44 (1949), 157–174.
26. Holsti, "The 1914 Case," pp. 369, 374–377.

of the message. Borrowing from psycho-linguistic theories, verbal analysts contend that the nature of messages is partly a function of the attributes of the sender. The message tells something about the life situation of the sender, his perceptions, and his way of thinking.[27] The notion that individuals and groups can be studied by analyzing their verbal output underlies much social science research; it is basic to all research done through questionnaires or interviews. A researcher stimulates verbal behavior by asking questions. He then infers characteristics and attitudes of the respondents from their verbal messages. Life histories, various projective tests, and word association tests do the same; if the stimulus word "administer" invokes in a student population associations of "medicine, sick, or dosage" rather than "estate, justice, or court," an investigator may well infer that he is dealing with medical students, rather than law students.[28] Additional available clues might validate the inference even further.

The third area about which inferences are often made is the effect of the message. The effects of messages may, of course, be quite apparent by the time the message is studied — a command to do X may have led to the doing of X. But at other times messages are studied before they have elicited a reaction, or before the reaction becomes widely known. When Russia verbally attacks China, calling her a dogmatist and war monger, there may be no immediate visible consequences. But foreign ministries around the world will try to infer from the messages what current and future relations between the Soviet Union and China may be like.

A further area in which inferential processes are used is deciphering the meaning of language. This has already been discussed in the second chapter, where it was pointed out that verbal behavior can be instrumental, carrying messages other than those which are explicit from the words. In that case, meanings are often inferred from the social context in which the words were conveyed. The social context becomes the "known" from which the unknown message meaning is inferred.

Inferences about Antecedents

Put broadly, "the content, form, and uses of the language of each community mirror its physical setting, what its members are aware of

27. Nunnally, "Individual Differences," p. 204; Davis B. Bobrow, "The Transition from International Communication to International Relations as Communication," APSA paper (1970), p. 17. Also see the literature on linguistic relativism cited in ch. 1, note 25, above.

28. Nunnally, "Individual Differences," pp. 218, 227.

and concerned about, and what their vicissitudes and successes with it have been. . . ." More specifically:

> The language reveals a host of social situations and processes — especially societal cohesion and separation; assimilation and ethnic diversity and conflict; social and cultural stratifications; all sorts of demographic, occupational, and other cultural specializations; social power and social control; kinds and levels of cultural development, as well as cultural history and texture; all historic contacts, including those by migration, invasion, and conquest; the social values, preoccupations, standards, and objectives; the size, complexity, and forms of social organization.[29]

Inferences about a message's antecedents may be derived in four ways. First, *the message per se* may permit inferences about the political and social context from which it originated. For instance, in the 1967-70 war between Nigeria and Biafra, the desperate appeal by Biafrans for food indicated not only hunger, but also dependence on outside assistance. One could further infer from this appeal that the fortunes of the Biafrans were declining, that much of the country was at starvation levels, and that Biafra's chances of military success were severely limited.

A study of United Nations debates permitted inferences about the nature and stability of political cleavages in the UN General Assembly. Debating patterns revealed definite bloc cleavages among the discussants. The verbal patterns also showed that alignments broke down when aggressive tendencies of particular countries were under discussion. In the pre-1967 Mideast debates, all countries were willing to agree that Israel had engaged in aggression, including the countries which had aligned themselves ideologically with Israel. This permitted inferences about the stability of bloc cleavages in various types of debating situations.[30]

Second, *changes in a stream of messages* over time may indicate that the conditions producing the stream of messages have changed. Analysis of May Day slogans in the Soviet Union from 1918 to 1943 revealed the decline of military slogans in favor of slogans of international cooperation. Verbal changes, corroborated by other data, convinced investigators that a change in policy had taken place. When nonverbal indexes of change are sparse or inaccessible, verbal indexes are a most welcome alternative.[31]

29. Joyce O. Hertzler, *A Sociology of Language* (New York: Random House, 1965), p. 35.
30. Graber, "Conflict Images," pp. 353–355.
31. S. Yacobson and Harold D. Lasswell, "Trend: May Day Slogans in Soviet

Likewise, a change in the images of African politicians in African literature between 1950 and the mid-1960's suggested a change in political perceptions among African intellectual elites. African politicians were first depicted as heroes leading their nations to independence. Later they were presented increasingly as villains, mismanaging the affairs of the nation and robbing the poor. From these changes in fictional characterization one could infer changes in public experiences and perceptions.[32] In the African context, nonfiction writing about incumbent politicians would not have been very helpful because it tended to be universally adulatory in response to censorship and other pressures.

During World War II, Alexander George and co-workers at the Federal Communications Commission tried to predict changes in German war policy by analyzing streams of messages sent by high German officials to the German public. These German messages initially rated Italy's military support highly. When the German High Command changed its tune and told the German people that Italy was not particularly important to the continuance of the war, the Federal Communications Commission analysts deduced that the Germans had begun to discount military support from Italy. They surmised correctly that German forces would shortly be withdrawn from Italy and that Germany would concentrate its military efforts on its home grounds.[33]

Third, *comparison of messages* of various parties may permit inferences about matters such as the degree of interdependence and cooperation among the parties, and the extent to which they share perceptions of danger from common enemies. Terry Hopmann used this type of comparative analysis to test cohesion within the Communist system.[34] Data about interaction among Communist powers are scarce, since there is little straightforward comment about such matters in Communist countries. Hopmann reasoned that certain aspects of cohesion might be inferred from similarity in verbal statements. The assumption was tested through a model of co-orientation in communication based on T. M. Newcomb's A-B-X model of interpersonal communication. The model predicts that two interdependent actors, A and B, will strive for consistency in their respective orientations toward X. When inter-

Russia," in Lasswell, Leites et al., *Language of Politics*, pp. 234–285; for other examples, see Pool, *Trends in Content Analysis*, pp. 27–40.

32. Bernth Lindfors, "The African Politician's Changing Image in African Literature in English," *Journal of Developing Areas*, 4 (1969), 13–28.

33. George, *Propaganda Analysis*, pp. 234–236.

34. P. Terry Hopmann, "International Conflict and Cohesion in the Communist System," *International Studies Quarterly*, 11 (1967), 212–236. Hopmann used semantic differential analysis for comparisons of verbal outputs; see ch. 5.

dependence increases, the symmetry in orientation toward X increases as well. If it could be shown that statements made by leaders of Communist countries about a common enemy become more similar in times of tension and less similar in calm periods, then tension-perceptions and levels of bloc cohesion could be inferred from verbal comparisons.

Accordingly, Hopmann compared official pronouncements about the United States during selected periods of tension and calm between the United States and Communist nations. Statements came from the Soviet Union, China, Albania, Bulgaria, Czechoslovakia, East Germany, Hungary, Poland, and Rumania. As predicted by the model, the results showed that the verbal evaluations of the United States by the nine countries were more similar during crisis periods. During low-tension periods, the average difference in evaluations among the nine countries was two and a half times as great as in times of high tension — 20 percent and 8 percent respectively.

Closer co-orientation in crisis applied only to attitudes toward countries whose threatening behavior had brought about the need for greater interdependence. Evaluations of uninvolved nations, such as North Korea and North and South Vietnam, remained disparate during the crisis. Even China and Albania, whose statements deviated widely from bloc norms in periods of low tension, verbally rallied to the bloc in high-tension periods. Hopmann's findings have been corroborated by the work of other investigators who use different countries, different incidents of accord and discord, and different time periods.[35]

Finally, searching messages for *specific content features* may also yield inferences about value structures of various societies. Political communicators try to stick closely to the cultural myths of their audiences; thus one can infer the myths of a society or group from the appeals which its popular leaders make. "The larger and more unknown his public, the more he (communicator) has to rely on attention-calling appeals. He fetches these from his knowledge of his public's ruling myth — Marxism for instance or America, the country of Freedom — and official social structure, and the method of its values' dissemination in old or modern communications channels. He must obviously stick closely to the basic structure of a community." [36]

---

35. For examples, see two articles by Ole R. Holsti, "East-West Conflict and Sino-Soviet Relations," *Journal of Applied Behavioral Science*, 1 (1965), 115–130; "External Conflict and Internal Consensus: The Sino-Soviet Case," in Philip J. Stone, Dexter C. Dunphy, Marshall S. Smith, and Daniel M. Ogilvie, *The General Inquirer: A Computer Approach to Content Analysis* (Cambridge: MIT Press, 1966), pp. 343–358.

36. Dovring, *Road of Propaganda*, p. 21.

From the cultural values of a group and the meanings which words and concepts have for it, one can often infer the group's life experience. Historical records show that in the Middle Ages the word "Hun" evoked terror among Central Europeans, but not among people in other parts of the world. From the reactions which historians have recorded, one can trace patterns of fear perception and infer invasion patterns of barbarian tribes. Studies of verbal treatment accorded to Jews, Turks, heretics, political leaders, and other subjects of intense feelings have also been used to infer experiences and cultural patterns of social groups.

Value structures of public assemblies and of their constituencies can be inferred from the values stressed in their debates. In the Middle East debates, for example, creation of an international police force was a frequent topic in the UN General Assembly. Discussants representing 71 out of 87 countries favored an international police force. Comparing the frequency and favorableness of attention given to this topic with that given to others, one could infer that proposals for an international police force stood a good chance of passage.[37]

Likewise, the study of UN debates showed a generally favorable appraisal of the United Nations as a conflict-reducing organization. Eighty-five percent of the speakers who mentioned the value of UN debate praised it; only 5 percent called it worthless or even harmful. Praise came from 63 countries, including all the parties to the Mideast conflict. Only 22 countries appraised any of the debates negatively. Analysis of these data, in the context of the usual verbal interactions in the Assembly, permits making inferences about members' support for the body. The validity and reliability of the results of debate analysis have been compared with results obtained through polling of members and through personal interviews. Regardless of method, the results were similar.[38]

Comparison of verbally expressed values may also be useful in detecting variations among societies or individuals. Hans Sebald attempted to infer variations in national character from a comparative study of national literatures, such as songbooks used in German and American schools.[39] He compared attitudes expressed in the songs toward a people's own society, other societies, authority, death, man-

---

37. Graber, "Conflict Images," p. 372.

38. Doris A. Graber, "Perceptions of Middle East Conflict in the UN, 1953–65," *Journal of Conflict Resolution*, 13 (1969), 477–480.

39. Hans Sebald, "Studying National Character through Comparative Content Analysis," *Social Forces*, 40 (1962), 318–322.

hood, work, family, nature, mating and courting, childhood, religion, and similar dimensions found in all cultures. He found that the features identified as "German" values resembled the characteristics of the authoritarian personality. "A large number of German songs emphasized authoritarian principles like absolute allegiance of the individual to the will of the nation; dutiful work as a road to success, freedom, and power, courage to fight to the end for the freedom of the nation."[40] Less than 1 percent of American songs placed the needs and goals of society above individual needs and goals; 36 percent of the German songs did. No American songs lauded heroic death, while over 8 percent of the German songs did.

Herbert Lewin compared the literature used by German Hitler Youth and the Boy Scouts of America in their respective character-building programs.[41] From the differences in these expressions of ideals, he speculated about the possible effects on the character of young members of these organizations. Inferences made from such comparative content-analysis findings about national character and the effects of the socialization process do, of course, require confirmation from other data if the validity and reliability of the verbal data are to become firmly established.

If the value structure of an individual or group is known, expression of these values can lead to inferences about who originated an unattributed message. Milton Rokeach and co-workers studied the values expressed in Federalist papers authored by Hamilton and Madison. They then searched for corresponding values in papers whose authorship was disputed. The resulting attribution of papers to Madison and Hamilton respectively corroborated conclusions reached by other investigators who had used different techniques for the same task.[42]

Inferences about Sources

Three sets of things can be inferred about a source from its messages. In the first place, one can infer the perceptual state of the sender — how he himself views reality, and how he appraises the perceptions of others. ". . . languages incorporate unique ways of cog-

40. *Ibid.*, pp. 321–322.
41. Herbert S. Lewin, "Hitler Youth and the Boy Scouts of America: A Comparison of Aims," *Human Relations*, 1 (1947), 206–227.
42. Milton Rokeach, Robert Homant, and Louis Penner, "A Value Analysis of the Disputed Federalist Papers," *Journal of Personality and Social Psychology*, 16 (1970), 245–250.

nitively organizing the world." [43] By becoming aware of the ideational organization of an individual's world, one can infer his mental state and thinking processes. For instance, when black leaders fill their statements with views which picture the white community as "the Enemy," one can infer their racial hostility. Constant and devout reference to the deity in the discourse of individuals or groups may lead to inferences about their religious outlook and fervor and their likely reactions to scientific findings contrary to religious injunctions. Use of professional or political jargon may link a speaker to groups without requiring specific information concerning the linkage.

Motives and perceptions of clients of public agencies have been inferred from their correspondence with these agencies. [44] Appeals received by Israeli Custom Authorities were examined to infer the clients' verbal strategies and perception of the agency. Appeals ranged from threats to blow up the agency if requests were refused to flattery and assertions that clients were doing the agency a favor by asking for good treatment. Pleas were of two basic types. Clients either raised profit motive considerations for themselves or the agency, or they referred to some norm which officials must uphold as a duty to the client or society. Analysis of the pattern of appeals revealed that one could infer the national origin of appellants from their communications. Appellants of non-Western origin were more likely to refer to the profit motive and to personal altruism of officials; they seemed to lack bureaucratic socialization and viewed and dealt with bureaucracy in ways more appropriate to primary personal relations. Westerners were more likely to appeal to formal regulations and impersonal norms.

It has been said that wars begin in the minds of men. National leaders' perceptions of reality, their fears, and their ideas about the intentions of others determine their decisions, regardless of whether their perceptions are correct. When Arabs talk frequently and intensely about the "offensive" weapons which Israel is staging near the Arab borders, one can infer that they are afraid of an imminent Israeli attack. In the absence of extensive heated comment on Israeli border fortifications, one can infer that fear and tension are low. The fact that

43. Julius Laffal, *Pathological and Normal Language* (New York: Atherton Press, 1965), p. 112. The imagery of poets has been used to infer traits of their personalities, because they presumably drew images from the objects which they knew best, to which they gave most thought, and to which they were most sensitive. *Ibid.*, p. 117.

44. Elihu Katz, Michael Gurevitch, Brenda Danet, and Tsiyona Peled, "Petitions and Prayers: A Method for the Content Analysis of Persuasive Appeals," *Social Forces*, 47 (1969), 447–463.

Arabs may call the weapons used "offensive" while Israelis would label them "defensive" may indicate differential perceptions of the intent behind the stationing of the weapons. Knowledge that differential perceptions exist, and inferences about their political consequences, may lead to important readjustments of policy.

Analyses of UN Mideast debates revealed that fear of war was expressed much more frequently by Eastern bloc countries than by members of the Western bloc. This knowledge could be used for inferences about differential threat perceptions and about policies based on these perceptions, or it might serve to infer propagandistic uses which various nations make of General Assembly debate, and the policy considerations underlying these uses. UN debate also showed a sharing of certain types of values among all the states represented in the United Nations. This information permits inferences about commonalities within the international system and actions which can be built upon these commonalities.[45]

Second, verbal output can also be used to infer the goals and motivations of the source. Goals expressed in UN debates about international cooperation and common attitudes toward preventive war and treatment of refugees permitted inferences about policy intentions of the nations involved. Communications by German elites to their people during World War II were studied to infer these elites' intentions, capabilities, priorities, and expectations; similar studies, done more or less methodically, are a staple in intelligence operations of foreign offices and defense departments around the world.

During the Korean War, China's goals in Korea and the steps likely to be taken to achieve these goals could have been inferred from available verbal materials. Public statements by Chinese leaders, commentaries in Chinese mass media, intelligence reports on troop movements and other strategic and diplomatic activities all revealed an initial lack of interest in the Korean War. The press was quite slow in reporting initial hostilities and gave them little prominence when they were finally published; it took forty-eight hours after the first announcement that war had erupted in Korea for Peking's news media to publicize the story, even though Shanghai papers had published the news earlier. When Peking papers did report it, they expressed confidence in North Korean victory and made no promises about Chinese aid.[46] After the initial neglect, anonymous military accounts

45. Graber, "Conflict Images," pp. 352–353, 359–364.
46. Allen S. Whiting, *China Crosses the Yalu: The Decision to Enter the Korean War* (New York: Macmillan, 1960), pp. 54–55.

about the American action began to appear gradually in the official newspapers; however, the expressed doubts about North Korean strength persisted, despite repeated slurs about non-Communist strength. "The imperialists look strong on the outside but are weak on the inside . . . (being) only 'paper tigers.'"[47]

By contrast, Peking reacted strongly toward American action in Taiwan. The Chinese press protested vigorously when the United States order the Seventh Fleet into the Taiwan Strait. The lag in publication of Korean news and the immediate publication of Taiwan news led to inferences about the comparative importance which China assigned to the two events. The inference of China's prime interest in Taiwan and only passing interest in Korea was further supported by evidence regarding China's troop dispositions at the time.

The subsequent change in Chinese policy was heralded by a sharply worded article in *World Culture* (*Shih Chih Shih*), a weekly publication closely associated with the Ministry of Foreign Affairs. *World Culture* alleged: "The barbarous action of American imperialism and its hangers-on in invading Korea not only menaces peace in Asia and the world, in general, but seriously threatens the security of China in particular. The Chinese people cannot allow such aggresive action of American imperialism in Korea. . . . North Korea's friends are our friends, North Korea's enemy is our enemy; North Korea's defense is our defense, North Korea's victory is our victory." Somewhat later, the Chinese press attacked Americans as "mad dogs."[48] Next a massive propaganda campaign was launched by Chinese news media, stressing the mutuality of Korean and Chinese interests and Chou En-lai's unwillingness to tolerate the invasion of China's neighbors.

Problems in inferring motivations and goals are well illustrated by another incident from the Korean War. After Republic of Korea units had crossed the 38th Parallel, Chinese premier Chou En-lai told India's Ambassador Panikkar that China would enter the war if U.S. troops crossed the 38th Parallel. American diplomats did not know whether this threat was real or a ruse. As Allen Whiting has noted, "The problem of communicating a threat is formidable, and in the context of the Korean war it is especially difficult. Peking had employed belligerent language with respect to liberation of Taiwan in the face of Seventh Fleet opposition, yet it had failed to make good its threat."[49] While some press comment had heralded subsequent action, other comments

47. *Ibid.*, p. 55.
48. *Ibid.*, pp. 84–85, 99.
49. *Ibid.*, p. 109.

had led to false expectations. For instance, after China entered the Korean War, the press discussed policies linked to a variety of outcomes of the fighting. It was impossible to infer which outcome the Chinese were actually anticipating; of course, this may have been an accurate picture of the situation, because China's goals were still flexible.

Finally, verbal output may reveal a great deal about the sender's personality. Psychologists are the most frequent users of techniques which analyze speech patterns to infer the personality of the source, including attitudes, needs, interests, and moods.[50] Certain types of language have been identified as paranoid or schizoid; tests for these types have been applied formally or intuitively to the verbal output of political figures such as Napoleon and Hitler.[51] Test results may indicate psychotic tendencies even when the general behavior of the individual remains within normal behavioral limits. Verbal analyses can also reveal insecurity, dishonesty, or rigidities in personality. Rigid attitudes which Secretary of State Dulles revealed toward the Communist leaders, and those which President Wilson displayed toward the Germans, indicated to political analysts that neither man would likely change his opinions. One could infer that as long as these men remained in power, U.S. policy would remain inflexibly hostile toward the Russians and Germans.

Psychological imagery in presidential inaugural addresses from 1905 to 1969 has been analyzed to assess the psychological characteristics of the presidents and to make predictions about how each would play his role.[52] Scoring methods originally developed for individual TAT protocols were used to locate images indicating achievement drives and power drives. The analysis yielded four types of presidents distinguished by their combination of low or high achievement drives with low or high power drives. Similarly, the values expressed by political leaders have been studied for the light they might shed on the leader's personalities. Psychologically oriented biographies have used this method; so have content analyses of the verbal output of such leaders

50. Nunnally, "Individual Differences," p. 218; James D. Barber, "Adult Identity and Presidential Style," *Daedalus*, 97 (1968), 949–950.

51. See Harold Lasswell, *The Psychopathology of Politics* (Chicago: University of Chicago Press, 1930), and the psychologically oriented biographies cited in note 53, below.

52. Richard E. Donley and David G. Winter, "Measuring the Motives of Public Officials at a Distance: An Exploratory Study of American Presidents," *Behavioral Science*, 15 (1970), 227–236. Also see the discussion of this study in ch. 7.

as Roosevelt, Stalin, Hitler, and Dulles.[53] So, too, the judicial philosophies and values of Supreme Court justices have been inferred from examination of their published opinions in legal cases.[54]

Inferences about Effects

The bulk of verbal communication involves the intent of a source to send a message which will have specific effects on a target audience and other audiences which are likely to overhear the communication. As discussed in the second chapter, the sender will examine the character of his audience and the situational context and then infer the effects which various types of messages are likely to have on the audience. He will encode the message in the manner that appears to be most effective.

When the sender is unable to observe the impact of the message or to learn about it indirectly, he may attempt to infer it from the verbal response. For example, if a plane hijacker is told by radio that a certain foreign country is no longer willing to give him asylum, one may infer that he received the message and believes it if he subsequently orders the pilot to reroute the flight to a different country, or if he inquires about the availability of other places of asylum.

If particular message effects cannot be observed, investigators may infer them by examining the effects of comparable communications on similar audiences in analogous situations. Investigators who were interested in the effects of Father Coughlin's radio speeches examined the appeals which the right-wing priest was using successfully with selected groups of listeners, hoping that discovery of the success formula would permit inferences about likely effects of similar messages on other radio audiences.[55]

Douglas Waples and Bernard Berelson studied emotionalism in the media during the 1940 presidential campaign to determine the effects

53. An example of this type of psychological biography is Alexander and Juliette George, *Woodrow Wilson and Colonel House: A Personality Study* (New York: John Day, 1956); a content analysis example is Ole R. Holsti, "Cognitive Dynamics and Images of the Enemy," in David J. Finlay, Ole R. Holsti, and Richard R. Fagen, eds., *Enemies in Politics* (Chicago: Rand McNally, 1967), pp. 25–96. Also see ch. 7.

54. Schubert, "Jackson's Judicial Philosophy," pp. 940–963. Schubert examined content variables, opinion variables, voting variables, and chronological variables. Also see Harold Spaeth, "The Judicial Restraint of Mr. Justice Frankfurter — Myth or Reality?" *Midwest Journal of Political Science*, 8 (1964), 23–28.

55. A. McC. and Elizabeth B. Lee, *The Fine Art of Propaganda: A Study of Father Coughlin's Speeches* (New York: Harcourt, Brace, 1939).

of such verbal stimuli on voting.[56] They found more emotional content in stories dealing with Franklin Roosevelt than in stories covering Wendell Willkie, his Republican opponent. Roosevelt's victory justified a tentative hypothesis that emotional media coverage may induce people to vote for the candidate on whose behalf their emotions have been stirred. Follow-up studies, including careful analysis of other factors co-occurring with emotional coverage, might confirm or disprove the usefulness of using emotional quality of media coverage as a predictor of election outcomes. The possibilities of developing measurement scales which would permit inferring specific consequences in the wake of verbal stimuli are manifold and tempting, although quite elusive.

Third-party reactions can be used to infer effects of messages on audiences. The impossibility of conducting audience surveys forced U.S. State Department officials to infer the reactions of Russian audiences to Voice of America broadcasts from comments made about the broadcasts by Russian sources.[57] The mere fact that VOA broadcasts were dignified with so much attention from Russian newspapers and radio broadcasts was taken as evidence that VOA reached important audiences and was deemed potentially influential. Soviet commentary addressed itself to specific types of images which the commentators apparently believed had been created by the broadcasts and which they presumably sought to destroy. The American analysts accepted the judgment of Soviet officialdom about the kinds of images produced in Soviet audiences, inferring the images from the description in the official comments. With limited opportunities to verify the inferences further, they remained questionable; but as the sole source for otherwise unobtainable information, they were a valuable tool in the armamentarium of international communications diplomacy.

SUMMARY

Beyond their manifest and latent meanings, words carry information about the social environment in which they have been sent and received. Political actors and analysts decipher these meanings to obtain information which is often unavailable in any other form. Deciphering

56. Douglas Waples and Bernard Berelson, "What the Voters Were Told: An Essay in Content Analysis," Graduate Library School, University of Chicago (1941), mimeographed.

57. Alex Inkeles, "Soviet Reactions to the Voice of America," *Public Opinion Quarterly*, 16 (1952), 612–617; Paul W. Massing, "Communist References to the Voice of America," *Public Opinion Quarterly*, 16 (1952), 618–622.

requires inferential reasoning: the knowledge gathered from the message is used to deduce additional meaning through logical processes which also take message context into account. Inferential reasoning is precarious because the analyst never knows whether he has included all relevant factors in his calculations. Nonetheless, it can be used with a high degree of success by knowledgeable, careful, and lucky analysts.

A prevalent approach to inference-making is logic-of-the-situation analysis. It is based on the assumptions that human behavior is purposive and rational within the limits set by incomplete information, and it further assumes that behavior is fairly regular (and hence predictable) when circumstances are constant. In the logic-of-the-situation approach, the analyst speculates about the circumstances in the situation at hand which were likely to produce the verbal data he is analyzing. He examines similarities between the message under consideration and past messages and the context which produced them. The assumption is that similar types of situations will evoke predictable messages from similar types of message-senders. The current message context is checked carefully for data which confirm that it is indeed similar to contexts which have produced comparable messages.

Four aspects of message contexts are generally examined. The analyst seeks information about the situational context in which sender and receiver were operating at the time of the communication. This involves such matters as investigating the power relations of the parties, their current economic status, and any unusual problems facing them. Further, the message transaction is analyzed in terms of general knowledge about human behavior, such as expected behavior changes under conditions of stress or behavior changes typically occurring at certain stages of the life cycle. General considerations are supplemented and modified by knowledge of idiosyncratic behaviors of the parties to the message transaction. Here the analyst looks for past behavior sequences and eccentricities. Finally, the idiosyncratic aspects of the communication situation are examined for communication context clues. For instance, a drastic shift from laudatory to derogatory verbal symbols in press references to a political actor would probably indicate a changed political context.

Verbal analysis permits the investigator to explore three ranges of inferential information: it provides him with clues to the social conditions and circumstances which produced the message; it yields data about the life situations, personalities, perceptions, and goals of the message-senders; and it permits speculation about the message's likely effects.

Information may come directly from the substance of one message stream and the underlying values it discloses — an appeal for food shipments may permit inferences about the economic plight of the sender and the value he places on human survival. Information may also emerge from a comparison of messages sent by the same source over a period of time. When a political leader's messages reveal a sharply rising sense of futility and defeat, one can make inferences about the state of affairs which gives rise to pessimism, and about the changing goals which may be in the offing. Another tactic involves comparing messages from a variety of sources; it may be used to infer ideological and situational differences or similarities among these sources, revealed by common or disparate characteristics in their messages.

5 Analysis and Measurement of Verbal Behavior

"When I use a word," Humpty-Dumpty said in rather a scornful tone, "it means just what I choose it to mean — neither more nor less."
— Lewis Carroll, *Alice's Adventures in Wonderland*

. . . Words strain,
Crack and sometimes break, under the burden,
Under the tension, slip, slide, perish,
Decay with imprecision, will not stay in place,
Will not stay still.
— T. S. Eliot, "Burnt Norton," *Four Quartets*

A number of approaches and techniques have been developed in the social sciences for the systematic study of verbal behavior. This chapter discusses the general nature of these approaches and techniques. Detailed instructions in their use are available in specialized books and manuals.[1]

RESEARCH DESIGN

Measurement of verbal behavior involves the same research decisions required in all scientific research: the formulation of a theory and of hypotheses on which to premise the investigation, choice of appropriate data-gathering and analysis methods, and choice of methods for interpreting the results. However, the nature of verbal behavior poses a number of special difficulties in making these decisions; this chapter highlights these problem areas.

Initial Decisions

The investigator of verbal behavior must first determine the precise objectives of his investigation. He may wish to analyze verbal output to obtain specified information expressed in messages; to make infer-

1. Examples are Philip Emmert and William D. Brooks, eds., *Methods of Research in Communication* (Boston: Houghton Mifflin, 1970), Ole R. Holsti, *Content Analysis for the Social Sciences and Humanities* (Reading, Mass.: Addison Wesley, 1969), and George Gerbner, ed., *The Analysis of Communication Content* (New York: John Wiley, 1969).

ences about the environment which produced the verbal behavior; and to test hypotheses about the nature and consequences of verbal behavior. He may focus his investigation on the message's source, substance, channels of transmission, or effects on different audiences.

The analysis may be designed to examine a society's patterns of expressed perceptions at a single time or over a prolonged period. Co-variation or interaction of verbal behavior and other types of behaviors and occurrences may be the focus of attention. Or one may wish to examine or compare the verbal output of selected communicators, with respect to single concepts or clusters of concepts. The analyst may be interested in the presence or absence of very specific data such as mention of new types of weapons, information about the status of internal transportation systems, and evidence of internal unrest. Or one may merely wish to record the substance of verbal behavior, along with identifying information regarding such matters as place and time of origination, authorship, and length. The bulk of historical research is done in this manner.

Psychological and social theories often are essential components in creating theoretical foundations for research designs for examining the effects of communications. For instance, an investigator trying to assess the effects of anti-Semitic messages by prominent black leaders on hitherto pro-black Jewish groups might look for Jewish messages reflecting tendencies toward dissonance reduction. Denials that the anti-Semitic messages had been sent, or downgrading of the leaders who sent them, might be considered verbal evidence that a dissonance effect had indeed been created.

Depending on his initial decisions about the objectives of the study, the analyst must then decide what types of verbal behavior will have to be examined and what strategies and tactics of examination will yield the best results. This may present him with a choice of using *syntactic* analysis, which examines style features; *semantic* analysis, which searches for meanings of verbal constructs; and *pragmatic* analysis, which examines causes and effects of verbal behavior.

Let us assume that an investigator wants to test the hypothesis that policies of military aggression are heralded by an increase in paranoid speech and in references to political ideology by the chief decision-makers in the aggressor countries. Several very important decisions have already been made — without necessarily ruling out alternative theories and hypotheses, the investigator has provisionally accepted the validity of a number of social science theories as premises for his investigation. From psychology comes the idea that paranoid individuals are prone to aggressive behavior. Political science contributes theories about the influence of ideologies on political action and about the impact of top leaders on military policies. Linguistics provides theories about the relation of particular speech formulations to behavior and psychopathologies of the speaker. The hypothesis thus has been formulated by combining insights from three fields of knowledge.

To test the hypothesis, additional important decisions must be made in order to create a research design. First on the list is the adoption or creation of measuring devices by which one can identify aggression, paranoid speech, and references to political ideology. The merit of the whole enterprise ultimately hinges on the validity and reliability of such measures. Other decisions include the choice of subjects whose verbal behavior is to be examined, and the choice of the sample of verbal behavior which is to be scrutinized.

Sample Selection and Data-Gathering

Let us assume that Adolf Hitler falls in the class of individuals whose verbal behavior will be included in the analysis. This choice may be dictated by the researcher's interest in modern (rather than ancient) politics, his desire to include a German leader in a cross-cultural analysis, and the practical consideration that a great deal of Adolf Hitler's verbal output has been preserved for examination. Other research goals would require different choices of subjects; a desire to stay within the American cultural context, or to concentrate on leaders below the head-of-state level, would exclude Hitler.

Once Hitler had been selected as a subject, the investigator might decide to observe his verbal behavior throughout his entire lifetime, or throughout his period in office, or only for short periods before and after military aggression. The basic assumptions and objectives of the study would be the guiding factors in these decisions. If it seemed theoretically important to relate each subject's speech patterns during periods of aggression to his general speech patterns throughout life, then a life-span examination would have to be made. If the historical period of his incumbency was of sole concern, then the study of verbal output could be limited to that time span. A primary focus on linking the event defined as aggression with the occurrence of paranoid and ideological speech would make an examination of selected periods of aggression and nonaggression sufficient.

The specification of a time frame is an important consideration in verbal behavior studies. Many investigators are interested in examining changes of verbal output over historically significant periods. Studies of newspaper and magazine output have concentrated on delineating changes in the description of such social perceptions as male and female character types and roles over decades and centuries.[2] Changes in the attention given to moral and motivational values in children's literature over several generations have been correlated with changes in the general public's moral and motivational attitudes during the same period.[3] Changes in topics discussed in newspaper editorials have been traced for various periods, as have changes in individual values detected in the verbal output of selected individuals. The investigator who traces changes in verbal behavior extending over lengthy periods may face difficult problems in getting comparable verbal data. Verbal output at different times and in different places may have been subjected to time-linked fashions of editorial treatment which distort the features he seeks to examine.

Instead of comparing verbal output across theoretically significant time periods, it is often useful to focus on output differences of various communicators during the same period. For example, the verbal outputs of Premier Khrushchev and President Kennedy have been compared during the same period with respect to the same international situation. This permitted a comparison of the philosophies and values which entered the decision-making processes of the two world leaders for the situation in question.[4] Likewise, speeches by old and new Bolsheviks in honor of Stalin's birthday in 1949 have been compared for similarities and differences in ideational clusters.[5]

Returning to our example of the study of verbal behavior as related to military aggression, the investigator must also decide whether the specific subject matter discussed by Hitler, and audience differences, affect the choice of verbal output to be examined. Would it be advisa-

2. See Morris Janowitz, "Content Analysis and the Study of the 'Symbolic Environment,'" in Arnold A. Rogow, ed., *Politics, Personality and Social Science in the Twentieth Century* (Chicago: University of Chicago Press, 1969), p. 158. Janowitz reports an analysis by Leo Lowenthal which showed a shift, over time, in perceptions of public heroes from idols of production to idols of consumption.

3. David C. McClelland, *The Achieving Society* (Princeton: Van Nostrand, 1961), ch. 2; R. de Charms and G. H. Moeller, "Values Expressed in American Children's Readers: 1900–1950," *Journal of Abnormal and Social Psychology*, 64 (1962), 136–142.

4. William Eckhardt and Ralph K. White, "A Test of the Mirror-Image Hypothesis: Kennedy and Khrushchev," *Journal of Conflict Resolution*, 11 (1967), 325–332. In testing bivariate hypotheses, it is very important to use controls.

5. Nathan Leites, Elsa Bernaut, and Raymond L. Garthoff, "Politburo Images of Stalin," *World Politics*, 3 (1951), 317–339.

ble to use private or public communications or both? Should the analyst limit himself to communications to selected audiences, such as addresses to party gatherings, or to cabinet members? Should he focus on predetermined subjects only? For example, all subject matter except foreign affairs might be excluded from the analysis.

There is little available theory to guide him in these decisions. In the Hitler examples, the psychological theory that paranoid behavior is most apparent when the individual is under stress might influence the investigator to observe verbal behavior during various stress periods primarily, using observations during calm periods as controls. Likewise, evidence that an actor's real perceptions, evaluations, preferences, expectations, intentions, and the like are best inferred from private utterances, rather than public speeches, may lead to a concentration on available private documents.[6]

Another data-gathering decision relates to the amount of verbal behavior which one wishes to examine. Survey research output produces limited amounts of verbal information. By contrast, the total amount of recorded verbal behavior related to an individual or situation may be vast, forcing the investigator into stringent sampling procedures. Decisions regarding the nature of the sample are made in light of the theories to be tested: one samples from the universe to which he wishes to generalize results. For instance, if the focus is on historical developments, sampling must be designed accordingly. For a study of cultural changes mirrored in verbal output, one might want to examine verbal behavior as reflected in newspaper editorials over a hundred-year span. For a situation-oriented study, one might wish to examine verbal behavior during particular types of incidents, such as a certain presidential election or series of elections. Or one might wish to sample a variety of cultures. Alternatively, for an analysis of subjects covered on the front pages of daily newspapers, one might select a completely random sample of front pages.

Data Interpretation and Validation

Interpretation of data may involve nothing more than a simple report of mention or nonmention of certain topics, frequency and length of discussion, and participation or nonparticipation of certain

6. Robert C. North, "Research Pluralism and the International Elephant," *International Studies Quarterly*, 11 (1967), 408. Also see John E. Mueller, "The Use of Content Analysis in International Relations," in Gerbner, ed., *Analysis of Communication Content*, p. 188. Mueller believes that written communications should be given more weight than unwritten ones.

communicators in a verbal interchange, along with impressionistic commentary about the significance of these observations. Or it may require a demonstration of how the data fit or fail to fit complex theories. In our example, if the researcher is testing the relation of paranoid and ideological speech to aggression, the data might show a causal connection between speech and action, a co-occurrence of speech and action with no proof of causality, no connection at all, or a negative relationship. Interpretation of the data would shed new light on the psychological and sociological theories linking aggression and paranoia as expressed in speech.

Standard interpretations have been developed for certain common aspects of verbal behavior. As a general rule, the relative frequency and recurrence of certain themes in a given body of verbal output indicates the degree of importance which the communicator places on these themes. Likewise, value judgments expressed or implied by the communicator are generally assumed to reveal his value perceptions, in the absence of discernible need for dissimulation.[7] Investigators assumed that personal letters written in Germany during bombing raids supplied genuine clues about the letter-writers' fears in the wake of the raids. They analyzed the frequency and depth of discussions of ill health, anxiety, and pessimism after a series of raids. The data, taken at face value, were then interpreted to indicate that day-time bombing raids aroused a great deal more anxiety than night-time raids and had more lasting effects in undermining German morale.[8]

Another decision which often faces the researcher concerns the interpretation of oral communication. Where features of oral delivery are known (such as pitch, intensity, and tempo), decisions must be made about using this information. Changes in pitch, a rasp revealing tension, or a tear-choked, breaking voice may be data which strongly affect the meanings assigned to verbal output. They may reveal vital information about the speaker and message which his words fail to convey, or try to obscure. These eight paralinguistic aspects are known to affect verbal meanings: increasing loudness and softness; raised and lowered pitch; spread and squeezed register; rasp and openness; drawl and clipping; increased and decreased tempo; laughing, crying, break-

7. The question of truth and lying is discussed more fully in ch. 1.

8. Dorwin P. Cartwright, "Analysis of Qualitative Material," in Leon Festinger and Daniel Katz, *Research Methods in the Behavioral Sciences* (New York: Dryden Press, 1953), p. 430. For other similar projects see Harold D. Lasswell, Daniel Lerner, and Ithiel de Sola Pool, *The Comparative Study of Symbols* (Stanford: Stanford University Press, 1952), pp. 79–81.

ing; kinesics.[9] Where the data consist of written transcripts of verbal output, the researcher may have to decide whether to use information about delivery features which may have affected the meaning and effect of the verbal output.

Raw material for verbal analysis is generally plentiful, but sometimes significant links in the chain of information are missing. In the case of an analysis of Hitler's verbal output, it might be very difficult to get samples of his verbal behavior before he assumed public office. Likewise, important documents produced during his period in office may have been deliberately censored or destroyed. There may be alternative means for getting the missing information; reports about the destroyed documents may be available in other records, or in the memoirs of co-workers. If second-hand reports are used, the researcher must be alert to likely distortions. A comparison of several different reports of the same verbal behavior may be required.

As in other areas of scientific investigation, the verbal analyst should try to validate his findings. Some analysts feel that all conclusions based on verbal data need nonverbal validation because of the uncertainties involved with interpretation of verbal data.[10] Genuineness of the verbal expression of anxiety in the German letters, and heightened fears of night-time raids, might be tested by checking physicians' records of treating patients with anxiety symptoms in the relevant period, or by checking suicide trends and rates of admission to mental hospitals. A finding of hostility among nations made on the basis of verbal data might be validated by the actual outbreak of armed or economic conflict among the nations in question. Where use of nonverbal measures is impossible, different verbal means of measurement may lend supporting evidence. Verbal analysis confirmed certain hypotheses about the verbal elements in Kate Smith's war bond marathons which had persuaded her listeners to buy bonds; audience interviews provided validation.[11]

9. Robert E. Pittenger and Henry Lee Smith, "A Basis for Some Contributions of Linguistics to Psychiatry," in Alfred G. Smith, ed., *Communication and Culture: Readings in the Codes of Human Interaction* (New York: Holt, Rinehart and Winston, 1966), p. 177.

10. Ole R. Holsti, "Content Analysis," in Gardner Lindzey and Elliot Aronson, eds., *The Handbook of Social Psychology* (Reading, Mass.: Addison Wesley, 1968), II, 606–607. For a brief discussion of a variety of validity checks, see the same author's *Content Analysis for the Social Sciences and Humanities*, pp. 142–148.

11. Robert K. Merton, *Mass Persuasion: The Social Psychology of a War Bond Drive* (New York: Harper, 1946).

There are a few areas in which verbal indexes have been so well validated that additional validations seem unnecessary; most of these concern the recognition of psychological states through verbal analysis. It is apparently possible to diagnose a schizophrenic's condition on the basis of his recorded verbal behavior, even without seeing the person or knowing anything else about him.[12] Daniel Ogilvie, Philip Stone, and Edwin Shneidman identified verbal characteristics of suicide notes which permitted them to distinguish phony from real suicide notes with 90 percent accuracy.[13] Richard Fagen reports an imaginary conversation between a Russian astronaut and his Soviet leader and compares this to a similar conversation between an American and his president. It would not require any supporting data to establish that two such communications — one indicating strong deference habits and the other exuding egalitarianism — came from different cultures.[14]

Strategies and Methods of Verbal Analysis

The various strategies and methods by which verbal behavior is commonly appraised can be classified into three modes of analysis: intuitive, quantitative, and qualitative. While it is heuristically useful to distinguish the three types, they are not truly distinct in practice; each approach usually contains some elements of the other two. Each mode of analysis must follow the steps outlined previously: a goal must be set for the investigation, a sample of verbal output must be selected for examination, it must be analyzed for clues it contains regarding the question at hand, and the findings must be put together and interpreted to answer the initial question. Since many of the average person's decisions are based on his analysis of the verbal behavior to which he is exposed, some of the methods are universally practiced. But like the man who did not know that he was speaking "prose" until someone told him so, most people are unaware of the complex verbal analyses which they perform repeatedly in the course of a day.

12. See Brendan A. Maher, *Principles of Psychopathology* (New York: McGraw-Hill, 1966), pp. 394–441, and sources cited there.

13. Daniel M. Ogilvie, Philip J. Stone, and Edwin S. Shneidman, "Some Characteristics of Genuine Versus Simulated Suicide Notes," in Philip J. Stone, Dexter C. Dunphy, Marshall S. Smith, and Daniel M. Ogilvie, *The General Inquirer: A Computer Approach to Content Analysis* (Cambridge: MIT Press, 1966), pp. 527–535.

14. Richard R. Fagen, *Politics and Communication* (Boston: Little, Brown, 1966), pp. 53–54.

Intuitive Methods

The technique of verbal analysis used most often by laymen and scholars alike is the intuitive method. It consists essentially of the research steps outlined earlier, performed in a relatively nonsystematic, informal, and often subconscious manner. The layman or scholar determines intuitively, or on the basis of his own past experience or his formally acquired knowledge of human behavior, what specific samples of verbal behavior are apt to contain the information he needs. He examines all or part of the verbal behavior he deems relevant to discern its manifest and latent content and meaning. For this process he uses ordinary decoding criteria, as discussed in the second chapter. Finally, he draws conclusions about the matter in which he is interested, applying his customary informal or formal methods of informational analysis.

To use a common problem in verbal analysis as an example: in an American election one might hypothesize that candidate D, a Democrat, is likely to be more pro-union than candidate R, a Republican. The basis of this hypothesis might be a comparison of such verbal data as party platforms in previous elections, impressions gathered over a number of years from the mass media, or the work of scholars. If one wants to use verbal analysis to discover whether candidate D is indeed more pro-union, one might select as a data base a meeting in which candidates D and R are discussing their respective positions. One would listen to their discussion, note and compare its substance, and determine whether to take it at face value or discount all or part as campaign rhetoric. Judgmental decisions would be made on the basis of a number of criteria, many of them intuitive, unexamined, and subconscious.

In the intuitive analysis of verbal behavior, the analyst is usually not even aware of the specific words which are being used. He gathers the meaning from the sense conveyed to him by combinations of words. Even in scientific analysis there is a recognition that "language is above all relational. The important thing about a symbol is the context of other symbols in which it occurs — which symbols precede it and which follow it." [15] If asked to repeat an idea which has just been expressed, the average observer (or the average speaker) is likely to vary the original words and word order in which the idea was couched. In ordinary communication situations, there are no rules or conventions which prescribe precisely the words and word orders which must be

15. Ithiel de Sola Pool, "Content Analysis and the Intelligence Function," in Rogow, ed., *Politics, Personality, and Social Science*, pp. 209–210.

used to convey specified meanings; hence there are no rigid rules for interpreting words and sentence construction. Meaning comes from an overall appraisal of the patterns produced by the various elements of the message.

However, while there are no precise rules, there are widely observed conventions about the use of style to convey meanings. A polite phrase at the beginning of a harsh demand may tone it down less than the same phrase uttered at the end of the demand. The sequence in which demands are phrased may affect the evaluation of their respective importance. Words with equivalent dictionary meanings may nonetheless carry different nuances which affect the meanings they convey. "Vary style and you will vary content slightly or greatly, inconsequentially or seriously." [16] The insightful analyst may be able to appraise accurately the meanings of style differences, using them as clues to judge whether the overall intent of the author is friendly, hostile, self-effacing, or domineering.

A decision to discount spoken promises as "campaign rhetoric" might be based on the vagueness or flowery quality of expression, on general skepticism about all promises made by politicians, on skepticism about the credibility of the particular speaker, or on the belief that promises concerning the subject matter in question are traditionally rhetorical. It would also involve judgments about the speaker's communication strategies. Was the message designed to convey the speaker's beliefs, or was it an instrumental message? If the latter, was it designed to convey implied messages or to act as a tool of persuasion? The last step would be to combine the impressions obtained from the verbal analysis into a final appraisal of the respective pro-union propensities of the candidates. Again, ordinary judgmental criteria would be used.

The Analysis of Situational Contexts

This ordinary process of verbal analysis involves many more judgments than meet the eye. Besides the steps outlined, it involves a complex, implicit simultaneous analysis of the total societal context in which the communication has occurred, an evaluation of each of the communicators and of their interactions, and judgments concerning the long-term and short-term objectives of the communication. [17] Lan-

16. George N. Gordon, *The Language of Communication: A Logical and Psychological Examination* (New York: Hastings House, 1969), p. 194.

17. Hugh Dalziel Duncan, *Symbols in Society* (New York: Oxford University Press, 1968), p. 17. Also see Hansfried Kellner, "On the Sociolinguistic Perspective of the Communicative Situation," *Social Research*, 37 (1970), 71–85. Klaus

guage rarely conveys adequate meanings by itself. "To hear the sentence, 'Castro is a Socialist,' spoken over the radio is to have little clue to its meaning if one does not know, among other things, whether Khrushchev, Adlai Stevenson, Robert Welch, or Norman Thomas is speaking, whether we are currently in a period of international tension or detente, and whether the program is beamed to Russia or North America." [18]

To makes sense out of communications, the analyst needs to know a good deal about the subject matter of discourse and the meanings which particular messages might convey.[19] One can readily illustrate the need for complex contextual appraisals by changing the locale of our example. Suppose that instead of dropping in at an election meeting in his home town, the investigator were suddenly transported to the Amazon to attend a gathering of Indians discussing the election of a village leader. He could listen to their words, but they would mean nothing to him; he would need an interpreter to translate their denotative meanings. But that would not be enough. The interpreter would have to supply the analyst with extensive background information about cultural patterns among the Indians and about behavior patterns and communication strategies of various candidates. Only after the analyst had become familiar with the cultural and situational context in which the language was used would he be able to grasp the meaning of the verbal behavior that he had observed.[20] Viewing the situation as a mediated stimulus-response model, context features would operate as crucial intervening variables. It would be difficult and time-consuming for an alien observer to learn to appraise these intervening variables properly.

Turning to real-life examples for a moment, Bryant Wedge has pointed out some typical difficulties in the process of analyzing cross-cultural communications between North Americans and Latin Americans. "The connotation of words, the feelings and associations which

Krippendorff, "Models of Messages: Three Prototypes," in Gerbner, ed., *Analysis of Communication Content*, pp. 101–102, lists the following essential information for capturing meaning: know source's information base; know source's behavioral characteristics, perceptions, and objectives; know nature of transmission facilities; know past and present interaction constraints within the communication system; know mechanisms of control of exchanged verbalizations; know source's information about interdependencies within the communications system.

18. Murray Edelman, *The Symbolic Uses of Politics* (Urbana: University of Illinois Press, 1967), p. 131.

19. Krippendorff, "Models of Messages," pp. 82–83.

20. See Kenneth E. Boulding, *The Image: Knowledge in Life and Society* (Ann Arbor: University of Michigan Press, 1956), p. 14.

they evoke, vary between the U.S. and Latin America. Consequently the very words which are used by or about the United States may contribute to the 'exploitative' image. The term 'capitalism' regularly evokes associations of 'exploitation.' . . ."[21] He also quotes John F. Kennedy's lament, voiced in June, 1961, after meeting Khrushchev: "The Soviets and ourselves give wholly different meaning to the same words: war, peace, democracy and popular will. We have wholly different views of right and wrong." Confident that he had gained some necessary cultural insights during the meeting so that he could interpret Soviet words in a Soviet cultural context, Kennedy added, "but at least we know better at the end where we both stand."[22]

The problems of incorporating cultural considerations in the appraisal of language are vividly shown when verbal output is translated into different languages. When translations of speeches made by UN Security Council members have been compared, they show that English, French, and Russian observers introduce different conceptual emphases into their rendering of a particular speech. Cultural differences apparently make it difficult to capture a common meaning based on the understanding of the speaker's culture.[23]

One delicate aspect of learning the cultural context of verbal behavior is to comprehend what elements of communication are not verbalized because they presumably are well known. "Most expressions contain an element which is assumed by the speaker to be as obvious to the listener as it is to himself, and an element to be imparted to the listener, who is assumed to be unaware of it."[24] Particularly with closely knit groups such as personal friends, conspiratorial groups, youth gangs, or political cronies, the sharing of meanings is often so great that very few words suffice to convey the desired information and elicit necessary responses. Very thorough study and observation of

21. Bryant Wedge, "Nationality and Social Perception," *Journal of Communication*, 16 (1966), 277.

22. *Ibid.*, p. 280.

23. Edmund S. Glenn, "Meaning and Behavior: Communication and Culture," *Journal of Communication*, 16 (1966), 249. Glenn and Wedge have developed a cognitive matrix to classify various national cognitive styles. See Edmund Glenn, Robert H. Johnson, Paul R. Kimmel, and Bryant Wedge, "A Cognitive Interaction Model," *Journal of Conflict Resolution*, 14 (1970), 39–43. Also see Edmund S. Glenn, "A Cognitive Approach to the Analysis of Cultures and Cultural Evolution," in Ludwig von Bertalanffy and Anatol Rapoport, eds., *General Systems Yearbook* (Ann Arbor: University of Michigan, 1966); and Bryant Wedge, "Communication and Comprehensive Diplomacy," in Arthur S. Hoffman, ed., *International Communication and the New Diplomacy* (Bloomington: Indiana University Press, 1968), pp. 24–47.

24. Glenn, "Meaning and Behavior," p. 250.

communicators and their perceptions of their audiences are required to know which unverbalized elements are nevertheless part of the total communication situation.

If an investigator must predict effects of verbal output, a thorough study of the cultural and situational context is particularly crucial. To lessen the chances of misjudgment, he may decide to use panels of experts to supplement his own appraisal. A study assaying the impact of radio speeches by presidential contenders Dwight Eisenhower and Adlai Stevenson intended to identify factors which would cause audience identification with the speaker. This involved judging the quality of personal interactions. A panel of experts was used, because group appraisals were deemed more accurate than individual judgments.[25]

In many situations a staggering variety of factors can alter effects; even the evaluation of known factors may become extremely complicated. During the Korean War, Premier Chou En-lai declared that China would enter the war if the United States invaded the Democratic Republic of Korea. Would serious threats of this nature deter a major power like the United States? In this case the content of the threat was known, as well as the setting in which it was uttered. The threat was made during a dramatic midnight meeting on October 2, 1950, when premier Chou En-lai summoned Indian ambassador K. M. Panikkar after Republic of Korea troops had crossed the 38th Parallel.[26] Given the fact that the threat was personally conveyed by a head of state to the official of another country, American analysts initially deemed it a serious announcement of contemplated military action by the Chinese. But before reacting to such a threat, further contextual information had to be considered. U.S. analysts needed to appraise China's military capabilities and the eagerness of Chinese military planners to jump into the fray, for if the Chinese had no ability or desire to carry out the threat, it would be empty.

The assessment of situational influences is far more complex and vexing in generalized verbal analysis than in verbal analysis based on survey research.[27] In survey research, the investigator carefully controls the verbal stimuli and some elements of the environment to which he

25. Hubert E. Knepprath, "The Elements of Persuasion in the Nationally Broadcast Speeches of Eisenhower and Stevenson during the 1956 Presidential Campaign" (Ph.D. dissertation, University of Wisconsin, 1962), p. 412.

26. Allen Whiting, *China Crosses the Yalu* (New York: Macmillan, 1960), p. 109.

27. Robert E. Mitchell, "The Use of Content Analysis for Exploratory Studies," *Public Opinion Quarterly*, 31 (1967), 234.

exposes selected audiences. Questions are worded and structured to produce answers that reflect only those dimensions which the investigator seeks to examine. Care is taken to avoid distortions which might result from extraneous factors, such as adverse reactions to the investigator or to the precise nature of the wording. By contrast, the general verbal analyst has no control over the circumstances under which his data are generated, the form in which they are phrased, or the situational context in which they are transmitted. Hence side effects from these uncontrolled variables may obscure what he seeks to examine. For instance, a comparison of the hawkishness of Secretary of State Rusk and Secretary of Defense McNamara failed because their respective statements were generated in response to different audiences; Rusk was responding to doves on the Senate Foreign Relations Committee, while McNamara was responding to hawks on the House Armed Services Committee. The desire to counterbalance each group obviously had tainted the secretaries' remarks.[28] Furthermore, some dimensions were unavailable for verbal analysis because the subject matter was never brought up by the speakers or the responses were unavailable.

Not all of the advantages lie on the side of survey research, however. By asking his questions in controlled settings and in relatively brief interviews, the survey researcher limits the kind of verbal output which he elicits. Moreover, his questions are based on his pre-judgments about the type of information which is relevant to his investigation and therefore confine the areas of knowledge which are tapped. On the other hand, the general verbal analyst deals with materials produced in natural settings; they may direct his attention to areas of knowledge which he would not have explored on his own.

Mutual Comprehension of Cultural Context

It is easy to exaggerate the difficulties which interpretation of cultural and situational contexts poses for verbal analysts. Most human communication occurs in standardized settings where the meanings and effects of verbal behavior are quite predictable.[29] For example, discussion of international affairs within national boundaries tends to be highly stereotyped. "National states provide social frameworks which powerfully determine the way in which other nations are viewed and

28. Mueller, "Use of Content Analysis," p. 190.
29. Smith, ed., *Communication and Culture,* p. 7; T. D. Weldon, *The Vocabulary of Politics* (Baltimore: Penguin Books, 1960), pp. 28–29.

interpreted." [30] Consequently, many people within given national boundaries share perceptions concerning the international environment and interpret messages similarly. They operate within a common semantic space which forces each participant "to express himself in the terms that are socially pre-defined as appropriate to the occasion." [31]

Communicators often know each other so well that they can identify each other's verbal output without being told the source.[32] Likewise, they know and often share each other's meanings and definitions of the situation. The impersonator who mimics the speech of another person can even capture precise forms of encoding likely to be used by that person. Word-association tests within the same culture confirm that there are large areas of agreement about the connotations of certain words.[33] It has also been shown that outsiders tend to adopt the language, interpretations, and even perceptions of the groups in which their communication behavior occurs.[34] This commonality of culturally learned and shared perceptions and understandings permits group members to communicate effectively through verbal messages; it also makes scholarly analysis of many aspects of verbal behavior quite feasible, provided the investigator understands the cultural community which he seeks to investigate.[35] Yet cultural contexts change so rapidly that even the native observer must be sure that he is applying contemporary interpretation-criteria to verbal materials. All too often native analysts apply outmoded standards; for instance, the denotations and connotations of such words as "colony," "patriotism," "conservative," or "liberal" have changed rapidly in recent decades.

An understanding of the cultural context includes an understanding of the strategies which different communicators may be using in a given situation. In the American cultural setting, communication strategies used by various politicians during elections are quite well known.[36]

30. Wedge, "Nationality and Social Perception," p. 273. Wedge cites studies by Hadley Cantril, Karl Deutsch, and Philip E. Jacob.

31. Kellner, "On the Sociolinguistic Perspective," pp. 80–82.

32. Erving Goffman, *Strategic Interaction* (Philadelphia: University of Pennsylvania Press, 1960), p. 9.

33. Julius Laffal, *Pathological and Normal Language* (New York: Atherton Press, 1965), pp. 10–13.

34. *Ibid.*, p. 24.

35. Gordon, *Language of Communication*, p. 120.

36. Robert Jervis, "The Costs of the Scientific Study of Politics: An Examination of the Stanford Content Analysis Studies," *International Studies Quarterly*, 11 (1967), 382–384. Jervis contends that "it is hard to find content characteristics which are independent of or insensitive to possible variations in communications strategy."

Potential presidental candidates generally deny their aspirations for the office at first. Experienced observers apply a rough-and-ready distortion coefficient which tells them that such denials should be discounted early in the race, but given more credence as deadlines for filing for candidacy in the primaries draw near.

Of course, common interpretation of a message does not necessarily imply a common response. As discussed in the second chapter, an announcement of an increase in income taxes and the elimination of sales taxes on food may be understood by an American audience drawn from all socioeconomic levels, but the effects of the message on the audience's support for government economic policies may vary widely, depending on how the proposed changes are evaluated.

Quantitative Methods

How do quantitative methods of verbal analysis differ from intuitive methods? Ithiel de Sola Pool's definition of content analysis gets to the heart of the matter: "Content analysis is a systematic and rigorous way of doing what humanistic students of ideas and behavior have always done, namely to look at what symbols are used in a body of text. Such observation of flow of symbols becomes content analysis of social science if some attention is paid to the procedure of observation." [37] In rigorous content analysis the investigator substitutes systematic, objective, usually quantitative procedures for haphazard, intuitive methods.

Systematic quantitative recording of data protects content analysis findings from distortions which spring from inaccurate or selective perception. It permits the investigator to submit large amounts of verbal data to examination by a variety of human and mechanical observers, all using identical rules for data selection and recording. Such recording also enables him to use various mathematical methods for analysis after data collection is complete. Some important verbal behavior patterns would probably not become apparent in intuitive content analysis. Factor analysis can be used to detect clusters of concepts; multiple regression analysis may make it feasible to predict the degree of change in communication variables which can be expected from a given change in the situation. Mathematical analysis techniques permit the development of mathematical formulas which can be used for future analysis and prediction of verbal behavior.

37. Pool, "Content Analysis and the Intelligence Function," p. 200. For other definitions see Holsti, *Content Analysis for the Social Sciences*, pp. 2–3.

The difference between intuitive and quantitative methods is most noticeable in the third step of the verbal analysis process, the examination of verbal output to record specified features. The other parts — initial formulation of the research problem, the selection of the sample, and the final interpretation of the data — also are generally handled with more rigor when investigators are sensitive to the imprecisions of intuitive processes. But the differences in these three steps are far less marked when one compares analyses performed by either subjective or objective methods; differences which do occur usually involve techniques of sample selection which may require the application of sampling theories.[38]

When an investigator is interested in rigorous quantitative analysis of verbal data and has selected the body of verbal output to be examined, he must choose a unit of analysis suited to his purposes. This unit may range from parts of a sentence to entire documents or groups of documents. Next he must specify relevant style or content variables and the methods which are to be used in identifying them. This may involve the preparation of elaborate codes and indexes. The possibilities are limited only by the researcher's imagination, creativity, and sense of what constitutes valuable information. The ultimate value of most verbal studies hinges on the insight and skill with which basic coding categories and indexes are selected and defined so that they are mutually exclusive and collectively exhaustive. If inappropriate categories are chosen, the investigator's research questions cannot be answered.

Studies of press coverage of the 1968 and 1972 presidential campaigns exemplify quantitative content analysis.[39] These studies examined the issues and presidential qualities which were reported by a sample of twenty U.S. newspapers during the last month of the campaign. The research sought to discover the amount and kind of information available to voters. Previous research had indicated that voters look at issues (including party identification) and at presidential qualities as primary decisional criteria. Recording and analyzing of newspaper presentation of issues and qualities therefore seemed to be a valid measure of the information available to voters for electoral decision-making.

38. For a brief discussion of the respective uses of random and purposive samples, see Holsti, *Content Analysis for the Social Sciences*, pp. 130–131.

39. Doris A. Graber, "Personal Qualities in Presidential Images: The Contribution of the Press," *Midwest Journal of Political Science*, 16 (1972), 46–76; and Doris A. Graber, "The Press as Opinion Resource during the 1972 Presidential Campaign" (forthcoming).

After criteria for choosing the sample of campaign stories had been determined, a coding scheme was devised through which a team of coders could decide precisely what portions of newspaper output needed to be recorded. This required a definition of what constituted an "issue" and a "presidential quality"; such simple distinctions needed for coding can present difficulties when they have to be operationalized. To use a different study as an example: William L. Dulaney, in an examination of deliberate race identification in newspaper crime stories, had to determine what constituted deliberate race identification. He decided to include all specific racial references, except that "if a detailed physical description, including race, was given of a wanted suspect, I assumed (though not necessarily correctly) that such information was published with the intent of generating leads that might assist in the apprehension of the suspect."[40] He also excluded stories which did not refer to race but which published photographs, stories which gave a suspect's address or the location of the crime which might reveal the racial composition of the neighborhood to the knowledgeable, or the suspect's affiliation with a particular group which would be racially identifiable.

To return to the campaign study, after a conceptual definition had been given to the categories "campaign issues" and "presidential quali-ties," a series of operational definitions was made of specific content variables to be included in the categories. Thirty-four issues and thirty-eight qualities were identified as subcategories for the 1968 study; in the 1972 study there were sixty-two issues and forty qualities. Pre-cise operational definitions, supplemented by examples, told coders how to identify each issue and quality: the code word "campaign tech-niques" was to be coded when "general strategy to be used in winning elections" was under discussion; the Watergate affair and other charges of malfeasance during the campaign were to be placed into two sepa-rate coding categories. Examples were given. Subsequent reliability tests indicated that the coding instructions permitted different coders to reach agreement on coding in better than 85 percent of their deci-sions; and the ability of a given coder to repeat his decisions in a second coding was even higher. Judgmental discretion had been reduced to a low level.[41]

40. William L. Dulaney, "Identification of Race in Newspaper Crime Stories," *Journalism Quarterly*, 46 (1969), 604.

41. For a discussion of ways to check coders' reliability, see Holsti, *Content Analysis for the Social Sciences*, pp. 135–142.

After coding was complete, it was possible to count the number of times that each issue and quality had been mentioned, rather than relying on an impressionistic appraisal. Since an average of 4,000 articles were coded for each election, with over 100 judgments made for each article, impressionistic computation would have been highly inaccurate.[42]

The ability to deal effectively with large numbers of variables in massive bodies of data pays additional dividends; it permits an investigator to compare large bodies of verbal output and thereby to detect long-term and large-scale verbal behavior systems. Anatol Rapoport, who has undertaken such comparisons, claims that there is "striking stability of large verbal outputs of individuals speaking or writing on the same topic, especially in the political sphere — a sad reflection, perhaps, on the rigidity of the corpus producers, but hardly disputable in the face of evidence."[43]

In addition to the mere recording of the absence or presence of statements about issues and qualities, the systematic coding scheme made it possible to record a variety of politically salient ways in which issues and qualities were mentioned during the campaigns. In the 1968 and 1972 studies data about qualities were tabulated to indicate whether the text stated positively or negatively that a candidate possessed or lacked the quality in question, or normatively that he ought to have the quality. Numerous qualitative classifications are possible; for instance, one can create evaluation categories which indicate whether content is approved or disapproved by the original communicator or by the reporter. This was done in the Hoover Institution's famous RADIR (Revolution and Development of International Relations) studies, which recorded political values and evaluations expressed in editorials in selected newspapers during the period from 1890 to 1950.[44] Or one can use analytical categories, as exemplified by a study of the Middle East debates which rated UN General Assembly speeches according to whether they were "conflict-creating" or "conflict-resolv-

---

42. One of the most massive manual coding operations ever undertaken was the content analysis of political symbols in prestige newspapers undertaken by Ithiel de Sola Pool and collaborators in the 1950s. The investigators examined 19,553 editorials in five newspapers over a sixty-year period. Each was checked for the presence or absence of 416 different political symbols. See Ithiel de Sola Pool, *The 'Prestige' Papers: A Survey of Their Editorials* (Stanford: Stanford University Press, 1952).

43. Anatol Rapoport, "A System-Theoretic View of Content Analysis," in Gerbner, ed., *Analysis of Communication Content*, p. 30.

44. Pool, *The 'Prestige' Papers.*

ing." [45] Stylistic categories present yet another approach: statements are classified as normative, comparative, imperative, or conditional. [46] Such classifications may greatly broaden the scope of subsequent analyses of the coded data.

Systematic coding also made it possible to record for each campaign issue or presidential quality a variety of data as to how, when, and by whom the point was raised, and the verbal context in which it was made. Recorded information included the name and date of the newspaper in which the issue or quality was mentioned, the candidate with whom it was associated, the person or group stating the issue or quality, and the frequency of co-occurrence of statements about issues and qualities in general, as well as about various candidates. After the data had been prepared for computers, it was possible to test a variety of theories by cross-tabulating certain variables. One could test the relationship of newspaper size, type of ownership, or party endorsement to the frequency of appearance of certain issues and presidential qualities; or one could compare the type of coverage given to a single issue, such as the Watergate affair, in all twenty papers, or in selected papers such as the *New York Times* and the *Washington Post*, or in editorials as compared to news stories. Such comparisons would be well-nigh impossible by the intuitive method if the initial focus had been on overall coverage in twenty newspapers.

Computer Content Analysis

Quantitative content analysts try to make coding instructions so precise that the coding process becomes almost mechanical. Coders who carefully check all of the specified contingencies should find that a given element of text unmistakably belongs in a particular category. In studies where it is possible to fully specify all contingencies and to

45. Doris A. Graber, "Perceptions of Middle East Conflict in the UN, 1953–65," *Journal of Conflict Resolution,* 13 (1969), 454–484.

46. Ole R. Holsti and Robert C. North, "Perceptions of Hostility and Economic Variables," in Richard L. Merritt and Stein Rokkan, *Comparing Nations: The Use of Quantitative Data in Cross-National Research* (New Haven: Yale University Press, 1966), p. 170. The Holsti-North study is an example of highly complex coding. To prepare their data for computer analysis, they coded the syntax, identifying for each statement the author, perceiver, agent and modifiers, the action and modifiers, direct object, target, and modifiers. They also precoded the time as current, past, or future, and stylistic categories to indicate mode of expression. In addition, they identified most words as strong or weak, active or passive, positive or negative in affect on a ± scale, so that they could submit their data to a semantic differential analysis.

eliminate all on-the-spot human judgmental aspects, coding can be performed by computers.

A good example of computerized verbal analysis is provided by the General Inquirer System developed by Philip J. Stone and his co-workers at Harvard. It has been used to study political topics such as the effects of Sino-Soviet relations on internal conflict within each country, presidential nomination acceptance speeches, and newspaper comment on the European and Atlantic communities.[47] As in manual coding, the investigator using the General Inquirer prepares a code-book or "dictionary" which gives precise instructions about the elements of text to be coded and how they can be recognized. The code-book is then stored in the computer. Since the computer lacks human judgmental faculties, the coding instructions need to be far more complete. While a human coder will generally detect the relevant meaning of a homograph (a word with a variety of meanings) from its context, the computer lacks this intelligence. To aid it, the General Inquirer System programs into the computer a process known as Key-Word-in-Context (KWIC). When a homograph appears, the computer automatically prints it in the context of the nearest words. For instance, the word "bit" may signify "a small amount," the past tense of the word "biting," a unit of storage space in the computer, or an appliance in the mouth of a horse. Since the words and syntactical structures associated with each meaning vary, one can program the computer to check for associated features of the word "bit" and choose the correct meaning on the basis of this additional information. Most words can be satisfactorily identified from just a few preceding and succeeding words. Instructions to the computer can also note the fact that most words have one strongly prevailing meaning.[48]

The assignment of particular meanings to words is further aided by the fact that the General Inquirer System works through a series of dictionaries adapted to the subject matter to be analyzed. The data used with the General Inquirer are restricted to verbal output generated in a relatively constant stimulus situation. The dictionary contains categories and subcategories into which the computer will classify

47. The system is described in Stone et al., *The General Inquirer*, Part I. For the political studies, see Part II, pp. 341–429. For a brief history of the General Inquirer system, see Erwin K. Scheuch and Philip J. Stone, "Retrieval Systems for Data Archives: The General Inquirer," in Merritt and Rokkan, *Comparing Nations*, pp. 448–449.

48. Philip J. Stone, "Improved Quality of Content Analysis Categories: Computerized Disambiguation Rules for High Frequency English Words," in Gerbner, *Analysis of Communication Content*, pp. 199–223.

words submitted to it. More than a dozen dictionaries have been developed.[49] Among them the Stanford Political Dictionary is designed for use with political materials; Namenwirth and Brewer have adapted the Harvard III Dictionary for the analysis of editorial comment on international affairs; the Need-Achievement Dictionary analyzes TAT (Thematic Apperception Test) responses, scoring need concepts whenever they are coupled with achievement concepts.[50]

Dictionaries containing 3,000 to 5,000 words have been found adequate for research conducted thus far; this fact has kept dictionary construction manageable. With the General Inquirer it is possible to instruct the computer to print out all words which were not coded initially because they had not been included in the dictionary. These leftovers can then be examined to determine whether they are inconsequential or should be added to the dictionary.

Since the position of a word within a sentence often affects its meaning, computerized coding usually necessitates precoding of the text so that the computer will know the grammatical relations of all words in the sentence. Sometimes text is rephrased into a set of simple statements to facilitate analysis. If much text is to be analyzed, this syntactic coding, along with key-punching the entire text, may be a time-consuming and expensive task. Consequently, computerized coding has thus far been used primarily for analyses of comparatively brief, rich textual materials. Advances in structural linguistics and visual word scanning devices hold great promise for reducing pre-coding labors.[51]

While dictionary construction and the usual procedures of precoding and key punching are quite tedious and time-consuming in computer analysis, the payoffs seem to be worth the price. The analysis gains in rigor because the investigator is forced to think through and

49. Scheuch and Stone, "Retrieval Systems," p. 449.

50. Stone, *The General Inquirer*, pp. 169–170; John Waite Bowers, "Content Analysis," in Emmert and Brooks, ed., *Methods of Research in Communication*, pp. 298–300. Each dictionary is designed to analyze text in light of different social science theories. For instance, the Harvard Psycho-Social dictionary uses Kurt Lewin's field theory of psychosexual symbolism, Osgood's dimensions of semantic space, and Leary's categories of interpersonal relations. Primary categories represent words in standard usage; secondary categories represent commutative and implicit meanings. Examples of primary coding categories are "self, other, job, role, male role, natural object, social place, or action norm." Examples of secondary coding categories are "overstate, sign-strong, male theme, danger-theme, peer-status, recreational." For more detailed explanation, see Scheuch and Stone, "Retrieval Systems," pp. 449–50.

51. See Pool, "Content Analysis and the Intelligence Function," p. 212.

spell out his research assumptions and procedures in unmistakable detail. His logical and procedural weaknesses become obvious — if not to him, then to others. Moreover, once documents have been fed into the computer, they can be subjected to analyses which may not have been anticipated when the material was originally stored. In manual content analysis, only the coding results and other observations, rather than entire documents, are normally recorded, so it is difficult, if not impossible, to test hypotheses which were not anticipated when the investigation was originally undertaken. Complex precoding procedures may also make it possible to test verbal features which are usually elusive in manual content analysis. For instance, syntactic coding of the keypunched text permits one to analyze the syntactic relationships among words which co-occur in the text, and possibly to discover important regularities.

Verbal Indicators

The dictionaries used for the General Inquirer System are based on the assumption that different types of verbal output contain key elements which permit investigators to make inferences about the message source and/or effects. These key elements, which constitute rudimentary models of verbal behavior, are important in most research projects which may be undertaken in the same subject area. For example, any dictionary which is to be used to investigate the psychological state of the source must provide ways of coding statements which refer to the source's feelings and evaluations about himself and his relationship to others; there must also be codes for recording the intensity of expressed feelings.

A number of specific verbal measurement techniques have been developed, based on the assumption that key elements of verbal output exist and are likely to be important for a wide range of investigations. A baseline of "normal" verbal output has been established for these indicators so that deviations can be properly measured.[52] A brief description of a few of these techniques follows, grouped under five headings: syntactic feature measures; paralanguage, kinesics, and silence measures; concept measures; interaction measures; and reaction measures. They have been used much more widely in psychological and sociological studies than in political analyses, although the increased

52. The chi-square statistic or analysis of variance is often used to confirm that differences in verbal samples are real and significant.

emphasis on behavior at all levels of politics is beginning to correct this imbalance.

Syntactic Feature Measures

Syntactic measures seem to be highly promising tools for political studies. Most of them were designed to assess psychologically relevant elements of speech, or to measure significant features such as creativity, sensationalism, or readability in textual materials. The Type-Token Ratio (TTR) is an example; it measures the number of different words found in a body of text, to determine the richness of vocabulary. Richness of vocabulary apparently correlates with a variety of mental states; the TTR for schizophrenics tends to be significantly lower than for comparable normal people. Improvement in the mental condition of schizophrenic patients can be accurately gauged by the degree of improvement in their TTR scores.[53] Disorientation, frustration, and suicidal intent can also be gauged successfully through use of the TTR. The tool is valuable for political studies in which an understanding of political deviance involves the determination of mental states.

It may also be important to assess the creativity of political leaders. Creativity can be measured through word-length indexes, indexes of abstraction which compare the ratio of abstract nouns to all the nouns the subject uses, and verb indexes which compute the ratio of finite verbs to total verbs. Sensationalism in news can affect mass and elite perceptions of the political world; it has been gauged through indexes of pausality which measure the amount of internal punctuation per sentence, and indexes of emotiveness which measure the ratio of adjectives plus adverbs to nouns plus verbs.[54]

Readability of textual political materials, including newspaper stories, may be significant in determining their impact on various audiences. It has been judged through computation of ratios of syllables to words, sentence-length measures, and redundancy measures. A widely used redundancy measure is "Cloze" procedure, which assumes that increased redundancy leads to increased comprehensibility. To judge redundancy in verbal passages, some words — usually every fifth word — are deleted from verbal passages. The reader is then asked to supply the missing information. The easier it is for the reader to fill in

53. Maher, *Principles of Psychopathology*, pp. 394–441.
54. A "finite" verb is a verb that can be used to form the predicate of a sentence. Mervin D. Lynch, "Stylistic Analysis," in Emmert and Brooks, eds., *Methods of Research in Communication*, pp. 328–329.

the words and restore the original meaning, the higher the message rates in readability.[55]

Measuring and comparing the use of articles, prepositions, conjunctions, and similar words has proved to be a highly useful tool in detecting personal idiosyncrasies in writing style. Using thirty words such as "upon," "whilst," and "enough," Mosteller and Wallace were able to prove that Madison, rather than Hamilton, was the author of twelve *Federalist Papers* which had been in dispute.[56]

Paralanguage, Kinesics, and Silence Measures

Paralinguistic features of language — tone, pitch, pace, etc. — affect the meaning of verbal communications; so do pauses of various lengths which may occur in individual speech or in interactions among speakers. Facial expressions, gestures, body position, or body motion may support, modify, or contradict what is being said verbally. "It has been estimated that in face-to-face communication no more than 35 percent of the social meaning is carried in the verbal messages."[57] Techniques have been developed to score these extraverbal and nonverbal aspects of speech and to develop interpretation systems to assess the interface of nonverbal and verbal expressions.

The kinetic scoring system developed by Ray L. Birdwhistell for recording body movements is an example of a carefully constructed measurement tool. Trained observers use specially devised kinesic symbols to record "kines," the smallest parts of body movements which have been found to carry meaning.[58] The pattern of which the kine is a

55. W. L. Taylor, " 'Cloze Procedure': A New Tool for Measuring Readability," *Journalism Quarterly*, 30 (1953), 415–433.

56. F. Mosteller and D. W. Wallace, *Inference and Disputed Authorship: The Federalist* (Reading, Mass.: Addison-Wesley, 1964). Milton Rokeach and associates used value analysis, discussed below, to reach the same conclusions. They focused on 24 key values, such as happiness, equality, peace, and social recognition. Milton Rokeach, Robert Homant, and Louis Penner, "A Value Analysis of the Disputed Federalist Papers," *Journal of Personality and Social Psychology*, 16 (1970), 245–50. Also see William J. Paisley, "Minor Encoding Habits, II: Extemporaneous Speech in the Kennedy-Nixon Debates," in *Old Papers in Communication*, no. 1, 1967.

57. Randall Harrison, "Nonverbal Communication: Explorations into Time, Space, Action, and Object," in James H. Campbell and Hal W. Hepler, eds., *Dimensions in Communication* (Belmont, Calif.: Wadsworth, 1966), p. 161. Additional factors which may affect the impact of verbal messages, and which have been investigated systematically, are architectural and other environmental settings, musical sound effects, the nature of transmission instruments such as telephones, radio, etc., and human clothing, adornments, and hairstyles.

58. Larry L. Barker and Nancy B. Collins, "Nonverbal and Kinesic Research,"

part, the "kinemorph," is also recorded. Gestures which involve simultaneous head, eye, and eyebrow motions may constitute kinemorphs. Kinemorphs are parts of more complex patterns called kinemorphic constructions.

By transcribing communication events verbally and kinegraphically, Birdwhistell was able to show that certain body movements always accompany specific language behavior. There are motions characteristic of questions, and motions which accompany declaratory statements; there are twenty-three different eyebrow positions, each carrying a separate meaning. As with verbal communication, Birdwhistell found that the meaning of nonverbal expressions varied, depending on the context in which the expression occurred, and on a particular communicator and his cultural background. Interpretation of kinemorphs therefore had to take context into account. In the age of television, when close-up pictures of politicians fill the screen, the impact of body language is apt to be substantial. Systematic kinemorphic analysis might shed light on campaign styles, identify elements of charisma, or indicate mental states such as embarrassment, anger, or elation.

Concept Measures

The assumption behind concept measures is that certain key concepts expressed in verbal output shed light on basic human characteristics. Standardized codes can tap these concepts; an example is Value Analysis, developed by Ralph K. White. White asserts that people of all cultures have four groups of basic values by which they appraise their own and other cultures.[59] The first group encompasses strength values such as independence, achievement, dominance, aggression, recognition, and strength. The second group is composed of moral values including morality, truthfulness, justice, religion, obedience, giving, tolerance, friendship, and group unity. Group three contains such economic values as prosperity, security, ownership, and jobs. The fourth group, "other values," deals with matters such as safety, emotional security, practicality, knowledge, determination, carefulness, and culture. White's Value Analysis provides a standardized method for identifying the kinds of values discussed in verbal output, and for com-

in Emmert and Brooks, *Methods of Research in Communication*, pp. 353–360. Also see Ray L. Birdwhistell, *Kinesics and Context: Essays on Body Motion Communication* (Philadelphia: University of Pennsylvania Press, 1970), essays 2, 11, 26, and 27.

59. Ralph K. White, *Value Analysis: The Nature and Use of the Method* (Glen Gardner, N.J.: Libertarian Press, 1951), p. 44.

paring positive and negative appraisals. The findings can tell the analyst a great deal about the value structure used by communicators to appeal to selected audiences. They also reveal real or ostensible attitudes of the communicator toward the objects under discussion.[60]

White has used value analysis to discover values stressed by political leaders, to measure hostility and conflict-mindedness, to study self-perception and ego ideals, and to study frustration. For example, an analysis of Richard Wright's autobiography *Black Boy* showed that references to authority figures were 100 percent negative, and that Wright disapproved of 89 percent of the people mentioned in his book. Self-approving references were low. From these findings, White made inferences about Wright's hostility feelings toward himself and others.[61]

In another study, public speeches of John F. Kennedy and Nikita Khrushchev were examined.[62] In 1,400 value judgments Kennedy stressed peace, military strength, non-aggression, and determination to defend the peace. Khrushchev, in 2,564 judgments, talked mostly about economic welfare, peace, achievement, and non-aggression. He combined peace and freedom into the concept of peaceful coexistence. He renounced international war but not class warfare. Mirror images prevailed. Imperialism and military aggression were identified by Kennedy with communism, and by Khrushchev with capitalism. Conflict-mindedness of the two leaders was measured by the percentage of judgments which denounced the other party for not adhering to certain values.[63] The index of denunciation was 17 percent for Kennedy and 21 percent for Khrushchev; by comparison, the denunciation index of Hitler's speeches was 32 percent, and of Franklin Roosevelt's speeches, 10 percent. Other indexes used to measure conflict-mindedness were based on the proportion of speeches which claimed that aggression was justified, statements alleging military potency, and the ratio of statements mentioning war to statements mentioning peace.

Other widely used concept measures for which standardized measurement techniques and interpretation rules have been established

60. *Ibid.*, pp. 82–83. White warns about the pitfalls of using manifest content without interpreting it in its proper context. He also discusses ways of checking the validity of verbal measures.

61. Ralph K. White, "Black Boy: A Value Analysis," *Journal of Abnormal and Social Psychology*, 42 (1947), 440–461.

62. William Eckhardt and Ralph K. White, "A Test of the Mirror-Image Hypothesis: Kennedy and Khrushchev," *Journal of Conflict Resolution*, 11 (1967), 329–332.

63. White, *Value Analysis*, p. 6, considers this the best single objective indicator of conflict-mindedness.

include the Discomfort Relief Quotient (DRQ), which assesses psychological states by comparing the frequency of mention of discomfort and relief, and the Positive-Negative-Ambivalent Quotient (PNAQ), which indicates how many statements are in each mode. Scales have also been developed to measure anxiety, hostility, and defensiveness as reflected in the communications of political leaders.[64]

Evaluative Assertion Analysis, developed by Charles Osgood, Sol Saporta, and Jum Nunnally, is a widely used general evaluation technique.[65] To eliminate bias, attitudinal objects whose evaluation is to be rated are replaced by nonsense syllables before the evaluation is coded. The text is then rephrased into a series of evaluative assertions. "The cunning, grasping party leaders led the nation to disaster," might become three statements: "The party leaders are cunning," "the party leaders are grasping," and "the party leaders led the nation to disaster." Judges would assign a direction and weight to each statement on a scale ranging from extremely favorable to extremely unfavorable. Then the assertions about each attitudinal object would be assigned a position on an evaluative scale.[66]

Probably the most widely known scheme of concept measurement is David McClelland's method for coding achievement motivation in children's literature. McClelland developed his indexes for measuring achievement motivation to test his theory that cultures in which achievement motivation was high in representative children's literature would show developmental features associated with high achievement. A series of research projects undertaken by him and others supported the theory and validated his method of measuring verbal cues to achievement motivation.[67]

Interaction Measures

Interaction measures range from simple schemes which merely record whether or not a statement has elicited a response, to sociograms of verbal interaction, to complex classification schemes which categorize and record patterns of interactive verbal behavior. A widely

64. Ole R. Holsti, Robert C. North, Richard A. Brody, "Perception and Action in the 1914 Crisis," in J. David Singer, ed., *Quantitative International Politics: Insights and Evidence* (New York: Free Press, 1968), pp. 123–158.

65. Charles E. Osgood, Sol Saporta, and Jum C. Nunnally, "Evaluative Assertion Analysis," *Litera*, 3 (1956), 47–102.

66. Bowers, "Content Analysis," p. 303.

67. McClelland, *The Achieving Society*; deCharms and Moeller, "Values Expressed in American Children's Readers."

used interaction measure which has been employed to study legislative committees and party caucuses is Interaction Process Analysis, designed by Robert F. Bales.[68] It divides verbal interactions into four
major categories: questions, answers, positive reactions, and negative
reactions. Each of these is subdivided into three categories. Questions
and answers are differentiated, depending on whether they refer to
requests for information, opinion, or suggestions; positive and negative reactions to messages are coded according to whether they involve
agreement or disagreement, tension or tension release, and antagonism
or solidarity. Bales asserts that all major aspects of group interaction
produced through verbal interchange can be scored with these twelve
categories. These include formulation of common definitions of the
situation to be solved, a common system for evaluating various possible
solutions, techniques of influencing group members, coping with tensions, arriving at decisions, and restructuring the group to permit it to
continue functioning when conditions have changed.

Bales's analysis measures the type of verbal interaction which has
occurred, but it does not analyze the content of verbal output expressed. Other schemes of interaction process analyses focus on analyzing social-emotional dimensions of the interaction, logical strategies
used by communicators, and interrelations between verbal stimuli and
their responses.[69] The content of interactions can be scored through
such schemes as Carr's Interaction Diagram, which rates the substance
of proposals made by group members according to the contributions
which they make toward solution of a given problem, and Sign Process
Analysis, which records the distribution of positive, negative, and neutral substantive remarks made by interacting group members in the
course of discussion.[70]

Reaction Measures

There are standardized ways of measuring syntax features, content
concepts, and verbal-interaction processes, but there are as yet few

68. Robert F. Bales, *Interaction Process Analysis* (Reading, Mass.: Addison
Wesley, 1950). A brief description can be found in Thomas W. Madron, *Small
Group Methods and the Study of Politics* (Evanston, Ill.: Northwestern University
Press, 1969), pp. 118–125. Also see ch. 9, below.

69. See Edmund J. Amidon, "Interaction Analysis," in Emmert and Brooks,
Methods of Research in Communications, pp. 373–425, and sources cited there.

70. Madron, *Small Group Methods*, pp. 130–135; Theodore M. Mills, *Group
Transformation* (Englewood Cliffs, N.J.: Prentice-Hall, 1964), ch. 2, pp. 19–41.
Also note Timothy F. Leary's classification system of interpersonal behavior in
Interpersonal Diagnosis of Personality (New York: Ronald, 1957), pp. 62–71.

well-developed procedures for measuring the reactions which verbal stimuli produce in their audiences. Reactions are usually inferred from overt action responses; however, many reactions may involve responses which are not expressed through overt behavior, so this procedure has severe limitations.

A widely used method for discovering how verbal and other stimuli are appraised by audiences is the semantic differential developed by Charles Osgood, George Suci, and Percy Tannenbaum. It is based on the assumption that individuals react to concepts and objects by appraising them along a finite series of meaningful dimensions in a multidimensional semantic space. For instance, a reader might react to a story about a politician by forming opinions about his sincerity, his power, and his inclination to use or refrain from using his power. Or he might react to a radio or television speech by the politician by evaluating the importance of its content and rating its persuasiveness.

The semantic differential method supplies an audience with scales for scoring relevant qualities of the object for which the investigator wants to know the audience's reactions. Test scores can then be compared. For instance, one can compare an individual's reactions to various stimuli, such as stories about two real candidates, or about a real and an ideal or hypothetical candidates, by asking the subject to rate the candidates for specified qualities after reading the stories. Different groups or individuals' evaluations of the same stimulus can also be compared. Republicans and Democrats may respond differently to a set of political concepts, such as the names of political candidates or specific policies linked to each party — Medicare, for instance, has much more favorable connotations for most Democrats than for most Republicans.[71]

However, comparative scores require careful interpretation, since the qualities chosen for comparison may have different meanings for different individuals and for different objects. The factors which move respondent A to code candidate C as "extremely powerful" may not be the same ones which move respondent B to make a similar evaluation. For A, the quality may mean legal power only; for B, it may mean actual coercive power. Likewise, "powerful" may refer to ability to control others when referring to a politician, to problem-solving ca-

71. Charles E. Osgood, George Suci, and Percy H. Tannenbaum, *The Measurement of Meaning* (Urbana: University of Illinois Press, 1957), pp. 18–30, 142. See also Lynch, "Stylistic Analysis," pp. 323ff., and Donald K. Darnell, "Semantic Differentiation," in Emmert and Brooks, *Methods of Research in Communication*, pp. 181–196, and sources cited there.

pacity when referring to a theory, and to physical strength when referring to an animal.

Experimentation with the semantic differential has shown that most stimuli are judged along three basic orthogonal (independent) dimensions or factors: evaluation along a positive-negative continuum, appraisal on the basis of activity or passivity, and judgment of strength or weakness. Semantic differential tests generally include scales to assess each of these three basic variables in order to get a well-rounded appraisal. Each scale normally involves a pair of adjectives with logically opposed meanings, aligned on a seven-point rating scale. The midpoint is neutral, indicating that the subject or object is judged to lean in neither direction. If the scale is experienced — inexperienced, the subject is considered neither (or both) if rated at midpoint. The remaining ratings indicate the degrees of experience or inexperience which characterize the subject in the rater's opinion.

Semantic scales are easy to use, reliable, and valid for gauging reactions to a wide variety of objects and concepts. However, differentials between scales do not actually measure the characteristics of the stimulus which is being appraised; rather, they measure audience perceptions of the stimulus. Since simple judgmental criteria apparently are not culture-bound, the semantic differential can be used to measure and compare evaluations of objects and concepts across cultures.[72]

Ordinary questionnaires and the Q-methodology, developed by William Stephenson, may also be used to judge how an audience perceives and evaluates a verbal stimulus. Q-methodology employs scales composed of rating statements which audiences are asked to sort according to the extent of their agreement with the statement. The statements are selected from previous verbal reactions to the topic under investigation or composed afresh to test particular behavioral theories. Generally, the sorters are instructed to maintain a fixed distribution on a rating scale with seven to eleven points, ranging from complete agreement to complete disagreement. The scales can be analyzed and compared to gain insight about the ways in which raters view persons or issues, or how they react to various types of verbal communication.

72. Darnell, "Semantic Differentiation," pp. 183–184. But note the questions raised on pp. 185–188 about the value of the semantic differential when used to measure meaning, rather than evaluation. For a discussion of cross-cultural uses of the semantic differential, see Charles E. Osgood, "Measurement of Meaning: An Exploration into Semantic Space," in Wilbur Schramm, ed., *Directions and New Findings in Communication Research* (New York: Basic Books, 1963), pp. 28–40, and Charles S. Osgood, William H. May, and Murray S. Miron, *Cross-Cultural Universals of Affective Meaning* (Urbana: University of Illinois Press, 1975).

Measurements can be taken at various times and under different conditions to test how these variations affect perceptions and meanings.[73]

Objections to Quantitative Analysis

A number of objections have been raised to the systematic, quantitative analysis of content. Many of them relate to long-standing imperfections in the methodology, such as the difficulty of devising sound coding categories, the tedium and energy expense of coding (often with comparatively small rewards in generalizable findings), and deficiencies in reliability and validity. Many of these shortcomings have already been ameliorated or corrected, and future improvements seem certain.[74] Consequently, methodological shortcomings in quantitative content analysis, while troublesome, do not seem unduly serious compared to shortcomings in other widely used social scientific and measurement techniques.[75]

More serious are objections to the fact that quantitative content analysis has often been restricted to the manifest meanings of words. This eliminates consideration of latent meanings which may be highly important in assessing a message. Investigators who have excluded latent meanings from coding and analysis schemes have feared that the reliability of coding would be sharply diminished if they strayed from manifest content; however, such fears seem no longer tenable. When it is important to include latent meanings in a particular analysis, manual as well as computer coding procedures can be devised to replicate some of the mental procedures which people perform when they code latent meanings.[76] This requires ingenuity in unraveling the steps in the judgmental process and systematizing them for the use of human

73. William Stephenson, *The Study of Behavior: Q Technique and Its Methodology* (Chicago: University of Chicago Press, 1953). Also see William B. Brooks, "Q-Sort Technique," in Emmert and Brooks, *Methods of Research in Communication*, pp. 165–180. For an excellent brief description, studded with examples, see Steven R. Brown, "Significance of Q Technique and Its Methodology for Political Science," MWPSA paper (1974).

74. See Pool, "Content Analysis and the Intelligence Function," p. 208.

75. For technical criticisms of content analysis, see Janowitz, "Content Analysis and the Study of the 'Symbolic Environment,'" pp. 160–162; and Irving L. Janis and Raymond Fadner, "The Co-efficient of Imbalance," in Harold D. Lasswell, Nathan Leites et al., eds., *The Language of Politics: Studies in Quantitative Semantics* (Cambridge: MIT Press, 1965), pp. 153–172.

76. See, for example, Donald H. Goldhamer, "Toward a More General Inquirer: Convergence of Structure and Context of Meaning," in Gerbner, ed., *Analysis of Communication Content*, pp. 343–355; and Stone, "Improved Quality of Content Analysis Categories," pp. 199–223.

and computer coders. It often involves provisions for modifying the manifest meanings in light of changing cultural and situational criteria. If past experience indicates that candidate A means the Ku Klux Klan when he talks of "extremist groups" to college audiences, and candidate B uses the same term for the Black Panthers when he talks to church groups, these situational meanings can be built into the quantitative coding system. An "if-then" coding scheme can be developed which specifies particular codes when certain conditions are known to have existed at the time of the creation of the verbal output.

Similarly, where communicators come from different cultures or are known to use particular communications strategies, the modifications which this knowledge entails can be built into the coding system. However, where the discovery of latent meanings requires analysis of complex social situations, it must be left for the final analysis process, after the manifest content has been coded. It may also be possible to formulate research designs which facilitate the discovery of latent meanings.

Another serious charge leveled against the usual methods of content analysis is that they are too quantitative. By limiting himself to asking quantitative questions — "How often?" "How much?" and "In how many combinations?" — the researcher severely restricts the aspects of verbal behavior which he can explore. Yet one must avoid an unduly narrow view of quantitative processes, for counting does more than search for high frequencies; it is a form of precise recording which creates nominal categories of presence or absence, or gross magnitudes. Once items are counted, the investigator can choose to ignore petty questions about frequency and explore the more general relational and qualitative aspects instead. Counting then serves merely as a systematic way of locating important data.

Some criticisms of quantitative content analysis center around the contention that undue emphasis is put on the importance of frequency of mention.[77] Frequent mention is not necessarily a sign that the concept in question is highly important to the sender or audience, that it will arouse much attention, or that it is more likely to herald action. Conversely, infrequent mention does not necessarily signify lack of importance. Each contention should be put into proper perspective.

Common sense confirms that one cannot mechanically judge the im-

77. Holsti, *Content Analysis for the Social Sciences*, pp. 5–12; Gilbert R. Winham, "Quantitative Methods in Foreign Policy Analysis," *Canadian Journal of Political Science*, 2 (1969), 198–199, discusses it in relation to international relations. Also see ch. 4, above, for a discussion of the validity of this inference.

portance of a topic by counting the frequency of its mention and measuring the time or space devoted to it. Nor can one say that all mentions are equally important, as would be implied if each were routinely counted the same in quantitative analysis. Moreover, each instance of mention is not an independent event. Once a concept has been expressed, that very fact may increase the chances for repetition because attention has been called to the concept. This, in turn, may reduce the chances for alluding to other concepts which may be far more important to the communicator and audience. Rhetorical styles or cultural conventions may call for the frequent use of certain concepts as matters of style rather than substance. Communist rhetoric is larded with references to imperialist aggressors when Western powers are discussed, even though the subjects of imperialism or aggression may not be at all central to the discussions.

High frequency cannot be equated with importance to communicators and audiences, and experienced content analysts do not automatically make this assumption. Once frequency or infrequency have been determined, it remains for the analyst to decide what significance, if any, should be assigned to these frequencies. This decision does not differ basically from judgments which need to be made in the physical sciences in determining what interpretation to place on a physical symptom. Just as an individual's elevated temperature may mean overheating, too much exercise, or fever caused by disease, so the frequency symptom may mean a variety of things. Surrounding circumstances need to be fully considered to discover the exact meaning.

It is equally naive to assume that frequency of verbal mention correlates very notably with behavior corresponding to the verbal announcement, for there may even be an inverse relationship. As Ithiel de Sola Pool points out, "the Russian Communists talk most loudly and frequently about democracy at the very time the dictatorship becomes more rigid and all embracing." [78] Again, this does not mean that frequency of mention and action are never related; it simply means that contextual factors must be examined to determine what inferences are warranted. [79] The same holds true regarding the relationship between infrequency of mention and unimportance. In many contexts, infrequency of mention is indeed a sign of unimportance, and a factor con-

78. Ithiel de Sola Pool, *Symbols of Democracy* (Stanford: Stanford University Press, 1952), p. iii.

79. See James M. Fendrich, "A Study of the Association among Verbal Attitudes, Commitment and Overt Behavior in Different Experimental Situations," *Social Forces*, 45 (1967), 347–355, and sources cited there.

tributing to unimportance. But the reverse may also be true. Two people can discuss a problem for hours with repeated mention of a variety of concepts; but let one of them call the other an offensive name, or mention an inappropriate concept, and this single verbal incident may overshadow everything else that has occurred, determining the outcome of the entire verbal interchange.

Qualitative Measures

A number of investigators believe that a systematic, directed search of selected documents for presence or absence of desired bits of significant information is often superior to quantitative analysis of large bodies of verbal output. A thorough study of the overall communications situation and appraisal of the verbal options open to leaders determine the documents and verbal features to be scrutinized.[80] After using both quantitative and qualitative methods in analyzing German wartime propaganda broadcasts. Alexander George has become a persuasive proponent of the priority due qualitative analysis: "Qualitative analysis of a limited number of crucial communications may often yield better clues to the particular intentions of a particular speaker at one moment in time than more standardized quantitative methods."[81] As an example, he cites a single speech by Goebbels after the battle of Stalingrad which talked about "counter-terror." The Federal Communications Commission analyst who made a qualitative analysis of the speech concluded that pogroms against German Jews were planned. The word "counter-terror" used in that particular linguistic and situational context became an important clue to German plans. Likewise, when a prominent German commentator warned that a U-boat victory gave no assurance that U-boats would remain significant factors in the war, this was interpreted as a downgrading of U-boats by the Germans. The importance of the source and the uniqueness of the remark alerted the analyst to its possible significance. A process of quantitative analysis might well have missed the cue because it occurred only once.

John Mueller cites the example of the Japanese surrender debates to show the importance of qualitative appraisal of unmentioned content. ". . . in the records of the Japanese cabinet debates about surrender in August 1945, the atomic bomb is barely mentioned, yet

80. See ch. 4, above.
81. Alexander George, "Quantitative and Qualitative Approaches to Content Analysis," in Ithiel de Sola Pool, ed., *Trends in Content Analysis* (Urbana: University of Illinois Press, 1959), p. 7. Also see Mueller, "Use of Content Analysis," p. 188.

commentators are reluctant to conclude that its existence had no bearing on the final decision." [82]

Qualitative analysis is valuable, but that does not diminish the usefulness of quantitative analysis. Rather, there is a case for both. For certain types of problems, quantitative analysis is the only suitable method. For instance, if one wishes to analyze long-term changes of mass perceptions as mirrored in the press, or in expressions by significant political figures, one should use quantitative methods. Repetition as such becomes an important factor, for whatever is repeated is more likely to affect a mass audience, through time, than what is mentioned rarely. By contrast, if one wants to trace particular decisions or the interaction of two speakers with respect to a particular topic, a qualitative, sharply focused approach may be preferable.

A marriage of the two approaches often produces the best results. For instance, text might be fed into a computer, using a General Inquirer Program, with instructions to print out every word which is not already in the dictionary or which is mentioned fewer than ten times. With these directions, a novel word like "counter-terror" in the Goebbels speech would be printed out and could be subjected to the type of qualitative analysis which the FCC performed. In fact, many single significant words which may have been missed by the FCC analysts might be retrieved through automated methods.

Overall, it seems that most obstacles to scientific content analysis lie in the realm of coding techniques. The basic idea that scientific measurement of verbal behavior is possible is well established by now, although doubters remain plentiful. The many misperceptions of verbal behavior that crop up when haphazard intuitive methods are used can obviously be reduced by employing the more systematic quantitative and qualitative methods. Further perfection of these methods should contribute immensely to the ease and accuracy with which verbal behavior studies can be conducted.

SUMMARY

This chapter has dealt with steps and problems in verbal behavior research from the initial research question, theory and hypothesis formulation, to decisions about the basic research design, sample and time-frame selection, to data collection and interpretation, and to final validation of the results. Difficulties common to social scientific re-

82. Mueller, "Use of Content Analysis," p. 188.

search are likely to occur at each step, but only a few of these pose un-usually serious problems in verbal behavior research.

Sample selection is one area of above-average complexity because of the vast quantity and wide dispersion of verbal data produced and accumulated by societies and individuals. Exceptionally stringent se-lection methods may be required to keep samples manageable, and great efforts may be needed to locate the complete universe of data from which a valid sample can be selected. When data span historical periods, significant changes in encoding and recording methods may impede accurate data-gathering.

The application of behavioral rules to verbal data is hampered by the fact that there are more unpredictable exceptions in verbal be-havior than in many other types of behaviors investigated by social scientists. For instance, the rule that frequency of certain themes in a given body of verbal data indicates the degree of importance which the communicator places on the topic has many exceptions which arise from a still incompletely identified array of variations in the circum-stances producing the communication. Similarly, paralinguistic features such as pitch, register, tempo, loudness, and breaking are known to modify verbal meanings. But there are as yet few validated instru-ments for measuring these features and for accurately appraising their modifying impact on the communication. Nonverbal corroborative evi-dence needed to validate the results of verbal analysis often is difficult or impossible to obtain. The politician whose perceptions have been culled from an examination of his private and public papers may have taken no nonverbal actions which confirm or refute the verbal evidence.

Three major, often overlapping modes of analysis are commonly employed in verbal behavior research: the intuitive method, the quanti-tative method, and the qualitative method. Most analysts using the in-tuitive strategy interpret meanings by appraising the interrelation of the various elements expressed in the message, rather than by ex-amining specific words contained in the message. They apply general interpretational rules to such features as stock phrases and verbal styles. All this is done against the background of informal situational context analysis: the use of social insight and judgment to predict reaction patterns which social stimuli are likely to produce in the cir-cumstances at hand. Familiarity with the social setting and with the senders and receivers permits laymen, as well as trained observers, to accurately appraise the social context of many messages. Most diffi-culties arise when the settings and parties to the message transaction are unfamiliar to the analyst, or when there are cultural disparities between the analyst and the communicators.

Systematic quantitative and qualitative methods of content analysis make the intuitive process rigorous, methodical, and objective and thereby free it from many inaccuracies and distortions. Content features are categorized and labeled according to a prearranged coding scheme designed to permit retrieval and analysis of all information elements needed for a particular research project. This allows accurate, detailed appraisal and comparison of bodies of verbal data whose size extends beyond the unaided memory span of the average individual. Systematic analysis also makes it feasible for groups of analysts to work jointly on projects, using identical analysis techniques, and it permits the use of time-saving information machines, including computers. In addition, quantitative content analysis makes possible the use of sophisticated mathematical techniques which may disclose obscure verbal patterns.

Qualitative content analysis involves the systematic, directed search of selected documents for presence or absence of a limited amount of presumably significant information. It differs from quantitative research by deemphasizing the potentially equal importance of all content elements, focusing instead on preselected key elements. Key elements are determined on the basis of a general psychological, sociological, and political analysis of the communication situation. Qualitative content analysis permits greater flexibility for considering latent as well as manifest meanings of messages.

Systematic verbal behavior analysis has profited from identification of a series of verbal indicators which provide standardized measures for discovering general characteristics of the message's sender or content. Fairly reliable verbal indicators are available for gauging a number of personality traits, mental conditions, and value structures. Indicators have also been developed to assess the nature and quality of interactions among communicators, and to appraise individual and group reactions to verbal communications. Likewise, the comprehensibility of messages to people at various educational levels, the degree of sensationalism of newspaper stories, and the degree of emotional content of campaign communications can be readily assessed by using standardized verbal indicators.

PART TWO

Verbal Behavior in Political Situations

Previous chapters have discussed the effects of verbal behavior, inferences which can be drawn from it, and ways of measuring it. This part will further illustrate these ideas with concrete examples drawn from politically oriented verbal research.

Since the verbal output of the mass media receives so much attention from the politically aware, and reaches so many political actors and observers, Chapter 6 begins with a discussion of mass media influence on politics. Attention will be directed to the ways in which mass media can create politically powerful verbal images of reality, and to the politically relevant inferences which one can draw from mass media images.

Chapter 7 concentrates on the verbal behavior of political elites, for reasons similar to those which led to a focus on the mass media. The predominant position of elites in the policy-making process makes their verbal behavior significant for its effects and for the inferences which it permits about politics at high levels. Through the mass media and direct contacts, elite verbal behavior reaches vast numbers of people who pay more careful attention to elite pronouncements than to most other types of political messages.

Still in accord with the principle that we are most interested in verbal behavior which is apt to have a major impact on politics, Chapter 8 deals with verbal behavior in public assemblies. It seeks to determine the effects which speeches may have on political interactions and outputs of such bodies, and on the audiences watching the proceedings and taking their cues from them. Again, inferences drawn from the speeches as to relationships among the participants, and concerning the political conditions which produced the speeches, are examined for the light they shed on the workings of otherwise obscure political processes.

Even within public assemblies, much business is done in small, face-to-face bargaining groups. Verbal behavior in such small groups differs considerably from assembly behavior, since the intimacy of a small group does not lend itself to the innuendo, diatribe, and posturing that so often pervades public proceedings. Verbal behavior in small groups has been examined closely by social scientists from various disciplines, especially in connection with collective bargaining. Some of these studies will be examined to determine their relevance for political negotiations in the small group.

Most verbal behavior is ephemeral; the sense and connotations of the message may be retained, but the specific words are forgotten almost as soon as they have been uttered. A multitude of terms and phrasings could be substituted for the specific words spoken. However, there are certain terms which have acquired very distinctive, highly emotional meanings for large groups of people. We call them "condensation symbols" because they condense a whole coterie of ideas and notions into symbolic words or phrases. They are familiar and widely used, and often in a stylized form. Colonialism, genocide, Hitler, black power, the American way, "Remember the Maine!" and "Make the World Safe for Democracy" are such symbols. Their prevalence and strong influence in politics necessitates an examination of their effects and the inferences which they call forth.

The criteria employed in selecting examples have been pragmatic. Findings presented are usually from studies of actual political events, rather than from laboratory experiments. The gap between the laboratory and the field is still too vast in most cases to establish strong, direct relationships between laboratory findings and political realities. Studies used here seem to be well-documented, careful in methodology, and interesting in subject matter. When choices were available, newer projects were preferred. The verbal studies here also pertain to significant problems at various political levels. While the end-product illustrates a variety of research techniques, balanced exposition of such techniques was not a prime consideration.

Except for occasional references to specific methodological problems, Part II does not attempt to analyze the controversial aspects of the research methods of the scholars whose work is reported. Many of the hypotheses involved in these studies require further testing before one can feel full confidence in the theories which have been developed.

6 Mass Media and the Verbal Definition of Political Reality

> More than 1000 state troopers and sheriff's deputies stormed Attica Prison today with guns blazing in an attempt to free 38 hostages held by rebellious prisoners.
> — *St. Louis Post-Dispatch*, September 13, 1971

> Having been largely thwarted in their attempt to turn university campuses into bases of revolutionary action, the New Left now is depending on a savage prison population to trigger enormous violence and undermine the official and public will to maintain law and order.
> — *The Independent American*, September–October, 1971

> There is blood on the hands of Governor Nelson Rockefeller, who ordered the National Guard to storm the prison at Attica, New York. The criminals are not in the cells but in the seats of state power.
> —*Daily World*, September 14, 1971

> Attica Prison in New York became the focal point for the exposure of this country's full turn toward fascism. The men that were killed there on September 13, 1971, all know, in varying degrees, that the state had no concern for their lives.
> — *The Black Panther*, September 25, 1971

The Mass Media Prism

Plato's allegory of the cave describes men who are chained in an underground den from childhood on; they can watch the scene of passing events only by observing shadows cast by a fire and listening to echoes of voices. Despite fantastic advances in communications technology, modern man is still chained in a perceptual cave. Most of his political knowledge comes to him second hand. He sees events as projected from the shadow play of the mass media.

How do the verbal images depicted by the media originate? As a play within a play. Events occur, like the Attica prison riot discussed in the opening quotes. These events are watched by trained and untrained observers whose observations, filtered through their perceptual screens, then furnish the raw material for verbal images presented in the mass media. If still or motion pictures are taken, the choice of scenes, camera angles, and verbal and written captions likewise imprints the material with the reporter's personal viewpoints. The media image consumer refilters media images through his own perceptual screens and makes them part of his personal image of reality. These images, largely verbally created, incomplete, and badly distorted, then become the primary basis for attitudes and actions by elite and mass publics.[1]

Like the men in Plato's cave, most people are unaware that they only rarely experience reality firsthand; somehow the verbal images, supplemented by selected pictorial images, seem to be the real thing. People are likewise oblivious to the fact that political leaders also rely on verbal reflections of the world, as selected and presented by the mass media, for their perceptions and appraisals of the political universe and for decision-making. In politics, dependence on reflected perceptions is especially great in foreign affairs, because it is impossible to attend all the events which occur around the globe.[2]

The need to form images based on descriptions presented by intermediaries is neither new nor highly regrettable. If people could not experience the world through the words and pictures of others, they would have to restrict their knowledge to those matters which they could observe themselves. Even today, in a world of rapid travel, the bulk of reality beyond one's doorstep cannot be readily observed. If the mass media do not furnish extra eyes and ears, unwatched reality escapes. The individual cannot respond to it because its stimulus never touched him directly.

The mass media are presenting an ever-widening spectrum of events to an ever-growing audience — with major political consequences. Most important, the mass media are at the very heart of the political process. By publishing some stories and omitting others from a vast pool of newsworthy events, and by determining the manner of presentation, mass media personnel thrust the limelight of political attention on some events to the exclusion of others. The nature of happenings predetermines some news choices — a major war or elections must be

1. On this point, see Johan Galtung and Mari Holmboe Ruge, "The Structure of Foreign News," *Journal of Peace Research*, 2 (1965), 64.

2. Bernard C. Cohen, *The Press and Foreign Policy* (Princeton: Princeton University Press, 1963), pp. 141–143, 210. Also see Einar Östgaard, "Factors Influencing the Flow of News," *Journal of Peace Research*, 2 (1965), 41, and sources cited there. Galtung and Ruge, in "The Structure of Foreign News," p. 64, point out that despite personal experience, professional contacts, and diplomatic dispatches, "the regularity, ubiquity, and perseverance of news media will at any rate make them first-rate competitors for the number-one position as international image-formers."

reported — but most choices are discretionary. The power to place events into selected contexts is equally vast and significant. News revelations can force politicians to act, or at least to go through the motions of action. Media publicity determines who and what becomes famous or infamous and who or what merits attention or oblivion.[3]

The mass media are "high-gain amplifiers" with phenomenally high rates of output compared to input.[4] One correspondent's perception of a given event can be beamed to literally millions of people and affect their political outlook. Most of their private discussions become abbreviated and simplified versions of media verbal images. Juan Perón's triumphant return to Argentina after decades of exile or the assassination of Senator Robert Kennedy in a California hotel, when filtered through the perceptual screens of a single individual or a handful of reporters, can become the shared reality of millions.[5]

This reality may be quite different from what the average mass-media consumer would have perceived, had he observed events first-hand. A study of press reports of political speeches presents a good example. Robert Scott and Wayne Brockriede analyzed the complete text of a speech made by Vice-President Hubert Humphrey in July, 1966, before a convention of the National Association for the Advancement of Colored People in Los Angeles.[6] In the speech, Humphrey identified himself with the anti–Black Power position of the NAACP. The speech, as excerpted in the electronic and printed mass media, so diluted the original that the media presentation deserved to be called a second speech occasion. The same held true when other speeches involving the Black Power concept were analyzed. Scott and Brockriede

3. Joseph T. Klapper, *The Effects of Mass Communication* (New York: Free Press, 1960), p. 104; Paul F. Lazarsfeld and Robert K. Merton, "Mass Communication, Popular Taste and Organized Social Action," in Lyman Bryson, ed., *The Communication of Ideas* (New York: Harper, 1948).

4. The phrase comes from Wilbur Schramm, "Information Theory and Mass Communication," in Alfred G. Smith, ed., *Communication and Culture: Readings in the Codes of Human Interaction* (New York: Holt, Rinehart and Winston, 1966), p. 523.

5. Karl W. Deutsch and Richard L. Merritt, "Effects of Events on National and International Images," in Herbert Kelman, ed., *International Behavior* (New York: Holt, Rinehart and Winston, 1965), p. 138. Norton Long ascribes to the newspaper "a great part in determining what most people will be talking about, what most people will think the facts are, and what most people will regard as the way problems are dealt with . . . to a large extent it sets the civic agenda." Quoted from "The Local Community as an Ecology of Games," *American Journal of Sociology*, 64 (1958), 256.

6. Robert Scott and Wayne Brockriede, *The Rhetoric of Black Power* (New York: Harper and Row, 1969), p. 78.

surmised that public reactions to the Black Power concept were reactions to media reality, rather than to the original speech reality.

Given human perceptual processes, which are subjective and linked to the individual's personal and social characteristics and past experiences, perceptual distortions are unavoidable. There are no unslanted verbal or pictorial presentations. Even when the facts which are stated are completely accurate, so many details are of necessity omitted from the description of any situation that the description becomes inaccurate It is important to recognize the unpalatable fact that objective reporting is impossible, along with the fact that this puts the mass media, whose versions of reality are widely disseminated and accepted, into an extremely powerful position.[7]

Other factors enhance this power position. Given the floodtide of stories culled from around the globe and even from outer space, it becomes increasingly impossible for media consumers to check media accuracy. Competing versions of the same story are seldom available. As in any monopoly situation, the information consumer can accept media images or reject them, but he can rarely produce his own version or obtain information that has not been covered in the media.[8]

By transmitting political news to an ever larger number of people, the mass media make possible mass action on the basis of widely shared perceptions. This may mean action by general mass publics, or, more likely, by selected publics of varying sizes who share common interests. Since much of the political news which the mass media present involves matters on which action is in progress or imminent, "the mass media, by providing a common reality on the basis of which people can interact, provide the agenda for public action."[9]

7. Allport and Postman's well-known experiments to test the psychology of rumor give graphic proof of the influence of prior attitudes on perceptual distortions. In one experiment, when viewers were asked to describe a picture which showed a white and black man standing in a train, facing each other, with the white man clutching a razor, the white respondents almost invariably reported the razor in the black man's hand. Gordon Allport and Leo J. Postman, "The Basic Psychology of Rumor," in Guy E. Swanson et al., eds., *Readings in Social Psychology*, rev. ed. (New York: Holt, 1952), p. 169.

8. In July, 1972, the *National Review* published "top secret" papers on the Vietnam war. The Justice Department immediately investigated the "leak." Other news sources relayed the information, including the Voice of America and the president's official news digest. Publisher William F. Buckley then confessed impishly that it had all been a planned hoax. *New York Times*, July 23, 1972.

9. George Gerbner, "Towards 'Cultural Indicators': The Analysis of Mass Mediated Public Message Systems," in George Gerbner, ed., *The Analysis of Communication Content* (New York: John Wiley, 1969), p. 126. Satish K. Arora and Harold D. Lasswell, *Political Communication: The Public Language of Political Elites in*

It is easy to overstate the importance of the mass media; their version of reality is widely disseminated, but this does not necessarily mean that it is listened to, understood, or accepted. Moreover, the mass media do not speak with a single voice on all topics. Competing versions of some controversial events may be available, even within the same medium. This weakens the monopoly power of individual news sources. Given these mitigating forces, one needs to ask what effect, in general, the mass media have on their audiences and on politics.

This complex subject has been investigated extensively by a number of scholars; most studies have focused on mass media effects on audiences, rather than on politics. Surveying much of the relevant literature in the field, Joseph Klapper found that the ultimate effect of the mass media on their audiences apparently depends on intervening variables, including audience predisposition, selective exposure, selective perception and selective remembering, the interaction of source and audience, contextual factors, time and situation factors before, during, and after message reception, group orientation of the audience, personality patterns, and competing implementation possibilities. In fact, "almost every aspect of the life of the audience member and the culture in which communication occurs seems susceptible of relation to the process of communication effect." [10] Or, as Bernard Berelson has facetiously put it: "Some kinds of communication on some kinds of issues, brought to the attention of some kinds of people under some kinds of conditions, have some kinds of effects." [11]

Berelson's point, of course, is that the mass media do affect their audiences, but the precise nature of the effect depends on the interaction of many variables. To understand the effect, one must first delineate the communication stimulus and then relate it to a particular audience at a particular time and place. The weight of research evidence supports the view that the media are particularly important in creating opinions on new issues: "communication content is more effective in influencing public opinion on new or unstructured issues, i.e.,

India and the United States (New York: Holt, Rinehart and Winston, 1968), p. 6, points out that mass media information is not as ephemeral as it may seem at first glance. "Since it is possible to store and retrieve print with comparative ease, a published newspaper has an impact on politics that goes beyond the immediate audience."

10. Klapper, Effects of Mass Communication, pp. 3–4.
11. Bernard Berelson, "Communication and Public Opinion," in Wilbur Schramm, Communications in Modern Society (Urbana: University of Illinois Press, 1948), p. 172.

those not particularly correlated with existing attitude clusters."[12] Even if they do not create the opinion, they are "highly efficient in imparting factual knowledge."[13] Moreover, fact and opinion transmission may be at its highest peak of effectiveness during political crises. "The apparent efficacy of the media in creating opinions on new issues suggests that their potential during a time of revolution or social unrest may well be enormous. Opportunities exist, at such a time, not only for the reinforcement of revolutionary views, but also for the introduction or definition of issues to which many audience members have given little or no attention."[14]

Besides creating opinions on new issues, the media may also reinforce opinions which are already held, thereby adding elements of stability and often rigidity to the political process. The media furthermore serve as major agents of political socialization and re-socialization, supplying much of the factual data which elites and masses use for opinion formation. Moreover, the accumulation of attitudes formed from information furnished by the mass media shapes the perceptual funnels through which future information is accepted and channeled or rejected.[15]

This chapter emphasizes the type of verbal environment which is created by the mass media and which is likely to influence politically significant reality perceptions which, in turn, may influence actual politics. Like Berelson, I am not prepared, at this early stage of mass communication knowledge, to claim specific effects for specific communications received by specific audiences. This is an admission that effects have not been sufficiently studied to make positive linkages, but it is not an admission that effects are nonexistent or that evidence for their existence is exceedingly weak.[16] I concur with Klapper's conclusion to his cautious analysis of mass media effects that "perhaps the greatest danger . . . is the tendency to go overboard in blindly minimizing the effects and potentialities of mass communications." Public

12. *Ibid.*, p. 176. The effects of foreign news coverage are analyzed in Øystein Sande, "The Perception of Foreign News," *Journal of Peace Research*, 3–4 (1971), 221–237.

13. Klapper, *Effects of Mass Communication*, p. 58.

14. *Ibid.*, p. 59. The effects of the mass media are particularly great in developing nations. For a brief discussion, see Ithiel de Sola Pool, "The Mass Media and Politics in the Modernization Process," in Lucian W. Pye, ed., *Communications and Political Development* (Princeton: Princeton University Press, 1963), pp. 234–253.

15. Klapper, *Effects of Mass Communication*, pp. 15–52; also see Kurt Lang and Gladys Engel Lang, "The Mass Media and Voting," in Eugene Burdick and Arthur J. Brodbeck, eds., *American Voting Behavior* (Glencoe, Ill.: Free Press, 1959).

16. Klapper, *Effects of Mass Communication*, p. 54.

relations efforts to get favorable mass media coverage, tight media control by totalitarian societies, and laws prohibiting pretrial publicity to preserve the impartiality of jurors and judges are but a few indicators of the pervasiveness of beliefs in the mind-shaping effects of the mass media.[17]

Major aspects of mass media coverage discussed in this chapter are: common distortion factors which skew mass media reality; the likely effects of skewed coverage on political action; and the use of mass media data as social indicators to infer the characteristics and actions of a given society.

GATE-KEEPING AND MEDIA REALITY

The mass media are faced with "the physical problem of riding the information torrent."[18] They must pick news stories rapidly from an almost limitless number of events to be reported. The average metropolitan general circulation newspaper in the United States, which is the most prolific single source of mass information about current affairs, can print only a tiny fraction of the day's happenings. Even the flow of wire service information, which already presents a narrowed stream of current worldwide information, must be sharply curtailed by newspaper gate-keepers. Generally, less than 10 percent of the wire service news is printed.[19] Mass media personnel also must decide the manner in which events are to be presented. From what perspective will the story be told? What sources will be used? What evaluations will be expressed or implied?

The following examples bypass the mechanics of gate-keeping — how the decisions are made to include or exclude certain stories, and how it is decided that stories will be featured from one angle rather than another. Nor will they dwell on the philosophies which presumably

17. Advertising and propaganda disseminated through the mass media also are predicated on a belief in the persuasiveness of mass media messages. See Cohen, *Press and Foreign Policy*; Dan P. Nimmo, *Newsgathering in Washington: A Study in Political Communication* (New York: Atherton Press, 1964); Douglas Cater, *The Fourth Branch of Government* (Boston: Houghton Mifflin, 1959); William L. Rivers, *The Opinion Makers: The Washington Press Corps* (Boston: Beacon Press, 1965).

18. Robert Manning, "International News Media," in Arthur S. Hoffman, ed., *International Communication and the New Diplomacy* (Bloomington: Indiana University Press, 1968), p. 160.

19. See Östgaard, "Factors Influencing the Flow of News," p. 59, and sources cited there for U.S. and foreign data. Also Manning, "International News Media," pp. 160–161.

underlie gate-keeping, or on normative considerations of what gate-keeping should and should not accomplish.[20] Rather, the focus will be on the results of gate-keeping in general, with specific examples to illustrate systematic distortions which ensue from normal gate-keeping processes, primarily in Western countries. The examples have been selected from the fairly narrow spectrum of studies which have attempted to analyze what slice of the available news pie was presented to the public, and in what shape and manner it was served. These examples reveal weaknesses in the mass communication process, because complete and impartial reporting of all important events is impossible. There are a large number of economic, technical, and journalistic considerations which effectively limit the choices which gate-keepers are able to make.

Narrow Ethnocentric Viewpoints

Our first example illustrates that mass media reality tends to depict the world from a narrow, familiar perspective, especially when it deals with remote events. ". . . by placing novel phenomena in a known

20. The gate-keeping function is analyzed in Warren Breed, "Social Control in the Newsroom," in Wilbur Schramm, ed., *Mass Communications* (Urbana: University of Illinois Press, 1960), pp. 178–194; David Manning White, "The 'Gate-Keeper': A Case Study in the Selection of News," pp. 160–171, and Walter Gieber, "News Is What Newspapermen Make It," pp. 172–180, both in Lewis A. Dexter and David Manning White, eds., *People, Society and Mass Communications* (New York: Free Press, 1964). Gate-keeping practices are compared internationally in Jacques Kayser, *One Week's News: Comparative Study of Seventeen Major Dailies for a Seven-Day Period* (Paris: Paul Dupont for UNESCO, 1953). There are many theories about the philosophy behind the gate-keeping function of the mass media, ranging from conspiracy theories which picture the media as controlled by narrow interests (business, political parties, or the military-industrial complex) to theories of ideological and social functions of the media, to purely journalistic criteria of newsworthiness. For an example of conspiracy theory, see Herbert Schiller, *Mass Communications and American Empire* (New York: Augustus M. Kelley, 1969), and Long, "Local Community." The influence of ideology on media gate-keeping is discussed in Arora and Lasswell, *Political Communication*, p. 7. Normative analyses of gate-keeping are generally based on an implicit or explicit assumption that the story actually presented used the wrong selection criteria and left out much which might have been included or substituted. Sins of omission and commission are pointed out to indicate how they distorted the reality against which the critic is measuring the story. Since the loss of information between happenings and their reportage is extremely great, such charges are easily provoked, made, and substantiated. Some of the basic standards against which selection has often been measured are responsibility; bias; attitudes toward law, people, and societal forms; comparison with medical data, census data, and adequacy of minority data. Examples are Thomas Franck and Edward Weisband, *Word Politics: Verbal Strategy among the Super Powers* (New York: Oxford University Press, 1972); Philip

conceptual environment, it suggests that the novel events can be understood, controlled, and predicted within the context of a familiar
order." [21] Stories come from a few sources which are usually selected
on the basis of their cultural or ideological affinity with the gate-keeper
and his public. This is where ethnocentric biases creep in. "The further
an individual is from the entity about which he is receiving information,
the greater are the cumulative biases that enter into his perception of
reality." [22] Put more generally, the more ambiguous the stimulus is for
the receiver, the greater the possibility that his perceptions will be
distorted.

The example comes from a 1965 study of mass media coverage of
the Congo, Cuba, and Cyprus crises in four leading Norwegian newspapers. The analysts, Johan Galtung and Mari Holmboe Ruge, found
that 91 percent of the news stories reported in these papers relied on
information furnished by four Western-controlled wire services: the
American AP (Associated Press) and UPI (United Press International),
the French AFP (Agence France Press), and NTB (Nordic), the Scandi-
navian wire service. Nordic receives its news primarily from the French
AFP and British Reuters. By relying on American, French, and British
sources, Norwegians were getting their political reality from a Western
perspective.[23] They learned little about how these conflicts were locally
perceived by the participants, or how major non-Western powers were
interpreting these situations. For instance, the news from Cyprus, as
seen through Reuters dispatches, reported Britain's relationship to the
conflict to the exclusion of other matters.

Galtung and Ruge speculated that there were six major perspectives
from which the various stories could have been told. One turned out
to be dominant — the perspective of major Western powers involved in

Green, *Deadly Logic: The Theory of Nuclear Deterrence* (Columbus: Ohio State
University Press, 1966); Paula B. Johnson, David O. Sears, and John B. McConahay, "Black Invisibility, the Press, and the Los Angeles Riot," *American Journal
of Sociology*, 76 (1971), 698–721.

21. J. Zvi Namenwirth and Thomas L. Brewer, "Elite Editorial Comment on
the European and Atlantic Communities in Four Countries," in Philip J. Stone,
Dexter C. Dunphy, Marshall S. Smith, and Daniel M. Ogilvie, *The General Inquirer: A Computer Approach to Content Analysis* (Cambridge: MIT Press, 1966),
p. 425.

22. Susan Welch, "The American Press and Indochina, 1950–56," in Richard
L. Merritt, ed., *Communication in International Politics* (Urbana: University of
Illinois Press, 1972), p. 228; also see the discussion of uncertainty absorption in
ch. 2, above.

23. For speculations about reasons for such orientations, see Östgaard, "Factors
Influencing the Flow of News," pp. 42–45. Many other papers rely on even fewer
sources because of financial stringencies. See Kayser, *One Week's News*, p. 93.

the conflict. Fifty-nine percent of all stories on the Cuban crisis viewed it in terms of U.S.-Cuban relations; 52 percent of all stories on the Congo pictured it from the viewpoint of Belgian relations to the Congo, and 54 percent of all Cyprus stories viewed it as Britain's conflict with a dependent country. The story was pictured far less frequently as part of the anti-colonial struggle of Cuba, the Congo, and Cyprus, or as a conflict among opposing factions within the country. Galtung and Ruge assert that the emphasis of the story was largely conditioned by the presumed interests of prospective readers; Norwegian readers presumably were interested in problems as viewed by Britain, Belgium, or the United States more than in problems as viewed by Cuba, Cyprus, or the Congo. The result of such selection criteria was a lopsided picture of these conflicts.[24]

Fragmentation, Inaccuracies, Sensationalism

The Western press's general criteria for newsworthiness have a crucial effect on the depiction of political reality. News must be interesting, simple to grasp, and have human interest appeal. It must emphasize the idealized values, as well as fears and concerns, of the surrounding culture.[25] If it requires distortions to fit into this procrustean bed, this is deemed defensible news practice. Since reading publics are intrinsically less interested in events from culturally distant nations, such events have to be highly newsworthy to be reported; this means that news from culturally distant countries, if reported at all, tends to involve sensational and strongly negative features. For instance, the most frequent theme in coverage of the United States by ten Mexican dailies in 1960 was that the United States was plagued with family problems, juvenile delinquency, and crime and sex problems.[26]

Since there is little background and build-up news, readers get the impression that events in far-off countries happen very suddenly and unpredictably.[27] Generally, only those events are reported which go

24. The problem plagues non-Western countries as well. Abu-Lughod reports that Arab readers in 1962 had much news available about the United States and Britain, but scarcely anything by and about the Eastern bloc. Ibrahim Abu-Lughod, "International News in the Arabic Press: A Comparative Content Analysis," *Public Opinion Quarterly*, 26 (1962), 608.

25. F. Earle Barcus, "Communications Content: Analysis of the Research, 1900–1958" (Ph.D. dissertation, University of Illinois, 1959), p. 241.

26. John C. Merrill, "The Image of the United States in Ten Mexican Dailies," *Journalism Quarterly*, 39 (1962), 207.

27. The deleterious effects of crisis-hopping are discussed in Cohen, *Press and Foreign Policy*, pp. 99–100, 241, 267, 272.

along with the cultural stereotypes shared by media personnel and their readers. To be considered newsworthy, stories from the less important countries will generally have to refer to

> people, preferably top elite, and be preferably negative and unexpected but nevertheless according to a pattern that is consonant with the "mental pre-image." It will have to be simple and it should, if possible, provide the reader with some kind of identification — it should refer to him or his nation or group of nations. This will, in turn, facilitate an image of these countries as dangerous, ruled by capricious elites, as unchanging in their basic characterictics, as existing for the benefit of top dog nations, and in terms of their links to those nations. Events occur, they are sudden, like flashes of lightning, with no build-up and with no let-down after their occurrence — they just occur and more often than not as a part of the machinations of the ruling or opposition elites.
>
> The consequences of all this is an image of the world that gives little autonomy to the periphery but sees it as mainly existing for the sake of the center — for good or for bad — as a real periphery to the center of the world. . . . Everything's relevance for everything else, particularly for us, is overplayed. Its relevance to itself disappears.[28]

As a consequence, remote and foreign events look undesirable and threatening, and proclivities toward ethnocentrism are enhanced.

While the distortions and omissions which ensue from gate-keeping are particularly striking in international reporting, they occur in domestic reporting as well. Even a fully publicized event such as an American presidential campaign suffers from serious omissions in presenting to the public those facts which most social scientists consider important for voting decisions. My own studies of press coverage during the 1968 and 1972 campaigns confirm this. I examined the type of information supplied by American newspapers about candidates and issues to determine the political images available to the average individual.[29] The investigation showed that campaign coverage dwelt heavily on personal attributes of the candidates, rather than on their professional qualifications; it failed to clearly stipulate the choices presented by the contenders, and it ignored a number of public issues which seemed very important to other observers. The issues of ecology in 1968 and full discussion of the Watergate affair in 1972 are examples.

---

28. Galtung and Ruge, "Structure of Foreign News," p. 84.
29. Doris A. Graber, "The Press as Opinion Resource during the 1968 Presidential Campaign," *Public Opinion Quarterly*, 35 (1971), 168–182; also see Maxwell E. McCombs and Donald L. Shaw, "The Agenda-Setting Function of Mass Media," *Public Opinion Quarterly*, 36 (1972), 176–187.

One cannot claim that an election might have had a different outcome if it had been discussed in terms of some of the untouched issues or the unmentioned dimensions of the candidates' personalities. Election research indicates that, in the United States, "typically about 80 percent, or more, of the voters have made up their minds about their vote before the campaign begins. . . . Some 70 to 85 percent will vote for the same party as in the previous election. . . ." [30]

This still leaves 15-30 percent open to possible media influence on their voting choices, and all of them open to changes in their political views which may not be immediately reflected in election choices. Voter turn-out, which may be crucial to election outcomes, also may be stimulated or discouraged by media-created images. Furthermore, potential voters who are cross-pressured as a result of exposure to mass media information may stay away from the polls. Beyond the voting decision, the impressions which people receive about candidates and issues may shape their general outlook on government. Campaign news may strengthen or weaken allegiances and reinforce or diminish previous political images which have been impressed on the public mind largely through mass media output.

Our final example of typical gate-keeping inaccuracies comes from an area of politics where complete facts are comparatively accessible and where there is a minimum of emotional or partisan involvement on the part of those who are gathering and reporting the facts. Even in this area, where one might expect rather accurate verbal pictures, distortions are widespread. Stories are incomplete and inaccurate, geared to capture interest rather than significance, and describing actions rather than the reasons for them or their significance.

These findings come from a study of reporting of U.S. Supreme Court landmark decisions. [31] Chester A. Newland examined coverage of *Baker* v. *Carr*, 82 Sup. Ct., 691, and *Engel* v. *Vitale*, 82 Sup. Ct., 1261, in sixty-three metropolitan daily papers. *Baker* v. *Carr*, the reapportionment case, overturned precedent and established that the federal judiciary could rule on the fairness of apportionment of state legislative districts. *Engel* v. *Vitale*, the prayer case, held that daily voluntary re-

---

30. Elihu Katz, "Platforms and Windows: Broadcasting's Role in Election Campaigns," *Journalism Quarterly*, 48 (1971), 306.

31. Chester A. Newland, "Press Coverage of the United States Supreme Court," *Western Political Quarterly*, 17 (1964), 15–36; also see David L. Grey, *The Supreme Court and the News Media* (Evanston, Ill.: Northwestern University Press, 1968), and Stephen L. Wasby, *The Impact of the United States Supreme Court* (Homewood, Ill.: Dorsey Press, 1970), pp. 83–99, 233–242.

cital of a nondenominational prayer in the public schools was unconstitutional.

Newland's sample showed that most stories about the court's actions were based on AP and UPI wire service coverage; hence information came from the pen of one of the two reporters who covered the Supreme Court beat for their respective wire services. However, some additional details had come in from reporters covering reaction to the opinions in Congress, the executive branch, the legal profession, and elsewhere. On the whole, "newspaper coverage on both cases was extremely sketchy and uninformative," particularly on the West coast. "Headlines were generally misleading on both opinions." [32] In a number of instances there were serious errors in the original stories, as well as in follow-up stories. For instance, it was claimed that the prayer decision had been based on the religious freedom clause of the Constitution, when in fact it was based on the establishment-of-religion clause. Arguments made in lower courts were erroneously attributed to Supreme Court justices.[33] Many readers learned practically nothing about the substance of the decisions; instead, they were treated to a medley of quotes from well-known personalities and "man-in-the-street" interviews. Extreme views were featured. In many instances the respondents, even the well-known persons, had not had time to read even excerpts of the Supreme Court opinions; consequently they gave surprisingly ill-informed replies. Without information sources of his own, the reader was at their mercy.

In the prayer case, opposition to the Court's ruling was featured. Prominent defenders of the decision "were scarcely noted when they spoke." [34] Defenses of the decision by the secretary of labor and the solicitor general were reported in only one of the sixty-three newspapers. Justice Clark's complaint that "popular misunderstanding was the cause of discontent," and that newsmen were largely to blame, was also ignored.[35]

Since the prayer case was relatively simple to grasp and emotionally stirring, it was featured far more than the more consequential reapportionment decision. Twenty-nine papers gave prominent coverage to the prayer decision, while only seven featured reapportionment. When the prayer decision was first published, it was allowed to deflect attention

32. Newland, "Press Coverage of the Supreme Court," p. 29.
33. *Ibid.*, p. 33. Where news is taken from news releases furnished by public relations men, inaccuracies may be even greater and more systematic. In some papers, public relations news releases constitute more than half of the stories.
34. *Ibid.*, p. 28.
35. *Ibid.*, p. 15.

from other important cases. "On June 25, 1962, the day of the prayer case, decisions were handed down with opinions in a total of 16 cases and in 257 memorandum cases. Although several of these decisions were of unusual significance, most were obscured by reports of reaction to the prayer case." Newland ascribes poor coverage to a lack of training of reporters who therefore do not understand the court's work; to the need for speed and brevity; and to the pressure to make stories sensational. He considers the resulting faulty reporting especially serious "because of the Court's ultimate dependence upon popular support for its authority and power." [36]

Obeisance to "Official" Views

Like other people, mass media reporters experience much of their reality second-hand. By the time they arrive on the scene of an unfolding event, much of the action may already have taken place. Even when the reporter can watch the event from start to finish, he must often get background and supplementary data from observations made by others who have knowledge unavailable to him; this forces him to find trustworthy sources for the missing information. Depending on the reporter's predilections, views about the trustworthiness of sources may vary widely. Available sources frequently are limited to public officials because of their superior access to news. In the field of foreign affairs, this generally means diplomats and military personnel abroad, or their domestic contacts in the State and Defense Departments and in Congress. Domestically, it means elected and appointed officials, particularly police officials in cases involving violence, disasters, or civil disturbances.[37] In many countries, including the United States, such "official" sources have traditionally been presumed to be accurate and their statements have been accepted at face value. Conflicting statements, if available at all, have born the onus of having to prove their own accuracy.

Unquestioned acceptance of official sources has marked consequences. When these sources are inaccurate, as happens frequently, false information may be widely accepted. Challenges to "official" accuracy are rare. The Kerner Commission, which investigated civil disturbances in 1967, discovered that official estimates of property damage in Detroit had been vastly exaggerated, yet "reporters uncriti-

36. *Ibid.*, pp. 31–34.
37. Sources of press information are discussed in Cohen, *Press and Foreign Policy*; Nimmo, *Newsgathering in Washington*; and Delmer D. Dunn, *Public Officials and the Press* (Reading, Mass.: Addison Wesley, 1969).

cally accepted, and editors uncritically published, the inflated figures, leaving an indelible impression of damage up to more than ten times greater than actually occurred." [38]

While such inaccuracies can have a significant impact on public perceptions, far greater effects may ensue from imprinting official reality on the public mind. If mass publics receive the official version of an event, the views held by established governments can readily become entrenched and are constantly reinforced by mass media offerings. Once the context of issues has become accepted, policy alternatives become limited. For good or ill, this leads to a hardening of established policy trends.

The reporting of the Vietnam War from 1950 to 1956 is a case in point. Analysis of the press coverage in the *New York Times, Washington Post, San Francisco Chronicle,* and *Chicago Tribune* has shown that all of these papers presented the same "official" reality in their news stories.[39]

> . . . the press insured that the reading public would view the war as a struggle between Communism and the free world, vital to the preservation of all of Southeast Asia, and perhaps all of Asia; that Ho Chi Minh and the Viet Minh were merely agents of Moscow and Peking whose primary means of gaining support was through terror and force, (although occasional reference was made to his nationalistic appeal); and of a gallant ally, France, fighting alongside the United States to preserve "liberty and justice for all."[40]

The press relied almost completely on administration sources for news stories; most of them were based on State Department press releases and interviews with American and French officials. Almost none came from on-the-scene reports by American reporters, though reports on the military situation occasionally came through French sources and from French reporters.[41] By relying almost exclusively on administration sources, reporters laid a foundation for the situation's later definition in accord with official views. The press taught the public that Indochina was an area vital to American interests, that it was

38. U.S. Government, *Report of the National Advisory Commission on Civil Disorders* (New York: Bantam Books, 1968), p. 365.

39. Susan K. Welch, "The Press and Foreign Policy: The Definition of the Situation," APSA paper (1970). Also see Welch, "American Press and Indochina," pp. 222–231. The *Chicago Tribune* was most critical of the official conceptualization of the situation. This was probably discounted by many readers as traditional *Tribune* isolationism.

40. Welch, "Press and Foreign Policy," p. 29.

41. Welch, "American Press and Indochina."

threatened by Communist aggression which must be stopped, and that the people of Indochina, if they knew the facts, would support the West rather than the Communists.[42] All questions and criticisms of the Indochina war aired in the press were analyzed within the same officially supported conceptual framework, with extensive quotes of the views of President Eisenhower, Secretary of State Dulles, and French civil and military officials.

Only much later did the press publicize other possible frameworks into which events might be cast. By that time, an unusual series of events had made a variety of official versions available, each espoused by recognized public leaders. Different policy options which fit these other frameworks then were publicized and considered for the first time. Mass and elite publics had to choose among these conflicting presentations of "reality" with little opportunity for independent reality testing. On the slender reed of these verbal "realities" weighty decisions about life and death of people and nations had to be made.[43]

Emphasis on Conflict and the Use of Force to Settle Disputes

Among systematic biases which skew political reality, the emphasis on conflict and the use of force to settle disputes has received a good deal of attention. Mass media of various countries have been compared for the emphasis they place on conflict behavior in news and entertainment offerings. Interest in this aspect of mass media coverage has been aroused because of strong public and professional beliefs that images of a world of individual and public violence beget individual and public acts of violence. Whether or not this is true remains a moot question, despite extensive investigations.[44]

The highlighting of conflict elements of a political situation can be illustrated through a study which compared the documentary record of a political event with its coverage in the *New York Times*.[45] Ray-

42. *Ibid.*, pp. 222–223.
43. See also John D. Cozean, "Profile of U.S. Press Coverage on Cuba: Was the Bay of Pigs Necessary?" *Journal of International and Comparative Studies*, 5 (1972), 18–53, and sources cited there. The conceptualization of American foreign aid in Indian and Pakistani newspapers has been traced by Carol Andreas, "To Receive from Kings: An Examination of Government-to-Government Aid and Its Unintended Consequences," *Journal of Social Issues*, 25 (1969), 167–180.
44. Robert K. Baker and Sandra J. Ball, *Violence and the Media: A Staff Report to the National Commission on the Causes and Prevention of Violence* (Washington: U.S. Government Printing Office, 1969); Klapper, *Effects of Mass Communication*, pp. 135–165.
45. Raymond F. Smith, "On the Structure of Foreign News," *Journal of Peace Research*, 6 (1969), 23–36.

mond F. Smith compared Indian White Papers recording the Sino-Indian border conflict of 1962 with coverage of the conflict in the *New York Times*. He found that despite its valiant attempts to cover all aspects of the situation, the *Times* concentrated on the more spectacular conflict aspects of the case. In the reality presented to its readers, violence was far more dominant than in the corresponding reality presented to White Paper readers.

Apparently emphasis on conflict is more characteristic of mass media in Western countries than their Communist counterparts. A story told in the Communist press thus creates realities different from those it creates when told in the non-Communist press. George Gerbner compared headlines covering UN General Assembly sessions between September 18 and October 14, 1960, in the *New York Times* and the Hungarian newspaper *Nepszabadsag*. Both are considered reliable and influential news sources. Gerbner found that the Hungarian paper focused much more on the substance of discussions than the *Times*, which featured contentious procedural matters.[46] Eighty-eight percent of the headlines in the *Times*, compared to 68 percent in *Nepszabadsag*, emphasized procedural disagreements. Fifty-two percent of the stories in the Times stressed conflict, 12 percent stressed agreement, and the remainder were neutral. In the Hungarian paper, only 7 percent of the stories focused on conflict, 39 percent focused on agreement, and the rest were neutral. Readers of the American paper would probably be impressed with the amount of conflict and attention to petty political matters in the Assembly, while readers of the Hungarian paper would be impressed with the constructive work which the body was doing. The difference in verbal reality could easily affect the attitude toward the UN of leaders and publics in these nations.[47]

Besides the stress on the existence of conflict among nations, the media also place strong emphasis on violence as the accepted means for settling international disputes. In the reporting of domestic conflicts, discussion of peaceful methods of settlement is far more common. Allan Coddington studied policies advocated by British newspaper

46. George Gerbner, "Press Perspectives in World Communication: A Pilot Study," *Journalism Quarterly*, 38 (1961), 321–322.

47. For similar data on television news coverage, see Benjamin D. Singer, "Violence, Protest, and War in Television News: The U.S. and Canada Compared," *Public Opinion Quarterly*, 34 (1970–71), 611–616. For comparative coverage of summit meetings, see Douglas Waples, "Publicity versus Diplomacy: Notes on the Reporting of the 'Summit' Conferences," *Public Opinion Quarterly*, 20 (1956), 308–314.

editorials dealing with conflict situations; [48] his sample consisted of ten national dailies examined over a twelve-day period. When international disputes were under discussion, the papers put little emphasis on settling them peacefully through such procedures as mediation or arbitration. Instead, force was stressed. By contrast, when domestic conflicts were at issue, procedures of mutual adjustment like conciliation and mediation were usually advocated. Force was rarely mentioned as a settlement option. The media images thus made it appear that settlement options differ, depending on the nature of conflict: for domestic conflict, peaceful options are readily available, while force is the common method for settling international disputes. The borderline between accurate description of present realities and self-fulfilling prophecy may be narrow.

Numerous surveys have brought forth evidence of a strong emphasis on conflict and violence in the American mass media, particularly television. This holds true of news and general information, as well as for fictional entertainment programs. Even when the mass media make a concerted effort to hold a true mirror to the world, the exigencies of news presentation and the dramatic impact of violent incidents result in overemphasis on violence.[49] Mass media coverage of racial conflicts in the United States in 1967 is a case in point. The Kerner Commission examined a total of 955 TV sequences and 3,779 newspaper articles, finding that, on the whole, the media had done a reasonably good job of depicting the disorders in a low key, thus reducing the chance of arousing dangerous fears and anxieties. Nonetheless, the reality presented by the media had been misleading. "We have found a significant imbalance between what actually happened in our cities and what the newspaper, radio, and television coverage of the riots told us happened . . . the disorders, as serious as they were, were less destructive, less widespread, and less a black-white confrontation than most people

48. Reported in Galtung and Ruge, "Structure of Foreign News," p. 88.

49. *Ibid.*, p. 69, cites a number of reasons why the mass media emphasize negative news. Negative events are easier to report because they are completed more quickly — for example, murder generally has a rapid start and ending. Negative news is less ambiguous and more consensual because most readers agree on what is definitely bad. Negative news is less predictable than positive news and therefore more unexpected and exciting. Studies have shown that people pay more attention to negative news. Ithiel de Sola Pool, *The "Prestige" Papers: A Survey of Their Editorials* (Stanford: Stanford University Press, 1952), p. 44, notes: "There seems to be a prevalent sixty-forty ratio between unfavorable and favorable judgments." For correspondents' feelings about the importance of stressing crises, see Östgaard, "Factors Influencing the Flow of News," pp. 49–50.

believed." "The overall effect," according to the commission, was "an exaggeration of both mood and event." [50]

In recent years the media have tried to make verbal reality more akin to actual happenings, but they have not made corresponding attempts in the entertainment field. The National Commission on the Causes and Prevention of Violence reported in 1969 that approximately eight out of every ten dramatic programs contained some violence, averaging nine violent incidents per hour; "television portrays a world in which 'good guys' and 'bad guys' alike use violence to solve problems and achieve goals. Violence is rarely presented as illegal or socially unacceptable. Indeed, as often as not, it is portrayed as a legitimate means for attaining desired ends. Moreover, the painful consequences of violence are underplayed and de-emphasized by the 'sanitized' way in which much of it is presented." The commission concluded that "a constant diet of violent behavior on television has an adverse effect on human character and attitudes. Violence on television encourages violent forms of behavior, and fosters moral and social values about violence in daily life which are unacceptable in a civilized society." [51] While the commission's conclusions have been disputed, there has been little argument about the fact that the world pictured by television is an orgy of constant violence. [52]

Much less attention has been paid to the fact that mass media often swing the other way when dealing with local events in small communities. Conflict is minimized, and an unreal world of sweetness and light is depicted. For instance, an analysis of news stories in eighty-eight Minnesota community newspapers showed that half of them did not report any local political conflict at all in February, 1965. [53] When conflict was reported, it dealt with governmental bodies in a generalized fashion. Only eight papers reported conflict involving named politicians or political parties, and only three covered local political controversies editorially. The authors of the study believe that this distortion of

50. U.S. Government, *Report of the National Advisory Commission on Civil Disorders*, p. 363.
51. *New York Times*, September 9, 1969.
52. Baker and Ball, in *Violence and the Media*, discuss the Commission's conclusions. Distortions also run in the opposite direction. Klapper (*Effects of Mass Communication*, p. 203) talks about the "myth world" of media entertainment fare which "is chiefly characterized by an overrepresentation of the wealthy and an underrepresentation of the lower classes, a lack of social problems, the triumph of rigid middle-class morality, and the prevalence of poetic justice."
53. Clarice N. Olien, George A. Donohue, and Phillip Tichenor, "The Community Editor's Power and the Reporting of Conflict," *Journalism Quarterly*, 45 (1968), 243–252.

reality is necessary to avoid stirring up community conflict. "The smaller community has fewer mechanisms for protecting the social order against the total disruption that might result from uncontrolled public dispute. Thus the community may look to the press as an instrument for tension management which therefore has a quite different role in social action compared with newspapers in larger communities." [54] The authors concede that "the small community press may be dysfunctional for social change in the very communities where change may be most crucial for future growth and prosperity." [55]

EFFECTS OF MASS MEDIA COVERAGE

All of the distortions discussed thus far potentially affect mass media consumers and politics; they are therefore not substantially different from the examples which follow. However, in the examples detailed below, the tie between the verbal stimulus and an action or attitudinal response appears to be somewhat firmer. Nonetheless, it always takes an inferential leap through uncertainty to postulate that audiences notice and respond to content features observed by the researcher.

Racial Stereotypes

The National Advisory Commission on Civil Disorders (Kerner Commission) has flatly charged: "By failing to portray the Negro as a matter of routine and in the context of the total society, the news media have . . . contributed to the black-white schism." "Far too often," according to the commission, "the press acts and talks about Negroes as if Negroes do not read the newspapers, or watch television, give birth, marry, die, and go to PTA meetings." If these mass media images affect the views of the average reader, as the commission believes they do, then white Americans "will neither understand nor accept the black American." [56] Prior to the large-scale rioting of the late 1960's, the mass media had failed to report the plight of Negroes; in part, this

54. *Ibid.*, p. 244. Communist countries make similar use of their mass media. Divisive stories and crime news are suppressed as socially harmful.

55. *Ibid.*, p. 251; also see Morris Janowitz, *The Community Press in an Urban Setting* (Chicago: University of Chicago Press, 1967).

56. U.S. Government, *Report of the National Advisory Commission on Civil Disorders*, p. 383. The effect of racial news on blacks is discussed in Philip Meyer, "Aftermath of Martyrdom: Negro Militancy and Martin Luther King," *Public Opinion Quarterly*, 33 (1969), 160–173.

neglect had permitted continuance of the social ills which contributed to the riots. "They [the mass media] have not communicated to the majority of their audience — which is white — a sense of the degradation, misery, and helplessness of living in the ghetto. They have not communicated to whites a feeling for the difficulties and frustrations of being a Negro in the United States. They have not shown understanding or appreciation of — and thus have not communicated — a sense of Negro culture, thought, or history." [57]

Sins of omission have been compounded by sins of commission. Stories about black citizens have cast them into stereotyped roles and images; a typical picture is presented by a study of the coverage received by blacks in several Los Angeles area papers from 1892 to 1968.[58] Before 1940 roughly half of all news about blacks could be classified as stereotypic, dealing with crime and anti-social actions by blacks, with sensational events such as accidents, conflicts, and natural disasters involving blacks, and with blacks as entertainers. About one-fifth dealt with various aspects of civil rights, and an average of 1 to 13 percent with interracial violence. The remainder were miscellaneous items. Many psychologists believe that widely publicized stereotypes, like the image of the irresponsible, lazy, violence-prone Negro, may become self-fulfilling prophecies. The stigmatized group is treated as if the stereotype were true. This, in turn, enhances the likelihood that the group will live up to the role set out for it.[59]

57. U.S. Government, *Report of the National Advisory Commission on Civil Disorders*, p. 383. In response to complaints that the media do not represent minorities, particularly blacks, and that black events can best be reported by black newsmen, media organizations in the United States have tried in recent years to include people from diverse ethnic backgrounds on their staffs. An interesting approach to coping with the problem of ethnically linked perspectives is Seattle's media council, which seeks to regularize communication between the media and black groups. Representatives of the media and of black groups meet regularly to make certain that black viewpoints are represented in the press, and to give the press an idea about the reaction of the black community to the type of news presented and the manner of presentation.

58. Johnson, Sears, McConahay, "Black Invisibility." While the sample used for the study seems inadequate — at best two issues per paper per year from 1892 to 1964, and 10-12 issues thereafter — the conclusions nonetheless correspond to the findings of other studies of racial coverage.

59. Stereotypes are also quite prevalent in international reporting. A study of ten Mexican newspapers in 1960 showed Americans as "people who are admirers of the businessman and athlete, who applaud physical prowess and care little for aesthetic values, who love a mechanical civilization, who have small interest in religion or in a high level of sexual morality, and who are prone to see Communists everywhere, especially where there is disagreement with American policy." Merrill, "Image of the United States," pp. 208–209.

By 1965-66, after the riots in the Watts ghetto, stereotypic news had dropped to 17 percent, with the percentage of anti-social acts down to one-sixth compared to previous coverage. Civil rights news had risen to 46 percent, and news about interracial violence to 19 percent. Investigators in other parts of the country reported similar changes in reporting trends.[60] While this new approach allegedly "began the difficult process of changing the public image of the black man among both whites and blacks," it created new and frightening stereotypes of its own. Emphasis on civil rights and interracial violence "bears with it the potential for badly frightening a white population that is quite naive and inexperienced about blacks. Press attention to the black community today is primarily devoted to its conflicts with the broader society, with its unhappiness with the status quo, and with its efforts to overturn it."[61]

Good Guys and Bad Guys

Even when they are not engaged in deliberate propaganda or editorializing, mass media often employ language which subtly conveys value judgments about the topic under discussion. Because of the subtlety of the verbal maneuver, it usually goes unnoticed. Consequently, the individual who might ordinarily resist more obvious persuasion, fails to summon his defenses. John Merrill examined ten successive issues of *Time* magazine, beginning in April, 1951, January, 1955, and November, 1962, to look for subtle value tags which might shape the images of Presidents Truman, Eisenhower, and Kennedy as portrayed there.[62] Based on coding developed by a panel of judges, Merrill found that there were 92 negative characterizations for Truman and one positive one; obviously *Time* was presenting an unfavorable picture of the man from Missouri. Truman's style was characterized by such words as "grinning slyly," "said curtly," "publicly put his foot in his mouth," "petulant," and "irascible President." Comparable stories covering President Eisenhower contained 81 positive expressions and one negative one. Eisenhower was praised as operating with a "happy grin," he "chatted amiably," and "cautiously pointed out," and he was possessed of a "serene state of mind." While Eisenhower was cast as a favorable figure, the image of John F. Kennedy was ambivalent.

60. See Johnson, Sears, McConahay, "Black Invisibility," p. 716, note 12, and sources cited there.

61. *Ibid.*, p. 719.

62. John C. Merrill, "How *Time* Stereotyped Three U.S. Presidents," *Journalism Quarterly*, 42 (1965), 563–570.

There were 31 positive expressions for Kennedy, paired against 14 negative ones. Words used for Kennedy's style were neutral and non-emotive. It was reported that he "contended," "insisted," "maintained," "promised." The image conveyed was of a confident, usually pleasant person. By contrast, Truman came through as a very unpopular, shabby politician who "stubbornly protected shoddy friends" and failed to give firm leadership to the country. Eisenhower as pictured in *Time* was a smiling, warm-hearted, sincere leader who wanted to keep his campaign promises, a statesman rather than a politician.[63] Besides value-laden phrasing, the stories were also slanted by emphases and omissions. Incidents and quotes which put Eisenhower into a favorable light were presented; for Truman the opposite course was followed. Comparisons of presidential popularity poll ratings with media ratings support the hypothesis that favorable coverage produces favorable images, while unfavorable coverage lowers poll ratings.

Value-tagging through judicious selection of materials to be published is a widely used tactic. In fact, George Gerbner contends that "the basic editorial function is not performed through 'editorials' but through the selection and treatment of all that is published . . . all editorial choice patterns . . . have an ideological basis and a political dimension."[64] While often unconscious, value-tagging through selection may be used deliberately to avoid the onus of more obvious value assignments which may be rejected as propaganda.

Radio Moscow's North American broadcasts, along with most other broadcasts beamed abroad for political purposes, have used the approach. Analysis of twelve Soviet news programs in 1962 showed that the chief persuasive technique was the selection of items.[65] Positive news was featured from the Soviet Union and the Eastern world in general; Soviet peace aims, culture, and progress were highlighted. By contrast, conflict, militarism, and imperialism were featured in news from the West. The language was not significantly slanted in the broadcasts. Loaded words, such as "colonialist puppet," "gangsters and Fascists," "bloodthirsty militarists" were used rarely. Nor were the facts distorted. But by alternating reports on the good aspects of the Soviet Union with reports on the bad aspects of the Western world, a striking contrast was produced.

63. *Ibid.*, p. 568.
64. George Gerbner, "Ideological Perspectives and Political Tendencies in News Reporting," *Journalism Quarterly*, 41 (1964), 495.
65. James Evartz Connolly, "A Rhetorical Analysis of the News on the North American Service of Radio Moscow" (Ph.D. dissertation, University of Minnesota, 1962), pp. 172–173.

Unfavorable publicity's adverse effect on national images has been measured through public opinion polls. News of the 1956 Soviet invasion of Hungary caused a 7 percent decline in favorable views toward Russia in Italy, a 9 percent slippage in France, and a 15 percent decline in Britain. Mass media reporting on German concentration camp atrocities in 1945 caused favorable evaluation of Germany by Americans to drop by 16 percent. Depending on the war news, the number of Americans who believed that Germany wanted to conquer the world fluctuated between 21 and 39 percent.[66]

Slanting through selection is also commonly used in verbal images publicized inside the Soviet Union. In addition, there is much value-tagging through direct value assignments. An analysis of 20,000 randomly chosen lines from twelve Soviet papers showed that adjectives most often used with communist matters were "great, glorious, grandiose, progressive." Western countries were tagged as "foul, shameful, ignominious, cruel, slanderous." This kind of semantic atmosphere is contagious: Soviet citizens "automatically react with the phrases and speech patterns with which they have been inculcated and that have become habitual."[67]

Just as people may absorb value judgments through using widely accepted value-laden linguistic codes, so people may absorb the value codes inherent in role-typing in the mass media. (General social roles, sexual roles, occupational roles, racial roles, etc., may all be included.) Because the mass media are deemed highly influential in setting role types for mass publics, a number of studies have investigated mass media role-typing. A study of *Newsweek* cover stories from 1935 to 1937 and again from 1959 to 1961 is an example.[68] Four character types were deemed worthy of the front cover spot. They were "Winners," "Independent Spirits," "Self-Sacrificing Public Servants," and "Villains." In the thirties, a significant number of cover figures were "Self-Sacrificing Public Servants"; there were few "Villains." This changed in the late fifties, when "Villains" climbed to attention at the expense of "Public Servants." The "Winner" and "Independent Spirits" categories

66. Deutsch and Merritt, "Effects of Events," pp. 153, 162.

67. Max Oppenheimer, Jr., "Some Linguistic Aspects of Mind Conditioning by the Soviet Press," *Journal of Human Relations*, 10 (1961), 30.

68. Lionel S. Lewis, "Political Heroes: 1936 and 1960," *Journalism Quarterly*, 42 (1965), 116–118. A number of studies of role-typing in telecasts have been undertaken since 1970; the roles of women, blacks, public officials, and policemen have received repeated attention. But few studies have been published, possibly because of weaknesses in research methodology. For a series of vignettes on mass media coverage of women, see *Journal of Communication*, 24, 2 (1974), 103–155.

remained fairly stationary. This type of widely publicized role-casting may contribute to the image which people have of their societies, and it may serve as a model which they seek to emulate.

An interesting attempt to measure interracial role and social distance in magazine short stories is reported by Earle Barcus and Jack Levin.[69] They developed a scale of closeness of social relationships and applied it to characters in biracial stories, both in magazines oriented toward black audiences and in general audience magazines. In both types the distance in role relationships was three times greater across racial lines than across all other social distinctions. The stories gave the impression that racial groups prefer to preserve social distances. If accepted as role models, they would serve to perpetuate the status quo of racial social distances.

Friends and Enemies

Our final example deals with verbal behavior which may be instrumental in propelling a nation into war. Historians have frequently assigned a major role to the mass media in drawing a country into war or keeping it out. American entry into the Spanish-American War has been blamed largely on the jingoist tone of the so-called Yellow Press; likewise, the media's failure to oppose pending military action in Vietnam and the Bay of Pigs invasion has been cited as a spur to military action which might otherwise have been prevented.[70] While it is well-nigh impossible to prove these charges, they seem quite plausible, since news leading to war usually covers subject matter on which people have neither independent knowledge nor ways to check the accuracy of mass media reports.

Schuyler Foster examined war news in the *New York Times* and Chicago newspapers from the outbreak of World War I in 1914 to American entry into the war in 1917.[71] Foster contends that the belligerent who is able to supply the most news to a given country is in a position to make his perceptions prevail and to win the support of the public. According to Foster, this is precisely what happened in the United States between 1914 and 1917.

69. F. Earle Barcus and Jack Levin, "Role Distance in Negro and Majority Fiction," *Journalism Quarterly*, 43 (1966), 709–714. The sample covered the period from April, 1964, to March, 1965.

70. See Cozean, "Profile of U.S. Press Coverage on Cuba," and sources cited there.

71. H. Schuyler Foster, "How America Became Belligerent: A Quantitative Study of War News," *American Journal of Sociology*, 40 (1935), 464–475.

Foster examined 11,000 newspaper items from sample newspaper issues. He recorded the channels which furnished the news, the subject matter discussed, the appeals presented to the public, and the belligerent with whom the news was concerned. During the first year of the war, 70 percent of the front-page war news published in the United States came from Germany's enemies; the proportion received directly from Germany did not exceed 4 percent. Britain had a virtual monopoly on cable news. The sinking of the passenger ship *Lusitania* by German submarines, which was considered quite influential in turning American opinions against Germany, was reported almost entirely by cables channeled through Britain. The same held true of news of the invasion of Belgium. News coming from German sources never exceeded 12 percent of the total before America's entry into war. Foster concedes that the heavy preponderance of news from anti-German sources was partly due to the fact that American ties with these sources were already strong; therefore, news polarization and the consequences ascribed to it may have been caused wholly or partially by existing attitudinal predispositions. Nevertheless, Foster believes that a better balance in news presentation — which should have been attempted in order to present a more well-rounded picture — might have delayed American belligerence or even forestalled it.

Initially, most war news originated in Europe; in 1914, only 11 percent came from American sources. By 1917 this had risen to 42 percent, and the news acquired a more American angle which was more likely to interest American readers. The news of military activities which might be of less interest to Americans declined from 72 percent to 22 percent. Instead, there was more emphasis on American complaints about damages suffered as a neutral power. American interests were being stressed collectively to show what the war was doing to America as a nation, rather than stressing the much greater damages which the war inflicted on the European powers.

As the crisis deepened, the general war news declined and the stories became more stereotyped, particularly when contrasting British and German actions. Value judgments became more common. The number of items which stressed conciliation declined, and discussion turned away from legalistic arguments to idealistic concerns. Foster believes this reveals media presentation's switch toward emotional appeals, nationalism, and the self-interest of the United States — a switch which made it more difficult to resist the urge to enter the war.

The claims made for the effects of mass media coverage of the war illustrate the typical difficulties of disentangling causes and effects.

Did the war news become more emotional and stereotyped because the United States was getting closer to war? Or did the United States get closer to war because the war news was becoming more stereotyped? The answer probably is affirmative for both questions. One may not be justified in blaming American involvement primarily on the manner of presentation of war news, but one is probably justified in claiming that the manner of presentation contributed substantially to increasing sentiment in favor of war.

INFERENCES FROM MASS MEDIA OUTPUT

When lay and scientific investigators allege that mass media output is motivated by certain considerations or leads to certain effects, they generally are making inferences. They infer the communicator's motives from his messages supplemented by information about the nature of the communicator and the situational context when the message was sent. Similarly, message effects are inferred from knowledge of the audience and the situation under which it has received or will receive a particular message. Such inferences are very common. This section deals with less common forms of inferences from mass media output which have proved valuable in political analysis — specifically, use of mass media data as social indicators from which actual and perceptual states of societies can be inferred; inferences about message antecedents; verbal clues to incipient war and revolution; and verbal indicators of community cohesiveness.

Social Indicators

Numerous investigators have argued that a society's or subculture's values and concerns can be deduced from the verbal output "expressed in the images, actions, and language" of its "most widely shared (that is, mass-produced and rapidly distributed) message systems." [72] The media publicize what major contenders for political power are saying, selecting those aspects which reporters believe to be of greatest interest to mass audiences. The mere fact of publication, in turn, tends to make audience interest and attention more likely. Hence "the sequence

72. The quote is from Gerbner, *The Analysis of Communication Content*, p. 129. Also see Harold D. Lasswell, Daniel Lerner, and Ithiel de Sola Pool, *The Comparative Study of Symbols* (Stanford: Stanford University Press, 1952). For a discussion of questionable aspects of such inferences, see Bernard Berelson, "Content Analysis," in Gardner Lindzey, ed., *Handbook of Social Psychology* (Reading, Mass.: Addison Wesley, 1954), I, 503–505.

of movements in history can be conveniently read by scanning the dominant symbols of successive periods."[73]

Analysis of media output can provide answers to four important questions about the status of a society. First, it can tell us what is public knowledge. By measuring the distribution and frequency of topics which the message system calls to the attention of the community, one can begin to estimate what publics know and do not know. Second, mass media analysis can tell the investigator what topics are labeled most important, and what the scales of priorities of a particular society seem to be. Likewise, mass media analysis can detect the values of a society by recording what is considered right and wrong. Finally, questions can be asked about what is related to what in mass media output. This shows what sorts of things are logically related, contingent on each other, or clustered together.

The Hoover Institute's RADIR studies, which examined mass media output from five countries over a sixty-year period, constitute the most massive attempt to answer these types of questions for various societies.[74] From sample editorials in French, German, English, Russian, and American "prestige" papers, investigators culled 105,000 occurrences of 416 symbols which appeared in 25,000 editorials published between 1890 and 1950. The investigators defended their sampling choices on the grounds that editorials in prestige papers such as the New York Times, the Times of London, and Izvestia are particularly "rich in the vocabulary of political ideology current among the elites of any given period of time," and that they are read by "the 'self-selected' elite who are most concerned with" and have the most influence over politics.[75] Moreover, editors of prestige papers came from the

---

73. Berelson warns: "It is difficult to know under what conditions inferences can be validly drawn about the total population or only about the particular audiences; to what extent they refer to the audience proper or to the producer's conception of the audience or to the producers themselves as (atypical) members of the audience; whether they legitimately apply to psychological variables in this sense; whether they are correctly based upon a conception of audience characteristics as a source of the content or as an effect of it or both; whether popular values are somehow identifiable, however roughly, as a direct quantitative function of content emphases. In short, the whole relationship between the content and audience characteristics allegedly 'reflected' in it is far from clear. At the least, it is far from a one-to-one relationship, and this fact in itself is a cautionary note against the over-interpretation of content data." Ibid., p. 505.

74. The studies are The Comparative Study of Symbols; The 'Prestige' Papers; Symbols of Democracy; and Symbols of Internationalism. The abbreviation stands for Revolution and the Development of International Relations.

75. Lasswell, Lerner, and Pool, Comparative Study of Symbols, p. 17. The validity of sampling a single elite newspaper in each nation has been questioned by J. Zvi Namenwirth. Namenwirth compared editorial positions regarding Euro-

same social and political backgrounds as most decision-makers and shared their political experiences.[76]

Various trends were examined and analyzed in the RADIR studies. Here the focus will be on indicators of nationalism and internationalism, on indicators of the self- and other-perception of nations, and on inferences which were based on analysis of these social indicators.

Trends toward nationalism or internationalism were assessed by the frequency of mention of national or international themes in newspaper content. The RADIR studies disclosed that international concerns were predominant in the five countries in the interwar period; European countries were the object of greatest attention, with the Far East, America, the Near East, and Africa following in that order. Before World War I and after World War II, press focus was on national concerns. The authors of the RADIR studies inferred that a shift in media attention from international affairs to matters of the nation's own foreign policy indicated domestic problems which forced a turn toward the nation's own problems, and rising fears of the outside world. The magnitude of symbol change allegedly corresponded to the magnitude of social and political change in the society in question.[77] Likewise, when there was rapid change of certain symbol patterns over a short period of time, one could infer that the society was in extreme flux.

In the Russian press seven symbols stressing old-fashioned military patriotism dominated Russian foreign affairs editorials from 1939 to 1949. "Fatherland," "War," and "patriotism" accounted for 69 percent of all political symbols used in editorials dealing with foreign affairs; "peace," "imperialism," "military occupation," and "armaments" were other dominant concerns.[78] No longer was the world described as a

pean unification and Atlantic issues in the *Times, Manchester Guardian,* and the *Daily Telegraph,* claiming that all of these are elite newspapers, although serving different elites. He found that the *Guardian* and *Telegraph* differed in their editorial approach from the *Times,* which had been used by the RADIR studies as representative of elite opinions. He recommended that "researchers should refrain from inferring national elite orientations from the investigation of only one national prestige newspaper." J. Zvi Namenwirth, "Prestige Newspapers and the Assessment of Elite Opinions," *Journalism Quarterly,* 47 (1970), 323. Namenwirth's research also revealed substantial differences between mass and prestige paper editorials. J. Zvi Namenwirth, "Marks of Distinction: An Analysis of British Mass and Prestige Paper Editorials," *American Journal of Sociology,* 74 (1969), 343–360.

76. Pool, *The "Prestige" Papers,* pp. 120–140. Also see Wilbur Schramm, ed., *One Day in the World's Press* (Stanford: Stanford University Press, 1959), p. 5.

77. Pool, *The "Prestige" Papers,* p. 64.

78. Ithiel de Sola Pool, *Symbols of Internationalism* (Stanford: Stanford University Press, 1959), pp. 44–52.

struggle between the bourgeoisie and proletariat; instead, the struggle now was between the Fatherland and the Imperialists. This was deemed evidence of "a highly nationalistic orientation . . . almost half of the instances of symbols relevant to foreign policy dealt not with foreign affairs themselves, but with national power . . . symbols of old-fashioned militaristic patriotism have been revived, while [other] symbols used for talking about the outside world have readily decreased in number." [79]

Knowledge of how nations perceive themselves and other nations may be valuable for making inferences about their relations with other nations. When the RADIR studies examined the frequency with which favorable and unfavorable references to one's own and other countries appeared in the editorials of the prestige papers, there were great variations in the favorableness of self-image.[80] As an overall figure, self-ratings were favorable 63 to 83 percent of the time during the sixty-year period. The British, whose favorable self-ratings averaged 65 percent for most of the period, dropped to a low of 21 percent during 1914-18, depicting a low ebb of self-image during World War I. By contrast, self-image was at 100 percent during Britain's heroic resistance to the initial Nazi onslaught of 1939-40. The average self-image of the French was higher, at 78 percent; it dipped to a low of 52 percent from 1945 to 1949. U.S. figures fluctuated between 60 and 72 percent favorableness. The Russians had a low 40 percent average rate of favorable comments before the revolution; they then dipped to a low average of 28 percent from 1918 to 1928 and hit a peak of 97 percent from 1946 to 1949, indicating a sharp rise in self-image beginning in 1929. Nazi Germany showed even higher rates of self-approval during World War II, possibly evidence of high morale among the leadership.[81]

The image of the outside world, as it appeared in editorial coverage, was never as favorable as the self-image. In the *New York Times* favorable comment about other countries reached a high of 68 percent during World War II, from 1942 to 1945, and a low of 11 percent from 1919 to 1929 during a period of American isolationism. The London *Times* had the highest average of favorable comment about the outside

79. *Ibid.*, p. 49.
80. Also see Arora and Lasswell, *Political Communication*, for self- and other images in India and the United States during the 1950's. Images discussed by the Arab press about the United States, Britain, France, the Soviet Union, and China are analyzed in Abu-Lughod, "International News in the Arabic Press," pp. 600–612.
81. Pool, The *"Prestige" Papers*, pp. 44–49.

world (49 percent) for the entire period, followed by 36 percent for the French papers, 23 percent for the Russian papers, and 22 percent for the German papers. Given such basically unfavorable views, prospects for international good will and trust seemed dim.[82]

Symbol analysis also gives clues to the relative popularity of various countries. The prestige papers rate Great Britain as the most popular country during the sixty-year period, followed by the United States, France, Russia, and Germany; these ratings were fairly constant. This type of popularity index could be useful in inferring the likely effectiveness of international policies of the five countries. For instance, Britain may have been perceived as a more successful negotiator or mediator than any of the other powers.

Inferences about Message Antecedents

Carefully documented analyses of inferences about message antecedents can be found in the work of Alexander George. George reports inferences made from German broadcasts during World War II and subsequent checks on the accuracy of these inferences. The messages which were broadcast in Germany from 1943 to 1944, at the time of the Cairo and Teheran conferences, provide an example. The broadcasts claimed that the conferences were designed to lead the German people to humiliation through another Wilsonian Fourteen Point plan. The German broadcasts commented on this plan with heavy sarcasm and ridicule; the inferences drawn by analysts about the motivations for this approach were "that the possibility of an Allied manifesto was taken seriously by the Nazi elite and . . . that the Nazi leadership feared that such a manifesto might have a serious effect on German morale." Subsequent study of German documents showed that these inferences had been correct.[83]

The analysts also inferred that the German people were dissatisfied with the restrictive information policy of their government. This inference was based on German broadcasts which explained in detail why certain political developments could not be broadcast. Using the rule that "qui s'excuse, s'accuse," the analysts deduced that justification of policy must have been prompted by complaints about secrecy.[84]

It has been suggested that the same rule could be applied to detect major changes in established policy, such as prospective breaches in

82. *Ibid.*, p. 45.
83. Alexander L. George, *Propaganda Analysis* (White Plains, N.Y.: Row, Peterson, 1959), pp. 216–217.
84. *Ibid.*, pp. 233–234.

treaties.[85] To prepare the public for policy changes, public officials make speeches and official declarations which they expect will be publicized through the mass media. Verbal analysts who are anticipating certain changes might then search the media for clues indicating that the public was being prepared for such changes. The intent to violate a disarmament treaty might be detected from negative comments about the treaty, alleging faults in the initial negotiations and forecasts of disastrous consequences.[86]

An actual example of this type of analysis, although done retrospectively, involved mass media clues to a tightening of security to stop the escape of East Germans to West Germany.[87] East German papers were checked for increased attention to the refugee problem, growing condemnation of refugees, and expressions of heightened governmental concern about the effects of political defection and the need for coercive action to stop defectors. Examination of the party newspaper *Neues Deutschland* for ten weeks before the closing of the border and the erection of the Berlin Wall showed most of the expected trends. The refugees who had earlier been characterized as foolish and shortsighted were later pictured as self-seeking traitors and criminals, unconcerned about harming their country. Stern measures were discussed for stopping the exodus. The changing trends in news coverage could have been used as indicators that East German policy had changed, and new coercive measures directed against the refugees were in the offing.

A preoccupation with certain crucial topics can lead to inferences about the psychological conditions which have produced this preoccupation. The RADIR studies of French press comments prior to World War II disclosed a steadily growing preoccupation with threats to France's security and with collective, nonviolent methods to cope with them. "Bolshevism," "Communism," "War," and "Left" were most frequently linked with discussions of menaces to national survival. Evidence of high threat perception led to inferences about the repercussions which constant emphasis on exterior threats were likely to have on French public opinion and defense policies. After World War II stress on security symbols declined, leading to inferences about basic

85. J. David Singer, "Media Analysis in Inspection for Disarmament," *Journal of Arms Control*, 1 (1963), 239.

86. *Ibid.*, p. 235.

87. Ernst F. Mueller, "Attitudes toward Westbound Refugees in the East German Press," *Journal of Conflict Resolution*, 14 (1970), 311–333.

changes in France's official outlook on the world, with Germany defeated and alliance with Russia a possibility.[88]

Symbol analysis may permit estimates of the degree of fear and tension within a country by examining expansion or contraction of the number of symbols which appear in newspaper editorials, and by checking the degree of polarization of judgments. Ithiel de Sola Pool contends that the number of symbols appearing in editorials narrows sharply when political elites perceive increased tension in their relationships with other countries. At the height of a crisis, "editorials concentrate intensively on four to six main symbols." By contrast, when the crisis still seems amenable to amicable solution, symbol usage grows more prolix. In totalitarian countries, where crisis perception tends to be high, the press concentrates on relatively few symbols.[89]

Besides the reduction in symbols, crisis times often are marked by a polarization of judgments. Extremes tend to grow at the expense of the middle. "As lines become rigid, judgments become rigid, too. In place of an atmosphere in which one could say of a given country or party that some of what it did was good and some was bad, there comes an atmosphere in which it verges on treason to speak well of the enemy or poorly of one's allies." Pool claims that "On the whole, uniformity of judgments seems to be a highly sensitive index of polarization of attitudes in the face of crisis. The correlation seems too clearcut to be accidental."[90]

Polarization of attitudes by one party can indicate probable trends in the attitude of the target of hostility. The other party will respond with a mirror image of hostility, or it will retreat from the positions which have brought about hostility. Symbol analysis can tell which policy has been chosen, though it cannot as yet predict or explain choices. Since the two alternatives lead to different verbal behavior, it is possible in times of crisis to "find increasing uniformity of judgment in some papers and decreasing uniformity in others."[91]

88. Pool, The "Prestige" Papers, pp. 78–79.

89. Ibid., pp. 25–27, 56–62.

90. Ibid., pp. 57–59. Also see G. Cleveland Wilhoit, "Political Symbol Shifts in Crisis News," Midwest Journal of Political Science, 13 (1969), 313–319. Wilhoit examined a sample of Associated Press wire tapes in 1964; confirming the RADIR study findings, he concluded that symbols of national community and executive decision-makers increased during foreign policy crisis, while symbols concerning rule-making and rule application and settlement of disputes decreased.

91. Pool, The "Prestige" Papers, p. 60. For examples of mirror images in foreign affairs and their consequences see Jerome D. Frank, Sanity and Survival: Psychological Aspects of War and Peace (New York: Random House, 1967), pp. 117–121.

Verbal Clues to War and Revolution

The degree of friendliness or animosity between political actors can be measured by analyzing the psychic distance expressed in their communications. Powers which are psychologically distant will express great hostility toward each other, while powers which are basically friendly will express little hostility. Furthermore, as Pool points out, "the degree of hostility expressed about the external world should be explained as a function of insecurity. Conversely, friendly attitudes toward the outside world are a function of satisfaction with the world as it is." [92] The RADIR findings, analyzed in historical context, support this conclusion.

Insecure countries are more prone to resort to military action. The possibility of overt hostilities is increased by the fact that "attitudes of friendship and hostility have been in considerable measure reciprocal; that is, psychic distance over time tends to be the same in whatever direction measured." Again the RADIR studies provided supporting evidence. Fifty-seven percent of all French editorials dealing with the United States were favorable to the United States, compared to 56 percent of all U.S. editorials dealing with France. Eighteen percent of all German editorials dealing with the United States favored it, matched by a 17 percent friendship rate in American papers for Germany. Britain expressed least hostility toward other nations, followed by the United States, France, Russia, and Germany, in that order.[93]

Karl Deutsch has suggested the possibility of establishing monitoring and early warning systems to analyze mass media output for evidence of mounting tensions so that preventive steps can be taken. "It should be possible to say whether the amount of attention given to a specific conflict area or to the image of a particular 'enemy' country is reaching the danger point, in the sense that continuing hostile attention in the mass media may tend to harden public opinion to such a degree as eventually to destroy the freedom of choice of the national government concerned." Deutsch considers the mass media a reflector as well as a cause of hostile attitudes. Through the images which they supply, latent attitudes of hostility can be transformed into "acute perceptions of a present conflict." [94]

92. Pool, *Symbols of Internationalism*, p. 14.
this conclusion.

93. *Ibid.*, pp. 4, 13. Pool checked out the possibility that these differences might reflect variations in journalistic style. He found that the non-hostile papers could be quite hostile in other matters, and vice versa.

94. Karl W. Deutsch, "Mass Communication and the Loss of Freedom in National Decision-Making," *Journal of Conflict Resolution*, 1 (1957), 201–202.

It may also be possible to infer revolutionary potential by analyzing value judgments publicized in the mass media. An elite's loss of faith in its value judgments seems to foreshadow an environment receptive to revolution. When the elites lose faith in their own myths and legitimacy, symbols which have always carried positive connotations in mass media coverage begin to carry negative ones. When the approval of prior values drops below 80 percent, the society has become revolution-prone, according to the RADIR studies. The Russian revolution was heralded by such a drop in majority symbol support. A similar drop occurred in the French press after World War II; even though it was not followed by revolution, RADIR analysts considered it a sign of ideological disintegration. Further tests of the theory, involving elite media output in pre-revolutionary and stable situations, are required before it can be used with confidence.[95]

Analysis of Community Cohesiveness

Among political scientists Karl Deutsch has been the leading exponent of attempts to trace cohesiveness and value-sharing among nations through an analysis of communication flows and mass media and elite verbal images.[96] Deutsch believes that a sense of community can be measured through expressions of "mutual sympathy and loyalties . . . 'we feeling,' trust, and mutual consideration. . . . partial identification in terms of self-images and interests; . . . mutual successful predictions of behavior, and of cooperative action in accordance with it. . . ." In nations who share a sense of community, there is a "perpetual dynamic process of mutual attention, communication, perception of needs. . . ." He and his co-workers have measured this cohesiveness through content analysis of mass media output.[97]

This type of analysis is exemplified in the measurement of desire for European and Atlantic integration in England, France, Germany, and the United States as it developed during 1953-63.[98] Editorial comments

95. Pool, The "Prestige" Papers, p. 56. Also see Crane Brinton, The Anatomy of Revolution (New York: Norton, 1938), for a discussion of symbol and value changes prior to revolution.
96. See, e.g., Karl W. Deutsch, Nationalism and Social Communication (New York: John Wiley, 1953), and Karl W. Deutsch et al., Political Community and the North Atlantic Area (Princeton: Princeton University Press, 1957).
97. Deutsch, Political Community, p. 36.
98. Karl W. Deutsch, Lewis J. Edinger, Roy C. Macridis, and Richard L. Merritt, France, Germany and the Western Alliance: A Study of Elite Attitudes on European Integration and World Politics (New York: Scribner's, 1967), pp. 240–244; Namenwirth and Brewer, "Elite Editorial Comment," pp. 401–427.

about the European and North Atlantic communities were traced in the London *Times, Le Monde,* the *Frankfurter Allgemeine Zeitung,* and the *New York Times.* The study revealed that interest in securing Atlantic integration had declined during the ten-year period, while interest in securing European integration had remained stationary. However, "the *New York Times* seemed to perceive a different world from that of its European counterparts." [99] Where European papers were skeptical of the prospects for integration, the *New York Times* was hopeful, idealistic, supra-nationalistic, and concerned about problems of East-West confrontation. It talked about merging military and economic agencies within the Atlantic community, while the European press seldom linked military and economic integration; European papers were mainly concerned with European economic and institutional problems, rather than with the Atlantic alliance and military problems. The world was viewed as multipolar rather than bipolar. Over the ten-year period, the attention and appraisal gap between the *New York Times* and the European papers widened steadily. To knowledgeable observers, it seemed that supranational integration had become primarily an object of U.S. interest and pressure and that the emphasis on military integration frightened Europeans, who preferred to concentrate on the economic aspects in European integration.[100] The growing disparities in views and the likely policy consequences probably were totally unknown to the average person who was exposed only to his own national press.

Relationships within the Communist bloc, as perceived by China and the Soviet Union, have also been measured through an analysis of press data. Peter Toma analyzed discussions of "revolution" and related concepts in the Soviet and Chinese press during June, 1963, and December, 1965, to find out how each country applied its concepts during a period of varying tensions with the United States. Toma also noted which Communist countries were cited as supporting or opposing Chinese or Russian views.[101]

Toma found that, according to Soviet and Chinese sources, eight countries supported Peking's position. In order of frequency, these

99. Namenwirth and Brewer, "Elite Editorial Comment," p. 420.
100. Deutsch, Edinger, Macridis, and Merritt, *France, Germany, and the Western Alliance,* p. 244.
101. Peter A. Toma, "Sociometric Measurements of the Sino-Soviet Conflict: Peaceful and Nonpeaceful Revolutions," *Journal of Politics,* 30 (1968), 732–748. Toma's data may be distorted by the fact that he used the *Current Digest of the Soviet Press* and the *New China Daily News Releases* as data bases. These may not be properly representative of the Russian and Chinese press.

were the Chinese People's Republic itself, Albania, and North Vietnam, cited as giving frequent support; North Korea, with a moderate amount; and Cuba, the German Democratic Republic, Poland, and Rumania, lending occasional support. Eleven countries were reported to side more or less frequently with the Soviet Union, including five which had also sided occasionally with China. In order of frequency of support for the Soviet position, they were: the Soviet Union, Yugoslavia, and Czechoslovakia with frequent support; Hungary and Bulgaria with moderate support; and the German Democratic Republic, Poland, Rumania, Mongolia, Cuba, and North Korea with occasional support. Slightly more than half of all the support statements were in favor of Peking's position. Toma inferred that Albania and North Vietnam were China's closest ideological allies, and Rumania and Poland were most distant. The Soviet Union's closest ideological partners were Yugoslavia and Czechoslovakia, with North Korea and Cuba the most remote. The findings contradicted impressionistic appraisals which had classed Hungary as a pro-Soviet moderate and the German Democratic Republic and Mongolia as pro-Soviet extremists. North Vietnam was more, rather than less, supportive of the Chinese viewpoint than North Korea.

SUMMARY

The information on which mass publics and political elites base their opinions about politics comes primarily from the mass media. The mass media in many countries enjoy vast discretionary powers in selecting this news supply, arranging it, and putting it into perspective; therefore they are one of the most potent political forces in the twentieth century. Media personnel can imprint the information supply with their own conceptions of political reality and of political priorities to which the political system ought to pay attention.

If mass media images are distorted or blurred or two-dimensional, media clients' pictures of the political world are erroneous, and their political responses may be inappropriate. The average news consumer can neither detect nor correct faulty images when the media are his sole source of information. He rarely knows whether important aspects of politics have been omitted from coverage and thereby excluded from political consideration and action. His sole control with respect to the information which reaches him through the mass media lies in his power to accept or ignore it, and to put his own interpretations on that to which he has chosen to pay attention. This power constitutes an important restraint on the political influence which the mass media enjoy, but it is a negative control only; it does not provide media clients with an alternate source for political information.

A number of common media practices lead to systematic distortions of important aspects of political reality and hence to faulty information bases for political decisions. Depicting the world from a narrow, parochial perspective is quite common in foreign affairs reporting. Events in other parts of the globe are depicted from the reporters' national perspectives, often with heavy emphasis on the relation of the event to Great Power politics. Indigenous viewpoints are ignored. In both domestic and foreign reporting, information essential for a full understanding of significant political events is often omitted because it does not meet the journalistic criteria of newsworthiness. These criteria demand that the material included in stories must be simple to understand, readily linked to prominent individuals, intrinsically interesting, and related to the concerns of the culture to which the story is presented.

The desire to ascribe stories to sources which are widely accepted as credible leads to unduly heavy reliance on government officials for news of political events, even when unofficial sources are readily available. The information supplied to media clients tends to favor presentation of official interpretations of political reality; in general, these interpretations support and serve to perpetuate the existing power structure and political philosophy. Conflicting views and philosophies held by people whose credibility has not been widely established rarely receive comparable coverage.

Other imbalances spring from disproportionately heavy emphasis on negative events. Minor disagreements, serious conflicts, and the use of force to highlight or settle disputes all are featured in ways which tend to exaggerate the ugly aspects of human discord. By dwelling on images of hostility, the media can transform latent hostile attitudes into acute perceptions which may then lead to actual hostilities. Preoccupation with the manifestations of discord often diverts attention from causes of the conflict and ways of settlement. Or conflict and other social problems may be unduly deemphasized for reasons which benefit media organizations but harm the long-range social and political health of their communities.

The impact of mass media images on their clients' perceptions has often been belittled because it is difficult to prove what people believe and how these beliefs were formed. However, there is extremely persuasive circumstantial evidence that the mass media contribute substantially to cultural images such as racial and sexual stereotypes, images of political candidates and public officials, and models for type-casting political heroes and villains.

The correspondence of mass media images to images held by mass and elite publics makes constant themes in news stories important social indicators. Mass media information discloses the actual and perceptual states of the societies which have produced the information. From an examination of substantial amounts of mass media information, one can infer what is publicly known, how it is rated in importance and evaluated, and how situations are perceived and structured. Patterns of symbols published in representative mass media may be used to infer the stability of political systems, the degree of cohesiveness of political communities, and the direction of political changes and of future policies. It seems feasible to monitor mass media output for signs of impending political chaos or war. If the relationship between specific types of mass media output and social and political developments can be firmly established, it may even become possible to forestall political disasters which have been foreshadowed by mass media coverage.

7   Verbal Behavior of Political Elites

> . . . in classical times when Cicero finished speaking, the people said,
> "How well he spoke" — but when Demosthenes had finished speaking,
> people said, "Let us march."
> — attributed to Adlai Stevenson [1]

> . . . two priests . . . were arguing whether it was proper to smoke
> and to pray at the same time. . . . To settle the matter they decided
> that both should write to the Holy Father for his opinion. Sometime
> later they met and compared notes. Each claimed that the Holy Father
> had supported his view. They were perplexed. Finally one asked,
> "How did you phrase your question?" The other replied: "I asked
> whether it was proper to smoke while one is praying; and the Pope
> answered, 'Certainly not, praying is serious business and permits no
> distractions.' And how did you phrase your question?" "Well," said the
> other, "I asked if it were proper to pray while smoking and the Pope
> answered, 'Certainly, prayer is always in order.'"
> — Told by Gordon W. Allport [2]

"Political elites," as the term is used in this chapter, are political decision-makers who hold or actively seek to hold widely publicized public
offices. The study of the verbal behavior of such political elites is particularly important because the game of politics is played so largely
with words — *their* words. Political decision-makers are important cogs
in the political communication networks of their polities. They process
vast amounts of verbal information, transmit or store and recall it, creating particularized meanings in the process. Most of their decisions are
verbally expressed and publicized and involve deliberate and purposive
selection, combination, and recombination of verbal data.

ACCUMULATION OF VERBAL CREDITS AND DEBITS

The score card of power of political actors is largely a verbal concoction. A reputation for power may occasionally require nonverbal

1. Quoted in Theodore White, *The Making of the President, 1968* (New York:
Atheneum, 1969), p. 87.
2. Gordon W. Allport, "Psychological Models for Guidance," in Floyd W. Matson and Ashley Montagu, eds., *The Human Dialogue: Perspectives on Communication* (New York: Free Press, 1967), p. 218.

evidence, but often its verbal strength suffices. Political elites seek to acquire verbal support from others primarily because of the personalities and power statuses of favored political actors, and because of the policies which those actors advocate. To be effective politically, a politician or political elite needs an aura of power. This involves creating various desirable reputations, and showing that these reputations are believed by powerful supporters, be they mass publics or powerful organizations or individuals. A political actor improves his chances for success if others believe that he has strength, intelligence, know-how, idealism, morality, decisiveness, influential backers, and a will to fight for the "right" causes.

Building Political Reputations

Political reputations are created partly by actions and partly by words, with the actions publicized primarily through words. Few people who considered John L. Lewis a powerful labor union negotiator were ever physically present when he was conducting negotiations. His reputation was verbally transmitted and embellished; if told appropriately, with the right conceptual linkages, audiences believed the story. Other impressions rest purely on verbal representations because they are deductions from actions and hence purely mental products. One cannot observe political "intelligence" or "stupidity." The politician must use verbal maneuvers to show his audience that his particular approach to the task was intelligent, in terms of verbally stated criteria which are believed by his audience to demonstrate intelligence.

Since the intellectual level of political appeals to mass publics tends to be low, this exercise often becomes a polemic which generates more heat than light. The great debates about U.S. policy in Vietnam were typical; "the debaters as individuals have no vested interest in structuring the terms of the debate in an 'objective' and sophisticated fashion. Their purpose, after all, is primarily hortatory. . . . The tendency then is for the debate to become a 'dialogue of the deaf'. . . ." As a result, "the complex intellectual structure underpinning the principal positions on the war has gone largely unexplored, and thus the full range of implications involved in these alternative approaches has not emerged clearly."[3] On public occasions talk often takes the place of action. As Norton Long has remarked scathingly: "The harassed citizens of the American city mobilize their influentials at a civic luncheon

3. Stephen A. Garrett, "The Relevance of Great Debates: An Analysis of the Discussion over Vietnam," *Journal of Politics*, 33 (1971), 479, 483.

to . . . exorcise slums, smog, or unemployment." We may smile at medieval peasants who combatted a plague of locusts by a high mass, or a procession of the clergy who damned grasshoppers with bell, book, and candle. But "our own practices may be equally magical." [4]

The power position of a political leader is also increased if he can demonstrate that he has a large or influential constituency; he may do so through winning elections, through engendering demonstrations, or through various forms of testimonials. Followers will be attracted partly by the personality myth and reputation ascribed to the political actor, and partly by the policies which he promises to bring to fruition.

Much of politics consists of defining political situations in specific terms and linking them to valued or unvalued goals in order to make them attractive and to be fought for, or unattractive and to be opposed. A political leader gains support by persuading others to view and value policies as he does; conversely, the leader who does not know how to marshal the right kinds of arguments may well lose his case.

President Lyndon B. Johnson believed that faulty verbal strategies lost him the confidence of the nation. The record seems to bear this out, although it does not prove that confidence could have been fully retained with better strategies. During his futile attempts to popularize the Vietnam war, President Johnson rarely addressed himself to the main arguments which extreme hawks and doves were making against his policies; nor did he stress the most appealing policy features, such as the ultimate strategic objectives on which most Americans could agree. He could have emphasized that U.S. forces in South Vietnam would help to contain China, that they would prevent major shifts in the world balance of power, and that they were protecting U.S. security interests. He shunned emotional appeals which might have been effective and talked abstractly instead. He avoided moving stories about the plight of the South Vietnamese driven from their homes by the invaders from the North, or atrocities committed by the North Vietnamese. Partly as a result of what Johnson himself called "my own shortcomings as a communicator," much potential public support for the war was apparently lost. [5]

A politician may also attempt to have his positions accepted for extraneous reasons, such as fear, hatred, or love for him as a person or

4. Norton E. Long, "The Local Community as an Ecology of Games," *American Journal of Sociology*, 64 (1958), 256.

5. Walter Bunge, Robert V. Hudson, and Chung Woo Suh, "Johnson's Information Strategy for Vietnam: An Evaluation," *Journalism Quarterly*, 45 (1968), 422–423.

for some other group. He may verbally create moods of anxiety or fear, calm and confidence, militancy or conciliation. In all cases he needs an astute command of verbal symbols to elicit support.[6] As Murray Edelman has said, through language a politician can "win the acquiescence of those whose lasting support is needed . . . it is the talk and the response to it that measures political potency, not the amount of force that is exerted. . . . That talk is powerful is not due to any potency in words but to the needs and emotions in men."[7] If the politician can advance the right kind of justification, he can win support both for himself as a person and for his policies. Hence he can influence, if not control, the allocation of political benefits.

Reinforcement of existing political beliefs and attitudes, and appeals to established needs, are likely to arouse the audience's interest and win its support. "Practical politicians usually recognize the emptiness of hortatory rhetoric that tries to activate interests other than those rooted in the material situation of the audience." Therefore "political argument when it is effective, calls the attention of a group with shared interests to those aspects of their situation which make an argued-for line of action seem consistent with the furthering of their interests."[8]

Since there are many different cognitive and emotional interests which can be tapped in any audience, it is possible to find effective appeals for most policies. A politician who seeks support for deescalation of a war can call attention to the large loss of life as part of the war, and to the heavy economic burdens. A politician interested in continuing the war can call attention to the even larger loss which may occur if the enemy is not defeated, and to the even greater economic burdens which would follow if the enemy's policies continue unabated. When the interests of a particular audience are divided or uncertain, a clever politician can keep his language vague enough so that different members of the audience can interpret it to support their respective points of view.

When political situations are so novel that audiences have few preconceived notions, trusted politicians ordinarily encounter few difficulties in gaining acceptance for their versions of reality. If the new information is presented within an acceptable conceptual framework,

6. Tactics to be used to manipulate verbal images are discussed extensively in Robert Jervis, *The Logic of Images in International Relations* (Princeton: Princeton University Press, 1970), pp. 174–219.

7. Murray Edelman, *The Symbolic Uses of Politics* (Urbana: University of Illinois Press, 1964), p. 114.

8. *Ibid.*, p. 123.

audiences who need to have opinions on the particular matter tend to follow the views of opinion leaders with whom they have learned to identify for a variety of reasons, such as shared ethnic or national background, common economic interests, or similar political views. The public's felt need for guidance in opinion formation presents politicians with unparalleled opportunities to win a wide following for themselves and their views.

The Weighty Words of Kings

If one defines political elites as the chief decision-makers in politics who ultimately determine and control the allocation of political values, one can argue that their verbal behavior is of extraordinary significance for three reasons.[9] First, the subject matter which political elites put into words includes topics of great political significance. A leader of the state may discuss questions of war and peace, economic security or insecurity, revolution or moderate change, justice or injustice for groups within the state. If he criticizes or praises a political figure or deed, or if he promises or threatens to act, or even if he merely changes a form of address, like calling "Communist China" the "People's Republic of China," people assign major significance to his remarks.[10] In fact, they may do so even if he denies that a particular verbalization was significant: "political leaders . . . do not retain control of words and phrases once cast abroad."[11] Because of the intrinsic importance of the matters with which political leaders deal, their views — and the matters which they treat with verbal neglect — are likely to be watched carefully.

This raises the second point. Not only do political leaders discuss vital questions; they also possess, within limits, the power and position

9. The rank order which individual actors occupy in the power hierarchy affects the political significance of their statements. William E. Griffith, "On Esoteric Communications: Explication de Texte," *Studies in Comparative Communism,* 3 (1970), 50, rates the weight and credibility to be assigned to statements by Communist leaders and institutions according to the following descending order of influence: personal statements by a universally recognized absolute ruler; major reports and resolutions of party congresses; reports emanating from the Central Committee; major ideological pronouncements in the party press and ideological journals, signed by pseudonym; official government statements; articles in elite academic or literary journals indicating major change.

10. Charles E. Osgood, "Conservative Words and Radical Sentences in the Semantics of International Politics," in Gilbert Abcarian and John W. Soule, eds., *Social Psychology and Political Behavior: Problems and Prospects* (Columbus, Ohio: Charles E. Merrill, 1971), pp. 118ff; also Jervis, *Logic of Images,* p. 197.

11. David Manning White, "Power and Intention," *American Political Science Review,* 65 (1971), 754.

to enforce their pronouncements.[12] Because of their roles, they can speak with an authority which may lie in their ability to physically force compliance — or, more frequently, in their audience's willing compliance with their requests. The views held by political leaders tend to be accepted by their respective mass publics. As Kenneth Boulding has put it, "the powerful also have some ability to manipulate the images of the mass towards those of the powerful." [13] The authority and power to act in accordance with pronouncements, combined with a wide sharing of official views, in turn lead to acceptance of official views as representing both leaders and followers. Statements by the leaders of a country or party or faction become the official view of that country, party, or faction.

Elite verbal pronouncements are also important because of their extremely wide audiences. The mass media tend to feature them, and people, aware of the source's power position, will pay attention to them. Wide publicity means that the verbal behavior of political elites constitutes a key element in most people's political environment; it also means that the value systems which are advocated by elites, or which form an implicit part of their verbal behavior, tend to become important parts of the shared value systems which form the basis for social cohesion.[14] Even when people have independent ways of arriving at adequate world views, they take the bulk of their cues about what is and ought to be in politics, and how it should be appraised, from the pronouncements of customary political leaders, despite the fact that they may not fully trust these leaders.

An example from international politics will illustrate how pronouncements of national leaders are publicized so that they become widely accepted as the official views of the country and its people. Nazli Choucri studied the parameters of nonalignment policies as expressed by President Nasser of Egypt, Prime Minister Nehru of India, and President Sukarno of Indonesia.[15] Each leader had made speeches about nonalignment at major international conferences attended by large numbers of world leaders, such as the Bogor Conference of 1954,

12. On the limitations which even top officials face in commanding obedience from their subordinates, see Richard Neustadt, *Presidential Power* (New York: John Wiley, 1960).

13. Kenneth E. Boulding, *The Image: Knowledge in Life and Society* (Ann Arbor: University of Michigan Press, 1956), pp. 121–122. Boulding defines "image" as "the total cognitive, affective, and evaluative structure of the behavior unit, or its internal view of itself and its universe."

14. *Ibid.*, p. 122.

15. Nazli Choucri, "The Perceptual Base of Non-Alignment," *Journal of Conflict Resolution*, 13 (1969), 57–74.

the Bandung Conference of 1955, and the Belgrade Conference of 1956. Each had also discussed nonalignment repeatedly before domestic audiences. The same themes had been stressed over and over again: nonalignment was not a policy born out of fear of the Great Powers; rather, it was good for the nonaligned countries because it enhanced their status and freedom of action in world politics and because it aided nation-building and domestic development. Because these leaders were highly respected in the nonaligned world, their conceptions of behavior suitable for nonaligned nations were widely accepted in their own countries as well as abroad. In Choucri's view, "the *perceptual orientation* of the national leadership may well be the most significant determinant of a state's alignment or non-alignment."[16] It receives wide support at home, and it forms a basis for the political calculations of other world leaders.

In the United States, the President's Committee on Campus Unrest has warned that "national leaders must recognize that what they say is also an implicit statement of the premises upon which government will act. When they seem insensitive to individual rights, they appear to imply that government will act insensitively." [17] The commission urged "public officials at all levels of government to recognize that their public statements can either heal or divide. Harsh and bitter rhetoric can set citizen against citizen, exacerbate tension, and encourage violence." [18]

While all public pronouncements by major political actors are deemed worthy of attention, there are certain speech occasions which have become especially significant in the tradition of a country or group. Speeches made on ceremonial occasions such as the inauguration of a new leader, or the opening of a legislative body, are examples; speakers choose such occasions to present significant messages to the largest possible audiences.[19] Political strategists vie for the opportunity to have their pet projects benefit from widely publicized official

16. *Ibid.*, p. 57.
17. U.S. Government, *Report of the President's Commission on Campus Unrest* (Washington, D.C.: U.S. Government Printing Office, 1970), p. 220.
18. *Ibid.*, p. 10.
19. John Kessel, "The Parameters of Presidential Politics," APSA paper (1972), studied State of the Union messages between 1946 and 1969. Kessel points out, "Speeches are important decision points in the political process. . . . Favorable mention of a policy gives visibility to it and confers presidential backing. . . ." Also, public messages give the president a chance "to focus congressional attention on his agenda, as well as to appeal to the general public" (pp. 3, 4). Also see John H. Kessel, "The Parameters of Presidential Politics," *Social Science Quarterly*, 55 (1974), 8–24.

attention. Since analysts of politics tend to watch these announcements for clues about the speaker's major political orientations, leaders are likely to select verbal images with greater than average care in order to convey the desired meanings.

Beyond the contemporary interest in these speeches and the impact they have on political opinions and actions, scholars have used them to trace developing political patterns. Marshall Smith analyzed twenty presidential nomination acceptance speeches between 1928 and 1964 for differences between Republican and Democratic candidates, changing trends over time, and particular differences between Goldwater and Johnson in 1964.[20] He noted decreased emphasis on domestic economic issues over time, and increased emphasis on foreign policy and on more diffuse domestic issues. Speech trends reflected political attention trends in the country, as recorded by historians. Smith also found decreasing stress on normative modes of behavior, moral imperatives, words of strength and authority; instead, there was more stress on needs and desires and goal-directed behavior. This, too, is in accord with recorded social trends of the period in question. While the speeches were partly a result of these trends, they also stimulated continuance and strengthening of these trends.

Political Rhetoric

Politicians tailor their rhetoric to a particular audience or audiences in order to achieve predetermined purposes and avoid undesirable consequences. Of course, "There is never certainty about how speeches will be received . . . a phrase can be a disaster or a priceless asset; it may catch the drift of things and mould a national resolve, or it may be so intolerable to the nation's mood that the person who utters it never shakes it off." [21] This section focuses on various aspects of rhetoric

20. Marshall S. Smith, with Philip Stone and Evelyn N. Glenn, "A Content Analysis of Twenty Presidential Nomination Acceptance Speeches," in Philip J. Stone, Dexter C. Dunphy, Marshall S. Smith, and Daniel M. Ogilvie, *The General Inquirer: A Computer Approach to Content Analysis* (Cambridge: MIT Press, 1966), p. 398. A comparable earlier study is J. W. Prothro, "Verbal Shifts in the American Presidency: A Content Analysis," *American Political Science Review*, 50 (1956), 726–739. Prothro analyzed the first acceptance, inaugural, and State of the Union speeches of presidents Hoover, Franklin Roosevelt, Truman, and Eisenhower to check changes in the use of New Deal terminology. Attitude expressions of various political elites below the top leadership level have also been studied for clues about past, present, and future political behavior of these elites. See, e.g., Robert C. Angell, Vera S. Dunham, and J. David Singer, "Social Values and Foreign Policy Attitudes of Soviet and American Elites," *Journal of Conflict Resolution*, 8 (1964), 33–491, esp. pp. 330–385, 424–485.

21. White, "Power and Intention," p. 754.

used by political leaders.[22] Three types of rhetoric are commonly used: the rhetoric of the statesman, the rhetoric of the rabble-rouser, and the rhetoric of the charismatic leader. Political leaders often combine elements of all three in varying proportions.

Speaking broadly, statesman rhetoric uses an approach of reasoned argument, setting forth all salient aspects of a situation with clarity and moderation. The statesman appeals to value judgments on an intellectual rather than an emotional plane. In cultures which prize notions of rationality, people do not fear the stateman's talk as defined here; they consider his type of speech-making as an exposition of facts and clearly labeled opinions which leaves the audience free to draw its own conclusions. By contrast, such people fear charismatic or rabble-rousing oratory because it seems to by-pass the rational faculties of the audience and to arouse often uncontrollable emotionalism and irrationality.

Charismatic rhetoric stresses sentiments which are deeply held by large numbers of people who may be afraid or unable to express them.[23] The charismatic leader may combine an appeal to emotional attachments to himself as a superman or savior with an appeal to various emotion-laden political and moral ideals. The effects are graphically described by a listener to Adolf Hitler's oratory:

> I do not know how to describe the emotions that swept over me as I heard this man. His words were like a scourge. When he spoke of the disgrace of Germany, I felt ready to spring on any enemy. His appeal to German manhood was like a call to arms, the gospel he preached a sacred truth. He seemed another Luther. I forgot everything but the man; then, glancing around, I saw that his magnetism was holding these thousands as one.[24]

Style may be more important that substance in charismatic rhetoric.[25] A charismatic speaker evokes associations and emotions by his allusions and other symbol-laden expressions. Charles de Gaulle reputedly was able to do this with the symbols "France" and "the French people." "He succeeded in establishing that cycle of identifications of France

22. For a timeless classic on political rhetoric, see Aristotle, *Rhetoric*, esp. Book I, chs. 1–8; Book II, chs. 1–11, 19–26, and Book III, chs. 1–19, in *The Works of Aristotle* (Chicago: Encyclopaedia Britannica, 1962), II, 587–675.

23. William H. Friedland, "For a Sociological Concept of Charisma," *Social Forces*, 43 (1964), 18–26.

24. Quoted in Hadley Cantril, *The Psychology of Social Movements* (New York: Wiley, 1941), p. 236.

25. Ann Ruth Willner, *Charismatic Political Leadership: A Theory* (Princeton: Center for International Studies, 1968), p. 104.

to himself, of himself to France, of the people with him, of himself and France to higher causes." He tried "to address himself to some of the highest qualities in men, a sense of sacrifice and responsibility and duty; he calls on them to find in the crisis an opportunity to grow, rather than to succumb to irrational fears, hatreds, and delusions so often flattered by demagogues." [26]

On a less elevated plane, Louisiana Senator Huey Long, that crossbreed of charisma and rabble-rousing, was particularly good at creating an easy, intimate style to ingratiate himself with his audiences. He "radiated warmth and attentiveness" to establish rapport with his audience, consciously violating canons of grammar and pronunciation to sound more like his listeners. He used the Bible as an authoritative reference to underline his morality, and he cited statistics and references to create the impression that his arguments were well researched and sound. "He could give the appearance of sweet reason, and he radiated common sense, which seemed to render his more radical or ideological statements harmless. . . ." [27]

Besides using the right words and allusions, charismatic rhetoric employs devices such as rhythm, repetition, and alliteration. Voice qualities and speech mannerisms are also important. Nkrumah's voice was "both deep and melodious, has a practiced resonance that audiences found attractive." [28] Stokely Carmichael's technique for capturing audiences involved shaking "his head, as he begins speaking and his body appears to tremble. His voice, at least in the North, is lilting and Jamaican. His hands move effortlessly. His tone — and the audience loves it — is cool and very hip. . . . No preacher harangue. No screaming. He speaks one tone above a whisper, but a very taut suppressed whisper." [29]

In rabble-rousing or demagogic rhetoric, anything goes. Appeals are entirely opportunistic; motives range from the highest to the basest; there is little concern for fairness or truth. As with charismatic rhetoric, style becomes a tool to arouse emotions. Since the subject matter of politics is rich in emotional connotations, it is easy to concoct emotional

26. Stanley and Inge Hoffmann, "The Will to Grandeur: de Gaulle as Political Artist," *Daedalus*, 97 (1968), 865, 869.

27. Ernest G. Bormann, "A Rhetorical Analysis of the National Radio Broadcasts of Senator Huey P. Long" (Ph.D. dissertation, University of Iowa, 1953). The quotes are from a description of Nkrumah, in David E. Apter, "Nkrumah, Charisma and the Coup," *Daedalus*, 97 (1968), 773, but fit the description which Bormann gives of Long's oratory.

28. Apter, "Nkrumah, Charisma, and the Coup," p. 773; Willner, *Charismatic Political Leadership*, p. 104.

29. Bernard Weintraub, "The Brilliancy of Black," *Esquire*, 73 (1967), 132.

appeals. The secret of success for the rabble-rouser, as for the statesman or charismatic leader, lies in his ability to interact intensely with
his audience and stir and move them.

Among rhetorical techniques used by most political leaders who must
appeal to mass audiences with diverse interests are evocative slogans
and expressions which can mean different things to different listeners.
In Nkrumah's Ghana," 'positive action' for example was C.P.P.'s [Con-
vention People's Party] 'revolutionary' program, which covered anything that seemed useful." [30] "Chronic repetition of clichés and stale
phrases that serve simply to evoke a conditioned uncritical response is
a time-honored habit among politicians and a mentally restful one for
their audiences." When this takes place, "men support or oppose as a
conditioned response whatever is accepted in their group as 'American,'
as 'segregation,' as 'socialized medicine,' or as 'standing up to Khrushchev.' " [31] Able political orators can create stirring new phrases to supplement old clichés; Winston Churchill kept British war morale high
by phrases like "Never in the field of human conflict was so much owed
by so many to so few," or "I have nothing to offer but blood, toil, tears
and sweat." [32] Whether stirring slogans or phrases are old or new, the
effect is similar. Under certain circumstances, "language becomes a
sequence of Pavlovian cues rather than an instrument for reasoning
and analysis." [33]

The dramatic qualities of speech are important. Because political
actors have to sway mass publics, "the parts they play before their
audiences canot differ greatly in formal aesthetic terms from the roles
enacted by the heroes and villains of popular entertainment." [34] For a
de Gaulle, "statecraft becomes stagecraft. . . ." [35] He knew that people
listened to him as they would to a great dramatic actor, and that they
vicariously shared his trials and tribulations, so he addressed them
accordingly. To Ghanaians, Nkrumah was "Show-boy." He had a fine
sense of personal drama which he conveyed to his listeners.

Threat and reassurance is the basic dramatic theme which seems to
underlie nearly all political rhetoric.[36] Politics has been described as

30. Apter, "Nkrumah, Charisma, and the Coup," pp. 774–775.

31. Edelman, *Symbolic Uses of Politics*, p. 125.

32. The first statement comes from a tribute to the Royal Air Force in the
House of Commons on August 20, 1940. The second comes from Churchill's first
statement to the House of Commons as prime minister on May 13, 1940.

33. Edelman, *Symbolic Uses of Politics*, p. 116.

34. Les Cleveland, "Symbols and Politics: Mass Communication and the Public
Drama," *Politics*, 4 (1969), 186.

35. Hoffmann, "The Will to Grandeur," p. 872.

36. See Edelman, *Symbolic Uses of Politics*, pp. 22–43, for examples of the use
of verbal threats and reassurances.

"an endless spectacle of threat and reassurance in which political actors try to assert order in ways calculated to impress audiences with their heroism, devotion, sincerity, dexterity, and other laudable qualities." As in a drama, the story unfolds as conflict between "principles of good and evil, security and danger, reassurance and anxiety, salvation and despair, order and disorder." [37] The leader talks about the perennial threats faced by any audience, and then about the way in which he will deliver them from the threats. He may probe a wide range of highly sensitive grievances to attract dissatisfied people with promises of a more satisfying society.

De Gaulle was at his best "when the circumstances were those of extreme and irremediable disaster, when the leader could appeal both to the present fears, anxieties, and sufferings of the people and to their hopes . . . when he could appear as the prophet, the unifier, the remover of roadblocks to and the guide toward the 'summits' of self-respect and greatness." In fact, it has been claimed that the essence of charisma is "communicated self-confidence," mixed with utopian mystique.

> The charismatic leader typically radiates a buoyant confidence in the rightness and goodness of the aims that he proclaims for the movement, in the practical possibility of attaining these aims, and in his own special calling and capacity to provide the requisite leadership. . . . This, indeed, may be the quality that most of all underlies their charisma and explains the extreme devotion and loyalty that they inspire in their followers; for people in need of deliverance from one or another form of distress, being in very many instances anxiety-ridden, easily respond with great emotional fervor to a leader who can kindle or strengthen in them a faith in the possibility of deliverance.[38]

Leaders like Lenin, Hitler, and Mussolini, whose rhetoric has been analyzed carefully, all projected boundless faith and righteousness to their audiences in times of great uncertainty and stress. Each blamed ills on a conspiracy of wicked people like the Jews, Catholics, Capitalists, Communists, Freemasons, and Jesuits. They depicted themselves as noble leaders who could defy these personified forces of evil.

When audiences lose faith in their leaders after actions fail to match promises, devotion may turn to hatred. As Judas warned Jesus in the rock opera *Jesus Christ, Superstar,* "You have set them all on fire — they think they've found the new Messiah — and they'll hurt you when they find they're wrong."

37. Cleveland, "Symbols and Politics," p. 186.
38. Quotes are from Hoffmann, "The Will to Grandeur," pp. 865–866.

Kenneth Burke has described four common forms of political drama enacted by political orators. One is the drama of guilt, when a society blames severe internal disorders and tensions on scapegoat groups, as happened to Jews in Nazi Germany. A second form is the drama of redemption, in which society is saved from terror and despair by a political leader and his panaceas. A third is the drama of victimage in which leaders and selected groups of people are depicted as the victims of evil forces; assassinated political leaders or victims of race riots are examples. Fourth is the drama of hierarchy; it depicts the social order as it should be organized, with the chiefs as chiefs and their followers as lowly Indians.[39] The rhetoric used in totalitarian societies favors the great dramatic tradition, featuring struggles between the principles of good and evil and personifying its villains and heroes. Rhetoric in democratic societies more commonly resembles a form of comic drama in which "language is used with an incantatory intensity to give its audiences cues as to how to experience an event."[40]

Because politicians manipulate language in order to elicit certain kinds of responses, language strategies can be studied within the framework of game theory.[41] If one knows the goals and skills of the speakers and the images they hold of their audiences, one can predict the strategies which they are apt to use in their efforts to elicit the desired responses. It is possible to forecast which common type of appeal a politician will probably use to involve his audience emotionally and intellectually, and to demonstrate that the politician is acting according to acceptable norms.[42]

If the audience is highly susceptible to traditional moral arguments, the speaker will probably emphasize these. A war of counter-insurgency can be justified by claiming that it is legal or required because of prior formal commitments. If the audience has missionary proclivities, a politician can try to make it feel that the war is part of a crusade which will save the world. If the audience believes that every society must be allowed political self-determination, the speaker may point

39. Kenneth Burke, *Language as Symbolic Action* (Berkeley: University of California Press, 1966), p. 39.

40. Cleveland, "Symbols and Politics," p. 194.

41. Vincent Lemieux, "Le Jeu de la Communication Politique," *Canadian Journal of Political Science*, 3 (1970), 360. Strategies which politicians use for persuasion in large assemblies and for bargaining in small groups are discussed in chs. 8 and 9.

42. Michael A. Weinstein, "Politics and Moral Consciousness," *Midwest Journal of Political Science*, 14 (1970), 189; Kjell Goldmann, "International Norms and Governmental Behavior," *Cooperation and Conflict*, 4 (1969), 173.

out how the war is aiding various groups of individuals in realizing their particular conceptions of a desirable society. If the audience responds to necessities, rather than to ideals, he may claim a utilitarian or historical-determinist reason, saying that the war is necessary in light of the inevitable workings of the international system.

"By the same token, politicians who oppose the war can argue that it is illegal or life-destroying, that it will further the imposition of undesirable political forms, that it will bar self-determination and that it is unnecessary in the light of the workings of international relations." Appeals can be aimed at exploiting distrust, if its seeds are present in the audience. "A politician will discredit an opponent by arguing that he uses legality when it suits him, that he is extracting personal profit from his crusade, or that he is denying certain groups their fair shares even while he claims to be even-handed." The opponent's claims that "he is acting in consonance with the imperatives of the system, his professional expertise, or in the light of secret knowledge" can be branded as lies by the mudslinger. "The opponent will respond by accusing the mudslinger of being either an incompetent dupe of the enemies of the state or an out and out subversive." Appeals may also be based on the personality of the political actor, rather than on his actions. A politician can be characterized as "honest, energetic, resourceful, trustworthy, dynamic, mature, soulful, understanding, compassionate, sophisticated, a red neck, *ad nauseam*." [43]

Of course, what is credible and effective varies from audience to audience within the same country, and even more so internationally. To predict reactions accurately, one needs to know audience idiosyncrasies. Harold Lasswell and Nathan Leites studied the verbal reactions of Communist leaders in various countries whenever the Communists had lost an election or a labor dispute. American politicians, under similar circumstances, would probably admit that the loss had occurred and would try to mollify and reassure their audiences by pointing out that the losses were moderate and that there were compensations. Instead, the Communist leaders took one of two extreme positions: they either denied that any setback had taken place and stressed only the good features of the situation, or they acknowledged the defeat and supplied self-criticism of their own tactics.[44] The Communist view that all failures are apt to involve malfeasance helps to explain the response.

43. All quotes are from Weinstein, "Politics and Moral Consciousness," pp. 190–192.

44. Harold D. Lasswell, Nathan Leites et al., eds., *The Language of Politics: Studies in Quantitative Semantics* (Cambridge: MIT Press, 1965), p. 345.

Likewise, Communist orators usually are far more subtle than their non-Communist counterparts in indicating policy changes to their audiences. A switch toward less militant approaches will be signaled obliquely by attacks on "dogmatism" or the "cult of personality." Attacks on "revisionism," or on "reformism," or praise for Stalin indicate turns toward conservatism.[45]

The persuasive rhetoric used by political leaders to win personal support and support for their policies from mass audiences is commonly termed "hortatory language." The hortatory style is reassuring *per se*; it creates the impression that large and important issues are being discussed, and that the public has a chance to participate in the decision-making process. People are reassured that important matters have been and will be carefully weighed according to acceptable criteria. The final decisions, whatever they may be, must therefore be supported because they were reached in the proper manner.

Other types of language employed by politicians for different occasions also use style to enhance the message's intended effect.[46] Legal language used for laws, treaties, and judicial decisions gives the impression of high precision and authoritativeness because it is rich in definitions and commands. Like hortatory language, it appeals to widely accepted basic values such as justice, order, and liberty. It makes the public feel that action is taken according to these canons. As lawyers know, legal language, despite its apparent precision and authoritativeness, is highly flexible and open to many different interpretations. Still, the form of the language reassures the public that the law stands firm and is being observed.

"Administrative language," used by governmental agencies for their directives, likewise abounds in authoritative-sounding definitions and precise commands. But unlike hortatory and legal language, its style does not dwell upon exalted purposes and public sharing of proclaimed values. For this reason it may annoy people, rather than stirring them or awing them into support.

"Bargaining language" offers "a deal, not an appeal. . . . A decision is to be made through an exchange of *quid pro quo's*, not through a rational structuring of the premises so as to maximize, or satisfy, values."[47] Bargaining language is designed to reach practical compromises,

45. Griffith, "On Esoteric Communications," p. 50.
46. The terminology and discussion are based on Edelman, *Symbolic Uses of Politics*, pp. 134–146.
47. *Ibid.*, p. 146.

seeking neither to reassure nor to edify publics. Therefore its use is restricted to closed encounters, remote from publics whose psychological needs require more ego- and ideal-nourishing verbal fare.

THE EFFECTS OF ELITE VERBAL BEHAVIOR

Rather than running through the gamut of possible effects discussed in the third chapter, we shall concentrate here on the structuring of political reality by political leaders through statements of political goals which become commitments; definitions of political situations which fix the direction and nature of political activities; and the production of policy justifications which may determine the kind of action which is politically possible.

The Binding Nature of Verbalized Goals

Political observers agree that "the repeated public expression of elite perceptions, even when consciously distorted, creates public commitments and expectations which decision-makers will probably feel compelled to fulfill; the alternative is a credibility gap with likely consequences for their security of tenure." [48] Furthermore, what elites pledge or announce may quickly become the basis for widespread and almost irrevocable action. The ordinary citizen engenders no such dilemmas in his own pledges or pronouncements. A public figure "gradually and unconsciously changes his values and beliefs towards consistency with what he feels he must say and do," particularly when his words have gained wide publicity.[49] Despite strong pressure toward keeping behavior consistent with verbal expression, skepticism about the binding effects of political pronouncements remains high.

Skepticism has been particularly high concerning promises made in American political party platforms. Gerald Pomper analyzed the content of major party platforms for all presidential elections between 1944 and 1964. An average of 47 percent of all platform statements dealt with future policy. When Pomper compared these pledges with actual party policy after the elections, he found that "platforms are not principally vague paeans to God, Mother and country . . . pledges are indeed redeemed." Depending on one's definition of fulfillment, between

48. Michael Brecher, Blema Steinberg, and Janice Stein, "A Framework for Research on Foreign Policy Behavior," *Journal of Conflict Resolution*, 13 (1969), 89.

49. Osgood, "Conservative Words and Radical Sentences," p. 118.

half and three-quarters of all pledges are fulfilled. ". . . only a tenth of the promises are completely ignored." [50]

The record of pledge fulfillment of the party in power was particularly good, averaging 80 percent fulfillment, compared to 40 percent fulfillment by the party out of power, which was apt to find it more difficult to stick to its promises. Pomper believes that the high fulfillment rate is a tribute to the constraining power of the pledged word. Controversial policies, like the Medicare Act of 1965, would not have been pursued vigorously, had they not been a matter of platform commitment.[51] Because of verbal constraints, the aphorism that "platforms are something to run from, not stand on" remains a canard.

Similar constraints may spring from State of the Union messages. John Kessel found a close correspondence between the verbal images of American politics in these messages and the ongoing political process. For instance, Kessel noted that presidents emphasize international activities during the first three years of office, but concentrate on domestic affairs, particularly social benefits and civil rights, during the fourth year's message.[52] Speeches announce the specific type of activity which is contemplated, such as executive action, legislative action, or the appointment of study commissions; this creates a well-publicized action agenda which cannot easily be ignored. Policies which have been given the presidential stamp of approval during public ceremonies create expectations for performance which give them precedence over less widely heralded policies.

Definitions of Political Situations

Political leaders' definitions of political situations are also bound to affect the policies which they will pursue. In fact, such definitions share all of the characteristics which make commitments binding. The need to verbalize political roles and situations forces leaders to choose among a variety of conceptualizations of the political universe and their part in it. Once these choices have been made and publicly stated, they become fixed orientations which are difficult to abandon. The role definition

50. Gerald M. Pomper, *Elections in America: Control and Influence in Democratic Politics* (New York: Dodd, Mead, 1968), pp. 158–159, 185–189.

51. *Ibid.*, pp. 150, 180, 193. Whether collective pledges which do not involve individual reputations differ in firmness from individual commitments remains a moot question.

52. Kessel, "Parameters of Presidential Politics," p. 9. For a relevant example from the Kennedy years, see Randall B. Ripley, *Kennedy and Congress* (Morristown, N.J.: General Learning Press, 1972), pp. 15–16.

becomes a verbal straitjacket limiting the direction of future policies.[53]

The significance of role definitions springs from the widely held expectations that they are genuine and binding. Scholars and politicians use them accordingly, as guides for analysis and action. K. J. Holsti, for example, investigated the foreign policy role definitions of seventy-one nations, as announced by their leaders.[54] Holsti examined the verbal output of top-level policy-makers such as presidents, foreign ministers, or their alter egos. He checked a total of 972 speeches, parliamentary debates, radio broadcasts, official communiqués, and press conferences for the three-year period from January, 1965, to December, 1967. Only general statements relating to overall policy stands were included in the study. Because countries with fewer than ten such statements for the test period were excluded, Latin American and Caribbean countries were somewhat underrepresented in the study.

The statements disclosed a surprising variety of role conceptions to which the seventy-one governments committed themselves. The average country claimed to fill four or five major roles — many more than one would anticipate from a perusal of the international relations literature which pictures most countries in only one major role. For instance, Canada saw itself as a faithful ally within the NATO system, a mediator within the world system, and a developer in the underdeveloped world, with active policies in all these areas.

The role which was mentioned most often and by the largest number of governments (76%) was that of collaborator in regional political subsystems. This role has been deemphasized in formal analyses of the international system which concentrate on the interplay among the Great Powers and the rest of the world. Fifty-five percent of the countries mentioned the role of independent actor, and 46 percent stressed the role of the supporter of liberation struggles. The concept of balancer in a balance-of-power system apparently has become an anachronism in current conceptualizations of policies. Except for de Gaulle, who viewed France as a balancer, it was scarcely mentioned among the roles named by other political leaders.

53. Different definitions of the war situation in Vietnam, and the corresponding policy options, are discussed in Ralph K. White, *Nobody Wanted War: Misperceptions in Vietnam and Other Wars* (Garden City, N.Y.: Doubleday, 1968). The importance of elite perceptions of political situations is discussed in Nazli Choucri and Robert C. North, "The Determinants of International Violence," *Peace Research Society Papers*, 12 (1969), 33–63. Choucri and North argue that "the leaders' perceptions of their nations' capabilities (accurate or inaccurate as the case may be) are equally, or perhaps even more critical than 'reality'" (*ibid.*, p. 35).

54. K. J. Holsti, "National Role Conceptions in the Study of Foreign Policy," *International Studies Quarterly*, 14 (1970), 233–309.

The sense of attachment felt by a country's leaders toward formal treaty alignments has also been tested through verbal analysis. Though Iran was formally an ally of the United States, its leaders never characterized the country as such in the period studied by Holsti. This may have indicated a possibly fatal unconcern with the alliance and its implications. Failure to include alliance support in policy pronouncements made attachment to the alliance appear weak, compared to other policies which were widely hailed. Likewise, policy consequences may ensue from the fact that Rumanian leaders never expressed support of the Soviet Union, although their country was part of the Soviet regional bloc; in contrast, Polish and East German leaders often stressed that they perceived their countries as members of the Soviet bloc.

Rather than focusing on definitions of general foreign or domestic policy roles, investigators may be interested in seeing how political leaders have defined the parameters of particular policies. They may watch public declarations about the military needs of a country because these needs are likely to generate pressures for certain policies. Assertions about the direction and nature of economic development may be scrutinized for information about the conditions which policies will be designed to meet. Warnings of coming reassessment of policies may be evaluated for the changing situational definitions which they may reflect.

The parameters of American "peace policies" as stated by American presidents from 1789 to 1966 have been examined for the light they might shed on past and prospective policies. Gene Edward Rainey analyzed inaugural and State of the Union addresses of all presidents up to 1966.[55] He wanted to ascertain what they identified as threats to the peace; what international conditions they labeled as conducive to peace; and what they alleged to be domestic prerequisites for international peace.

Rainey discovered that presidential addresses rarely mentioned threats to U.S. peace. Fear perceptions, which have played so large a part in the foreign policy pronouncements of other nations and which have molded their international behavior, were of minor importance in American political rhetoric. American presidents generally were not concerned with the international environment for peace and the institutions needed to enhance it. The period between 1920 and 1929 was an exception, as was, to an even greater degree, the 1940-49 period. Between 1949 and 1966 presidential comments about international insti-

55. Gene Edward Rainey, "The American Image of Peace" (Ph.D. dissertation, American University, 1966).

tutions and the international environment in general as peace factors declined steadily.

The story was different for discussions concerning the relations of U.S. domestic conditions to a policy of peace. Internal conditions which might affect peace were of some concern from 1840 to 1849, 1900 to 1909, and 1920 to 1929 and, more strongly, from 1950 to 1959, followed by a sharp drop in interest. Factors which were postulated as important for the maintenance of peace were: disarmament, ethical and moral behavior, mutual understanding, democratic form of government, legitimacy of government and the rule of law, trade, prosperity, and the creation of a sense of international community. Legitimacy and ethics were mentioned most consistently as conditions which would bring about peace. Since 1930, the creation of a sense of international community has also been stressed. Emphasis on democracy, prosperity, and disarmament as peace factors was comparatively slight — in fact, during the early years presidents apparently believed that armed strength and peace went together.

Looking at more particularized situational definitions, elite conceptualizations of specific policies have been analyzed to assess the rationale behind the policies and likely developments in light of the rationale. Analysis of speeches by major U.S. policymakers involved in formulating the Marshall Plan showed that twelve major themes were stressed as rationales for the policy.[56] Dominant themes were the national interest of the United States, the need to counter the threat of Communism, and the need to assure European economic recovery. The national interest theme was generally worded, without specifying how the national interest would benefit. In fact, there was even some mention of the fact that the plan might be harmful to the economic interests of the United States.

The Communist threat was stressed most strongly in March, 1948, following the Communist coup in Czechoslovakia and the death of Foreign Minister Jan Masaryk. Many of the arguments were directed toward Congress, where the program was under consideration. The need to assure European recovery was put into the context of the political and economic consequences of breakdown in Europe, rather than emphasizing the human plight which might follow economic

56. Gilbert R. Winham, "Perceptions of Administrative and Congressional Elites in Decision-Making: A Case Study of the Marshall Plan," APSA paper (1969); also see Nazli M. Choucri, "The Perceptual Base of Non-alignment" (Ph.D. dissertation, Stanford University, 1967), and Robert Curtis Gray, "The Social Construction of the Cold War: Image and Process in Soviet-American Relations, 1941–1947" (Ph.D. dissertation, University of Texas at Austin, 1975).

collapse. Verbalizations of these various situational definitions by decision-makers and their acceptance or rejection by influential audiences determined the ultimate alignment of political forces for and against the plan, the specific commitments which were authorized, and the fate of policies related to the Marshall Plan.

The Need for Acceptable Policy Justifications

There is yet another way in which words define the arena for political action. To sustain support for themselves and their policies, politicians must justify policies in terms of acceptable norms; when acceptable norms are lacking, it may become very difficult to gain support, and politicians then may deem it advisable to abandon the policy. As Richard Snyder has said, "The decision to perform or not to perform a given act may be taken on the basis of socially available answers to the question 'what will be said?' " [57]

After Egypt's nationalization of the Suez canal, British leaders tried to avoid open collusion with Israel because they felt it could not be verbally justified to their constituents. They therefore delayed the Franco-British invasion until they could assume the peacemaker's guise. "In a sense, the British government searched for an acceptable justification. Having found one, its actions were modified accordingly." [58] Achievement of Britain's military and political objectives was hurt by the need to delay until an acceptable justification had been found.

Likewise, President Kennedy refused direct U.S. participation in the 1961 Cuban invasion because it would have been difficult to justify this after abstinence had been pledged.[59] As a result, the air cover for the Cuban invasion was inadequate. This contributed heavily to the failure of the venture. Similarly, in the Cuban missile crisis of 1962, an air strike was ruled out partly because American political leaders had opposed the principle of large nations attacking small ones and felt that they could therefore not give adequate rationalization for such an airstrike. The blockade was chosen instead, even though it was deemed militarily less effective. This illustrates that "there is a continuous interaction between considerations of what to do, and what to say. . . . Statecraft, from this point of view, is the art of combining the desirable and the justifiable." [60]

57. Richard C. Snyder, H. W. Bruck, Burton Sapin, *Foreign Policy Decision-Making* (New York: Free Press, 1962), p. 146.
58. Goldmann, "International Norms," p. 192.
59. *Ibid.*, p. 193.
60. *Ibid.*, p. 183.

A number of rationalizations can occasionally be used to justify normally unacceptable conduct, but they lose their effectiveness if used too often. Among them are the excuses that the conduct in question is a one-time occurrence, that it was done by unauthorized people, that damaging concessions were made in anticipation of concessions by the other side, that the issue did not seem important to the actor and he did not realize that it mattered to the other side, and that the actor misinterpreted the other's intents and desires.[61]

INFERENCES AND PREDICTIONS

The importance of political elites in the process of politics has made it inevitable that their verbal output would be the object of close scrutiny, interpretation, and inferences about its implications. What does *it* mean? What does *he* mean? What does it imply? — these are constant questions. Inferences are made about the antecedents of the message which caused the political leader to say what he did, about the clues which the message supplies as to the personality and actions of the decision-maker, and about the probable effects of the message. This section focuses on studies which try to infer or predict significant personality traits and policy propensities from the verbal output of political elites.[62] The discussion of inferences and predictions is preceded by a brief review of the problem of dissimulation and a general discussion of the impact of a decision-maker's operational codes on policy outputs.

Are Decision-Makers' Words Meaningful Data?

Because language is a political tool used to manipulate audiences and to structure situations, there always lurks the suspicion that manipulation involves dissimulation. Words are not to be trusted. They may become binding, but this does not mean that they mirror the speaker's real thoughts. Some of these doubts have already been dealt with in the initial chapters, where it was indicated that, because of its many disadvantages, outright lying is less frequent than generally believed.[63] If a speaker lies, his falsehoods still reveal much about his perceptions and reasoning processes.[64]

61. Jervis, *Logic of Images*, p. 198.
62. The studies by K. C. Holsti, G. E. Rainey, and G. R. Winham, discussed earlier in this chapter, are also relevant.
63. Jervis, *Logic of Images*, pp. 70–112.
64. See ch. 1, above.

A number of tests are available for determining the credibility of a government leader's statements. The speaker may have a well-known reputation for truthfulness or untruthfulness; it may be possible to check the accuracy of this reputation by carefully analyzing the situations which have given rise to it. In this analysis one must accurately distinguish between ritualistic and other types of communication, because the former require different truth criteria. One must also resist the temptation to automatically label professions of good intentions by one's enemies as falsehoods. Between 1935 and 1939, when Adolf Hitler and Franklin Roosevelt stated similar goals for their countries (such as safety, independence, strength, morality, justice, and non-aggression), Hitler, as well as Roosevelt, may have been telling the truth.[65]

The speaker's position in the power structure may also be a measure of credibility. The higher the authority and the greater the reputation for credibility of his office, the more dangerous it would be for the speaker to be caught in a lie. Hence statements by the highest officials are more likely to be true, particularly when they concern domestic matters, rather than foreign policy.[66] Likewise, the frequency of repetition of a statement, and the frequency or infrequency of public refutations of it, are clues to its credibility. A leader's statement is more likely to be true if he makes it frequently and if it is rarely contradicted by him or by others. The dispersion of statements is important, too; statements which broadcast the same message to many different audiences under many different conditions are more likely to represent the truth than statements which are made to only one particular kind of audience or on one particular type of occasion. Hitler's successive claims that each of his aggressions was Germany's "last territorial demand in Europe" were obviously contradicted by his oft-asserted claim that "common blood belongs in a common Reich." [67] General MacArthur's glowing public statements that the Inchon landings during the Korean War promised to be highly successful were refuted by his simultaneous private admissions that the success of the landings was doubtful.

65. Ralph K. White, "Hitler, Roosevelt, and the Nature of War Propaganda," *Journal of Abnormal and Social Psychology*, 44 (1949), 162. The fact that Hitler's verbal output was steeped in expressions accusing Germany's enemies of persecuting her may explain why he felt it necessary to abandon his professed ideals. If Germans, including himself, believed his words, then "a peace-loving Germany, with an all-good, all-wise leader" was "surrounded by dangerous, warmongering, diabolical enemies" (*ibid.*, pp. 165–166, 170).

66. Goldmann, "International Norms," p. 187; Jervis, *Logic of Images*, p. 79.

67. White, "Hitler, Roosevelt," p. 169.

What about the influence which individual decision-makers exercise over the decision-making process? If politics is an inexorable process which moves by the weight of its own momentum, does it really matter whether we know how individual political leaders conceptualize politics? If individuals' verbalized perceptions do matter, how does one judge the effect of these perceptions on policies for which a bevy of top officials share responsibility?

In answer to the first question, students of decision-making agree that elite conceptualizations of the political process are significant in many different circumstances.[68] How elites "structure and analyze issues of public policy will . . . affect the political process by which decisions on those issues are reached." In each case, the issues involved, the particular position and influences of the decision-maker, and the situational constraints entailed in the decision are variables that must be considered. Elite views are particularly significant for major, non-routine decisions. In routine decisions, institutional values and procedures tend to prevail. But "during an unanticipated situation in which decision time is short, and information is ambiguous, the attitudes of a small group or even a single official will take on added significance." [69]

A political actor's perceptions of his own role also may be an important variable.[70] A man like John Foster Dulles, who felt that responsibility for foreign policy was largely on his shoulders, will be more likely to try to make his conceptions prevail than a man like Dwight D. Eisenhower, who believed in delegating much decision-making authority to his subordinates. Conceptualization of the weight that one's own views do carry and ought to carry is largely a factor of personality, but it is also affected by institutional role conceptions and

68. Robert D. Putnam, "Studying Elite Political Culture: The Case of 'Ideology,'" *American Political Science Review*, 65 (1971), 679. As noted earlier, "decision-makers act in accordance with their perception of reality, not in response to reality itself." Brecher, Steinberg, and Stein, "Framework for Research," p. 81.

69. Ole R. Holsti, "Cognitive Dynamics and Images of the Enemy," in David J. Finlay, Ole R. Holsti, and Richard R. Fagen, *Enemies in Politics* (Chicago: Rand McNally, 1967), pp. 88–89; also see Sidney Verba, "Assumptions of Rationality in Models of the International System," *World Politics*, 14 (1961), 102–103.

70. Role conceptions as predictors of political action are discussed by Heinz Eulau in John Wahlke, Heinz Eulau, William Buchanan, and LeRoy Ferguson, *The Legislative System* (New York: John Wiley, 1962), p. 243. Eulau says: ". . . roles or role orientations are at least relatively stable points of reference in terms of which a legislator will conduct himself and give meaning, both to himself and others, to his behavior. Even if, at this stage of research and development, we cannot in every case link roles or role orientations to behavior, the fact that legislators do articulate what they think they should do by virtue of their relations among themselves and between themselves and clienteles suggests that roles are effective indicators of behavioral possibilities."

practices. In societies opposed to cults of personality and devoted to group decision-making, the conceptualizations held by individual leaders are likely to count for less.[71] Hence a combination of socialization and role requirements may often "outweigh, if not eliminate, the effects of personal factors in organizational decision-making."[72]

It is not uncommon to find that the norms which one can deduce from the statements of individual decision-makers are shared by their close associates in the decision-making process. This happens partly as a result of interactions of decision-makers within political organizations, partly as a consequence of the fact that like-minded people attract each other in the formation of decision-making groups, and partly because decision-makers in the same cultural setting are exposed to the same values and constraints.[73] When the foreign policy statements of leaders in various countries during the incipient stages of World War I were compared, the record showed that the perceptions expressed by top-level decision-makers within the same nation were quite similar. Variations due to individual differences were extremely small, even among decision-makers who occupied a variety of roles.[74] Hence the views expressed by prominent elite-members could be deemed representative of the statements by the members of their decision-making groups.

Inferences from "Operational Codes"

If one concedes that the views of top decision-makers profoundly influence the focus of political attention and the direction and shape of major policies, then one can expect to draw important inferences from a study of their policy statements.[75] The term "operational code" refers to the basic outlooks which political leaders have expressed about the nature of the political system and about the value of various

71. Goldmann, "International Norms," pp. 160–170, 185.

72. Ole R. Holsti, "Individual Differences in 'Definition of the Situation,'" *Journal of Conflict Resolution,* 14 (1970), 303. Also see J. David Singer and Paul Ray, "Decision-Making in Conflict: From Inter-Personal to Inter-National Relations," *Bulletin of the Menninger Clinic,* 30 (1966), 300–312; Verba, "Assumptions of Rationality," pp. 93–117.

73. Herbert C. Kelman, "The Role of the Individual in International Relations: Some Conceptual and Methodological Considerations," *Journal of International Affairs,* 24 (1970), 7.

74. Holsti, "Individual Differences," p. 309.

75. Kenneth Boulding believes that the images which are part of the operational codes of decision-makers are exceedingly primitive in international affairs. "The national image, however, is the last great stronghold of unsophistication. Not even the professional international relations experts have come very far towards seeing

types of policy approaches.[76] Analysis of statements by decision-makers or analysis of the party creeds or ideologies to which they profess allegiance has been the most widely used tool in the search for operational codes. It has been supplemented by case studies of political action in which premises for action were inferred from the choices leaders made among sets of policy options.

Various approaches have been used in studies of operational codes. Some studies seek to assess operational codes of individual decision-makers; others focus on high-level decision-making groups. General dimensions of belief systems about human nature and human interaction have been examined, as well as attitudes related to specific policies or specific political actors. Still other studies concentrate on the nature of reasoning processes of political actors, and on their psychological needs for power and achievement. Following are examples of each, beginning with a study of the operational code of Secretary of State Acheson and the inferences it permits.

David McLellan examined Acheson's general philosophy about the nature of politics, as well as his beliefs about means and ends to reach political goals.[77] To tap Acheson's basic philosophy about politics, McLellan searched his verbal output for answers to the following questions: What is the essential nature of politics and the fundamental character of opposing political forces? What is the probability that

the system as a whole, and the ordinary citizen and the powerful statesman alike have naive, self-centered, and unsophisticated images of the world in which their nation moves. Nations are divided into 'good' and 'bad' — the enemy is all bad, one's own nation is of spotless virtue" (*The Image*, p. 131).

76. The concept of "operational codes" was developed by Nathan Leites for *A Study of Bolshevism* (Glencoe, Ill.: Free Press, 1963). The "operational code" is part of a person's general belief system used in filtering, classifying, and evaluating information. "It embraces what is perceived as knowledge about past, present, and future states of the world, as well as attitudinal elements, established goals and preferences" (Goldmann, "International Norms," p. 163). The value which decision-makers place on each other's operational codes is discussed in Jervis, *Logic of Images*, pp. 174–180. Also see Alexander George, "The 'Operational Code': A Neglected Approach to the Study of Political Leaders and Decision-Making," *International Studies Quarterly*, 13 (1969), 191, 197.

77. David S. McLellan, "The 'Operational Code' Approach to the Study of Political Leaders: Dean Acheson's Philosophical and Instrumental Beliefs," *Canadian Journal of Political Science*, 4 (1971), 52–75. Objections have been raised to the practice of arbitrarily specifying the dimensions of operational codes. Harold and Margaret Sprout, "Environmental Factors in the Study of International Politics," *Journal of Conflict Resolution*, 1 (1957), 320, contend: "At best, the analyst's inferences regarding his subject's images or the milieu and his orientation to it rest invariably and inescapably on more or less arbitrary decisions as to the relevance and weight to be given to various kinds of evidence perceived and filtered through the analyst's own (and usually several intermediaries') culture-biased spectacles." Also see George, "The Operational Code,'" p. 197.

political actors can achieve their fundamental political values and aspirations? Is man able to control historical development, or is the course of history inexorable and man a helpless pawn in the process? If man is not a pawn, at what point can he control or dominate historical development? What is the role of chance in human affairs?

Acheson's public and private speeches supplied consistent answers to all these questions. He did not visualize the nature of politics as a conflict among irreconcilable forces; peaceful coexistence among all world political systems seemed possible. Acheson also apparently believed that Americans could control their destiny. He expressed the view that control could be achieved by building strong international organizations like NATO, to keep America's enemies in check and deal with them from a position of strength.

A second set of five questions probed Acheson's beliefs about the means for achieving policy goals. Acheson's statements were examined for views on these topics: Which is the best way to establish the objectives of political action? What is the most effective strategy to pursue these objectives? How are political risks calculated, controlled, and accepted? What is the best chronology to follow in pursuit of objectives? Finally, what is the utility and role of different appropriate means in this pursuit? Acheson alleged, among other things, that pragmatic politics, rather than the postulation of moral absolutes and abstract considerations of power politics, would bring the most desirable results. He also judged methods short of war adequate to achieve all needed goals. Since Acheson's mode of operation coincided with his verbalized beliefs, McLellan concluded that knowledge of his operational code permitted valid inferences about his likely appraisal of political situations which he had not discussed publicly, and about his probable mode of political operation. Confidence in the validity of Acheson's statements was enhanced by the fact that his public statements were essentially consistent. Interviews with his friends and associates in the United States and abroad, as well as contacts during a six-month internship in Acheson's office, confirmed the conclusions derived from the verbal analysis.

The belief systems of groups of decision-makers, rather than of individual leaders, have also been scrutinized for policy-relevant information. J. David Singer was interested in discovering possible changes in the operational codes of American and Soviet foreign policy elites.[78]

78. J. David Singer, "Soviet and American Foreign Policy Attitudes: Content Analysis of Elite Articulations," *Journal of Conflict Resolution*, 8 (1964), 424–485.

He wanted to verify whether there had been changes in operational codes between 1957 and 1960 toward eliminating war as a policy option. Leaders of both countries seemed to have settled for intense but peaceful competition in diplomacy, economics, and propaganda. Empirical evidence of such a shift, Singer believed, might change the interpretations and inferences drawn from political statements and actions of the U.S. and the U.S.S.R. "The more clearly each sees the other's assumptions, expectations, and preferences, the less likely one is to make the move that leads the other to upset the tenuous balance." [79]

Singer extracted four basic aspects of elite operational codes from foreign policy statements.[80] Elite views about the nature of the international system were ascertained through statements describing the system as dominated by harmony or conflict, and setting forth mutual relationships as struggles between ideologies, social systems, or power centers. Likewise, Singer looked for statements about the causes of war, and about the expected interactions between nations with different social and political characteristics. Like McLellan, he searched for statements about the predictability of international events and about the possibility of control over national destinies. The second major focus concerned statements assessing the contemporary distribution of power within the international system, predicted developments, and the elites' rankings of their respective nations within this system. A third area concerned each elite's belief about suitable means of political action. Did they believe in fighting aggressive or preventive wars? Did they consider the military a major foreign policy instrument? A fourth series of questions related to reciprocal evaluations of each other's operational codes. How did each elite characterize the foreign policy beliefs and practices of the other?

Singer's analysis disclosed that each side apppeared to be substantially concerned with aspirations for world domination. Twenty-four percent of the Soviet items accused the United States of having world domination as its primary goal, while 31 percent of American items made the same assessment of the Soviet Union. The military was seen as a major foreign policy instrument of the opponent in 59 percent of the Russian statements and 28 percent of the American statements.

79. *Ibid.*, p. 425.
80. Singer's assumption that one can use newspaper and magazine articles as accurate reflections of elite perceptions is open to question. For Soviet foreign policy views he used *Pravda, Kommunist*, and *International Affairs*; for U.S. elite views he used the *New York Times, Department of State Bulletin*, and *Foreign Affairs*.

Elites in each country considered the other side devoted to the theory of preventive or preemptive military strikes, the comparative figures being 100 percent for all Soviet items discussing the topic, and 90 percent for all relevant American items. Information that policy-making elites expressed beliefs of this nature is useful for predicting both Russian and American reactions to a variety of policy moves by the other side.

Rather than using a deductive approach, deriving specific political actions from general political beliefs, one can take the inductive route, inferring general policy outlooks from a study of particularized statements about a specific political situation. Ole Holsti's study of the appraisal of the Soviet Union by John Foster Dulles is an example.[81] The study was based on verbatim transcripts of the publicly available statements of Secretary of State John Foster Dulles, made during the years 1953 to 1959. It included 122 press conferences, 70 addresses, 67 appearances at congressional hearings, and 166 other documents. These sources were relatively evenly distributed over the six-year period. Since a contemporary figure was concerned, Holsti was able to supplement his data with interviews and questionnaires addressed to Dulles's personal associates. All of them concurred that the written public record truly pictured the secretary's political perceptions which underlay his policy decisions.

Analysis of the Dulles record showed that he conceived of the Soviet Union as being dominated by the Communist party, whose unalterable aim was world control. Although the amount of hostility shown by the Soviet Union varied from time to time, Dulles believed that its goals were undeviating and that relaxations in hostility merely reflected internal difficulties, primarily economic, within the Soviet Union. The proper policy response to decreased Soviet hostility, therefore, was increased, rather than reduced, Western pressure to bring about a further weakening of the U.S.S.R. Dulles also believed that the Soviet people were suppressed by their own evil government and would be good friends of Americans were it not for the influence of their government. When Dulles discovered that his beliefs in imminent Soviet economic collapse were incorrect, he did revise his estimates of Soviet economic prowess, but he never revised his overall conception of the bases of Soviet policy.

Taken as a whole, the Dulles record showed that the secretary

81. Holsti, "Cognitive Dynamics," pp. 25–96. Also see Ole R. Holsti, "The Belief System and National Images: A Case Study," *Journal of Conflict Resolution*, 6 (1962), 244–252.

viewed the world in terms of good and evil. The policy of the United States and the Western powers was morally right and therefore good, and the policy of the Soviet Union was evil.

> Dulles' image of the Soviet Union was built on the trinity of atheism, totalitarianism, and communism, capped by a deep belief that no enduring social order could be erected upon such foundations. . . . Upon these characteristics—the negation of values at or near the core of his belief system—he superimposed three dichotomies. (1) The "good" Russian people versus the "bad" Soviet leaders. (2) The "good" Russian national interest versus "bad" international communism. (3) The "good" Russian state versus the "bad" Communist party.[82]

Dulles had publicly outlined the framework of his views of the Soviet Union before he became secretary of state. His later reactions were predictable, especially since his style of single-handed foreign policy-making was aided and abetted by President Eisenhower. It was unfortunate that Dulles subscribed to a "bad faith model," because "perceptions of high hostility are self-fulfilling." As Holsti points out, "inherent bad faith models in effect rule out the existence of data which might challenge the model itself; they even deny the possibility that such information might become available in the future."[83] A country saddling itself with a man of Dulles's convictions had little chance, if it so desired, to reduce tensions with its greatest adversary.

It may be possible to forecast changes in the style of political leadership in a country by comparing political images expressed by established and ascending political leaders. For example, leadership images voiced by members of the Soviet Politburo were studied in 1951, as they appeared in *Pravda* and *Bolshevik* magazine in honor of Stalin's seventieth birthday.[84] At that time, older leaders like Malenkov, Molotov, and Beria still described Stalin in terms of the old Bolshevik ideology, stressing the party and state as the important units to which the achievements of the Stalin period should be credited. The younger leaders, such as Voroshilov, Mikoyan, Bulganin, Kosygin, Kaganovich, and Khrushchev depicted Stalin as a folk hero and father figure. This image of Stalin as the people's leader, rather than the old Bolshevik image of party chief, indicated their acceptance of the cult of personalism which Stalin had fostered during his reign. It also revealed their orientation toward appeals to the masses, rather than to party leaders.

82. Holsti, "The Belief System," p. 247.
83. Holsti, "Cognitive Dynamics," p. 95.
84. Nathan Leites, Elsa Bernaut, and Raymond L. Garthoff, "Politbureau Images of Stalin," *World Politics*, 3 (1951), 317–339.

The findings of the study subsequently were used to compute a political distance index for each Politburo member in relation to Stalin's expressed policies.[85] The index showed the least distance between Stalin and the old-time leadership, and increasing distance with the other leaders, Khrushchev being the most distant. "The power struggle immediately succeeding Stalin's death clearly confirmed the inferences made."[86]

Yet another device for gauging a leadership's perceptions and operational codes is the examination of the verbal justifications it gives for major policies. Michael Brecher used this approach to examine the foreign policy images of the leaders of eight middle-size or middle-power countries, four of them developed and four underdeveloped. In each case, he examined the justifications given for major decisions in four policy areas: military-security, political-diplomatic, economic-developmental, and cultural-status.[87] In the case of Sweden, for instance, justifications for the 1963 military decision to abstain from nuclear weapons production were coded and categorized according to such underlying conceptions as whether they related to military or economic capability, or to global or sub-global politics. Swedish leaders justified their abstention from nuclear weapons production by seven types of arguments; most important was stress on Sweden's traditional nonaligned role in global politics, her obligation to contribute to interbloc detente, and her desire to avoid nuclear proliferation. Next were arguments relating to competing pressures from workers, intellectuals, the military establishment, and the business community. Third was concern about alienating the Soviet Union. Fourth was the desire to keep Scandinavia free from military conflict. Fifth was the argument that conventional military capabilities were regarded as adequate for Swedish defense. Sixth was pressure from Swedish conservatives and liberals; last was a negative cost-benefit balance.

Analysis of these and other policy justifications yielded a number of potentially powerful leads to policy predictions for middle powers. Brecher concluded that such countries do not seek military and economic power as primary policy objectives; in fact, economic and military considerations enter only rarely into decisions other than those

85. Klaus H. Krippendorff, "An Examination of Content Analysis: A Proposal for a General Framework and an Information Calculus for Message Analytic Situations" (Ph.D. dissertation, University of Illinois, 1967).

86. *Ibid.*, p. 118.

87. Brecher, Steinberg, and Stein, "Framework for Research," pp. 75–101. The countries examined were Canada, Israel, Poland, Sweden, India, Nigeria, Tunisia, and the UAR.

directly concerned with these matters. Middle powers favor the maintenance of detente among the superpowers. In domestic politics, decision-makers in developed states are acutely concerned with pressures
springing from interest group demands; in developing nations, interest
group demands are paid far less heed. Pressures from competing elites
are rarely cited in policy justifications by either developed or developing nations.

Brecher believes that the pattern of justifications, based on study of
various major decisions over an extended period, gives an accurate
view of policy images and operational codes of the leaderships of the
eight countries. Even if decision-makers carefully chose and ordered
the justifications initially, with ulterior purposes in mind, they are likely
to have become "prisoners of their articulated images." [88] At the very
least, "the study of justifying-statements appears to be particularly useful for the identification of customary norms." [89] The reasons cited for
a policy are tailored to be plausible and intellectually, morally, and
emotionally appealing to the audiences whom the leaders expect to
reach.

A somewhat different use of rationalizing statements by political
leaders led to insights into their conceptualizations of the Cuban missile crisis. Graham Allison examined the conceptual models implicit in
the interpretations which these decision-makers gave to the crisis.[90]
"The regularities show what analysts think about the character of problems, the categories into which it should be placed, the type of evidence which is relevant . . . clusters of such related assumptions constitute basic frames of reference or conceptual models in terms of
which analysts both ask and answer questions. . . ."[91] An interesting
feature, common to all the conceptual models of the Cuban crisis, was
the fact that they tried to fit all actions into a rational framework. There
was no room for the unique, unplanned event; every part of the action
in the Cuban missile crisis was somehow explainable either by the motivations of the actors or by organizational or bureaucratic necessities
within the country in question.

The close linkage between a political analyst's conceptual model of
action, his policy recommendations, and his predictions of future events

88. Ibid., p. 89.

89. Goldmann, "International Norms," p. 188.

90. Graham T. Allison, "Conceptual Models and the Cuban Missile Crisis,"
American Political Science Review, 63 (1969), 689–718.

91. Ibid., p. 689. A fuller discussion can be found in Robert D. Putnam, The
Beliefs of Politicians: Ideology, Conflict, and Democracy in Britain and Italy (New
Haven: Yale University Press, 1973).

is demonstrated by a study which examined the views of twenty-two academic analysts of Soviet foreign policy. Those analysts who saw the Soviet Union bent on world domination interpreted specific policies in much more ominous ways than those who considered Russian aims as limited and non-expansionist. Policy recommendations were closely linked to basic images. If the Soviet Union is seen as "expansion-minded without limit, extremely expansive, militant, and immoral in implementation . . . relentlessly initiatory, motivated by lust for power, posing mortal danger to the rest of mankind," only one policy avenue is open. The democracies "must remain stronger than the Communists. . . . They must counter promptly, steadily, the initiative of the other side, without squeamishness as to means. . . ."[92]

Inferences from Psychological States and Characteristics

The reasoning processes evident in the verbal output of political elites have been scrutinized for clues they might hold for predicting decisions. Presumably, from basic reasoning processes one can reconstruct the way in which an individual puts together available bits of information into a coherent world view, and what he sees as causality and purpose. From this knowledge, one can infer the person's underlying, often unexpressed, philosophy and his personality make-up. An individual whose verbal output is concerned with the appearance of events, rather than with the events themselves, can be presumed to believe that there is little reality distinct from perception; there is only conjecture, surmise, belief. A psychologist might characterize such a person as "relativistic, fearful of commitment . . . divorced from reality, alienated from others."[93] He would also know that it would be rather difficult to change that person's outlook. Other conclusions, equally relevant for assessing the implications of a leader's personality traits, might be drawn if the person's verbal output indicated insecurity or paranoia.

Edwin Shneidman has used examination of reasoning processes to

92. William Welch, *American Images of Soviet Foreign Policy* (New Haven: Yale University Press, 1970), pp. 267–269. To arrive at a measure for judging the accuracy of the various appraisals, Welch chose "to look to and to array whatever pertinent general statements of Soviet goals are to be found in the most authoritative documents, such as Party programs, state constitutions, the 1957 and 1960 manifestos, speeches at Party congresses, and other gala affairs. . . ." Using such data he determined, among other matters, that the political goals of the Soviet union did not include world conquest.

93. Edwin S. Shneidman, "Logical Content Analysis: An Explication of Styles of 'Concludifying,'" in George Gerbner, ed., *The Analysis of Communication Content* (New York: John Wiley, 1969), p. 278.

compare the political potential of Richard Nixon and John F. Kennedy. Shneidman examined the reasoning style of the first two Kennedy-Nixon debates. He concluded that "Kennedy and Nixon . . . independent of the *content* of their thoughts or the issues they were discussing, each would *process* the issue through his mind in ways quite different from the other." [94] From these differences, a psychologically trained observer could infer differences in style and operation which might be expected from the two candidates in office.

Robert Putnam applied similar analysis techniques to interview protocols and questionnaires which contained the verbal conceptualizations of various policies by a sample of British and Italian national legislators. [95] Putnam coded the answers along twelve different dimensions, each assessing politically relevant aspects of the legislator's reasoning processes. These concerned such matters as the extent to which the focus of discussion was on broad social and moral principles, or on specific situations and details; and the extent to which reasoning was deductive from general political or social or economic theories, or inductive from concrete experiences. Note was taken of whether the respondent evaluated the benefits of policies in terms of losses and gains to particular groups, or to the entire society, or in terms of technical or financial practicality, or of administrative efficiency. References were recorded to past or future utopias, political feasibility, acceptability, or particular ideologies. The context into which an issue was placed was analyzed, as were presence or absence of moralistic evaluations of blame or credit for particular events.

On the basis of this type of analysis, Putnam identified "ideological" politicians and then tested whether they had the types of political characteristics usually attributed to ideologues. It was possible to distinguish an ideological style characterized by a focus on general principles, deductive reasoning, and a stress on ideas, but it was not possible to associate this style clearly with ideological political behaviors as defined by a number of investigators; hence the expected inferences from style to mode of operation could not be made. The study did reveal marked national distinctions in reasoning processes between Italians and Britishers, as well as differences in thinking styles among age groups. For instance, Italians tended to view policies in more general terms than their British counterparts, and were more prone to reason deductively; while Britons were more concerned with technical practicality and policy costs, Italians were more concerned

94. *Ibid.*, p. 266.
95. Putnam, *Beliefs of Politicians*, pp. 651–681.

with moral principles and future utopias. No inferences about likely actions linked to these different thinking processes were tested.

Familiar psychological tests have also been applied to measure politically relevant psychological characteristics. If one can measure the achievement drives and power drives motivating presidential candidates, one may be able to predict the manner in which they will handle the presidency. Accordingly, Richard Donley and David Winter coded the inaugural addresses of American presidents from 1905 to 1969 in order to measure needs for achievement and power.[96] Inaugural speeches were chosen because they presumably record the candidate's fundamental concerns, hopes, fears, and aspirations and establish a distinctive tone and atmosphere for the incoming administration. Inaugural speeches were assumed to contain imagery which showed what the candidates wished to preserve and what they wished to change.

The verbal analysis revealed four types of presidents: one, the high achievement, high power motivation type, was likely to be strong and active and seemingly ruthless at times. Theodore Roosevelt, Wilson, Franklin Roosevelt, Kennedy, and Johnson fit into this group. The second group was high on achievement and low on power motivation, which meant that it wanted high achievement but lacked political skills. In this group Hoover was representative. In the third group were high power, low achievement personalities who would seek office for personal ends. No twentieth-century president up to 1969 fit in this group. The fourth group consisted of presidents who were low in achievement as well as in power motivation and hence fairly inactive; Taft, Harding, Coolidge, and Eisenhower fit into the category. The authors concluded: "In general, the motive levels expressed in a particular President's Inaugural speech are closely related to the overall record of that President's term of office, regardless of the particular issues, crises, or political situation that confront the President . . . verbal measures of motives are related to long-term trends of choice and action, even in very complex situations."[97] The only president for

96. Richard E. Donley and David G. Winter, "Measuring the Motives of Public Officials at a Distance: An Exploratory Study of American Presidents," *Behavioral Science*, 15 (1970), 227–236. The use of speeches which might possibly be ghostwritten was justified on the grounds that the presidents "select the writers, they give ideas, they approve or disapprove of wording; and they add the final touches, phrasing and imagery" (*ibid.*, p. 229). TAT protocol scoring procedures were used.

97. *Ibid.*, p. 233.

whom the hypothesized findings did not work out was Woodrow Wilson, who turned out on these scales to be high in power motivation and low in achievement motivation, even though other analysts have considered him high on both. Donley and Winter feel that their methodology can be used for inferring politicians' likely future actions, as well as for analyzing the past.

Studies have indicated that political decision-making is strongly affected by the degree of fear perception of political leaders.[98] At the international level, fear perception tends to lead countries into irrational, often violent policies. It reduces the amount of communication between opposing leaders and the number of policy options each side takes into consideration, and it produces hostility reactions in others. The more hostile the leadership of the putative enemy is perceived to be, the more hostile and fearful his presumptive targets become. Painstaking analysis of the events leading to World War I showed that, as threat-perception increased, the likelihood of a war decision also increased.

Critical decisions leading to war were made when threat perceptions were at a peak without knowledge of reciprocal threat perceptions in other countries. In fact, in 1914 all nations felt wronged and considered themselves the targets of undeserved hostility.[99] Since prospective conflict may be predictable by measuring the amount and direction of threat and hostility perception expressed by leaders in a given system, it has been proposed that verbal measures of threat perception be applied to current political situations to detect mounting fears among political leaders. If fears are detected early enough, preventive measures may halt fear escalation.[100]

98. See, e.g., Ole R. Holsti and Robert C. North, "History of Human Conflict," in Elton B. McNeil, *The Nature of Human Conflict* (Englewood Cliffs, N.J.: Prentice-Hall, 1965), pp. 155–171; Richard A. Brody, "Some Systemic Effects of the Spread of Nuclear Weapons Technology: A Study through Simulation of a Multi-Nuclear Future," *Journal of Conflict Resolution*, 7 (1963), 720–721, 726, 738–740.

99. For similar psychological conditions during the Suez crisis, see Randolph M. Siverson, "International Conflict and Perceptions of Injury: The Case of the Suez Crisis," *International Studies Quarterly*, 14 (1970), 157–165.

100. Stephen Withey and Daniel Katz, "The Social Psychology of Human Conflict," in McNeil, *Nature of Human Conflict*, pp. 83–84. A discussion of indicators of threat perception is found in Ole R. Holsti, "The Value of International Tension Measurement," *Journal of Conflict Resolution*, 7 (1963), 612–614. For a study which is critical of various extant measures of stress, see Eleanor L. Norris, "Verbal Indices of Psychological Stress," in Robert P. Abelson et al., eds., *Theories of Cognitive Consistency: A Source Book* (Chicago: Rand McNally, 1968), pp. 417–424.

SUMMARY

Politicians do most of their work through words. They gain support for their election or appointment to office and for their policy recommendations by talking persuasively to constituents, external publics, and colleagues in the world of politics. If they enjoy the confidence of their audiences, their verbal claims require little or no proof — in fact, once politicians have established good verbal rapport with their audiences, they may become opinion leaders whose words are accepted almost automatically, particularly during political crises when anxious people want guidance. Followers usually need nothing more than words to spread and enhance the political reputations of their leaders.

To be persuasive, words must be properly chosen and delivered to convey the types of messages and moods which will elicit the desired responses from a given audience. This involves understanding and meeting the predispositions and needs of the audience at the time the message is delivered. Political leaders' skills in finding the right words at the right times to convey suitable ideas play a crucial part in their political successes and failures.

Three factors make the pronouncements of major decision-makers especially potent. The subject matter often involves affairs of the greatest political significance to the society; top leaders usually have not only the persuasive powers, but also the physical resources to see that their words are enforced and their plans come true; and large audiences ordinarily are aware of the words of top leaders and are likely to take them as cues for their own beliefs and behaviors. Consequently, leaders are generally viewed as official spokesmen for their constituencies. Pronouncements which leaders make on significant ceremonial occasions, such as inaugurations, are particularly influential because they are widely publicized as official and binding commitments which indicate a leader's or political elite's beliefs and intentions.

Political leaders employ various forms of political discourse, ranging from the reasoned arguments of statesman rhetoric, to the emotional appeals of charismatic oratory, to the deceptive or irresponsible promises of demagogic speeches. All are attempts to persuade audiences to accept the speaker's views, but each genre appeals to different response mechanisms in the audience. Regardless of the type of rhetoric which a political speaker uses, he must try to make his speeches dramatic enough to capture the audience's attention. Some variation of the threat and reassurance theme commonly serves the purpose; the political leader first arouses anxieties and fears, then quiets them by promising to take appropriate action to protect the audience from the threat. Depending on the make-up of the audience, verbal strategies may call for appeals ranging from moral and idealistic suasion to catering to the basest self-interests. To assure wide understanding and nearly automatic responses, tested phrases and clichés abound.

Once they have been widely publicized, verbal pronouncements by political elites readily become binding commitments, because the status of the sender lends weight to the message. Audiences believe that a pronouncement heralds present or future reality, and they adjust their own beliefs and actions accordingly. These substantial responses make cancellation of the verbal commitment costly in terms of physical and psychological readjustments and potential credibility gaps between political elites and their constituencies.

Political folklore to the contrary notwithstanding, commitments expressed in the platforms of the major political parties in the United States and in major presidential pronouncements have been reasonably accurate indicators of later action. In cases where political elites have committed themselves publicly to the definitions of political situations, these definitions have guided subsequent action. When political elites have proclaimed public needs of their societies, when they have indicated causal sequences, when they have stated publicly what policies needed to be adopted and why, these pronouncements have led to widely shared perceptions which have shaped the policies adopted by their societies. At times, political leaders cannot find believable and acceptable rationales for policies for which public support is essential. Such policies may then have to be held in abeyance until suitable verbal justifications can be evolved.

Study of patterns of verbal pronouncements by political elites and individual leaders permits a number of important political inferences. A study of "operational codes" — basic views about how the political system is structured and how it operates — allows an analyst to predict political leaders' likely responses to specific situations which may arise in the future. Conversely, a study of a leader's verbal reactions and conceptualizations in response to specific situations may permit the analyst to infer the general principles by which the leader is guiding his actions. Analysis of patterns of justifications and of rationalizations of political acts permits inferences about the conceptual models which political elites are using in their thinking. Likewise, reasoning processes and psychological traits evident from verbal output may provide clues to the political actors' perceptions and may permit inferences about action patterns which can be expected from them.

In sum, the words of the mighty are worthy of close attention: they become widely adopted patterns of thought for their followers; they guide current politics; and they strongly affect the range of political options which will become available in the immediate future.

8 Verbal Behavior in Public Assemblies

Near the close of the 1951 session, Senator Matthew Neely of West Virginia rose to his feet, pointed to a hundred-pound stack of *Congressional Records* upon his desk which recorded the session's proceedings, and accused his colleagues of being "irrepressible windbags." Comparing the Senate to the Tower of Babel, he beseeched all senators with speeches in their bosoms to deliver them during recess "in highly secluded places . . . where the only auditors will be hoot owls, turkey buzzards, and shitepokes. These, when vexed, as they certainly would be, could take the wings of the morning, noon or night and fly far, far away."
— quoted by Donald R. Matthews[1]

. . . the Senate is in some respects at a crucial nerve-end of the polity. It articulates, formulates, shapes, and publicizes demands . . . its organizational flexibility enables it to incubate policy innovations, to advocate, to respond, to launch its great debates, in short to pursue the continuous renovation of American public policy. . . .
— Nelson W. Polsby[2]

Chapter 6 emphasized that verbal behavior becomes important when it is submitted to large audiences which accept this verbal output as their own definition of reality. Chapter 7 showed that utterances of influential persons receive wide attention and acceptance due to the source's official status and its power to act or secure compliance in accordance with its pronouncements. Verbal behavior in public assemblies is important for all these reasons. Insofar as it is widely disseminated by the mass media, it becomes part of the verbal reality experienced by large numbers of people. Insofar as the members of public assemblies are powerful members of political elites, capable of enforcing their views, what they say becomes significant. Since these aspects have already been examined in the previous chapter, no further elaboration is needed.

Rather, this chapter scrutinizes the debate process as such. Is public verbal behavior in assemblies — as distinguished from private talks

1. Donald R. Matthews, *U.S. Senators and Their World* (Chapel Hill: University of North Carolina Press, 1960), p. 243.
2. Nelson W. Polsby, "Policy Analysis and Congress," *Public Policy*, 18 (1969), 65–66.

among members — important for the work carried out by these assemblies? What specific functions are performed by public debate? What constraints on debate in public assemblies arise from the fact that these assemblies lack privacy? What verbal effects result from the interactions in a debating format?

At the outset, "public assembly" must be defined and contrasted with the small bargaining groups which will be discussed in the following chapter. "Public assembly" here identifies any political gathering whose deliberations are likely to become a matter of current public record. This includes such obviously public bodies as national and state legislative assemblies, international assemblies like the United Nations or the Organization of African Unity, public mass meetings, political conventions, and open and publicized sessions of subordinate bodies of such gatherings. UNESCO in the United Nations, or congressional committees and subcommittees in the U.S. Congress are examples of the latter. Since the choice of studies of verbal behavior in such assemblies has been determined by the availability of published research, there is heavy reliance on data from legislative assemblies.

Assemblies vary in their degrees of "publicness," depending on the ease of access to the assembly and the likelihood of mass media coverage. A congressional session is more likely to attract an audience and wide mass media coverage than a congressional subcommittee session, simply because the meeting place is larger, better known, and usually more accessible, and because the proceedings presumably are of interest to a wider audience. An opening session of the United Nations, attended by heads of state, is bound to receive more media coverage and visitors than a routine session of a subcommittee of UNESCO. The constraints imposed on debate by the public nature of the meetings will vary, depending on the degree of publicness. By contrast, the deliberations of small bargaining groups and other nonpublic gatherings, discussed in the next chapter, are likely to be shielded from the gaze of outsiders. No verbatim records or even minutes may be kept, let alone published, so the participants can behave as if there were no outside audience.

Public Debates — Wheat, or Chaff?

When one reads about verbal behavior in the world's most public assemblies, such as the United Nations, Congress, or Parliament, one is struck by the frequent assertions that public debate in these bodies is "useless babbling." [3] Worse, it has been claimed that the business of some legislative bodies "is actually impeded, not assisted, by at least nine-tenths of the speaking that takes place." [4] One is also struck by descriptions of the poor attendance and cursory attention of the membership during debates. Eugene Eidenberg and Roy Morey capture the observers' impression of futility during the opening debate on the important 1965 Education Bill, when the only two senators present were "huddled in a corner in deep conversation." [5] Donald Matthews calls the audience for Senate debates "pitifully small and often inattentive." [6] The picture is similar for other public bodies.

The rate of use of the written record of debates is no more encouraging. When Anthony Barker and Michael Rush surveyed 104 members of Parliament in 1967, to find out if their sparse attendance at debates was counterbalanced by reading the debate record, less than one-tenth of the respondents claimed to read the published speeches regularly. An additional one fifth claimed at least to skim the record. [7]

Derogations of the value of debates in public assemblies are contradicted by counterclaims and indexes which imply that debate is important, after all. Members of public assemblies vie for the right to speak, and when they speak, they spend much time in carefully preparing their remarks. As busy people, one would hardly expect them to waste a great deal of time and effort in a fruitless exercise. Nor would American congressmen seek to have even undelivered speeches published in the *Congressional Record* if they considered speeches a total waste. The value placed on the right to speak can also be gauged by the great weight assigned to a chairman's power to determine who shall or shall not be heard during assembly debates. Assemblies like the Senate are extremely jealous of the right of unrestricted speech; this attitude is reflected in senators' opposition to rigorous cloture rules. When parliamentary bodies adopt rules to ex-

3. Bertram M. Gross, *The Legislative Struggle* (New York: McGraw-Hill, 1953), p. 365. Also see Anthony Barker and Michael Rush, *The Member of Parliament and His Information* (London: George Allen & Unwin, 1970), p. 131; Matthews, *U.S. Senators*, p. 243; and Norman V. Walbek, "National Public Foreign Policy Orientations as Expressed in U.N. General Assembly Debate: Notes on a Neglected Research Area," International Studies Association Paper (1971), p. 2.

4. T. F. Lindsay, *Parliament from the Press Gallery* (London: Macmillan, 1967), pp. 76, 81.

5. Eugene Eidenberg and Roy D. Morey, *An Act of Congress: The Legislative Process and the Making of Education Policy* (New York: Norton, 1969), p. 162.

6. Matthews, *U.S. Senators*, p. 246.

7. Barker and Rush, *Member of Parliament*, p. 146.

pedite business by limiting debate, it is common for the membership to quickly reverse these rulings.

Like insiders, outside audiences accord importance to debate in public assemblies. Large numbers of people vie for the right to attend sessions of public assemblies in order to listen to the verbal proceedings. While mass media coverage omits much of what is said, it is a rare session of a public body which does not receive at least some coverage.

Two factors largely explain the contradictory evaluations of public debate. First, most of those who claim that verbal behavior in public assemblies is not important would be willing to modify their statement by adding "most of the time." "Floor action is irregular. It fluctuates between deadly dullness and high drama, routine ratification of committee action and momentous decisions." [8]

The other reason for skepticism about verbal behavior in public assemblies springs from differing criteria for gauging speech importance. Traditionalists think of parliaments as great deliberative bodies where speeches display measures' merits in the grand manner. Argument and retort finally hammer out each major decision. Obviously, there is little of this kind of verbal interchange in today's public assemblies; those who look nostalgically to some of the great debates of the past rightfully complain that eloquent oratory has become a lost feature of public decision-making. Public assemblies' duty to arrive at decisions through public debate has been largely abdicated to committees and subcommittees, where debate has shriveled to a puny verbal exercise, far removed from the stirring oratory of yesteryear.

If one considers public debate to hammer out decisions as the only assembly function which deserves the label "important," then verbal behavior in public bodies is not generally important, because it is not "a direct and immediate exchange of ideas, facts, and arguments in the spirited manner of parry and counterthrust." [9] On the other hand, if one recognizes that verbal behavior in public bodies performs a variety of functions, then one can find other areas of activity which deserve to be called important. The mere fact that certain issues are publicized through debate, while others remain shrouded in silence, is highly significant. Only those issues which are verbalized or which can be inferred from verbalization can be included in the process of conflict resolution and policy-making. The way in which issues are verbally defined and in which various parameters are stressed will

8. Gross, *Legislative Struggle*, p. 364.
9. Robert G. Lehnen, "Behavior on the Senate Floor: An Analysis of Debate in the U.S. Senate," *Midwest Journal of Political Science*, 11 (1969), 507.

shape the discussion and policy outcomes.[10] Prudent verbal formulations can forestall conflict which might otherwise arise. Astute questions may draw forth significant political commitments.[11]

Careful management of silence is also an important aspect of the debating process. The skillful debater knows what *not* to debate, as well as the fine art of proper debate timing. The 1957 Federal Aid to Education Bill passed Congress by avoiding discussion of the explosive parochial and private school issues. In similar debates in 1949 and 1950, the chances for agreement had been destroyed by an extensive airing of the issue of federal aid for those schools.[12]

Debates are also important for the light they shed on the moods and views of various political actors on a given issue at a particular time, and the impact these moods are likely to have on future events. An analysis of UN General Assembly debates covering the Arab-Israel confrontation in the Middle East revealed that only a few issues were singled out by debate participants as essential preconditions for solution of the conflict.[13] One could therefore infer that there was a reasonable chance for reaching compromises along a wide spectrum of issues. From the debates one could also infer the degree of consensus among assembly members on values and norms of international conduct, and the solidarity which various member nations felt or wished to express for the Eastern or Western political bloc. Studying debate patterns over time, one could trace consistencies and changes in group and individual patterns and then attempt to assess the significance of these stable or changing patterns in the political life of the nations involved.

Debate may also reveal the role perceptions of the participants. A study of Senate committee debates showed that various senators viewed themselves as playing the role of chairman, district represen-

10. D. A. Strickland, "On Ambiguity in Political Rhetoric: Defeat of the Rat Control Bill in the House of Representatives, July, 1967," *Canadian Journal of Political Science*, 2 (1969), 340, 344.

11. Michael W. Kirst, *Government without Passing Laws: Congress' Nonstatutory Techniques for Appropriations Control* (Chapel Hill: University of North Carolina Press, 1969), p. 46.

12. Richard F. Fenno, Jr., "The House of Representatives and Federal Aid to Education," in Robert L. Peabody and Nelson Polsby, eds., *New Perspectives on the House of Representatives* (Chicago: Rand McNally, 1962), pp. 305–307. While silence can help, it can also hurt. The bill was ultimately killed, despite earlier successes, because of lack of verbal support from the White House.

13. Doris A. Graber, "Conflict Images: An Assessment of the Middle East Debates in the United Nations," *Journal of Politics*, 32 (1970), 371. Also see Walbek, "National Public Foreign Policy Orientations."

tative, or party members; this information gave valuable insights into the legislative and representational process in the committee.[14]

VERBAL BEHAVIOR AS INTERACTION IN A PUBLIC SETTING

How do the constraints of publicness and the interactions of various debate participants affect the verbal behavior which occurs in public assemblies? Several major influences will be discussed in the setting of public assemblies, but the reader should bear in mind that the constraints of publicness and interactive influences occur in other settings as well. Expressions by members of political elites, as well as by mass media, are public and interactive in the sense that senders seek to gauge and meet the expectations and idiosyncrasies of their intended audiences.

Adhering to Accepted Norms

Because utterances in public assemblies are public and readily observable by large audiences, the framers of such utterances usually feel compelled to project idealized images of public life. Approved patterns of behavior for a particular job, as defined in the actor's culture, will be enunciated. Actors often feel compelled to make themselves appear strong, righteous, and devoted to valiantly defending the legitimate interests of their constituency in public assemblies. This makes for a great deal of posturing, and it militates against compromises. Consequently, genuine bargaining is rarely possible in open sessions of public assemblies.

The resulting rigidity of positions is enhanced by the notion that public figures, acting in public, must follow widely sanctioned morally and legally sound policy principles. Past actions and future plans and policy proposals must be defensible in terms of these principles. This may make it difficult to abandon a stated position because the good, strong, moral political actor loses face when he yields on a matter of principle.

Analysis of UN General Assembly debates indicates the kinds of values which are commonly stressed in international public assemblies, particularly in well-publicized sessions. The most frequent themes are "legality, internationalism, and emphasis on the United Nations." Speakers also stress "the themes of peace, human rights,

14. Ralph K. Huitt, "The Congressional Committee: A Case Study," *American Political Science Review*, 48 (1954), 340–365.

colonialism, national sovereignty, national rights, nationalism, and a negative orientation to force." [15] These choices are not completely ritualistic but involve some deliberation, as shown by the fact that there are telltale variations in emphasis on these themes among the UN membership. Castro's Cuba and Nkrumah's Ghana did not stress the need for the rule of law, mirroring their disdain for the established international legal scene; instead, Cuba put unusually heavy stress on themes of anti-colonialism and self-determination. [16]

The need to posture as a figure of strength, acting on the most unexceptional principles only, detracts from the air of reality characteristic of debate in public assemblies. The audience is well aware that some of the debate is ritualistic, discounting it accordingly, but since the audience rarely knows precisely where reality presentation ends and ritual begins, it finds it difficult to decode messages delivered in public assemblies. When a speaker prefaces his request for money for a project by "I am in favor of economy but I am not in favor of false economy," it is hard to tell whether he is or is not economy-minded. [17] When he proclaims that a policy which benefits his constituency was designed primarily to benefit the entire community, verification of his claim to altruism may be well nigh impossible.

On the other side of the ledger, publicity for the proceedings in public assemblies partly counteracts the pressures toward posturing. In a body like the United Nations, the positions which representatives express are considered to reflect the official position of their country. Such positions are violated only at the peril of loss of credibility in the international assembly; therefore nations are careful to state only those positions to which they can adhere with minimal twisting of the verbal record. Moreover, expressed norms often beget conforming behavior. In the final analysis, however, public debate is liable to greater pressures toward distortion than are other forms of verbal interchange; consequently, public debate is not generally valued highly as an accurate medium for information transmission.

In democratic societies the norm that debate should permit all viewpoints to be heard may further obscure the thrust of public debate. [18]

15. Walbek, "National Public Foreign Policy Orientations," pp. 23–26. Walbek contends that the striking similarity in expressed values is "perhaps the strongest evidence for the existence of a public culture in the U.N. to which all nations conform."

16. *Ibid.*, pp. 14, 27–28.

17. Richard F. Fenno, Jr., *The Power of the Purse: Appropriations Politics in Congress* (Boston: Little, Brown, 1966), p. 16.

18. This requirement is usually taken very seriously, even in committees of legislative assemblies. *Ibid.*, p. 21.

In many debates more time is given to the exposition of minority views than to the exposition of the majority position. If allotted time is equated with strength and pervasiveness of expounded views, observers may be left with the impression that the majority view is more contested than it actually is; mass media reporting often enhances this misperception. Even policy-makers may be confused by the apparent balance of views and may give greater weight to the minority than is due to it.[19]

Maintaining a Productive Interaction Climate

Most public assemblies are goal oriented, with certain tasks to perform within a limited period of time. These tasks may be the framing and passing of laws or resolutions, the selection of political leaders, or the settling of disputes among members or their constituencies. To accomplish these tasks, despite conflicting interests and personalities among the members, verbal behavior must be judicious, permitting continuous fruitful collaboration and compromise.[20] Many of the formal and informal rules of public assemblies are directed toward maintaining a productive interaction climate. They include rules to force relevancy of the discussion and rules to systematize the order in which various viewpoints may be expressed, with time allotments to majority and opposition views. But the bulk of formal and informal regulations are concerned with fostering an atmosphere of decorum, if not friendliness, on the assumption that politeness and formality guard against anger and that anger decreases the willingness of parties to cooperate and seek agreement.

There is little firm evidence that the arousal of anger really destroys the spirit of negotiation, though a number of experiments and laboratory tests do indicate that fear and anger reduce the ability to achieve group goals. Fear may also lead to an avoidance reaction; information is shut out, and there is a refusal to consider relevant issues. Other experiments seem to show that fear arousal may actually enhance willingness to negotiate. Fear arousal may also spur information acquisition by fearful parties, thereby increasing the possibility of finding likely solutions.[21] It has even been argued that angry verbal inter-

19. On this point, see Peter G. Richards, *Parliament and Foreign Affairs* (Toronto: University of Toronto Press, 1967), p. 106.

20. Gross, *Legislative Struggle*, p. 371. For typical rules, in this case from the Indian Parliament, see A. R. Mukherjea, *Parliamentary Procedure in India* (London: Oxford University Press, 1967), pp. 168–173.

21. Irving L. Janis, "Effects of Fear Arousal on Attitude Change," in Leonard Berkovitz, ed., *Advances in Experimental Social Psychology* (New York: Academic

changes may be a desirable surrogate for physical combat. "If we learn
. . . to express hate in symbolic ways, we may not need to fight. Perhaps we should encourage, not discourage, diplomats to become highly
skilled in cursing. The press might be taught not to deplore international cursing, but to regard it as the critic does a play. Diplomats
might be trained to dramatize, not to mask, differences. As we learn
to express hostility short of war, our chances of survival might increase." [22]

But even though the impact of anger on negotiation effectiveness is
questionable, commonsense notions that anger harms negotiations are
very pervasive.[23] Therefore most assemblies demand that members
must refrain from personal attacks of any kind, so the form of address
is often impersonal and stylized. Members of the U.S. Senate are not
addressed by name but by position, "the senior Senator from Maine,"
or "the gentleman from Wisconsin." Religious and ethnic slurs are
ruled out; the motivations of members of the assembly and their
personal intelligence or integrity are beyond public reproach. When
opposition is expressed, it is often accompanied by protestation of
respect for the opposed party. The language may be stilted and florid,
such as: "Mr. Chairman, I will have to object to this amendment offered by my good friend from North Carolina. He is one of God's
noblemen in my book; but there are times when you just have to take
issue with your good friends and this is one of those times. . . . I hope
that the gentleman will not feel too bad if his amendment is defeated." [24]

Though not covered explicitly by formal or informal rules, members
ordinarily couch issues in language which is unlikely to anger partici-

Press, 1967), III, 169–171. For a diplomat's impressions of the adverse effects of
barbed language on specific negotiations, see Arthur Lall, *Modern International
Negotiation: Principles and Practice* (New York: Columbia University Press,
1966), pp. 148–150, 233–235.

22. Hugh Dalziel Duncan, *Symbols in Society* (New York: Oxford University
Press, 1968), p. 108.

23. Constantin Melnik and Nathan Leites, *The House without Windows: France
Selects a President* (Evanston, Ill.: Row, Peterson, 1958), p. 268, describes a two-
stage process in the French Parliament. When decisions involve a great deal of
emotion, it is discharged during first-stage verbal interchange. In the second stage,
with emotions already effectively vented, reason and common sense come to the
fore.

24. Fenno, *Power of the Purse*, p. 447; also Gross, *Legislative Struggle*, p. 370.
For similar attitudes in the French Parliament, see Melnik and Leites, *House without Windows*, p. 104. Paul Lutzker, "The Behavior of Congressmen in a Committee Setting: A Research Report," *Journal of Politics*, 31 (1969), 148, calls the relative absence of negative social-emotional interactions in congressional committees
"the single most startling finding" of his research on interaction patterns.

pants in the debate. Members develop "accepted ways of disagreeing which minimize, rather than exacerbate, interpersonal friction."[25] When discussions fail, assembly members often attribute the failure to intemperate language and indelicate phrasing of issues.[26] A subject like abortion or compulsory sterilization may be discussed successfully in medical terms, but not from religious or moral vantage points; limits set on immigration are more palatable when debated in terms of the national economy than when dealt with in terms of ethnic or racial balance. Arguments on procedural grounds are less inciting than arguments on substantive issues.[27]

Moderation of hostility in public debates may be more apparent in times of crisis than in times of political calm. A study of the Mideast debates in the United Nations General Assembly over a thirteen-year period showed less heated oratory and fewer accusations at the time of greatest tension.[28] At other times, there was far more expression of intolerance and ill will. When Norman Walbek analyzed the verbal behavior of eleven nations during comparatively relaxed General Assembly sessions in 1955, 1960, and 1965, he found a fair amount of heated debate. He concluded that immoderate expressions were part of a deliberate strategy: "expressions of intolerance are calculated ingredients in a national official's bargaining behavior, an attempt to communicate unwillingness to compromise on the issue at hand."[29]

Sometimes emotions are aroused deliberately to speed up or delay assembly action. Thunderous applause for a prospective leader can make a doubtful selection more certain; delegates may become infused with the idea that an epic moment is at hand, that they must cast aside their differences and proceed with unanimous or near-unanimous action.[30] On other occasions, "a deep, tense hush can be as moving as the loudest tumult."[31]

Conversely, undesired action can be impeded by circulating stories

25. Richard F. Fenno, Jr. "The Appropriations Committee as a Political System," *American Political Science Review*, 56 (1962), 322.

26. For a more complete discussion of such norms and compliance with them, see Fenno, *The Power of the Purse*, pp. 24ff.

27. *Ibid.*, pp. 446–448.

28. Doris A. Graber, "Perceptions of Middle East Conflict in the UN, 1953–65," *Journal of Conflict Resolution*, 13 (1969), 472–480.

29. Walbek, "National Public Foreign Policy Orientations," p. 12. The oratory of the following countries was examined: Colombia, Cuba, Ghana, India, Sweden, Thailand, USSR, United Arab Republic, United Kingdom, United States, and Yugoslavia.

30. Melnik and Leites, *House without Windows*, p. 167.

31. Lindsay, *Parliament from the Press Gallery*, p. 53.

which arouse negative emotions. Constantin Melnik and Nathan Leites describe a session in the French Assembly where "news and false rumors spread: assassination, pitfalls, murderous maneuvers, stabbings in the back." The work of the assembly was almost brought to a halt. Working conditions "are extremely unfavorable, for the necessary atmosphere of calm is utterly lacking. . . . This makes things particularly difficult for the top leaders. If the leader takes part in the impassioned discussions of the rank and file, follows their emotional eddies . . . he must abandon all hope of serious action. . . ."[32] In the session in question, the leaders resorted to the tactic of postponing major decisions until the small hours of the morning, when many members had left the assembly and fatigue had cooled the ardor of those remaining.

The Give and Take of Debating

The nature of his audience strongly influences what a speaker will say and how he will say it. The speaker may utilize an intellectual choice process, with a number of behavioral criteria to predict the type of communication which will be most appealing to his audience; or he may rely on an intuitive, empathetic process, sensing what his audience wants to hear. Either case involves substantial restraints on the speaker's freedom to choose his verbal output. Audience reaction, real or fancied, is a major influence in producing public speeches.[33] A public speaker often must cope with a multiplicity of audiences, each requiring different verbal fare. A contributor to congressional debates speaks at one and the same time to his colleagues in Congress (both of his own party and of the opposition) and to his constituents at home; he may also speak to national and even international audiences. The need to consider all these audiences may force him to compromise on what he wants to say or to talk in vague generalities which offend no one and which can be interpreted to mean a variety of advantageous things to different audiences.

A good example of the influence of audiences on the speaker is presented by a study of speeches by John Foster Dulles, the chief Ameri-

32. The chief purpose of the session was the election of a new French President. Melnik and Leites, *House without Windows*, p. 127.

33. Raymond A. Bauer, "The Communicator and the Audience," *Journal of Conflict Resolution*, 2 (1958), 67–77; Paul W. Keller, "The Study of Face-to-Face International Decision-Making," *Journal of Communication*, 13 (1963), 72–73. Johan Kaufmann, *Conference Diplomacy: An Introductory Analysis* (Dobbs Ferry, N.Y.: Oceana Publications, 1968), pp. 162–168.

can negotiator for the Japanese-American peace settlement. In public speeches to general audiences, Secretary Dulles postured as a spokesman for the free world, stressing general policy and security considerations. He tried to make the treaty seem noncontroversial and to focus on public consensus, properly anticipating that this would aid in the treaty's ratification.[34] In speeches before the Senate, Dulles stressed the need for creating a new Japan, and for establishing prospective policies towards Nationalist and Communist China which he felt were likely to foster Senate approval for the treaty. Before foreign audiences, the secretary emphasized the need for collective security against the Communist threat.

The leadership in the Senate Foreign Relations Committee pursued the same verbal tactics as the secretary. It pictured the settlement as largely nonpolitical and noncontroversial and tried to keep discussion brief and low-key. It asked Dulles no embarrassing questions and even helped him to call attention to the most appealing features of the treaty.[35] Opposition speakers pursued different goals with influential audiences. They chose a tactic of attacking the treaty, often bitterly, along lines which have been characterized as a "flight from relevancy." Senator Jenner of Indiana intemperately appealed to right-wingers by calling the treaty "part of the Hiss-Acheson-Lattimore design for the sell-out of Asia, and the wrapping up of our military might in the coils of the United Nations." [36]

Once debate has begun, subsequent speakers must speak within the context of the preceding remarks. They may be precluded from touching upon certain issues because prior speakers have already exhausted the patience of the audience on these topics or have given them a slant which cannot readily be counteracted. The debate may have taken an unexpected turn, making some otherwise relevant issues no longer relevant. A debate which begins on the high plane of general public good may have to remain on this plane, whereas a debate which deals with more particular interests may permit a variety of speakers to air the concerns of smaller constituencies.

When various debate participants have assumed certain roles, others may feel that they must assume an opposing or totally different role. Ralph Huitt's study of Senate committees showed that discussion order

34. Bernard C. Cohen, *The Political Process and Foreign Policy: The Making of the Japanese Peace Settlement* (Princeton: Princeton University Press, 1957), pp. 134–137.

35. *Ibid.*, pp. 148–154.

36. *Ibid.*, pp. 171–173.

strongly influenced the role which various participants took in debate. Once the chairman role, the role of advocate of constituents, or the role of advocate of party interests has been preempted, later speakers seek different roles.[37] In this sense, interaction during debate may create its own momentum. Previous verbal output shapes future verbal output.

Some debates are not truly interactive. In UN proceedings there may be relatively little connection between the pronouncements of various delegates, because speeches are prepared in advance, before delegates know what others plan to say.[38] Likewise, legislative meetings may be merely "a forum for the presentation of views" operating under "a norm allowing statements to be made by any participant and then ignored." [39] Nathan Polsby believes that "the essence of the Senate is that it is a great forum, an echo chamber, a publicity machine." [40] Interaction to produce legislation is secondary.

One other feature of the interaction process deserves mention. Public debate is often criticized for straying from truth and the canons of relevancy. However, the interaction process contains a built-in remedy: in most public assemblies there is a chance for instant rebuttal of any outright falsehoods, including instant ridicule of obviously spurious statements. Speakers find it advisable to adhere to a straighter and narrower line of truth and relevancy than might otherwise be the case. Bluntly put, "No one likes to be made to look and feel an ass" or a liar in front of a wide audience.[41] Instant rebuttal during face-to-face confrontations is a far more powerful restraint than long-range impersonal rebuttal.

Elements of the Verbal Interaction Process

Elements in the verbal interaction process may affect its quality; among those which have been studied are the socio-emotional climate created by verbal interaction, the succession of tasks accomplished during debate, and the patterns of substantive positions surfacing at various times during public debates. While the body of descriptive

37. Huitt, "Congressional Committee," pp. 344–353; also see Lutzker, "Behavior of Congressmen," pp. 160–161.

38. Graber, "Perceptions of Middle East Conflict," pp. 474–476.

39. Lutzker, "Behavior of Congressmen," p. 156.

40. Polsby, "Policy Analysis and Congress," p. 63.

41. Lindsay, Parliament from the Press Gallery, p. 78. Also see R. L. Friedheim, J. B. Kadane, and J. K. Gamble, Jr., "Quantitative Content Analysis of the United Nations Seabed Debate: Methodology and a Continental Shelf Case Study," International Organization, 24 (1970), 480–482.

data is growing, few theories linking particular debate patterns to final policy results have been advanced and adequately tested.[42]

Paul Lutzker used Bales' Interaction Process Analysis to study interaction patterns within House and Senate subcommittees involved in the Higher Education Act of 1965.[43] He tried to assess the socio-emotional climate created by debate, and to rate the contributions which debate made to the work of the committees. Each participant's verbal output was coded for six socio-emotional qualities and six task-related qualities; each group of qualities represented three pairs of polar opposites, such as showing tension or releasing it, or asking for opinions as against giving opinions.[44] The contributions of each participant to the interaction process were then charted. Lutzker found that social-emotional statements, especially negative ones, constituted only a small part of the verbal output of congressional subcommittee members. In Lutzker's view, deemphasis of socio-emotional issues assured that the interaction climate was friendly and businesslike.

In the typical situation scored by Bales, problem-solving groups had gone through three phases.[45] An emphasis on problems of orientation came first, followed by emphasis on evaluation of these problems, and on problem solutions. Debating patterns in the Higher Education subcommittees were different — problems of orientation and evaluation were emphasized, but solutions were largely ignored. Lutzker concluded that the subcommittees served not as problem-solving bodies, but as forums for the presentation of views. Efforts to find solutions appeared to be spread over the work of several committees concerned with the Higher Education Act, rather than being concentrated in a single committee.[46] Lutzker believes that interaction process analysis, if tailored to the needs of public assemblies, can shed a good deal of light on the verbal interactions which occur in such assemblies. If

42. Lutzker, "Behavior of Congressmen," p. 166.

43. *Ibid.*, pp. 140–166.

44. Social-emotional pairs were: (a) shows solidarity with group, raises other's status *versus* shows antagonism, defies other's status; (b) shows tension release, jokes, laughs, *versus* shows tension, asks for help, withdraws; (c) agrees, shows passive acceptance, understands, *versus* disagrees, shows passive rejection, formality. Task-oriented pairs were (a) asks for orientation, information, repetition, *versus* gives orientation, information, etc.; (b) asks for opinion, evaluation, analysis, *versus* gives opinion, evaluation, analysis; (c) asks for suggestion, direction, possible ways of action, *versus* gives suggestion, direction, possible ways of action. Lutzker, 'Behavior of Congressmen," p. 144. A bibliography on interaction process analysis appears on p. 143.

45. Robert F. Bales and Paul A. Hare, "The Diagnostic Use of the Interaction Profile," *Journal of Social Psychology*, 67 (1965), 239–258.

46. Lutzker, "Behavior of Congressmen," pp. 156–157.

emerging patterns can be correlated with certain desired debate outcomes, interaction process analysis may become a useful tool for planning debates and predicting outcomes.[47]

Patterns of substantive position statements emerging during public debate have been studied by Diane Clemens. She analyzed verbal interactions during the Yalta conference (February 4–11, 1945), concentrating on the kinds of proposals made by participants and the progress toward bilateral and tripartite decisions in the wake of these proposals.[48] The five major issues which were discussed at Yalta were German reparations, German dismemberment, the fate of France, the fate of Poland, and the nature of the United Nations. Debate on each issue was analyzed on a day-by-day basis. A special symbol was devised to indicate which delegation's proposal was the basis for discussion on that day. For each day, the relative position of the participants, as expressed in their statements, was diagrammed. Perfect agreement was charted as overlap, while diametrically opposed positions were given the widest possible spatial separation.[49]

Among other findings, the study showed that the initial proposals concerning the solution of a particular issue had a better chance for adoption than later proposals; countries whose proposals became the original basis for discussion thus stood the best chance of having them prevail. (The Soviets made the main proposal in three out of five issues and saw their proposal carry the day.) When two of the three powers could agree, they invariably were able to sway the third power. There seemed to be little difference between agreements that proceeded from general principles to particulars, and those which reversed the process.

The study showed that analysis of interaction patterns "suggests several configurations which were usually found preceding agreement and indicates some of the circumstances which foster a high incidence of consensus." [50] If it is generally valid in other debates, such a finding

47. *Ibid.*, p. 166.

48. Diane S. Clemens, "The Structure of Negotiations: Dynamics and Interaction Patterns of the Crimean Conference," *Peace Research Society Papers*, 11 (1968), 57–65. Although military security reasons kept the conference proceedings from immediate publication, they were intended to be public and handled accordingly. Partial publication occurred the following year. For her analysis, Clemens used official government records, notes of American conference participants, and memoirs.

49. Unfortunately, the report does not indicate how perfect agreement and total disagreement were measured.

50. *Ibid.*, p. 63–64. Also see Lloyd Jensen, "Soviet-American Bargaining Behavior in the Postwar Disarmament Negotiations," *Journal of Conflict Resolu-*

could have major policy implications. From the descriptive standpoint, the Clemens study gives a fresh view of negotiating procedures and interactions. What actually took place, as judged by scientific content analysis, differed from the impressionistic accounts of major historians of the Yalta conference. [51]

Another approach to the study of interaction is content analysis geared to discovering the peace-making potential of verbal activities. Content analysis has been used to ascertain whether verbal interchanges during the Mideast debates were conflict-creating or conflict-reducing. Speeches were judged to be conflict-creating if they made no proposals for conflict settlement and used intemperate language; speeches were rated as conflict-resolving if they were relatively moderate in tone and contained proposals for conflict resolution.[52] Heavy stress on East-West or Arab-Israeli bloc alignments was viewed as evidence of inflexibility, making compromise in bloc-linked disputed issues less likely.

The study analyzed conflict-creating and conflict-resolving characteristics of 848 speeches. "Looking at the verbal climate, one is struck by the prevalence of moderation and sustained efforts towards conflict resolution. In crises, even more than in noncrises, speeches were usually moderate and delegates were more ready to praise than condemn." [53] Despite frequent references to bloc lines, compromise across these lines seemed possible. These are valuable findings about verbal interactions in the United Nations, if anger-arousing speeches are dysfunctional for conflict resolution, and if speeches must contain pro-

---

tion, 7 (1963), 522–541. Jensen studied patterns of substantive concessions and retractions of concessions in Soviet-American disarmament negotiations, 1946–61. His work is discussed more fully in the next chapter. For debate patterns on questions of control over the continental shelf and seabed, see Friedheim, Kadane, and Gamble, "UN Seabed Debate," pp. 479–502.

51. See, e.g., Herbert Feis, *Churchill, Roosevelt, and Stalin: The War They Waged and the Peace They Sought* (Princeton: Princeton University Press, 1957); John L. Snell, ed., *The Meaning of Yalta: Big Three Diplomacy and the Balance of Power* (Baton Rouge: Louisiana State University Press, 1956).

52. Graber, "Conflict Images," pp. 454–484. "Extremely immoderate speeches were those which used terms like barbarism, atrocities, and genocide to characterize the actions of another country. . . . Speeches were coded as immoderate if charges of illegal activity, violation of the Charter, or deliberate deception were made in somewhat more temperate language. . . . Speeches were classed as moderate if they contained no abusive language, accusations of criminal behavior, or charges of unjustifiable violations of the norms of international conduct to which the members had given approval." Using these criteria, "72 percent of all speeches were moderate, 23 percent immoderate, and only four percent were extremely immoderate" (*ibid.*, p. 476).

53. *Ibid.*, p. 482.

posals for settlement and avoid pledges of adherence to fixed bloc positions in order to contribute to peace-making.[54]

AUXILIARY FUNCTIONS OF ASSEMBLY DEBATES

Thus far, when talking about the functions of public assemblies, reference has been primarily to their most obvious tasks, such as debate over the substance of pending laws in legislative assemblies and debate over measures to solve conflicts in international bodies. We now turn to ancillary and less obvious functions which are sometimes of equal or greater political significance than formal assembly activities.

Broadly speaking, verbal behavior in public assemblies serves three types of auxiliary purposes. "Intra-systemic functions" relate to the functioning of the assembly as such. Verbal behavior may also serve the personal goals of individual members; it then performs "ego functions." Finally, verbal activities in public assemblies may be intended to serve a variety of functions for audiences outside the assembly. These are "extra-systemic functions" which may be only remotely related to the specific business before the assembly.

Intra-systemic functions can be demonstrated with data collected in studies of legislative assemblies and their committees. These data, with some modifications, are relevant for other public bodies, such as mass meetings and international conferences.[55]

Information Dissemination

An important auxiliary purpose of debate in public assemblies is the dissemination of information to assembly members. "Floor statements are often the quickest and most effective methods of passing the word around among other members of Congress. . . ."[56] Various speakers pass on items of information which they want their assembly colleagues

---

54. For support of these hypotheses, see James N. Rosenau, ed., *International Politics and Foreign Policy* (New York: Free Press, 1961), p. 126; David J. Finlay, Ole R. Holsti, and Richard R. Fagen, *Enemies in Politics* (Chicago: Rand McNally, 1967), pp. 5–6; Dean G. Pruitt, "Definition of the Situation as a Determinant of International Action," in Herbert Kelman, ed., *International Behavior* (New York: Holt, Rinehart and Winston, 1965), pp. 395–398; and Lewis A. Froman and Michael D. Cohen, "Threats and Bargaining Efficiency," *Behavioral Science*, 14 (1969), 147–159.

55. Some of the similarities in functions and operations of various types of governmental bodies are discussed in Heinz Eulau and Katherine Hinckley, "Legislative Institutions and Processes," in James A. Robinson, ed., *Political Science Annual, 1966* (Indianapolis: Bobbs-Merrill, 1966), pp. 85–189.

56. Gross, *Legislative Struggle*, p. 366.

to know. They do this in a highly selective manner, calculating intended impact in relation to the business at hand, or in relation to other purposes. A skillful speaker can make even irrelevant remarks appear relevant in order to avoid running afoul of debate rules which require information to be related to the assembly's agenda. Speakers may also choose to convey information which obscures, rather than clarifying. Among the inspiration for such tactics is the fact that ". . . issues, acts, and personalities, once sufficiently beclouded, serve better as objects of *projection*: obscurity lends mystique, and the mystique excites all kinds of saved-up grievances and wishes. Given a little mystique, the stage is set for excitement and the discharge of tensions. . . ."[57]

In a public assembly, the information dissemination process is not as controllable as individual speakers would like it to be. Fellow participants who want to help or hinder the speaker, or who possess political goals of their own, may bring out matters which a given speaker would like to have kept shrouded in silence. Legislative hearings or question hours are particularly suited for forcing into the open information which speakers may be reluctant to reveal. The chief aim of debates or hearings may be to draw out information which would otherwise be unavailable or unnoticed by assembly members. Again, a good deal of the information exposed in this manner may have little or nothing to do with the ostensible purpose of the debate or hearing.[58]

How much value do members of public assemblies place on the information transmission function? The evidence is scant.[59] In their 1967 interviews of members of the British House of Commons, Anthony Barker and Michael Rush tried to ascertain what use members made of information available in public speeches. They asked fifty-five Conservative and fifty Labour members whether they often listened to speeches by backbenchers, as distinct from speeches by the top leadership. The idea was that attendance at routine sessions was more indicative of information seeking than was attendance at glamor events. Only 17 percent of the answers were positive, with newer members attending more frequently than old-timers. Speeches were praised more

57. Strickland, "On Ambiguity in Political Rhetoric," pp. 388, 340.

58. Kirst, *Government without Passing Laws*, pp. 26–29. For an example of irrelevant questioning designed to show official neglect of the Internal Communist threat in the United States, see Telford Taylor, *Grand Inquest: The Story of Congressional Investigation* (New York: Simon and Schuster, 1955), pp. 117–120.

59. Most descriptive and questionnaire-based discussions refer to general reaction to debate and do not single out the information transmission function. For favorable appraisals of various conflict-resolving functions served by UN debate, see Graber, "Conflict Images," pp. 477–480.

often for their entertainment value than for their informational content. Speakers noted for sarcasm or rebellious views were sought out more often than speakers known for dispassionate analyses of issues. Many members characterized public debate as stale, claiming that it mostly reiterated well-known facts.[60]

Some distinction was made between attendance at debates in general and attendance at debates directed toward specific items of policy-making. When the respondents were asked how they rated the House of Commons as a source of information in "one of your own special fields of interest," one-third ranked it as "valuable" and an additional one-fifth as "sometimes valuable." This amounted to a 52 percent favorable response. Members valued debate in their own chamber more highly than debate in the House of Lords. Only one-third of the Commons membership attended debates in the House of Lords more than twice a year. Many never attended at all and few read the proceedings of the upper chamber.[61]

Building Loyalties and Disloyalties

Much verbal behavior in public assemblies is directed toward the goal of building or destroying factional loyalties; in fact, students of the public scene often consider this the prime function of public debate. "Public debate is necessarily only a method of giving unity and morale to organizations. It is ceremonial and designed to create enthusiasm, to increase faith and quiet doubt . . . to reconcile the spiritual conflicts within an organization and to attract followers to that organization by appealing to their prejudices." [62]

Loyalty is built in different ways. Talk may be designed to create confidence in the ability and fairness of advocates of specific courses of action; it may aim at constructing an *esprit de corps* for the whole body or for a particular faction.[63] Talk is intended to build feelings of personal or factional allegiance which will then carry over to measures proposed by the trusted individual or faction. In the passage of measures, "personal relationships bulk large. . . . It all depends who the

60. Barker and Rush, *Member of Parliament*, pp. 133–139.
61. *Ibid.*
62. Thurman W. Arnold, *The Folklore of Capitalism*, rev. ed. (New Haven: Yale University Press, 1964), pp. 379–380. The historical primacy of the consensus-building function is discussed by Gerhard Loewenberg, "The Influence of Parliamentary Behavior on Regime Stability," *Comparative Politics*, 3 (1971), 177. Loewenberg also cites the views of John Stuart Mill, Walter Bagehot, and Carl Friedrich. Also see Gross, *Legislative Struggle*, p. 366.
63. Matthews, *U.S. Senators*, pp. 244–245.

person is . . . you're not going to take a project of a guy who will gouge you. It's the human element." While it "would of course be next to impossible to demonstrate the effects of personal factors, . . . observers have no doubt they are important." [64]

Richard Fenno describes the way in which the House Appropriations Committee seeks to create trust in Congress. The committee has developed a standard rhetoric which stresses that it has acted in accordance with overall House expectations; that its membership is experienced and well qualified; that the members of the committee have worked hard; that they possess the facts; and that there is agreement across party lines. These norms are widely approved by Congress. The committee's effectiveness has been enhanced by its ability to convince Congress that the committee has heeded the norms.[65]

Even when the debate addresses itself more directly to the merits of agenda items, psychological considerations are paramount. Speakers emphasize the aspects which are rationally or emotionally acceptable to those colleagues whose support is at stake. They do not generally attempt to construct the ideal case for an agenda item.[66]

Instead of helping to build one's own position and faction, verbal behavior may be directed to attacking the opposition and destroying its consensus. In fact, much of the speaking time in public assemblies is taken up by attempts to discredit the other side. As in consensus building, several approaches are available. One can attempt to destroy personal or factional allegiance by casting aspersions on the personal integrity, wisdom, or motivations of opposition members. Or one can place the measures advocated by the opposition into an unappealing light. Such efforts may force parties, even those who had not intended to enter a particular verbal fray, to present counterarguments. During the UN debates of Korean events, the Russians boycotted the initial sessions but felt compelled to return to the conference table to rebut the anti-Communist arguments presented by the United States.[67]

Building a Record for Future Action

The arguments advanced in public assemblies may look beyond immediate political gains to building a record for future action. When the Senate Foreign Relations Committee held hearings on the Japan-

64. Fenno, *Power of the Purse*, p. 608.
65. *Ibid.*, pp. 438–440.
66. On this point see Huitt, "Congressional Committee," pp. 340–351.
67. Allen S. Whiting, *China Crosses the Yalu* (New York: Macmillan, 1960), p. 73.

ese peace treaty, members made a deliberate effort to question Secretary of State Dulles in a manner designed to answer all foreseeable future objections to the treaty. Dulles was given an opportunity to express himself on interpretations of various treaty provisions, in order to lay the basis for later judicial and negotiated interpretations of the precise meaning of these provisions. The rationale behind the treaty provisions was fully explored so that it would be available if the treaty were to become a model for other treaties.[68]

Debate permits assembly delegates to present their views for the historical record to prevent faulty inferences from their "yea" or "nay" votes. Delegates who favor a measure for reasons which differ from those already expressed can publicize their own views. In parliamentary bodies like the British House of Commons, where voting follows strict party lines, debate may be the only opportunity for members to air dissent. Peter Richards cites the Common Market debates as showing substantial differences within each party, despite the fact that the vote adhered rigidly to party lines. The debate record then becomes an important document for reporting intra-party differences and gauging the possibility of future modification of Britain's Common Market policies.[69]

The rationale by which a policy is publicly justified may provide desirable or undesirable precedents for future action. Rationales used to explain American foreign policies to various assemblies and to the world at large are illustrative. Thomas Franck and Edward Weisband claim that the United States mismanaged its verbal strategies in the Cuban missile crisis, and in the subsequent intervention in the Dominican Republic, by choosing rationalizations which branded it as a brutal aggressor in the eyes of many domestic and foreign observers. Worse, the rationalizations, which stressed the right of regional systems to preserve their ideology by force, later facilitated Soviet aggression. The Brezhnev Doctrine, used to justify Soviet intervention in Czechoslovakia, "faithfully echoes official U.S. pronouncements made during the covert overthrow of the government of Guatemala, the Cuban missile crisis, and the invasion of the Dominican Republic. Thus the Soviets were able to claim credibly that the principles upon which they were acting were those we ourselves had devised to justify our conduct in the Americas, and that by our rhetoric we had implicitly signaled our con-

68. Cohen, *Political Process*, p. 154. On the uses of such records for political maneuvers and in courts of law see Kirst, *Government without Passing Laws*, pp. 6–7, 149.
69. Richards, *Parliament and Foreign Affairs*, p. 105.

sent to their application in the case of Czechoslovakia." [70] Since the United States had previously used the justification, it was, in effect, barred from contesting the Russian action.

The authors contend that the invasion of Czechoslovakia would have been unlikely if the United States had not supplied the Russians with a ready-made rationale. Although this probably overstates the case, there is no question that American statements proved helpful in the Russian maneuvers. "Conduct explained by principles inconsistent with those applied previously in similar circumstances, tends to transform the system . . . the other superpower in the future will expect to have recourse to the same principles." [71]

Tactical Verbal Maneuvers

Last, but not least, verbal maneuvers may serve a number of tactical goals. They may be used as a ruse to arouse false expectations, or as a smokescreen to conceal matters that might otherwise be exposed. A speaker can stress one aspect of a problem to give the impression that this will be the main line of attack. His opposition may then prepare counterarguments to meet the initial thrust, only to discover that the speaker has switched to a different line of attack. The switch may catch the opposition off guard and destroy its case.

It is not at all uncommon to use verbal maneuvers to delay action or stop it entirely. Filibustering in the U.S. Senate is probably the most famous example of using lengthy, largely irrelevant speeches to physically exhaust the opposition and thereby kill off the business under consideration. Records of the successful use of the filibuster and estimates of the many measures which were not pushed because of the threat of filibuster testify to the impact of this tactic on the governmental process.[72] Even short of filibustering, measures can be "talked to death" by exhausting an assembly's patience with needless discussion. Conversely, lengthy and wearisome debate may force passage of a measure, merely to halt further discussion.

The use of verbal maneuvers to delay action and thereby give a chance for the opposition to rally has been less fully documented. Bertram Gross cites one instance which occurred in 1945. The House of Representatives had passed a bill for the compulsory control of the civilian labor force. When the measure came up in the Senate, it was

70. Thomas Franck and Edward Weisband, *Word Politics: Verbal Strategy among the Super Powers* (New York: Oxford University Press, 1972), pp. 6–8.
71. *Ibid.*, pp. 6–8, 47, 122.
72. Gross, *Legislative Struggle*, pp. 373–375.

expected to pass. In hopes of gaining time for the opposition to rally, Senators Joseph O'Mahoney and Wayne Morse made lengthy Senate speeches. These speeches were later credited with allowing time for labor and business interests to launch a counterattack against the measure and ultimately deprive it of Senate support.[73]

Gratification of Ego Functions

To point out that many people, particularly politicians, like to hear themselves talk is no startling revelation. Some observers have intimated that most speech-making in public assemblies can be credited, wholly or in part, to the desire for personal, group, or national ego inflation. People talk because it makes them feel important or because they think it will please their friends. People also talk to deflate the egos of others, either because this enhances their own ego or serves their personal or political purposes. Likewise, people talk to "let off steam"; this cathartic function has been called "a quasi-ritualistic means of adjusting group conflicts and relieving disturbances through a safety-valve."[74] When people talk to reduce intrapsychic tensions, other purposes, such as knowledge transmission or conflict resolution, may become entirely secondary.[75]

It is, of course, impossible to determine how many speeches are motivated, primarily or partly, by a desire to gratify personal needs. Data from the U.S. Congress suggest that the practice may be less widespread than is generally believed. For instance, Robert Lehnen's study of ten senatorial debates found that only a minority of senators participated at all, and even those few generally spoke only in debates that were of special interest to them.[76] The senators seemed more interested in the goal of the debate than in sounding off on any pretext. In fact, Lehnen was able to characterize senators as "generalists," who were people who would talk on three or more issues; "specialists," who would talk on one or two issues; and "non-talkers," who made no verbal contribution at all to the ten debates under examination. Lehnen found that there were only fourteen generalists, compared to forty-five specialists and forty non-talkers.

Other investigators have found similar self-restraint in speech-mak-

73. *Ibid.*, p. 368.
74. David B. Truman, *The Governmental Process* (New York: Alfred A. Knopf, 1951), pp. 372–377.
75. A. James Gregor, *An Introduction to Metapolitics* (New York: Free Press, 1971), p. 317.
76. Lehnen, "Behavior on the Senate Floor," pp. 511–512.

ing. In a debate on the federal aid to education bill, less than 20 percent of the Senate membership participated. Those who spoke were knowledgeable — primarily members of committees and subcommittees concerned with a particular aspect of the bill.[77] Apparently the desire for ego inflation is held in check partly by the norm that those who speak should have special knowledge of the matters which they are discussing.

Speeches are sometimes made primarily to pay off a political debt of support or opposition or to earn political credit with colleagues. A speaker will talk to support or oppose a measure as a gesture of friendship or enmity for colleagues, rather than to express concern for the measure. He may fully expect that his friends will repay the favor in the future when measures of concern to him can benefit from verbal support by others.

Another personal motivation for speaking is the desire to remain in the political limelight. A legislative chamber may be "in a way, a theater where dramas — comedies and tragedies, soap operas and horse operas — are staged to enhance the careers of its members. . . ."[78] Congressmen face reelection every two years, but their congressional duties often keep them from returning home to their constituencies for campaigning. Therefore they are tempted to speak in Congress or other assemblies for the prestige and publicity which such verbal activities bring. At such times, when campaigning purposes may be uppermost, a congressman says things designed to impress his home constituencies. Many of the speeches which are read into the *Congressional Record* appear to be motivated by a desire for personal political publicity, rather than by a desire to accomplish the work of Congress.

Outside Publics as Debate Targets

Speakers in public assemblies are highly conscious of the fact that their speeches are available to outside publics through direct attendance or mass media publicity. Furthermore, much of what is said in public assemblies becomes a matter of permanent record. Given these facts, speakers utilize the public forum to address outside publics. Congress is sometimes used as a political campaign forum; public negotiations, like disarmament conferences, may serve to denounce opposing countries and praise one's own.

77. Eidenberg and Morey, *Act of Congress*, p. 143. Also see Fenno, *Power of the Purse*, pp. 436–437.
78. Polsby, "Policy Analysis," p. 64.

Few data indicate how much attention is paid to the verbal activities of public assemblies by the general public or by specialized audiences. Available data on attention paid to mass media and on levels of public knowledge tend to make one skeptical about many people's attentiveness to public assembly proceedings, and the fact that even the membership in these assemblies often pays little attention to the verbal behavior enhances that impression.[79] Matters ignored by the mass media are particularly unlikely to reach outside audiences. However, political effects of assembly messages may not depend primarily on the numbers of listeners — who the listeners are, what positions they hold in various power hierarchies, and how they will use these positions may be more important than sheer numbers.

Most extra-systemic functions performed by public debate are quite similar to intra-systemic functions. Take information transmission. Public assembly speakers air matters with which they want the public to be familiar; in fact, the exposition of competing viewpoints for the benefit of the public has often been called the chief function of legislative bodies like Congress.[80] Beyond the desire to disseminate information, speakers may wish to build outside support or opposition for certain decisions. Much of the public debate on Vietnam in Congress, and even in public negotiating sessions, was largely an attempt to mobilize public opinion for or against specific policies. Likewise, members who cannot hope to win in the voting game may still be able to score with external audiences, and at some future time such external support may be convertible into votes in the assembly.[81]

Attempts to create support and opposition take various forms. Support or opposition may be sought for individuals, or for factions, or for the entire public body. The appeals may be directed toward individuals or groups or mass audiences. Strategy may call for building external support or opposition for a given measure in hopes that feedback from outside publics will enhance the chances for passage or defeat of the measure by the assembly. Speakers may also try to use debate to affect the manner in which a measure will be executed.

The prevailing pattern of success or failure in appeals to outside

79. However, Barker and Rush, *Member of Parliament*, p. 136, found that 86% of the members of the House of Commons read newspaper accounts about Commons debate. For most of them, particularly old-timers, it was their only contact with the bulk of debates.

80. Cohen, *Political Process*, pp. 175–176.

81. On this point see Lindsay, *Parliament from the Press Gallery*, p. 80; also Chester L. Cooper, "The Complexities of Negotiation," *Foreign Affairs*, 46 (1968), 454.

publics may be of great significance for the general stability of political systems.[82] A well-functioning political system ordinarily requires that its constituents believe that public bodies are competent to cope with governmental problems, and that measures taken by public bodies and their officials deserve support. If public debate convinces large publics that their government is functioning poorly, public trust is sapped and the system is weakened.

The need for maintaining trust in government often tempts political leaders to omit from debate facts which may betray governmental incompetence; it also induces them to make unfounded reassuring statements about the government's ability to cope with problems. In the process, publics who are reassured may also be misled, with little opportunity for discovering where facts end and fictions begin.[83] When potential audiences have conflicting needs, this situation may severely curb what can be said in public assemblies. Many abstentions from public debates and even from voting can be explained by the need to avoid offending important external audiences.

The difficulty of attracting the attention of external audiences tempts members of public assemblies to make their messages "newsworthy" so that they are quoted in the mass media and noted by the desired outside publics. The result may be a "football stadium psychology" where scoring points becomes more important than reaching agreement.[84] Messages may be oversimplified or made unduly dramatic, as occurred during congressional debate of the 1967 rat control bill, when much of the debate was directed to external audiences. Since debate was phrased to arouse emotions which clouded issues, rather than clarifying them, it contributed to the ultimate defeat of the measure. "Representatives who impress the folks back home with their eloquent phrases, or perhaps their severe castigation of their enemies, are not always the most effective in achieving national objectives. . . ."[85]

The temptation to be dramatic can lead to extremes of character assassination. Alan Barth has described Senate subcommittee interroga-

82. Loewenberg, "Influence of Parliamentary Behavior," p. 180.

83. Murray Edelman, *The Symbolic Uses of Politics* (Urbana: University of Illinois Press, 1965), pp. 22–43.

84. The phrase is used by Dean Rusk in "Parliamentary Diplomacy — Debate Versus Negotiation," *World Affairs Interpreter*, 26 (1955), 83–88.

85. Discussion of the rat control bill is covered in Strickland, "On Ambiguity in Political Rhetoric," pp. 338–339. The quote refers to UN debates and is from Chadwick F. Alger, "Decision-Making Theory and Human Conflict," in Elton B. McNeil, *The Nature of Human Conflict* (Englewood Cliffs, N.J.: Prentice-Hall, 1965), p. 286.

tions of Owen Lattimore, a respondent during hearings designed to discredit the Communist movement before the American public. Because senators felt that the case had to be made dramatically to impress the public, extremely hostile and misleading questioning was used to defame Lattimore and picture the Communist movement as vicious. Other congressional hearings have followed similar patterns.[86]

On many occasions, extra-systemic functions may be the sole or primary task performed by debate in public assemblies. "Bilateral diplomatic meetings or multilateral conferences may be arranged for the purpose of stalling or creating a decoy which gives the illusion that a government is seriously interested in bargaining, while it really desires no agreement. . . ." Likewise, "a government may enter into diplomatic negotiations primarily for the purpose of making propaganda; it uses a conference not so much to reach agreement over a limited range of issues as to make broad appeals to the outside public, partly to undermine the bargaining position of its opponents."[87]

The U.S.–North Vietnamese negotiations in Paris are a case in point. These negotiations dragged on for years, stylized like a kabuki play, with little progress toward their ostensible goal—a negotiated peace. It was quite apparent that both sides were using the conference for distributing propaganda to a world audience: to contrast their own political virtues with the opposition's vices. Some observers charge that most public debates in the United Nations are nothing but propaganda ploys "designed primarily for public domestic and international consumption, not for the information of other delegates. The many conferences on disarmament and arms control since World War II have similarly been exploited for propaganda purposes."[88] This is too sweeping an indictment. Careful content analysis of the Mideast debates in the United Nations between 1953 and 1967 provides evidence that debates can be moderate in tone, designed to reduce conflict through discussion, rather than fanning it by appeals to outside audiences.[89] There is no reason to suspect that the Mideast debates are unique in this respect.

86. See Alan Barth, *Government by Investigation* (New York: Viking Press, 1955), and Taylor, *Grand Inquest.*

87. K. J. Holsti, *International Politics: A Framework for Analysis*, 2nd ed. (Englewood Cliffs, N.J.: Prentice-Hall, 1972), p. 189.

88. *Ibid.*; also see Joseph L. Nogee, "Propaganda and Negotiation: The Case of the Ten-Nation Disarmament Committee," *Journal of Conflict Resolution*, 7 (1963), 510-521.

89. Graber, "Conflict Images," pp. 472–484.

THE SCOPE OF DEBATE EFFECTS

A good deal has been said thus far about the purposes of verbal behavior in public assemblies without paying much attention to effects.
The remaining pages of this chapter will present empirical studies and
impressionistic observations which try to assess whether public debates
really matter. A graphic way to determine whether debate in public
assemblies has any effect on politics is to imagine what would happen
if there were no public debates. What form would a particular legislative measure or other agreement have taken if its supporters and opponents had not been allowed to speak, or had not been known to have
the option to speak? Few would contend that it would have made no
difference at all on the shape of crucial, controversial measures and on
opinions about their substance and political context. Debate impact
needs to be measured by more than passage or rejection of a measure.
When a wide variety of related consequences are considered, debate
does indeed make a sizeable difference.[90]

Whether the effect is good or bad is a quite different, often disputed
matter. The American political folklore that debating leads to better
final decisions is questioned by critics like Thurman Arnold: "The notion that legislation becomes more expert because of prolonged public
discussion of proposed measures is an illusion which follows the notion
that public debate is addressed to a thinking man through whose decisions organizations have group free will. All prolonged public discussion of any measure can do is to reconcile conflicts and get people used
to the general ideal which the measure represents."[91]

Is Anybody Listening?

To say that public debate does make a difference is not to claim that
all or even most of the debate purposes discussed earlier are fulfilled.
In fact, there seems to be more wasted effort in public assembly debates than in other forms of verbal behavior discussed thus far. As
Bernard Cohen has said about the Senate, most discussion "has little
effect on the members or on the legislation that is being debated."[92]

90. Ronald Butt, *The Power of Parliament* (London: Constable, 1967), pp.
441–444, suggests raising the hypothetical question. Also see Gross, *Legislative
Struggle*, p. 365, and Lehnen, "Behavior on the Senate Floor," p. 507. It is
instructive to compare societies where public debate is limited, or where opposition parties and factions are not allowed, with societies permitting open public
debates.

91. Arnold, *Folklore of Capitalism*, p. 380.

92. Cohen, *Political Process*, p. 175.

Intra-systemic and extra-systemic information transmission furnishes a good example of massive wastefulness. First, the opportunity to reach audiences at all, even internal ones, is usually heavily dependent on erratic mass media behavior. Except for special high-interest audiences who seek out particular information, only those few aspects of assembly behavior which the mass media cover well have a chance to be widely heard. Good mass media coverage still does not assure attentive audiences, even when the debate subject will seriously affect those audiences.

Speech effects have often been claimed but rarely proven. When stirring rhetoric is followed by actions which conform with the aims of the rhetoric, this has led to assertions that the rhetoric caused the behavior. But it is equally possible that the rhetoric reflected predispositions already present in the audience. Similarly, Richard Fenno has presented data to show that Congress is more likely to approve actions of the House Appropriations Subcommittee following verbal assurances that the subcommittee has reached its decisions unanimously. But Fenno's data do not prove a cause-and-effect sequence. There was no proof that it was the verbal assertion of unanimity, rather than the subject matter, which brought about a climate favorable to acceptance. In fact, one may well reason that the aspects of the measure that led to its unanimous acceptance by the subcommittee were also persuasive for the parent body.

Cause and effect linkages can be more readily established in the realm of interaction climates. Whiting relates a typical story about the Russians at the United Nations during the Korean debate in August, 1949. Ambassador Jacob Malik seemed to proceed on the assumption that rude and hostile speeches would make Russia's enemies yield to her demands, but rudeness brought no concessions. After the Indian ambassador, Sir Benegal Rau, had warned Malik that his verbal tactics were increasing tensions and reducing chances for agreement, the Russians switched to more polite verbiage. Thereafter, the interaction climate seemed vastly improved and progress was made toward resolving conflicts.[93]

Influence on Decision-Making

The power of speeches to change opinions has been demonstrated in a number of laboratory situations, but there have been few field tests. I know of no studies which have tested the effects of speech-making

93. Whiting, *China Crosses the Yalu*, p. 73.

in public assemblies by interviewing audiences to ascertain their attitudes prior to a speech and repeating the interview after the speech. There have been attempts to measure opinion change as a result of political campaigning which involved some speeches to political gatherings, but the results have not shown any impressive changes in opinions traceable to verbal activity of the candidates in public assemblies.[94]

Political folklore gives little weight to the persuasiveness of public speeches. Senator Carter Glass has been quoted as claiming that in twenty-eight years of legislative experience he had never known a speech to change a vote.[95] Thurman Arnold says categorically: "Public argument never convinces the other side, any more than in a way the enemy can ever be convinced." And a British commentator states that "it is doubtful whether such giants as Disraeli or Gladstone ever persuaded an opponent to vote for them."[96] Systematic analysis of Senate debates on ten issues led to similar conclusions; however, the analysis also showed that debate on amendments occasionally did change minds, apparently because amendments presented novel situations in which no prior opinions had been formed. On controversial bills, the amount of debate on amendments always exceeded comments on the bill as such, presumably because there was a better chance to affect the amendments than the bill.[97]

The study also showed that the remarks of the floor manager of a bill, however brief, seemed decisive; "his specific opposition to a proposal usually forecast its defeat."[98] Likewise, speeches by party leaders in Congress were more likely to affect the fate of measures than were speeches of more ordinary members.[99] Such observations indicate the great influence which the role of the speaker can have on the impact made by his words. Arguments of committee chairmen or party leaders tend to be persuasive not only for their substance, but also because the

94. Campaign effectiveness is discussed and documented in such works as Jay G. Blumler and Denis McQuail, *Television in Politics: Its Uses and Influences* (London: Faber and Faber, 1968), and Angus Campbell, Philip E. Converse, Warren E. Miller, Donald E. Stokes, *The American Voter* (New York: John Wiley, 1964).

95. Gross, *Legislative Struggle*, p. 366.

96. Lindsay, *Parliament from the Press Gallery*, p. 77. When Huitt studied the interaction of members of Senate and House committees during debates, he observed that members came "with a ready-made frame of reference. Facts which were compatible were fitted into it: facts which were not compatible, even when elaborately documented, were discounted, not perceived, or ignored" ("Congressional Committee," p. 354).

97. Lehnen, "Behavior on the Senate Floor," pp. 507–510.

98. *Ibid.*, p. 510.

99. Fenno, *The Power of the Purse*, pp. 469–470.

chairman is presumably knowledgeable, because the mores of Congress endorse support for his views, and because the speaker's political power makes it advisable to comply with his wishes.

Verbal strategists in public assemblies are keenly aware of political and tactical maneuvers which increase the chances that political speeches will be persuasive. Sound choices of speakers, arguments, timing, and sequencing are essential. When the controversial 1965 Education Act was under consideration, floor managers maneuvered debate in such a way that groups opposed to the principle of federal aid to education received little chance to air their views. This prevented debate on basic principles which could have killed the bill. Opponents of the bill then skillfully attacked weak spots in the measure on which its supporters had not unified their position. As a result of these verbal maneuvers, the fate of the bill seemed in doubt. Representative Brademas of Indiana was able to parry this thrust through astute questioning which permitted the bill's supporters to emphasize issues on which they could agree and around which they were able to unify their positions. Supportive party leaders were able to secure passage of a number of motions which shortened the period of debate, reducing the chances for expressing dissonant opinions. All in all, clever verbal tactics played a major part in shepherding the bill successfully through Congress.[100]

A number of scholars have contended that general debate comes too late to affect policy-making. Debates in Congress, for instance, follow extended prior discussions by subcommittees. "By the time a bill comes to the floor, the things that Congressmen say generally reflect a well-developed line-up of forces, and the opposing lines are generally drawn tightly enough to resist major changes that may be attempted through speech making alone."[101] Because of the presumed expertise of the subcommittees, the arguments against their positions may have little impact, and would-be challengers may feel that exposition of their viewpoints is useless because the parent body will publicly reject their ideas. A procedure of brainstorming sessions by the full assembly, preceding committee discussion, has been proposed. However, where the range of issues discussed by public assemblies is wide and complex, few members can acquire expertise in even a few of the issues likely to arise. Then it becomes questionable whether any procedural changes can bring about more informed general discussion.

100. Eidenberg and Morey, *Act of Congress*, pp. 125, 129, 167.
101. Gross, *Legislative Struggle*, p. 366. Also see Woodrow Wilson, *Congressional Government*, 9th ed. (Cleveland: World Publishing, 1965), p. 148; Butt, *Power of Parliament*, p. 441.

The Case for and against Debating

The general value of public debate for achieving the goals of public bodies is a matter of controversy. Many observers contend categorically that debate is generally helpful, while others argue the opposite. Evidence can be cited to support either point of view, which indicates that both may have merit. Chadwick Alger claims that discussion in a public forum is essential for the resolution of international conflicts. Participation in public assemblies helps the members to clear up misconceptions about viewpoints held by representatives from other countries and clarifies their reasoning. In the United Nations "all nations represented are continually thrown together in the discussion, lobbying, negotiation, and debate of the common agenda. During this activity each nation has an opportunity for contact with all others, in contrast to the limited choices available elsewhere." [102] Delegates may discover some common bonds with their enemies and some cleavages from their friends. Exposure of such cross-cutting conflicts increases delegates' overall willingness to search for mutually acceptable solutions.[103]

Other observers have made similar claims for domestic bodies, pointing out that assembling people with diverse views allows unparalleled insights into the real nature of conflicts dividing them. Debate can then be structured to deal with the real difficulties, as perceived by the members.[104] The view that wide public debate is helpful is part of the prevailing democratic credo in many societies; in line with it, there has been a steady and sharp trend toward institutionalizing public assemblies and publicizing the debate record.

Laboratory evidence indicates that the mere act of assembling people enhances chances for agreement. Roger Brown and others have noted a tendency toward convergence of opinions within groups. "There seems to be an almost ineradicable tendency for members of a group to move towards agreement. It occurs when there is no instruction to reach a consensus. It occurs when there is no opportunity to argue. It even occurs, incipiently, when members do not know one another's opinions but can only guess at them. It occurs when the positive relations among the members are very weak." [105] Brown explains

102. Alger, "Decision-Making Theory," pp. 274, 278.
103. Chadwick F. Alger, "Non-Resolution Consequences of the United Nations and Their Effect on International Conflict," *Journal of Conflict Resolution*, 5 (1961), 140.
104. Alger, "Decision-Making Theory," p. 276; also Huitt, "Congressional Committee," p. 364.
105. Roger Brown, *Social Psychology* (New York: Free Press, 1965), pp. 657–669.

this on the basis of Heider's principles of balance. Members of a group seek to balance their feelings of group solidarity with their attitudes toward the opinions held by the group. As a result, group decisions tend to be different from individual decisions prior to group discussion.

However, arguments that a wide exposition of all viewpoints leads to more thoughtful decision-making and compromises which can accommodate a variety of factions are counterbalanced by contrary evidence. Thus Brown's studies led to the conclusion that "group decisions following discussion are consistently riskier than individual decisions." [106] This result contradicts widely held notions that a group has a moderating influence on decisions; it may be explained by the proposition that people are bolder when they have group support and more cautious and conventional without it. Some of the most heinous political crimes, such as massacres, have been planned and executed by groups. If boldness leads to greater risk-taking, this may suggest that decisions involving individual responsibility are safer. The question of the respective quality of public assembly versus executive decision-making has periodically rocked American politics. Groups dissatisfied with presidential decisions have claimed that congressional decisions, because of their joint and public nature, would be more moderate and thoughtful. The evidence, thus far, is inconclusive.

Other risks of debate are illustrated by a study of discussions during the Naval Disarmament Conference of 1927. Public airing of problems incited hostilities, rather than settling them. "The very discussion of the subject of arms control aroused on all sides feelings of jealousy and suspicion, which had hitherto been largely dormant or even non-existent." [107] The discussions revealed how far apart the parties really were. This discovery might have been beneficial, were it not for the fact that the negotiators at the time did not realize the wide discrepancies between themselves and therefore departed with bitter feelings when the conference accomplished nothing. [108]

Public debate can also serve to harden positions. For example, UN debates on colonialism forced the colonial nations to defend and harden their stands; the positions which they took publicly were dictated by a desire to appease home constituencies. [109] Misunderstandings and in-

106. *Ibid.*, pp. 657–660.

107. David Carlton, "Great Britain and the Coolidge Naval Disarmament Conference of 1927," *Political Science Quarterly*, 83 (1968), 575.

108. *Ibid.*, p. 596.

109. Alger, "Decision-Making Theory," p. 286. Also Rusk, "Parliamentary Diplomacy." On the other hand, if nations publicly commit themselves to a new

ability to communicate may also make public assemblies counterproductive. This was demonstrated earlier by Edmund Glenn's comparisons of French, English, and Russian versions of the same UN speeches which revealed systematic differences in conceptual emphasis. The tensions in debates which can arise from different interpretations of verbal materials and from mutual misperceptions may exacerbate conflict, rather than reduce it.[110]

How does one measure the effectiveness of a public debate? D. A. Strickland has devised a simple test, based on the assumption that the primary purpose of public assemblies is to reach decisions. Any debate which yields more agreement and fewer factions is labeled "productive"; any debate which yields less agreement and more factions is "unproductive." Strickland used this test in analyzing the debate on the rat control bill in the House of Representatives in 1967. The debate had failed to increase agreement. To test the contribution to debate outcome made by various statements, Strickland developed a vagueness measure to indicate whether statements shed light on the issue at hand or clouded the picture.[111] By this test, the overall rate of clarity was high in this particular debate, with proponents of the measure making clearer arguments than its opponents. Still, the debate was ineffective in reducing opinion divergencies because issues which were brought to the fore dealt with extraneous matters, such as federal encroachment on local control, or the need for general pest control laws. Opponents inquired sarcastically whether rats were a "type of migratory wild life? Should the federal government be responsible for controlling other biting creatures such as bugs and squirrels?"[112] Such arguments diverted attention from the main issues. Strickland complained that politicians were hiding "snugly in thickets of obscurantism" so that "the posing of issues and the sequential effects of irrelevancy and ambiguity" instigated "a degenerative repertoire even where the ostensible issue and the political context call for responsible deliberation."[113]

position, this may counteract hardening of previous attitudes. Alger, "Non-Resolution Consequences," p. 139.

110. Edmund S. Glenn, "Meaning and Behavior: Communication and Culture," Journal of Communication, 16 (1966), 266–270.

111. "Vague" statements were defined as "utterances which, in context, do not seem to contain any information or which contain several unresolved meanings." Strickland scored utterances with no vagueness as 0, utterances containing innuendo, double entendre or puns as 1, and utterances with vague or multiple meanings beyond that category as 2. Strickland, "On Ambiguity in Political Rhetoric," p. 340.

112. Ibid., p. 343.

113. Ibid., p. 344. Huitt also stresses clarity of debate as an important index of effectiveness; "Congressional Committee," p. 347.

Kenneth Boulding proposes a more impressionistic measure to gauge the likelihood of reaching agreement through debate. He contends that there is a critical watershed in opinion cleavages in groups. If opposing opinions are on the same side of the watershed, then debate is likely to bring the opinions together to a consensus, while opinions on opposite sides of the watershed are more likely to be driven apart.[114] Boulding provides no tests to measure where the watershed lies in a given set of issues. In some cases, the precise wording used in formulating positions may make it simple to determine whether opposing positions fall on the same side of the watershed or on opposite sides. If consensus is desired, a compromise verbal formulation which takes this into account may make it possible to avoid crossing the watershed.

SUMMARY

Sparse attendance at public debates and unfavorable comments about them give the impression that they are largely a waste of time. Still, people vie for the right to speak, and the proceedings of public assemblies are widely reported. Several factors explain the paradox. First, the significance of debate has been judged by many yardsticks, besides the most obvious one of assessing its contribution to clarification of the subject under discussion. Depending on what aspects of debate effects are measured, the evaluation of its importance may vary considerably. Second, the range of significance of debates varies widely: some are trivial and fleeting, others fateful and lasting. Merely bringing certain matters to public attention through the words of official spokesmen in an open forum may have important consequences. This explains why politicians often strive eagerly to have certain matters brought out in debate, forcing speakers to take a stand, or why they seek to suppress other matters from debate in hopes of avoiding public alignment of proponents and opponents.

The fact that assembly debates are public and interactive imposes constraints on their conduct. In the political culture of the United States, speakers must stress ideal norms of behavior, morally and politically, regardless of the practicability of these norms. On the one hand, this need may lock speakers into untenable stands on issues, to the

---

114. Kenneth E. Boulding, *The Image: Knowledge in Life and Society* (Ann Arbor: University of Michigan Press, 1956), p. 133. For similar lines of reasoning, see also Carolyn W. Sherif, Muzafer Sherif, and Roger Nebergall, *Attitude and Attitude Change* (Philadelphia: W. B. Saunders, 1965), and Carl I. Hovland and Milton Rosenberg, eds., *Attitude Organization and Change* (New Haven: Yale University Press, 1960).

detriment of subsequent political bargaining; on the other hand, the obvious unreality of the idealized posture raises vexing questions about the boundary between political ritual and reality. Posturing is partly restrained by the desire to avoid public commitments, and by the fear of having rhetorical bubbles instantly pricked by the barbs of verbal rebuttal.

Because verbal pronouncements in public assemblies reach large and often diverse audiences, speakers find it difficult to tailor their communications to the needs of particular audiences. They may decide to be vague to leave meanings uncertain, or ambiguous to permit a variety of politically useful interpretations of the message. Studies of debate patterns have revealed a number of verbal strategies by which speakers seek to accomplish their purposes in public settings, but these studies have not yet produced theories to predict the types of messages generated under given circumstances, and the types of verbal interchanges likely to yield particular results.

Certain restraints are imposed on debates by the need to maintain a good climate for verbal interaction within an assembly. Formal debate procedure, stylized forms of address, and informal guidelines help preserve politeness and calm. Many of these rules are based on the assumption that avoidance of anger and fear enhances the prospects for successful verbal interaction. Techniques have been developed for tracing and categorizing patterns of verbal interaction, but little is known about the effects of these patterns on the impact of verbal interactions in public assemblies.

Aside from airing views on the topic under discussion in a public assembly, debate serves a number of other intra-systemic, extra-systemic, and ego-enhancing functions. Intra-systemic functions include information dissemination to members, building or destroying the unity of assembly factions, preparing for future political actions, and providing official rationales and justifications for actions. Tactical maneuvers are also common, such as verbal smokescreens to distract attention from a topic and deflect it to another, and filibusters designed to delay or obstruct action completely.

Public assemblies may also be used as forums for addressing outside publics. Purposes of address include attempts to disseminate information to outsiders, efforts to build up support for certain policies, or endeavors to inspire confidence in the political system. The desire to appeal to outside publics may tempt speakers into flamboyant verbal behavior in hopes of attracting wide and prominent mass media coverage for their remarks. At times, public meetings are arranged or conducted primarily for their propaganda value in swaying external audiences. As in public pageants, speakers unfold carefully prepared scenarios before audiences who presumably are dazzled by the status of the actors and the solemnity of the setting.

Speakers may also talk solely or partly to enhance their psychological well-being and their own political fortunes. They may attempt through their speeches to affect the careers of their political friends and enemies in order to gain future support or destroy potential opposition.

The effects of debates in public assemblies on internal and external audiences depend on many factors besides the substance and quality of the messages. It matters how, when, where, and by whom arguments are made. The speakers' political status is especially important; messages by floor managers of bills and by party leaders carry an extra increment of persuasiveness which messages from less strategically placed individuals lack. The timing and sequencing of messages which regulate the flow of debate help determine the success or failure of propositions under discussion; hence politicians vie for the opportunity to control debate flow, and they entrust it to those most highly skilled in the techniques of verbal maneuvering. To steer debates toward successful outcomes, debate managers must also control the subject matter of discussion to avoid unduly divisive topics, or the excessive hardening of positions while verbal battle-lines are drawn.

Given the fact that public debates accomplish a wide variety of purposes for a large array of participants, criteria for measuring success or failure must carefully delineate the types of goal achievements by which the debate is to be judged. Whether or not the effects are generally valuable or disadvantageous is an unanswerable question. Public debate is a tool; the desirability of the end product depends on the norms and goals of particular observers.

9 Verbal Behavior in Small Bargaining Groups

> . . . most conflict situations are essentially *bargaining* situations.
> They are situations in which the ability of one participant to gain his
> ends is dependent to an important degree on the choices or deci-
> sions that the other participant will make. . . .
> The "obvious" outcome depends greatly on how the problem is
> formulated, on what analogies or precedents the definition of the
> bargaining issue calls to mind, on the kinds of data that may be
> available to bear on the question in dispute.
> — Thomas C. Schelling, *The Strategy of Conflict*[1]

> The compleat negotiator . . . should have a quick mind but un-
> limited patience, know how to dissemble without being a liar,
> inspire trust without trusting others, be modest but assertive, charm
> others without succumbing to their charm, and possess plenty of
> money and a beautiful wife while remaining indifferent to all tempta-
> tions of riches and women.
> — Fred Charles Iklé, *How Nations Negotiate*[2]

THE NATURE OF SMALL BARGAINING GROUPS

The Consequences of Small Size and Privacy

A definition of "small bargaining group" will indicate how this chapter differs from the preceding one. "Small" is used in two senses; most
importantly, it refers to the immediate audience of the verbal behavior.
In a small bargaining group, the audience which will hear the communication is limited to the group in attendance. This intimate setting,
remote from the limelight of publicity, permits far greater frankness.
Negotiators like Clemenceau, Orlando, Lloyd George, and Wilson, at
the Paris Peace Conference of 1919, chose to gather in a tiny room to
exclude large numbers of aides and reporters. They were seeking the
benefit of a small group meeting to expedite the conduct of their business.[3] Bargainers in a small group need not worry about possible im-

---

1. Thomas C. Schelling, *The Strategy of Conflict* (London: Oxford University Press, 1968), pp. 5, 69.
2. Fred Charles Iklé, *How Nations Negotiate* (New York: Praeger, 1964), p. 253.
3. Jack Sawyer and Harold Guetzkow, "Bargaining and Negotiations in International Relations," in Herbert Kelman, ed., *International Behavior* (New York: Holt, Rinehart and Winston, 1965), p. 493.

mediate effects of their words on outside audiences. They need not impress the galleries by firm statements of non-negotiable positions which typically issue from open gatherings and which reduce the chances of compromise. Instead, they can concentrate on reaching agreement.

The Cuban missile crisis illustrates the point. "Although the Security Council meetings offered the most obvious points of contact between representatives of the two sides, these formal meetings were almost entirely given over to rhetorical debate and did not, for the most part, facilitate effective communication. On the other hand, the headquarters setting in New York furnished a useful context for less formal contacts between Stevenson and Zorin as well as among members of their staffs." [4] Away from the glare of publicity, it was possible to make concessions, reach compromises, and lay the groundwork for settling the dispute.

Second, the fact that there are only a few participants in small bargaining groups seems to make such groups better suited for decision-making. "One of the more fundamental notions of group discussion is that the process becomes unwieldly when the members can no longer sit around the table facing each other . . . if the group can be kept in size where members can talk in conversational tones, without spending much effort in trying to locate a respondent, the efficiency of the group is improved." [5]

Members of small groups also interact more smoothly; "smaller groups inhibit expressions of disagreements and dissatisfaction more than large groups . . . as size increases, there will be decreasing cohesiveness." [6] So, too, it is easier to assess one's collaborators and opponents in a face-to-face situation. In a more intimate setting, one can more readily "communicate a way of life, a set of attitudes, an approach to adversity, integrity, empathy, common sense." [7] One can also usually get feedback more readily than in a public setting, where negotiators may have to await formal instructions before making a reply. With

4. Oran R. Young, *The Politics of Force: Bargaining During International Crises* (Princeton: Princeton University Press, 1968), p. 139. Also see Arthur Lall, *Modern International Negotiation: Principles and Practice* (New York: Columbia University Press, 1966), p. 331.

5. Gerald M. Phillips, *Communications and the Small Group* (New York: Bobbs-Merrill, 1966), p. 42.

6. E. J. Thomas and C. F. Fink, "Effects of Group Size," *Psychological Bulletin*, 60 (1963), 375. The findings were based on laboratory experiments. Also see Erwin P. Bettinghaus, *Persuasive Communication* (New York: Holt, Rinehart and Winston, 1968), pp. 200–202, and sources cited there.

7. Jeremy J. Stone, *Strategic Persuasion: Arms Limitations through Dialogue* (New York: Columbia University Press, 1967), p. 4.

ready feedback, uncertainties can be clarified on the spot and the participants can be more certain that they understand each other.[8] However, in some small bargaining groups, the negotiators receive such rigid instructions that instant feedback is precluded. Sometimes Russian negotiators have not been free to agree to punctuations of minutes of proceedings without authorization from their home office.[9]

Reaching Agreement through Group Interaction

This brings us to the second element of the definition, "bargaining." As used in this chapter, small bargaining groups are interacting primarily to reach a specific agreement — framing a law or portions of law, designing executive or administrative procedures, drafting a treaty, or settling a boundary dispute. The essence of the bargaining process lies in the presentation of a variety of viewpoints by members of the group, and ensuing verbal interaction to narrow alternatives to a single common choice. This chapter is chiefly concerned with the verbal aspects of this process whereby decisions are reached through explicit verbal bargaining.[10]

Of course, larger groups may also strive for agreements, but, as discussed in the previous chapter, goals other than decision-making are often most important in public assemblies. A speech which has propaganda effects on an outside audience or establishes a record for the future may fulfill its major purposes, even if no converts are won in the assembly and no decisions are reached. In small bargaining groups, motives other than reaching agreement are not lacking, but they tend to be less prevalent and tempting.

The designation "group" indicates that a number of people are jointly and interactively involved in the decision-making process. It

8. Harold J. Leavitt and Ronald A. H. Mueller, "Some Effects of Feedback on Communication," in A. Paul Hare, Edgar F. Borgatta, and Robert F. Bales, eds., *Small Groups: Studies in Social Interaction* (New York: Alfred A. Knopf, 1965), pp. 442–443.

9. K. J. Holsti, *International Politics: A Framework for Analysis*, 2nd ed. (Englewood Cliffs, N.J.: Prentice-Hall, 1972), p. 206.

10. For a general discussion of communications variables in decision-making, see Michael Haas, "Communication Factors in Decision Making," *Peace Research Society Papers*, 12 (1969), esp. pp. 67–80. Tacit bargaining is discussed in Thomas C. Schelling, *Arms and Influence* (New Haven: Yale University Press, 1966), pp. 137–150. Charles Walcott and P. Terrence Hopmann, "Interaction Analysis and Bargaining Behavior," APSA paper (1972), p. 1, describe bargaining as involving the offer of "tentative formulas for mutually agreeable exchanges of values," attempts to "modify the preferences of other participants," and attempts to "resolve differences and to arrive at mutually satisfactory solutions."

is "two or more people who, for a given period of time, are concerned with a mutual goal and who devote their efforts during this time to the achievement of that goal." [11] Usually there is face-to-face interaction in a joint meeting so that group dynamics come into play. Our focus on bargaining in small face-to-face groups does not mean that all bargaining takes place in such units; some or all bargaining may occur without face-to-face communication of the parties. As a matter of fact, in many situations bargaining is a mixed process, with part of it taking place in groups and part of it occurring in other settings.

The Berlin crisis of 1948–49 provides an illustration. When the Russians were barring Western access to Berlin, negotiations to solve pending problems took place through a combination of group meetings and other forms of message transmission. There were high-level exchanges of formal notes emanating from the heads of states, foreign ministers, and ambassadors in distant capitals; these notes tended to be stiff and "to imprison each side a degree more tightly in the web of argument." [12] There were also informal interchanges, such as ostensibly offhand remarks by Secretary of State Dean Acheson, and offers conveyed by Premier Stalin in answering interview questions by an American newspaperman. And there was a formal Security Council debate. During the 1961 sequel of the crisis, Premier Khrushchev made a number of sabre-rattling speeches and President Kennedy did the same; each was intent on communicating important bargaining information to the other side. None of these communications involved a small group setting.

Discussions by the protagonists with third parties represented at the United Nations were meant to relay information to the other side without direct and formal contacts. Indirect bargaining was supplemented by a number of direct encounters which illustrate the wide variety of small bargaining groups which may become involved in settling a particular dispute. There were face-to-face meetings at high levels involving ambassadors, foreign ministers, and heads of state. There was an abortive four-power conference of financial representatives, and a session of the Council of Foreign Ministers which met in London. At a somewhat lower level, there were meetings of the military governors of Germany and the commandants of Berlin. The Allied Control Commission for Germany convened, as did the Berlin Kommandatura. On the most informal level, there was the famous washroom encounter between Ambassadors Philip Jessup and Jacob Malik at the United Na-

11. Phillips, *Communications and the Small Group*, p. 7.
12. Young, *Politics of Force*, pp. 118–130. The quote appears on p. 130.

tions. This least formal of all contacts was later credited with being the decisive step in breaking the ice on blocked negotiations.[13]

Small group bargaining is particularly important in politics because most political transactions, especially in a democracy, ultimately take place in small groups. As Gerald Phillips has observed, "Small group methods dominate our decision-making, problem solving and information-seeking activities."[14] Reputedly, "in government . . . there are more planning groups and committees than there are people on the government payroll."[15] Much of the work of legislative assemblies is done by committees and subcommittees. Likewise, executive organizations work through problem-solving committees which are set up to analyze particular problems, decision-making committees which are charged with deciding policies, and planning committees which are entrusted with planning the work of a particular organization.

Even at the top levels of government, where decisions are presumably made by highly placed individuals, most decisions spring from a small group process and involve the interaction of various (often clashing) opinions. "Rarely can advocates of a particular policy prevail without engaging in processes of negotiation, bargaining, and coalition-building."[16] When President Kennedy made decisions regarding the Cuban missile crisis or the Bay of Pigs invasion, he assembled a small group of advisors for the decision-making process. Even President Johnson's very personal decision to leave the presidency after only one term was reached with the help of a group of advisors.[17]

The Limits of Small Group Effectiveness

One reason for the popularity of small group bargaining in the Western world is the fact that political folklore pictures talking in small groups as one of the best ways to settle disputes.[18] In fact, some people believe that all disputes are solvable, if groups interact properly. Scientific evidence about the effectiveness of the group process in bringing about solutions in general, and desirable solutions in particular, is

13. *Ibid.*
14. Phillips, *Communications and the Small Group*, p. 10.
15. *Ibid.*, p. 120.
16. Alexander L. George, "The Case for Multiple Advocacy in Making Foreign Policy," APSA paper (1971), p. 10.
17. Phillips, *Communications and the Small Group*, p. 10.
18. Laura Nader, in a postscript to Burton's article, contends that preference for face-to-face interaction must be considered a cultural attribute which may vary from culture to culture. John W. Burton, "Resolution of Conflict," *International Studies Quarterly*, 16, (1972), 55.

scanty; most of it rests on laboratory findings, rather than on field studies. Laboratory studies show that it is easier to develop trust and cooperation in face-to-face group settings than when no meeting takes place. Morton Deutsch found that college students who had an opportunity to meet face-to-face in a situation which motivated them to maximize their own gains chose a cooperative solution in 59 percent of the cases, instead of the 13 percent rate prevalent when no face-to-face communication had taken place.[19] In a similar experiment J. L. Loomis discovered that, in addition to increased cooperation, students who communicated face-to-face expressed more trust in each other. Other laboratory experiments have shown the importance of trust in reaching satisfactory settlements.[20]

The records of a number of international crises also reveal that when small group bargaining was used, along with other forms of bargaining, the face-to-face negotiations accomplished their purposes better than other methods. The case of the Cuban missile crisis has already been mentioned; other examples come from East-West confrontations in Berlin and from the Taiwan Strait crisis of 1958, where "the formal sessions at Warsaw proved entirely irrelevant."[21]

Even when face-to-face meetings do not solve a problem, observers often feel that the personal contact has helped to create a climate more favorable to future conflict resolution. Participants can gauge how strongly opposing sides feel about particular questions; they can test what is really understood by the other side and what is unclear. They may learn which issues may benefit from future negotiations and which issues present little hope for compromise.[22]

When face-to-face negotiations do not succeed, disappointment tends to be acute because of the high initial expectations. "We expect our threats to be efficacious, our warnings to be sobering, our offers to be enticing, our guarantees to be reassuring, and our logic to be airtight. But it is always possible that our threats will seem provocative, our warnings laughable, our efforts insignificant, our guarantees flimsy, and our logic self-serving."[23]

19. Morton Deutsch, "Trust and Suspicion," *Journal of Conflict Resolution,* 2 (1958), 265–279. The bulk of small group research involves cooperative groups where all members stand to gain by a common solution. The study of groups involved in zero-sum or mixed-motive bargaining has generally been neglected. See Walcott and Hopmann, "Interaction Analysis," p. 2.

20. J. L. Loomis, "Communication, the Development of Trust, and Cooperative Behavior," *Human Relations,* 12 (1959), 305–317.

21. Young, *Politics of Force,* p. 121.

22. Stone, *Strategic Persuasion,* p. 61.

23. *Ibid.,* p. 8.

There are many reasons why bargaining groups may fail. Their creators, though endowing them with all the necessary characteristics, may not really intend to use them for bargaining. Some American presidents have used their cabinets as interactive decision-making bodies, while others used them merely as a forum for the presentation of reports. In the latter case, one could hardly expect group decisions to emerge. Soviet-American disarmament negotiations, even in their more private phases, likewise have often been nothing but "parallel monologues in which the basic appeals are made to the galleries of world public opinion, rather than across the table to the opposition." [24]

Some of the sources of misunderstanding which may abort small group bargaining are long-standing differences in perception about the nature of the problem, reinforced by differing perceptions of ongoing developments. Prior predispositions about changing political realities may prove troublesome, as may miscalculations about the motivations and strengths and weaknesses of various parties whose interests are under consideration. As Oran Young remarked in regard to well-designed but ineffective bargaining efforts in the Taiwan crisis of 1958 and the Berlin crisis of 1961, "There is no necessary correlation or causal connection between sheer communication and genuine understanding." [25]

The interaction process within small groups which produces bargains is also strongly affected by the parties' overall perception of the interrelationship of the constituencies which they represent, and of their personal role interactions. Group members may be basically antagonistic to each other for political and personal reasons, and hence more intent on expressing that hostility than on searching for agreements; they may be basically friendly and eager to reach agreement and willing to pay a price for it; or they may take an intermediate stance. [26]

Put in the terminology of game theory, negotiations may be viewed as a zero-sum game or positive-sum game. [27] In the zero-sum game, each

24. Lloyd Jensen, "Soviet-American Bargaining Behavior in the Postwar Disarmament Negotiations," *Journal of Conflict Resolution*, 7 (1963), 522.

25. Young, *Politics of Force*, p. 144.

26. The effects of basic attitudes on bargaining outcomes are discussed in Henry A. Landsberger, "Interaction Process Analysis of the Mediation of Labor Management Disputes," in Hare, Borgatta, and Bales, eds., *Small Groups*, pp. 490–94. Landsberger concludes that "ultimate success of the session could be partially predicted from the parties' state of mind when they embarked upon the session: the more hostile their expressed feelings, the less likelihood of success" (*ibid.*, p. 493).

27. Schelling, *Strategy of Conflict*, pp. 88ff.; Harvey A. Hornstein and David W. Johnson, "The Effects of Process Analysis and Ties to His Group upon the

side believes that its own gains are the other side's loss and vice versa. If this view is taken, each side tends to rigidly hold out for its optimum gain. If a positive-sum game is conceptualized, the parties believe that solutions are possible which permit simultaneous gain for both. Such an outlook facilitates arrival at a mutually satisfactory solution. In a mixed game, parties share some goals and clash on others; success in negotiations then depends on sensitivity to each other's interests and willingness to compromise.

Bargaining within the Common Market is a good example of successful interaction in a bargaining relationship where perceived gains and losses are mixed. The positive-sum approach is more likely to characterize routine domestic legislative and administrative situations, while the zero-sum approach often characterizes bargaining to solve already existing conflicts, especially those which concern distribution of resources. The zero-sum approach is quite common in international bargaining and is likely to lead to bargaining failures.[28]

Another factor which may mitigate against the effective use of small groups for decision-making is the intragroup role perception of the delegates. As in public assemblies, delegates may see themselves primarily as representatives of constituencies whose interests must not be surrendered, rather than as members of a group charged with performing a cooperative task. In some groups there is a progression from the delegate role to the group member role, if the group's operations develop group loyalty. Elected officials (in contrast to appointed or self-selected ones) are least likely to succumb to such group influences.[29]

To encourage the development of group spirit, during the Cuban missile crisis President Kennedy developed what has been called the "collegial style of policy making."[30] Rather than bringing together advisors from different branches of government to plead the cases of their constituencies, he created a special *ad hoc* group to constitute a new body. Each member was requested to think through the whole crisis, not only his special concerns. This approach helped to "maintain a broad-gauged atmosphere in which all relevant political, military, in-

Negotiator's Attitudes toward the Outcome of Negotiations," *Journal of Applied Behavioral Science*, 2 (1966), 450ff.; Holsti, *International Politics*, pp. 193–94.

28. Schelling, *Strategy of Conflict*, p. 21.

29. Seymour Scher, "Congressional Committee Members as Independent Agency Overseers: A Case Study," *American Political Science Review*, 54 (1960), 911–920; Ralph K. Huitt, "The Congressional Committee: A Case Study," *American Political Science Review*, 48 (1954), 344ff. Huitt discusses different roles played by senators in their committee work.

30. George, "Case for Multiple Advocacy," pp. 24–25.

telligence, and diplomatic considerations could be identified, and the relationship among them kept in mind in devising and assessing alternative courses of action." [31]

Even when small bargaining groups work effectively to reach decisions, there may be reasons for dissatisfaction. The privacy and secrecy which these groups enjoy may encourage shady dealings. Unscrupulous negotiators may be "plotting for private gain at the public's expense (as in the case of log-rolling, bribery, secret treaty negotiations, and often slate making). . . . To the extent that it is suggested that the participants are engaged in making deals to promote the interests of their own services, agencies, or economic groupings, these proceedings are looked upon with suspicion, rather than favor." [32]

Despite such reservations about small group bargaining, and despite the fact that many small groups do not function well, the fact remains that the most successful bargaining interactions normally occur in small groups. The folklore that it is easier to reach agreement in face-to-face bargaining groups than in other kinds of meetings is supported by the evidence, particularly in Western settings. Whether or not small group deliberations yielded a better result than a different form of negotiation in any particular case cannot be known, for history plays most of its dramas only once. We cannot test whether a change of setting for the cast of characters would have yielded a happier ending.

INTERACTIVE BEHAVIOR IN SMALL GROUPS

Creating a Productive Interaction Climate

Since small bargaining groups, as defined here, are comparatively remote from the limelight of publicity, many of the constraints imposed by publicity do not apply. There is little need for posturing, for appealing to outside audiences, for guarding against public exposure of ill-tempered behavior. Yet publicity is not the only curb on unrestrained interaction. Every social setting, including the small group setting, imposes restraints on the individuals involved in it. These restraints spring from internalized cultural norms of proper behavior, from the necessity to behave in a manner which makes group goal achievement possible, and from the consequences of human interaction in groups.[33]

31. *Ibid.*, p. 27. Also see Alexander L. George, "The Case for Multiple Advocacy in Making Foreign Policy," *American Political Science Review*, 64 (1972), 751–785.

32. Murray Edelman, *The Symbolic Uses of Politics* (Urbana: University of Illinois Press, 1964), p. 147.

33. See James D. Barber, *Power in Committees: An Experiment in the Govern-

In most groups, particularly in Western culture, there is an implied norm of reciprocity in group settings. The individual expects that the actions which he feels at liberty to take may be reciprocated by others,[34] so he limits his behavior to actions which he would not mind having reciprocated. He restrains personal invective, steers clear of topics and conceptualizations which might obstruct the group's progress, and limits verbal input to allow others to participate in the discussion.

If a group member puts little value on achieving the goals set for the group, the force of these restraints subsides. Moreover, there is some controversy about the value of various behavioral norms in furthering group decision-making. Russian negotiators have frequently felt that rudeness served important bargaining purposes better than polite conduct — "Khrushchev's infamous shoe in the United Nations was used as a gavel, not as a cudgel to hit an antagonist."[35] Rudeness "may serve as a counter-offensive to discourage the enemy, it may be a defense against inner temptations to reveal one's weaknesses . . . or it may reassure oneself that one is not succumbing to the temptation of entertaining good feelings towards the enemy or of imputing such feelings to him."[36] While Western democracies have heeded the adage that more flies are caught with molasses than with vinegar, the great totalitarian powers of the twentieth century have acted otherwise. Their negotiating style has been characterized by the use of intemperate language, arbitrary and rigid interpretations of agreements, and frequent deception.[37] Their high rate of failure to reach agreements may testify to the ineptness of these tactics if reaching agreements was, in fact, their goal. In the 1970's Russian and Chinese negotiators have changed their bargaining styles somewhat in the direction of greater politeness and moderation.

In some respects, constraints on hostile behavior are more severe in small groups because members tend to develop personal ties to each other. Personal liking for group members may prevent individual participants from expressing hostilities linked to conflicting official posi-

---

mental Process (Chicago: Rand McNally, 1966), pp. 110ff., for a discussion of the development of an integrative group culture. Erving Goffman, Strategic Interaction (Philadelphia: University of Pennsylvania Press, 1970), p. 136, notes that "internalized standards constitute the chief enforcement system for communication in society."

34. For a discussion of cultural differences in group norms, see Brenda Danet, "The Language of Persuasion in Bureaucracy: 'Modern' and 'Traditional' Appeals to Israel Customs Authorities," American Sociological Review, 36 (1971), 847–859.

35. Iklé, How Nations Negotiate, p. 116.

36. Ibid., pp. 90, 116. The quote is based on studies by Nathan Leites.

37. Holsti, International Politics, pp. 202–206.

tions. An atmosphere of mutual acceptance and cooperation may make disagreement difficult and may even foster uniformity of opinion. On the other hand, a small group can also engender greater hostility among its members because more intimate contact allows personalities to rub and clash more readily. In such cases there may be much more expression of hostility than one would find in a public assembly because the constraints imposed by an outside audience are lacking. Joint decision-making may become impossible.

Fred Iklé has compiled some "rules of accommodation" which must be obeyed to keep the negotiating atmosphere relaxed. They are based on the "shopkeeper" approach, which assumes that agreements can be reached through compromise, that compromise is "a sensible, fair, and rational way of reaching agreement over contentious issues," and that "expressions of good will toward the opponent, as well as frankness and candor in discussions, will produce an atmosphere conducive to compromise." [38] Iklé's rules prescribe that: "unambiguous lies must be avoided, explicit promises have to be kept, invective is never to be used, explicit threats must not be issued, agreements in principle must not be blatantly violated when it comes to the execution of details, and mutual understandings must not be deliberately misconstrued later on." In addition to these "hard" rules, there are "soft" rules which may occasionally be violated. Among them are rules that "the opponent's domestic difficulties should not be exploited in public, debts of gratitude should be honored . . . motives should not be impugned, and the discourse ought to be reasonable in the sense that questions are answered, arguments are to the point, facts are not grossly distorted, repetition is minimized, and technical discussions are kept on a factual level." [39]

In the small group setting, it is not only easier to compromise, but also easier to sense what sorts of compromises are necessary and at what point in the proceedings they can be made to greatest advantage. Verbal clues are supplemented by paralinguistic clues and knowledge of the idiosyncrasies of group members. [40] Experience with the dynamics of a particular group allows the members to accurately judge the precise verbal formulations that will lead to a helpful interaction climate.

The physical setting in which the group meets is also significant for creating a sound interaction atmosphere. John Burton of the Centre for

38. Quotes from *ibid.*, p. 200. "Shopkeeper" approach is a phrase coined by Harold Nicolson, *Diplomacy*, 3rd ed. (London: Oxford University Press, 1963), pp. 52–54.

39. Iklé, *How Nations Negotiate*, p. 87.

40. On the importance of paralinguistic cues in small group communication, see Goffman, *Strategic Interaction*, p. 9.

the Analysis of Conflict at University College, London, contends that placing a bargaining group into an academic setting will predispose the participants to behave with proper academic decorum, detachment, and impartiality.[41] Others advocate the seclusion of a remote resort, preferably with awe-inspiring scenery, or meeting in a place rich in relevant historic memories. Public buildings may provide an edifying setting, primarily through their architecture and decorations. Bargaining sessions have often occurred in surroundings rich in creature comforts — including the proverbial wine, women, and song — designed to induce pleasant moods in the participants. This type of staging is more easily arranged for a small group than for a large public assembly.

The Interplay of Verbal Stimuli and Verbal Responses

Thus far, this chapter has covered general factors springing from the interactive setting and certain general rules which set bounds to acceptable interactive behavior. It has not dealt with the substance of the process — the selection, formulation, and interplay of verbalized ideas in group bargaining sessions — and its effects on the group's operation. Unfortunately, research is quite meager in this area.

Although the processes and effects of interactions among members of small groups have received extensive study, particularly by sociologists, little effort has gone into analysis of message interchange as such, despite the fact that exchange of messages is the chief mode of interaction of small groups. When verbal behavior has been studied, emphasis has been on the messages' effects on group members, and on the mode of speech, rather than on the messages' substance and interplay. For instance, Bales' Interaction Process Analysis (discussed in the previous chapter) focuses on the part verbal interaction plays in accomplishing a group's goals. The analyst codes the verbal mode and apparent effect of propositions submitted to the group, and he notes whether people made suggestions, asked questions, gave evaluations, or built or destroyed personal good feelings. Yet, the substance of the verbal interchange which produced these results is not recorded or analyzed. We do not know the nature of the suggestions, the thrust of questions and evaluations, or the subject matter which influenced personal rapport.[42]

41. John W. Burton, "Resolution of Conflict," p. 22.

42. Research methods for group analysis are discussed by Karl E. Weick, "Systematic Observational Methods," in Gardner Lindzey and Elliot Aronson, eds., *Handbook of Social Psychology* (Reading, Mass.: Addison Wesley, 1968), pp. 357-451. For analysis of verbal behavior, see esp. pp. 381-401. An interesting modification of Bales' analysis, IPS (Interaction Process Scores), is discussed in

A brief review of various group analysis techniques will indicate how heavily group interactions depend on the interplay of particular messages. Yet the importance of the substance of messages responsible for the verbal interaction dynamics is implied rather than expressed, and few guidelines are provided for appraising message content. A description of Interaction Process Analysis notes that "the interactionist counts and classifies both verbal and non-verbal communications and then applies content analysis to the results in order to predict disunity, power struggles, and conflict between task and socio-emotional ideals," [43] but it does not stress the importance of particular verbalizations. If verbal behavior can reveal disunity, struggles for power, and socio-emotional status, it does so through specific verbal formulations which affect group interaction. Since production of particular verbal expressions is a deliberate process, a group which does not want to display hostility can conceal it and use other statements to create a different verbal climate with other interaction consequences.

A variant of Interaction Process Analysis, Sign Process Analysis, measures the interaction climate created by group discussions. The analyst examines the interrelation of positive, negative, and neutral remarks. Negatively phrased statements presumably hamper the achievement of group goals, while positively phrased statements may help the group to reach agreement. This implies — without explaining the possibilities — that a change in phrasing can decisively affect the conduct of the group's business. When a half-rainy day becomes half-dry, more than the weather may be improved.

In the sociometric approach to small group study, various research techniques, including analysis of verbal interactions, are used to discover interpersonal affinities and rejections within groups. Again, this indicates the large role of words in creating and reflecting human interaction patterns. Sociometricians assume that "groups of individuals who are favorably disposed towards each other will operate more effectively than those where individuals manifesting hostility are present." [44] Consequently, sociometry has been used both formally and informally to compose groups likely to engage in friendly communication and hence expected to interact effectively.

Edgar F. Borgatta, "A Systematic Study of Interaction Process Scores, Peer and Self-assessments, Personality and Other Variables," *Genetics-Psychology Monographs*, 65 (1962), 219–291. Also see Walcott and Hopmann, "Interaction Analysis," pp. 4–7, for their BPA (Bargaining Process Analysis), developed to study bargaining in international groups, such as test ban negotiating groups.
43. Phillips, *Communications and the Small Group*, p. 44.
44. *Ibid.*, p. 43.

Still another approach to the study of group dynamics is psychiatric gaming analysis. "Communication in a small group can be understood as a multiplayer game . . . an ongoing series of complementary, ulterior transactions progressing to a well-defined outcome." People tend to have patterns in their personal communications and to expect patterned responses. These "standardized verbal responses in which there are regular moves in response to regular moves can be referred to as the 'interaction game.'"[45] Through the study of verbal interchanges, transactional psychiatrists identify the verbal game played by groups; many such games have readily predictable results.[46] Group members may be unaware of the game into which they may have stumbled through the use of phrases whose impact they did not fully fathom. Once they become aware of the verbal stimuli which elicit certain responses, they can play interaction games to maximize gains and minimize losses. Examples of verbal games which are frequently played in politics are "Sweet Reason" and "I Want My Way." In the former, group members verbalize areas of agreement and gloss over disagreements; in the latter, one or several group members use standard phrases to indicate that they will not budge from their stated position.[47]

Phenomenological analysis, cognitive theories, and systems analysis likewise rely heavily on the study of verbal interactions in small groups. In phenomenological analysis, the emphasis is on the group as an entity, rather than on interaction of individual group members. However, verbal interaction of group members is analyzed because it gives the group its character so that one can talk about group opinions and group decisions. Cognitive theories explain the interactions of group members primarily on the basis of verbal communications transmitted and received by group members. A member's reactions to verbal interchange in the group will vary depending on whether new units of information are consonant or dissonant with what he already knows, largely through verbal transmissions.[48] Systems analysis "is based on the belief that alteration in agenda or procedure of a group can alter the quality of its output."[49] Since much of a group's agenda involves verbal interaction, this approach, too, places heavy emphasis on the type of verbal interaction which takes place within a group.

45. *Ibid.*, p. 111.

46. The technique is discussed fully in Eric Berne, *The Structure and Dynamics of Organizations and Groups* (Philadelphia: J. B. Lippincott, 1963).

47. Phillips, *Communications and the Small Group*, p. 112.

48. For a full discussion, see Leon Festinger, "Informal Social Communication," *Psychological Review*, 57 (1950), 271–292.

49. *Ibid.*, pp. 47–50.

Social scientists have discovered some regular interaction patterns in their analyses of verbal interactions in small bargaining groups. For instance, Bales' Interaction Process Analysis detected regular verbal steps by which group members move sequentially from initial statements of problems to final decisions.[50] During group meetings, the rates of giving information tend to be highest in the first third of the meeting, while rates of giving opinions are usually highest in the middle portion. Rates of proposing solutions are low in early periods and high in the last third of the meeting. Rates of both positive and negative suggestions tend to increase throughout group sessions, possibly as a result of members' greater familiarity with each other, resulting in lowered inhibitions.

When solution of human relations problems were discussed in laboratory settings, Bales found that the group's verbal maneuvers fell into four main categories: positive reactions, negative reactions, problem-solving, and questions. In 96 laboratory group sessions, an average of 56 percent of all verbal maneuvers related to problem-solving. Half of the time a speaker's first remark was a reaction to the problem. Positive reactions outnumbered negative ones by two to one. However, in groups which began on a high note of consensus, group spirit tended to drop at the intermediate stages, only to rally at the end.[51] At present, such findings are primarily of academic rather than practical interest. But if norms of successful interaction can be discovered, it may be feasible to devise measures for judging whether a particular verbal interaction is suitable for reaching the desired goals.

Analysis of verbal interchanges in actual meetings may pave the way for discovering the elements of successful and unsuccessful interaction. The previous chapter discussed studies of verbal interaction patterns in public bodies, like the UN General Assembly and the Yalta conference. Here evidence from less publicized gatherings will be added. Lloyd Jensen studied the patterns of substantive concessions and retractions of concessions in Soviet-American postwar disarmament negotiations from 1946 to 1961. It was his thesis that "the essence of bargaining is a willingness to make concessions in order to enhance agreement. Concessions thus provide one possible indicator of the propensity of a nation to negotiate seriously on disarmament. . . ."[52]

50. Robert F. Bales, "How People Interact in Conferences," in Alfred G. Smith, ed., *Communication and Culture: Readings in the Codes of Human Interaction* (New York: Holt, Rinehart and Winston, 1966), pp. 95–99.
51. *Ibid.*, pp. 95–102.
52. Jensen, "Soviet-American Bargaining Behavior," p. 522.

In seven selected negotiating sessions, the United States made 82 percent of its concessions in the first third of the session, the Soviets made 75 percent in the final third. Jensen believes that "far more effective bargaining could be established if concessions by both sides were staggered throughout the negotiations."[53] In 1946, 1948, 1957, and 1960 the pattern was for concessions to be reciprocated within the same session. Between 1949 and 1952 reciprocal concessions were delayed by one session. If there were no counter-concessions in the same session, the next session tended to be barren, with concessions resumed in the following one. "A general proposition would seem to be that if concessions are not reciprocated during a given round of negotiations, then a nation will reduce its level of concessions during the next round. . . ."[54] A study of successful and unsuccessful aspects of individual and group bargaining patterns during initial negotiating rounds might have helped in perfecting debate tactics in later ones.[55]

Controlled Communications

The study of debating patterns has not yet yielded adequate scientifically verified norms for conducting small group bargaining. However, available studies and inferences drawn from various interaction theories have produced a number of experimentally tested working hypotheses. The work of John Burton and co-workers at the Centre for the Analysis of Conflict at University College, London, and Leonard Doob and associates at Yale University provides highly sophisticated examples.[56] Both investigators assembled small groups of people, rep-

53. Ibid., p. 530.
54. Ibid., p. 528.
55. Also see Robert F. Bales and F. L. Strodtbeck, "Phases in Group Problem-Solving," Journal of Abnormal Psychology, 47 (1951), 485–495. Charles A. McClelland, "Verbal and Physical Conflict in the Contemporary International System," APSA paper (1970), reports correlations between verbal defense, verbal aggression, and physical aggression in 7,655 conflict events between 1966 and 1970, with inconclusive results.
56. Relevant studies are John W. Burton, Conflict and Communication: The Use of Controlled Communications in International Relations (New York: Free Press, 1969); Leonard W. Doob, Resolving Conflict in Africa: The Fermeda Workshop (New Haven: Yale University Press, 1970); Ronald J. Fisher, "Third Party Consultation: A Method for the Study and Resolution of Conflict," Journal of Conflict Resolution, 16 (1972), 67–94; Robert R. Blake, Jane Mouton, and Richard L. Sloma, "The Union-Management Intergroup Laboratory," Journal of Applied Behavioral Science, 1 (1965), 25–57. The purpose of the laboratory, which guided bargaining among highly antagonistic union and management representatives, was to "bring to an explicit level the assumptions, attitudes, and feelings that exist among members" by discussing "how that group performs —

resenting parties involved in active political conflict, to work out solutions in a setting designed to produce optimum results.

John Burton's experiment was conducted in the fall of 1966 when a group composed of six social scientists, two Greek Cypriots, and two Turkish Cypriots gathered for a one-week meeting at University College, London, to search for solutions to the Greek-Turkish intercommunal conflict in Cyprus. A university setting was chosen to give an atmosphere of privacy, detachment from the world of politics, and an air of impartial, scientific investigation. The setting was deemed highly important in creating a receptive frame of mind so often lacking in more ordinary bargaining situations. "Participants would be free to express their views openly and to get to know and respect each other as individuals. The atmosphere fostered mutual trust, a sense of shared values, and commitment to a common task. . . ." [57]

But the most important aspect of the experiment was control of group communications to avoid harmful debate, encourage fruitful verbal interchange, and make available expert advice on group interactions and conflict theories. "Communication between parties by itself does not solve conflicts. The form of communication, and the behaviour of the parties during communication, determines its outcome." [58]

When serious conflicts are at stake, ordinary bargaining sessions often produce highly repetitive and stereotyped discussions. "Alternative versions of the historical record are recited, old accusations and justifications are rehearsed, and fine legalistic points about rights and wrongs are debated." [59] As Oran Young remarked about negotiations during the Berlin crisis: "The constant emphasis of both sides on efforts to apportion the blame for the crisis itself was . . . vain and inconclusive. Each side had accumulated a web of interpretations and attitudes allowing for a consistent explanation of each new event in its own terms, that had made it almost impossible to appreciate the basis of the opponent's position . . . the Berlin crisis is hardly recognizable as the

how its behavior is motivated, what its conduct has been, what its intentions, purposes, and goals are" (*ibid.*, p. 32). Also see Hornstein and Johnson, "Effects of Process Analysis," p. 451, for a discussion of ways to create "an incentive for change by highlighting the cooperative interests of the negotiators and by providing satisfying experiences in alternative behaviors which could lead to these goals."

57. Herbert C. Kelman, "The Problem-Solving Workshop in Conflict Resolution," in Richard L. Merritt, ed., *Communication in International Politics* (Urbana: University of Illinois Press, 1972), p. 175.

58. John W. Burton, "The Analysis of Conflict by Casework," in *The Yearbook of World Affairs, 1967* (London: Stevens & Sons, 1967), p. 30.

59. Kelman, "Problem-Solving Workshop," p. 190.

same clash from reading the exegetic material promulgated by the two sides." [60]

To avoid this type of argumentation and begin on a more constructive note, Burton's group started with each party's exposition of its own perceptions of the conflict. This phase of calm, factual presentations was designed to probe the normally hidden real causes of conflict, including its domestic roots.[61] Participants were encouraged to "share their definitions of the conflict, their perceptions of their own and others' goals and actions, and their assessments of the costs and benefits of alternative conflict resolutions." [62] These are subjects highly prone to mutual misperceptions or ignorance and neglect. The social scientists steered the discussion to clarify points, examine causes, and prevent accusations and other inflammatory talk. It seemed particularly important to avoid expressions of strong feelings which could become major barriers to interpersonal communication. In the wake of hostile expressions, "There will be just two ideas, two feelings, two judgments, missing each other in psychological space." [63]

In the second phase, the social scientists presented various models of conflict and asked group members to discuss their applicability to the Cyprus situation. Members were encouraged to view their specific problem in a larger, generic setting. Assessments could then be made on the basis of dispassionately analyzed general knowledge rather than on the basis of the specific, highly emotional situation which had led to conflict.

During the third phase, the social scientists submitted general examples of conflict resolution and again asked the parties to draw specific parallels to the Cyprus situation. The purpose was to present for discussion a wide spectrum of options from which the conflicting parties could ultimately select the most appropriate ones. When specific solutions were under discussion, the social scientists took pains to point

60. Young, *Politics of Force*, p. 122.
61. Burton, *Conflict and Communication*, pp. 22, 49.
62. Kelman, "Problem-Solving Workshop," p. 171.
63. Carl R. Rogers and F. J. Roethlisberger, "Barriers and Gateways to Communication," *Harvard Business Review*, 30 (1952), 29. Rogers advocates that bargaining rules should require that each subsequent speaker may state his case only "*after* he has first restated the ideas and feelings of the previous speaker accurately and to that speaker's satisfaction" (*ibid.*, p. 30). Mediators often serve a role analogous to the social scientists in Burton's experiment. They are outside the emotional field created by the conflict and guide communication, and they may interject proposals which the parties could not be expected to make on their own. See Oran Young, *The Intermediaries: Third Parties in International Crises* (Princeton: Princeton University Press, 1967), pp. 38–54.

out why options which seemed reasonable to one party might not seem reasonable to the other; this again broadened the scope of verbalized information to include aspects of the problem which are normally slighted by bargaining groups.

The assumptions guiding Leonard Doob's experiment were quite similar. In the summer of 1969 Doob, along with William J. Foltz and Robert B. Stevens and several experts in sensitivity training, assembled a group of representatives from Ethiopia, Kenya, and Somalia at Fermeda, a Tyrolean mountain resort, in order to discuss solution of a border conflict among the three countries. As in the Burton experiment, a secluded setting was selected, and the group operated under the tutelage of impartial social scientists. But, unlike the Cyprus workshop, the Fermeda experiment began with a series of regular T-group sessions to sensitize the participants to their own interpersonal behavior and to group processes in general. The T-group sessions were supplemented by training in leadership roles, role-reversal techniques, and cooperation and competition strategies. The guiding idea was that group members function imperfectly unless they first become sensitive to each others' needs and familiar with the process of group interaction.

The border conflict was not mentioned at all during this initial period. It was introduced during the second part of the sessions, when the social scientists guided discussions in a manner quite similar to the Burton approach. They drew attention to information which provided insights into mutual perceptions; they drafted proposals for fresh solutions following careful political analysis of the situation; and they tried to curb hostile, accusatory interactions.

After completing the workshops, participants in both experiments agreed that they had gained new insights into group interactions, the nature of conflict and conflict resolution, and the various facets of the specific conflict under discussion. They had discovered new areas of common interest and explored mutually beneficial solutions to the conflict at hand. But since they were not directly involved in the negotiations at the governmental level, it was not certain how much of their work would be reflected in official bargaining.[64]

64. The representatives invited to the London meeting had been selected by top decision-makers in their communities. The Fermeda workshop participants were influential community leaders from governmental and academic circles, but they had not been selected by political leaders. Burton's critics have disputed the importance of communications failures in coping with international conflict. See Ronald J. Yalem, "Controlled Communication and Conflict Resolution," *Journal of Peace Research*, 3–4 (1971), 265–271; and the critique at the end of Burton, "Resolution of Conflict," pp. 36ff.

Burton believes that controlled communications procedures can be used to prevent conflicts, as well as to settle them. Once areas of potential friction have been identified, prospective antagonists can meet to define problems which are likely to arise in the future. They can assess their respective perceptions and projections of future events and then devise methods to avoid anticipated clashes. Social scientists attending controlled communications sessions can supply information about trends in world society, likely changes in the countries with conflicting interests, and other relevant information. Because controlled communications lead to insights into the basic nature of political problems, settlements are apt to be mutually acceptable; they rest on a shared analysis of circumstances, and they are not adopted reluctantly in an atmosphere of strife, or under the shadow of threats or fears of failure. In Burton's opinion, informal gatherings of members of the British Commonwealth during its early years were quite similar to his proposed controlled communications sessions.[65]

MAJOR ELEMENTS OF THE BARGAINING PROCESS

Small bargaining groups go through a series of procedures designed to bring about the agreements that the meetings were intended to produce. These procedures are heavily dependent on verbal interaction. This section delineates how verbal behavior at various stages of the bargaining process accomplishes the group's work.

The Significance of the Agenda

Many students of the bargaining process agree that the ideas discussed and the order in which they are verbalized strongly affect bargaining outcomes. The agenda must be carefully composed to yield "saliencies and focal points on which mutual expectations can center."[66] It is not necessary to spend time discussing the effects of topic choices and omissions, since previous chapters have already indicated why these decisions are crucial.[67]

The careful selection of agenda items does not assure that the members of the bargaining group will avoid time-wasting irrelevancies. "There are no rules against repetition, illogical reasoning, unanswered

65. Burton, *Conflict and Communication*, pp. 100–102.
66. Young, *Intermediaries*, p. 53.
67. See esp. chs. 1 and 3. Also see Young, *Intermediaries*, pp. 41–42; Haas, "Communication Factors," p. 76.

questions, irrelevant arguments, and pointless speeches." [68] When such tactics are used, they may exasperate group members and make the negotiating climate tense. But there is little recourse in written and unwritten bargaining rules to stop unproductive or counterproductive practices as long as they do not constitute an outright abandonment of agenda items under discussion.

Stalling tactics may be helpful in some types of bargaining contexts, such as labor disputes, when the parties view their positions as highly antagonistic. "Non-linear behaviors such as delays, retrogressions, resistances, and crises" may permit the parties to let off steam and clarify mutual expectations. In fact, indirection may be "willfully incorporated into the verbal system. . . . The communicant at the conference table knows better than to scorn non sequiturs — gaps can be made more telling than words — or to grow impatient with long-winded sentences." [69] The ability to say in twenty words what could be said in two or three may become a prized asset which keeps the parties talking and, in the process, readies them for negotiations which might otherwise be impossible.

The order of discussion is important because verbal interchange produces a chain-like reaction in which each prior exchange becomes the setting for what follows. The setting and mood, particularly at the outset, strongly affect bargaining outcomes. For example, an agenda which places some items of easy agreement first may help to get the bargaining process off to a good start. In fact, an agenda may deliberately include items inserted primarily to ease negotiations; these are of interest to the parties but generally are not crucial to the main contest. Ability to reach decisions on them, often through a trade-off in concessions or other tactics, may produce a propitious psychological climate for the ongoing negotiations. Rather than starting with easy items, one may choose to tackle the toughest items first, if one anticipates initial good will and enthusiasm which may wane later. The most auspicious order of discussion for a given type of negotiations remains controversial. There have not been enough studies to give guidelines for the wide variety of bargaining situations and settings which occur in politics.

Information Inputs

At the outset of every bargaining session, the emphasis is on supplying information about the questions at issue. This information includes

68. Iklé, *How Nations Negotiate*, p. 117.

69. Ann Douglas, *Industrial Peacemaking* (New York: Columbia University Press, 1962), pp. 35–37.

"facts" describing the problem and its setting, as well as data about mutual perceptions and preferences. Chapter 3 discussed how various conceptualizations of a given problem can create divergent realities with radically different consequences. "The formulation of an issue may stake out the starting points and limits for concessions, fix the bench marks for evaluating gains and losses, and circumscribe the areas where pressures, threats, and inducements can be used." No wonder that "delegates may spend more time and effort in trying to agree on what the issues are than in settling them." [70] It makes a good deal of difference, for example, whether electronic surveillance of political figures is examined as an effort to protect national security or as an invasion of civil rights.

What constitutes the optimum amount of information to be submitted to a bargaining group has remained a controversial issue among students of small bargaining groups. Western political folklore claims that group decisions benefit when information input is as wide and varied as time and comprehension limits of group members will allow. Decision-makers presumably can make the best choices when they can select from the most complete array of facts and options. Behavioral scientists have contended that simplistic categorizations of others increase, especially in terms of hostile-friendly dimensions, when information supply is reduced in a bargaining situation.[71] Simplistic categorizations frequently produce inaccurate predictions of behavior. These, in turn, cause uncertainties and misjudgments that are bound to impede successful bargaining.[72]

Restrictions on information input into bargaining groups are often imposed to eliminate discordant information which may endanger group consensus, or which is likely to meet with group disapproval or disbelief. Members may also withhold such information to protect their own status in the group. While some students of group processes consider this type of information restraint beneficial, others deem it exceedingly dangerous. On the basis of his studies of decision-making groups within the executive branch, Alexander George became concerned about the deleterious effects of constraints on raising discordant

70. Iklé, *How Nations Negotiate*, p. 218.
71. Alden E. Lind, "Perceptions and Political Bargaining," APSA paper (1969), p. 33.
72. Also see Harold H. Kelley and J. W. Thibaut, "Experimental Studies of Group Problem Solving and Process," in Gardner Lindzey, ed., *Handbook of Social Psychology* (Reading, Mass.: Addison Wesley, 1954), II, 335–385, where a number of studies are reported which seem to indicate that group judgments are better if the group is exposed to a variety of opinions.

issues and unpopular perceptions and options in discussions. George examined U.S. foreign policy decision-making, much of it conducted in small groups, in a series of major foreign policy crises between 1950 and 1965.[73] On the basis of this examination, he identified "malfunctions" of the decision-making system which led to decisions flawed because of inadequate or inaccurate information.

Among serious malfunctions afflicting small group decision-making, George cited achieving consensus too early and readily, without exploring all options fully. This malfunction was most prevalent when pressure to reach quick decisions was great. A second malfunction involved submission of only a limited number of divergent options and hypotheses for group consideration. For instance, the option of withdrawal from Vietnam apparently was not discussed by President Johnson and his advisors because it seemed unacceptable in light of the prevailing definitions of the war situation. Important options may be ignored by decision-making groups when there is no advocate willing to submit them; this, too, deprives group members of the chance to consider a complete array of options.[74]

George believes that decision-making groups should be constructed in such a way that the widest possible assortment of opinions is represented and likely to be introduced into group discussions. Since this "multiple advocacy system" gives an equal chance of adoption to all proposals, the advocates of various viewpoints must be carefully chosen so that they are fairly equal in influence, competence, information, and bargaining and persuasion skills. If advocates are unequal in those respects, the options which they propose do not have equal chances for serious consideration by the group.[75]

Observation of bargaining groups in action has cast some doubt on the notion that bargaining always becomes more successful when more information is made available. Too many facts and options may actually be more confusing than enlightening — in fact, one well-known bargaining strategy is to overload group discussion with reams of data so that the opposing side, overwhelmed with undigestible "facts," will

73. George, "Multiple Advocacy" (APSR), pp. 751–785. The crises were the North Korean attack on South Korea in 1950; the Indochina crisis in 1954; the Bay of Pigs incident in 1961; the Cuban missile crisis in 1962; the multilateral force decision regarding NATO in 1964; the Vietnam escalation in the spring of 1965; and the Dominican intervention in 1965.

74. Ibid., pp. 769–773.

75. Ibid., p. 759. Also see Irving L. Janis, Victims of Groupthink: A Psychological Study of Foreign-Policy Decisions and Fiascoes (Boston: Houghton Mifflin, 1972), esp. pp. 197–222.

capitulate. If it does not, the sheer inability to cope with vast quantities of data may force group members to weigh the information cursorily, making snap decisions based on preconceptions, rather than on reasoned judgments.[76]

It may also be wise to restrict some types of information which may poison the bargaining atmosphere. As discussed earlier, restraint may ensue from the normal interaction process in which the parties sense the inappropriateness of mentioning certain matters. It may be purposive withholding to prevent unwanted considerations from entering the picture. The withheld information may be extraneous to the case at hand, such as information about failure in concurrent negotiations, which, if publicized, could engender a mood of pessimism. It also could be information involving the parties and case at hand, but not essential to the bargaining in question. For example, it has been shown that labor disputes are settled more quickly when there is a dearth of information about the respective motives of labor and management. By contrast, bargaining positions of both sides should be fully known.[77]

Without settling the argument about the merits of extensive versus limited information, one can at least say that the amount and kind of information presented will affect the outcome of bargaining. To settle the quantity argument, one would have to examine bargaining outcomes in comparable situations on the basis of amounts and kinds of information made available to the bargainers. Few social scientists have as yet undertaken this difficult task. One attempt along this line is a study of foreign policy decision-making by Michael Haas. Haas tested the relationship of twenty-seven communications variables to choices of violent foreign policies, in the hope that this kind of study would show what patterns of verbal activities were apt to be linked to specific types of decisions, such as decisions to use violence.[78]

Information Evaluation

"The processes of obtaining and sharing relevant information and of identifying and inventing alternative options" are followed — and overlapped — by information evaluation. Information evaluation involves "examining relationships among available information and evaluating

76. John W. Burton, *Systems, States, Diplomacy and Rules* (Cambridge: Cambridge University Press, 1968), p. 73; Lind, "Perceptions and Political Bargaining," p. 27.

77. Sawyer and Guetzkow, "Bargaining and Negotiations," pp. 496–497.

78. Haas, "Communication Factors," p. 76.

the relative appropriateness of alternative options with reference to stated objectives and values." This in turn is followed — and over-lapped — by procedures for making final choices.[79] Evaluation of in-formation and policy options entails more than analysis of the various arguments in terms of a given logic; it also involves emotional reactions to the manner in which the various group members have presented their cases and appraisal of the seriousness with which negotiators have put forth their respective proposals and are willing to abide by their positions.

There are few general guidelines for evaluating the verbal informa-tion presented in small bargaining groups, beyond the general guide-lines for message decoding and interpretation discussed in earlier chap-ters. Evaluation remains more of an art than a science, combining analytical skills with empathy and intuition.[80] One of the few attempts to systematize evaluation focused on using verbal cues to appraise the inten-tions of parties in the negotiating process.[81] The parties were Russian and American negotiators participating in disarmament negotiations. The study, conducted by Lloyd Jensen, was based on the assumption that a party which is ambivalent about a distant goal will make conces-sions while the goal is remote. When the goal approaches, the reluctant party will avoid it by refusing further concessions. Statements made during negotiations could be examined for concession patterns to de-tect "approach-avoidance bargaining."

The verbal record of over 400 sessions during a five-year period showed the parties' early tendency to reciprocate offers of conces-sions.[82] When agreement seemed imminent, the Soviet Union started to retract its offers; the United States continued concession statements for a while, but then stopped. A study of approach-avoidance patterns dur-ing early bargaining sessions should have been a cue to the United States that the U.S.S.R. was not really interested in coming to a final agreement. "In view of the increasing recalcitrance of the Soviet Union

79. Quotes from a note in George, "Multiple Advocacy" (*APSR*), p. 757, which defines the three phases of decision-making outlined by organizational theorists such as Herbert Simon, James March, Richard Cyert, and others.

80. See chs. 2, 4, and 5. Some of the difficulties in information evaluation are discussed in Philip Green, *Deadly Logic: The Theory of Nuclear Deterrence* (Columbus: Ohio State University Press, 1966), pp. 188–190.

81. Lloyd Jensen, "Approach-Avoidance Bargaining in the Test Ban Negotia-tions," *International Studies Quarterly*, 12 (1968), 152–160.

82. Jensen coded proposals approaching the other side's position as conces-sions, and those withdrawing from it, after previous agreement, as retractions. A five-point concession and retraction index was developed to gauge the magnitude of concessions and retractions. *Ibid.*, pp. 153–156.

on the test ban issue, it is remarkable that the United States was caught off guard by the Soviet resumption of testing in September 1961." [83]

An index of agreement may also be useful in gauging the seriousness of the parties in reaching a settlement. Jensen constructed such an index to compare rates of agreement between the proposals of Soviet and American disarmament negotiators during various years of the post-war disarmament negotiations. The index showed that agreement increased progressively over the years, despite many stalemated sessions. Jensen argues that despairing U.S. negotiators could have concluded from this information that ultimate agreement was possible, even though the rate of progress would be slow. The fact that a limited nuclear test ban agreement was finally signed in 1963 supported the validity of the index.[84] The Soviet Union's change of attitude between 1961 and 1963 followed nuclear tests which had reduced the value previously assigned to atmospheric testing; besides, new detection devices had made it easier to monitor treaty breaches.

Final Choices

The next stage in the bargaining process, following the "talking-out requirement" which defined and reconnoitered the "negotiating range," consists of narrowing options.[85] "Negotiation is a process of refining and reducing alternative positions until a unique combination is reached that is acceptable to all parties." [86] Various types of statements can be used during this phase. Parties can simply acknowledge that their positions coincide on some of the options under consideration, or they can agree, explicitly or tacitly, to eliminate some of the previously discussed options by ignoring them. Parties can make concessions and counter-concessions by agreeing to accept some of their opponents' stated positions,[87] or there may be a compromise whereby a middle ground is adopted. Many of these mutual adjustments may require extremely careful phrasing to convey fine shadings of meanings acceptable to opposing sides.

83. *Ibid.*, p. 156. Jensen contends that the amount of attention paid to the test ban issue was a further cue that the Soviet Union had lost interest and had decided to resume testing.

84. Jensen, "Soviet-American Bargaining Behavior," p. 531.

85. Quotes from Douglas, *Industrial Peacemaking*, p. 42.

86. William Zartman, "Convergence and Power: An Approach to the Analysis of Negotiations," APSA paper (1969), p. 5.

87. *Ibid.*, pp. 8–9, 12. Zartman warns that in judging the amount of concession and convergence, one must remember that initial positions often are tactical stands which are deliberately extreme.

When bargaining patterns among members and prospective members of the Common Market were analyzed, the pattern of concessions parried by counter-concessions seemed prevalent. Agreement was reached first on larger principles, followed by agreement on lesser questions and then on details. If the negotiations on larger principles became bogged down, attention was shifted to settling details first.[88]

The process of gaining group concurrence for final decisions depends largely on verbal efforts designed to change the dissenters' perception of the decision, rather than on attempts to change the dissenters' value structures. At this point the search for an acceptable solution becomes an effort to make a solution appear acceptable; dialectic merges into rhetoric.[89] After studying bargaining among members of the Common Market, William Zartman identified four ways in which Common Market members, meeting in small groups, attempted to talk each other into changed perceptions. Two of these involved carrot-and-stick methods, and the other two eliminated all competing options by picturing them as out of reach.[90] In the "carrot" approach, one option was made to appear more attractive than its alternatives through emphasis on attractive features which had received insufficient attention earlier, or had not been mentioned at all. Sometimes additional benefits were attached to the desired decision. The "stick" approach involved the same process in the negative, with the danger of negative results used as the motivating force.

To reduce the number of available alternatives, a group member could make it appear that one alternative had already been chosen or eliminated by citing definite commitments which had already been made. A bargainer might refer to previous treaty agreements as precluding acceptance of certain options, or he might claim that particular choices had been foreclosed by the march of events or were beyond the capacity of the bargaining powers. Arguments about whether a forthcoming nuclear test ought to be stopped could be ended promptly by an announcement that the test had already taken place or that the testing nation lacked the necessary physical resources.

When enough alternatives have been eliminated and bargaining positions are close, the parties may be able to settle the remaining differences by procedural or mechanical means. Parties may be willing to accept midpoints or round figures, or previous agreements or initial offers, or similar reference points. These convenient (if often illogical)

88. *Ibid.*, p. 20.
89. Phillips, *Communications and the Small Group*, p. 9.
90. Zartman, "Convergence and Power," pp. 8–9.

settlement points satisfy prevailing notions that it is fair to split differences. However, it may require persuasive skills to convince group members that the differences are really split rather than settled to the advantage of one side.

"The manipulation of perception of events or situations in order to shape the bargaining calculations of other parties" can be extremely difficult.[91] Even when mutual perceptions are fully understood, the parties rarely know precisely what type of verbal stimuli will be needed to change these perceptions. "A bargaining situation is just the type of stimulus field to which we would expect people to respond differently." [92] Besides, most individuals resist changes of their perceptions. In a debate, each side has preconceived notions and tends to listen selectively. As Anatol Rapoport has poetically phrased it, "Medea, Macbeth, Don Quixote and Faust are all irreversibly committed to their respective world images, and blindness of their commitments is the essence of their tragedies." [93]

Few studies deal with generalities of perception which may indicate to bargainers the type of verbal images to which their opponents are most susceptible. One of the few studies of general perceptual approaches is Bryant Wedge's work in analyzing cross-cultural differences in perception. Wedge and co-workers developed a cognitive matrix which "in its simplest form, permits us to describe twenty-five distinct patterns of logic and reasoning. . . ." [94] The matrix was developed through "the identification of the most common or modal pattern of thinking and social discourse among a given population." It was "based on the analysis of the styles of argument and presentation which are normally used in attempting to teach or convince others." [95]

According to this matrix, predicated on verbal measures, Brazilians tend to have a universalistic view of the world. For them "global ideal-

91. Young, *Politics of Force*, p. 394.
92. Lind, "Perceptions and Political Bargaining," p. 22.
93. Anatol Rapoport, *Fights, Games and Debates* (Ann Arbor: University of Michigan Press, 1960), p. 260.
94. Bryant Wedge, "Communication and Comprehensive Diplomacy," in Arthur S. Hoffman, ed., *International Communication and the New Diplomacy* (Bloomington: Indiana University Press, 1968), pp. 39–40; also see Edmund Glenn, "A Cognitive Approach to the Analysis of Culture and Cultural Evolution," in Ludwig von Bertalanffy and Anatol Rapoport, eds., *General Systems Yearbook*, (Ann Arbor: University of Michigan Press, 1966), XI, 115–132; and Edmund Glenn, Robert H. Johnson, Paul R. Kimmel, and Bryant Wedge, "A Cognitive Interaction Model to Analyze Culture Conflict in International Relations," *Journal of Conflict Resolution*, 14 (1970), 35–48.
95. Wedge, "Communication and Comprehensive Diplomacy," p. 42.

istic theory determines to a very high degree the perception of any kind of evidence." [96] Case particularism characterizes American perceptions. Americans pay close attention to the evidence and settle cases on their individual merits. Wedge claims that Dominicans are so particularistic in their outlook that they cannot think in terms of generalizations. On the basis of the study of cognitive matrixes reflected in verbal arguments, he predicted (correctly) that Dominican students would be more resistant to the universalist appeal of Marxist theory than Brazilians. Wedge's approach, applied to the bargaining setting, could show group members what types of appeals were apt to be most fruitful in gaining acceptance of group decisions.[97]

BARGAINING TACTICS AND TECHNIQUES

The remainder of this chapter is devoted to a brief review of those few verbal bargaining techniques and tactics which have received substantial scholarly attention. Specifically, it will examine the relevancy of game theory and its principles in planning successful verbal tactics, and the use of noncoercive and coercive persuasion techniques. The section closes with a reminder of the importance of bargaining contexts for the success or failure of specific tactics and techniques.

The Relevance of Game Theory

The concerns of game theory, as Thomas Schelling has defined them, are games of strategy "in which the best course of action for each participant depends on what he expects the other participants to do." [98] Since the concerns of bargaining are similar, some students of the bargaining process have contended that game theory furnishes insights as well as rules for small group bargaining tactics. Other scholars disagree and argue that the approach is not suitable for the real-life conditions under which most small groups operate. Specifically, they claim that most small group interactions are mixed-motive games, rather than the zero-sum games which are a prime concern of game theoreticians.[99] Besides, some basic assumptions which underlie game theory are not met in most small group bargaining. Take the assumption

96. *Ibid.*, p. 40.
97. *Ibid.*, p. 43.
98. Schelling, *Strategy of Conflict*, pp. 9–10.
99. See pp. 256–257 above for description of various types of games. Also see Young, *Intermediaries*, p. 48.

that the parties have full information about the problem at hand.[100] Political bargaining situations tend to be highly complex, involving large amounts of relevant information. In most situations, even with complete cooperation by all parties, the bargainers will not have full information about the problem.

Nor is political bargaining a rational choice process as visualized by game theory. The negotiators do not generally make a payoff matrix for themselves and systematically line up their alternatives to choose the one that minimizes their losses, and they do not expect their opponents to do this, either. Rather, they wishfully anticipate that the other side will fail to be as clever as they are, or that it will be susceptible to being talked into a choice which may not be the best for it. In real life, it is even uncertain what are genuinely the best choices. "Precise utilities cannot be assigned to alternative positions or outcomes. Many positions cannot be expressed either as a single quantifiable item or as several quantifiable and relatable items."[101] In fact, utilities of outcomes may vary from day to day, depending on changes in outside circumstances, perceptions, or membership in the bargaining group.

Nonetheless, although the realities of bargaining do not permit full use of gaming rules, many concepts derived from game theory help in analyzing bargaining situations.[102] Game theory points to the importance of the opening move, which shapes the kind of game that will be played subsequently; bargainers likewise need to be concerned with the precise way in which negotiations are started. Making a first move permits a group member to set the general trend of negotiations by defining the proposal from which bargaining will proceed. On the other hand, making the first move, without the information furnished by the other's move, also presents disadvantages. If he misjudges the opposition's demands, the first mover may be unduly generous. If the other side moves first, its weaknesses may become apparent and useful to the opposition.[103]

Game theorists use the concept of a "manifest contract zone" or "bargaining zone." This is the "range of positions each of which is preferred

100. For a brief summary of objections, see Zartman, "Convergence and Power," pp. 4–5.

101. *Ibid.*, p. 3.

102. Schelling, *Strategy of Conflict*, p. 162, cautions that the mathematical structure of the payoff matrix should not be allowed to dominate bargaining analysis. Empirical research is needed to discover the rules of mixed-motive games.

103. Carl Stevens, *Strategy and Collective Bargaining Negotiations* (New York: McGraw-Hill, 1963), p. 39.

by both parties to 'no agreement,' and both know this." [104] Each party tries to choose the most desirable position in the manifest contract zone. This concept is very helpful in analyzing what actually happens in the initial phases of bargaining. "The first transaction between the parties is given over to an exhaustive determination of the *outer limits* of the range within which they will have to do business with each other." [105]

Among examples of rules for bargaining developed on the basis of game theory are the "large demand rule," the "minimum demand rule," and rules regarding ritualistic sparring. [106] "The large demand rule provides that the initial bargaining demand and counterdemand are in excess of the least favorable terms upon which each party is willing to settle, and in excess of what each expects the agreed-upon position to be. Both parties know this." Asking more than one expects to get leaves room for concessions. Flexibility to retreat from an announced position is essential if a party commits itself to bargaining. "A few bargaining relationships, however, feature what may be termed the 'minimum' demand (or 'maximum' concession), which is an initial bargaining proposal virtually identical with the least favorable terms upon which a party is willing to settle." [107] If used, it ends the bargaining game. The other party is presented with a take-it or leave-it choice. Knowledge that the verbalization of one's minimum demands will preclude further bargaining may save bargainers from inadvertently stumbling into this position. The minimum-demand opening offer may be a very bad move in those situations in which both sides must show to their constituents that they gained something from negotiations. Labor-management negotiations are an example.

Game theory indicates that in many types of negotiations, such as labor-management negotiations, ritualistic sparring may be required in the early phases. "There are vehement demands and counter-demands, arguments and counter-arguments. Each side shows prodigious zeal for exposing and discrediting its opposite, and sooner or later there almost inevitably comes from each side a conscious, studied, hard-hitting critique of the other. These attacks are typically vigorous and spirited; not infrequently they are also derisive and venomous." If the parties know that this "outward appearance of deep and irreconcilable cleav-

104. *Ibid.*, p. 36; also see Schelling, *Strategy of Conflict*, p. 22, and Coral Bell, *Negotiation from Strength* (New York: Alfred A. Knopf, 1963), p. 221.
105. Douglas, *Industrial Peacemaking*, p. 20.
106. Stevens, *Strategy*, p. 33. The rule is particularly applicable to labor disputes.
107. *Ibid.*

age" between them is normal during the initial phases of negotiation, they can assess its significance accordingly.[108]

Noncoercive Persuasion Techniques

Game theory has tended to deemphasize the tactical role of persuasion and to stress the significance of coercion.[109] By contrast, in small group bargaining the parties often prefer tactics of non-coercive persuasion. These include a variety of verbal strategies designed to cater to the psychological needs of other group members, as well as to exploit their weaknesses and prejudices. A few of these are here outlined to indicate their general nature and show why they form part and parcel of the verbal factors which influence bargaining outcomes.[110]

Experiments and field studies have shown that, in order to be persuasive, group members must make themselves personally acceptable to the group as trustworthy, reasonable sources of proposals.[111] A wide variety of verbal assertions can do the trick, including such tactics as linking oneself and one's proposals to sources trusted by the members whose support is being wooed, and using the right kind of language in terms of comprehensibility, emotional quality, allusions, and style.[112] "Egg-head language" may fill a group of laborers or farmers with distrust; highly educated individuals, in turn, may respond unfavorably to speeches that abound in grammatical errors.[113] "Whitey talk" including phrases like "you people" and references to racial stereotypes may alienate black group members and deter blacks from accepting group decisions.[114] "You persuade a man only insofar as you can talk his language by speech, gesture, tonality, order, image, attitude, idea, *identify-*

108. Douglas, *Industrial Peacemaking*, pp. 14–15.

109. Stevens, *Strategy*, p. 67.

110. One of the best discussions of persuasion techniques is the pioneering study by Carl I. Hovland, Irving L. Janis, and Harold H. Kelley, *Communication and Persuasion: Psychological Studies of Opinion Change* (New Haven: Yale University Press, 1953). Also see Winston L. Brembeck and William S. Howell, *Persuasion: A Means of Social Control* (New York: Prentice-Hall, 1952); Bettinghaus, *Persuasive Communication*; Kenneth Burke, *A Rhetoric of Motives* (New York: Prentice-Hall, 1950), pp. 43–69; and Hugh Dalziel Duncan, *Communication and Social Order* (New York: Bedminster Press, 1962), pp. 225–241, which deals with persuasion techniques used by Adolf Hitler.

111. Gary Cronkhite, *Persuasion: Speech and Behavioral Change* (Indianapolis: Bobbs-Merrill, 1969), p. 75.

112. On the nature of appropriate language and the structure of effective messages, see Bettinghaus, *Persuasive Communication*, pp. 139–143, 147–166.

113. *Ibid.*, p. 162.

114. Jack L. Daniel, "The Facilitation of White-Black Communication," *Journal of Communication*, 20 (1970), 136–137.

ing your ways with his. Persuasion by flattery is but a special case of persuasion in general." [115]

Group members in search of support for their views must avoid the impression of manipulating their listeners.[116] Most listeners like to feel that evidence is submitted to them to permit choices, rather than to elicit automatic acceptance of conclusions formulated by others. This does not mean that a speaker cannot indicate the conclusions which his associates ought to reach on rational or political grounds, but group members must be made to feel that they are yielding to the logic of the situation, rather than to the machinations of a group member.

The logic used and the sources quoted must strike a responsive chord in the audience. This does not mean that the logic must follow formal canons of reasoning; it does mean that it must conform as closely as possible to previous thought processes and experiences of the group. It must also provide them with a socially acceptable rationale for the decisions so that they can defend them when questioned.[117]

The motives to which group members appeal must be geared to take advantage of the cultural and personal psychological predispositions of the group. Appeals may be made to reason, to emotion, to cultural norms, to personal or group profit, or to moral strictures and a sense of obligation.[118] Since most people like to humor their friends and displease their enemies, a verbal indication that a decision will please friends and anger enemies may make it highly attractive. So, too, people like to think that they are consistent in their positions and that their positions are consistent with their self-image and their image of the world. Therefore, statements are more persuasive if they conjure up verbal images which show the advocated position to be consistent with other views held by the individual, and with his overall world view. They are especially persuasive if they reduce existing cognitive inconsistencies. In many situations, appeals to basic emotions such as hate and fear or love, admiration, and pride are productive. They may be directed toward interpersonal, intergroup, or intersocietal feelings. Timing and sequencing properly geared to the bargaining setting are crucial in all appeals.

Since bargaining sessions involve face-to-face interactions, group

115. Burke, *Rhetoric of Motives*, p. 55.
116. Cronkhite, *Persuasion*, p. 77.
117. Stevens, *Strategy*, pp. 73–75.
118. Elihu Katz, Michael Gurevitch, Brenda Danet, and Tsiyona Peled, "Petitions and Prayers: A Method for the Content Analysis of Persuasive Appeals," *Social Forces*, 47 (1969), 447–453.

members must be prepared to duel verbally with dissidents and opponents, with a verbal defense against the other side's thrusts, as well as a verbal offense directed at the weakest chinks in the opponents' armor. When the force of arguments seems to be equally persuasive on all sides, expressions of confidence in one's own argument and avoidance of expressions of doubt may provide the winning edge. Evidence for this view comes from an experiment in which quality and quantity of arguments, personality of speakers and listeners, and all other persuasion factors were carefully matched.[119] The speakers who most often expressed confidence in their views and least often voiced doubts turned out to be most persuasive. No wonder the label "confidence man" has been coined for swindlers who exude confidence to bilk their victims!

Coercive and Deceptive Persuasion Techniques

If the opportunity presents itself for threats, deceptions, and lies, are these sound verbal tactics? The answer is moot.[120] Many game theorists and other scholars have presented speculations as well as some evidence that they are, indeed, effective. Commenting about the use of threats, George Kent contends, "The liberal would like to believe that using such threats is disadvantageous. Conservatives, and considerations of pure bargaining theory, suggest that the threatener will be better off." [121] Coral Bell praises the sabre-rattling tactics of Secretary of State Dulles as a good way to show Communist negotiators that the West had both the will and the capacity to defend itself. "It is in will rather than in capacity that the Western powers have characteristically shown themselves most deficient." [122] Threats demonstrate willingness to act and infuse negotiators with a sense of danger which will sharpen their desire to come to a peaceful agreement. Herman Kahn talks about

119. Harvey London, Philip Meldman, and A. Van C. Lanckton, "The Jury Method: How the Persuader Persuades," *Public Opinion Quarterly*, 34 (1970), 182.

120. Herman Kahn, *On Escalation: Metaphors and Scenarios* (New York: Praeger, 1965), p. 251, notes that coercive measures are more common at high political levels than at low ones.

121. George Kent, *The Effects of Threats* (Columbus: Ohio State University Press, 1967), p. 24. Kent argues that every bargaining situation contains the implied threat that negotiations will be broken off, even when no explicit threats of any kind are made. Presumably parties who enter negotiations expect some gain from them. This makes knowledge that negotiations may be broken off and the gain forfeited a threat which coerces the parties into reaching agreement. Also see George Kent, "Determinants of Bargaining Outcomes," *Peace Research Society Papers*, 11 (1969), 23–42, and Bell, *Negotiation from Strength*, pp. 96–98.

122. Bell, *Negotiation from Strength*, p. 98.

posturing and bluffing to inveigle the other side into concessions. "Every technique and trick that can be used to make more likely the other's adaptation may be important if the escalation [of war danger] grows sufficiently intense." [123]

If agreement, regardless of its nature, is preferable to no agreement, then coercive tactics may be sound. However, a number of studies have shown that threats impair the ability of parties to communicate adequately with each other and that decisions reached while parties felt threatened are often irrational; [124] hence the bargains struck as a result of threats may be unsound. On the basis of laboratory simulations, Morton Deutsch and Robert Krauss state categorically that "the availability of threat clearly made it more difficult for bargainers to reach a mutually profitable agreement. Indeed, Bilateral Threat presents a situation so conflict-fraught that no amount of communication seems to have an ameliorating effect." [125]

Threats may also produce psychological reactions against yielding to force — which means they can prevent, rather than encourage, agreement. Threats also tend to make political positions more rigid, contracting the bargaining zone. A threatening party must work its offers around the threat, because threat abandonment may impair its credibility. [126] More study is needed to determine the circumstances under which threats were followed by the desired results, the conditions under which they produced failure, and what desirable and undesirable side effects were involved.

The major disadvantage of lies and deceptions springs from the credibility problem which they create if detected. Especially when the bargaining situation involves a lengthy period or a sequence of encounters, it is unlikely that numerous falsehoods and dissimulations will remain secret and unsuspected. Once the credibility of a party has become impaired, future negotiations suffer because his word is not

123. Kahn, *On Escalation*, p. 250.

124. See Lewis A. Froman and Michael D. Cohen, "Threats and Bargaining Efficiency," *Behavioral Science*, 14 (1969), 147–153; Robert C. North, "When Deterrence Fails," APSA paper (1963), pp. 4–9, 12; Green, *Deadly Logic*, pp. 200–203; Haas, "Communication Factors," p. 80; and Sawyer and Guetzkow, "Bargaining and Negotiations," pp. 498–499.

125. Morton Deutsch and Robert M. Krauss, "Studies in Interpersonal Bargaining," *Journal of Conflict Resolution*, 6 (1962), 73–74.

126. Sawyer and Guetzkow, "Bargaining and Negotiations," p. 485; D. D. Hoefner, "Some Effects of Guilt-Arousing and Fear-Arousing Persuasive Communication on Opinion Change," *American Psychologist*, 11 (1956), 359; Harold H. Kelley, "Experimental Studies of Threats in Interpersonal Negotiations," *Journal of Conflict Resolution*, 9 (1965), 79–105.

trusted. Uncertainty about the truth or untruth of statements and offers may lead to dangerous miscalculations. Lack of credibility may also force a party with a reputation for bluffing and lying to buttress most of its assertions by signs and signals which attest to their accuracy. This may be difficult and costly in the long run, like the proverbial burning of bridges to demonstrate that retreat is impossible. Coercive verbal tactics and deceptions, like physical coercion, need to be carefully considered; while they may be highly effective, they have deleterious side effects, immediately and in the long run.

Bargaining Context as Intervening Variable

This discussion of various verbal tactics has emphasized that their effects depend on the bargaining context. It may be well to point once more to a few important situational factors and to reemphasize that they constitute intervening variables in the verbal stimulus-response process. What particular verbal patterns will evolve and be effective or ineffective depends on the subject matter with which the parties are dealing. A meeting to settle a hotly contested boundary dispute usually engenders more high-powered verbal tactics than a school board meeting called to fix the price of a lunch program. It also makes a difference whether the problem under discussion involves a one-time decision, or is part of a continuous interaction in which many future encounters are anticipated.

The personalities and interaction of the negotiators likewise are extremely important variables in the flow of negotiations.[127] The process of interaction will create a climate of antagonism or cooperation which will influence reciprocal verbal behavior and negotiation outcomes. Verbal skills of the negotiators and leadership patterns which develop in the group also contribute to the type of negotiating climate which is created; so do external settings and influences.

Power relations among the parties are another significant factor. How such relations affect interaction depends partly on cultural predispositions and norms. In a culture which bids the strong to defer to the weak, great power may carry minimal weight, but in most situations speakers with high status and the ability to command political resources tend to prevail over those of lesser status and resources.[128]

---

127. For the importance of even minor personality factors, see Jerome D. Frank, *Sanity and Survival: Psychological Aspects of War and Peace* (New York: Random House, 1967), p. 202.

128. Jerald Hage, Michael Aiken, Cora B. Marrett, "Organization Structure and Communications," *American Sociological Review*, 36 (1971), 860–871.

Turning to communications factors, the positions verbalized at the start of the bargaining process may determine the bargaining boundaries and the subject matters which will receive attention. Communications patterns tend to develop their own momentum thereafter. Attempts to change the course of a set pattern may be like swimming upstream — strenuous and at times impossible.

Evaluation of the bargaining outcomes also influences verbal tactics. When cases seem lost or about to be lost, parties may employ verbal ammunition different from that used when success seems in hand. How the parties evaluate the outcome of bargaining depends on their logics, value structures, and goals. If the bargaining parties have antagonistic objectives, their vantage points will determine whether they call the outcome successful or unsuccessful.

Some group members will evaluate bargaining outcomes simply by whether or not a decision was reached, regardless of the nature of the particular decision. Others will compare the initial position with the final position and call the negotiations successful if a change in the intended direction has been brought about. The bargaining process as such may be deemed beneficial even without changed positions; the outcome of negotiations may also be appraised by whether or not violence was avoided, especially in the field of international affairs. Regardless of the measure used to judge the bargaining outcome, most participants in small groups agree that verbal factors are a decisive influence on the final decisions.

Summary

The study of verbal interactions in small bargaining groups is particularly important for understanding politics, because most governmental decisions are produced by such groups. Members of small bargaining groups meet face-to-face to develop proposals and then pare, shape, and amalgamate them into a package which most of the members are willing to accept. The number of participants and the privacy of the discussion setting make it easier to reach decisions in small bargaining groups than in public assemblies. Fewer individuals need to be placated; the intimacy of the setting permits greater frankness and reduces posturing; and the complications arising from appeals to outside audiences can be avoided. Since verbal behavior in small groups is guided by implied norms of reciprocity, the participants usually treat each other with courtesy and consideration, even though the moderating pressures of public exposure are lacking. But rudeness and threats are not ruled out if they appear useful to some members under the circumstances.

Political folklore in Western countries has it that bargaining in small groups is the best way to reach agreement. However, this does not mean that small bargaining sessions always succeed. Various factors may be responsible for failure to reach agreement: there may be no real desire to arrive at an acceptable solution; there may be mutual misunderstanding of basic attitudes toward the problem at hand; or there may be unbridgeable clashes of interests or totally incompatible personalities. How the players view the bargaining game is also crucial. If they regard it as a zero-sum game, chances for success are small; if they view it as a positive-sum game, the likelihood of success is greater. Prospects for success of mixed-sum games are intermediate.

Scholars and practicing politicians have paid far more attention to evolving rules of successful bargaining behavior in small groups than in public assemblies. This fact may reflect their evaluation of the comparative importance of verbal activities in the two types of bodies. Most of the "rules" rest on common-sense appraisals of the vagaries of the negotiating process, rather than on scientific analysis. Various steps in the bargaining sequence have been described and analyzed, from the construction of a sound agenda to the procedures for final evaluation of verbal activities. The choice of subjects to be aired (or ignored) and the order of discussion have been carefully scrutinized, as have the opportunities for various verbal conceptualizations of problems. The optimum amount of information to be introduced during bargaining has remained a controversial subject. Some experts recommend that all relevant issues be raised, with input from a wide array of advocates representing different interests. Others prefer to limit input in order to avoid information overloads and to evade discordant issues.

Several approaches can produce the final narrowing of options to an acceptable package. Carrot-and-stick tactics alternately offer rewards and threaten penalties; patterns of concessions matched by counter-concessions are also possible. Persuasion may be directed toward changing the parties' perceptions of solutions, rather than altering their value structures. A knowledge of the cognitive matrices of the negotiating parties may help in judging the most persuasive types of verbal approaches.

In studying the interplay of verbal stimuli in bargaining sessions, more emphasis has been placed on participants' attitudes toward the group's objectives or toward each other, or on the forms and types of statements that have been made, than on the verbal reality created to bring about the effects. This emphasis has diverted attention from the substance of messages, and from the possibilities of controlling bargaining outcomes through manipulating substance.

Group analysis techniques whose verbal aspects are briefly explored in the chapter include Interaction Process Analysis, Sign Process Analysis, Psychological Gaming, and Phenomenological Analysis. They also include experiments in Controlled Communications. In these experiments, social scientists guide the discussions of parties in conflict to bare the roots of the conflict, permitting the parties to develop solutions free from the blinding effects of verbal pyrotechnics. Regrettably, most verbal analysis techniques have been used primarily for studying verbal interaction patterns in laboratories, rather than in natural settings.

Beyond the general rules used in verbal decoding, few measures have been developed for evaluating information received during bargaining sessions. A party's ambivalence toward agreement has been appraised by tracing verbal signs of approach-avoidance bargaining. If a party's verbal stances become more uncooperative when its stated goals are approached, the party has been judged ambivalent about reaching a solution. Game theory has also proved useful in analyzing bargaining tactics. Although small group bargaining in political settings generally does not meet a number of important assumptions of game theory, many game theory concepts are nonetheless applicable. Game theory's stress on the consequences of the initial move is relevant to small group bargaining; so are the concepts of the manifest contract zone, small and large demand rules, and the interpretations to be placed on ritualistic sparring.

Game theory stresses the use of coercive tactics in zero-sum games and neglects non-zero-sum games. By contrast, most students of bargaining prefer to view small group bargaining as a mixed-motive game in which noncoercive tactics are preferable. These tactics employ more or less scientifically grounded principles of persuasion which have been quite fully described both by scholars and by practicing politicians.

A good deal of scientific evidence has been gathered to determine whether coercive and deceptive tactics are productive or counterproductive for bargaining success in the short or long run. The results are unclear. Much apparently depends on the idiosyncrasies of the situations and the identities of members of the bargaining groups. Bargaining context thus is a crucial intervening variable which must be carefully assessed in evaluating the likely impact of verbal stimuli generated during bargaining sessions.

10 Condensation Symbols in Politics

> . . . it is possible to think of utterances which are intended to effect immediate and radical changes in the communications system itself in which they are uttered . . . to set up patterns of choric incantation shared by the speaker and his responding audience, which transform the relations between them, the roles and identities of both, and the matrices within which psychic mobilization and political action become possible. When speech thus transforms the communications system, the utterance becomes a "happening" in its own right.
> — J. G. A. Pocock, *Politics, Language and Time*[1]

> As I pass through my incarnations
>   in every age and race
> I make my proper prostrations
>   to the gods of the Market Place;
> Peering through reverent fingers,
>   I watch them flourish and fall,
> And the Gods of the Copybook Maxims,
>   I notice outlast them all.
> — Rudyard Kipling, "The Gods of the Copybook Maxims," stanza 1

The Nature of Condensation Symbols

A verbal condensation symbol is a name, word, phrase, or maxim which stirs vivid impressions involving the listener's most basic values. The symbol arouses and readies him for mental or physical action. Thus a reference to "my country" triggers a host of informational and affective connotations about the national unit where a person was born. As the opening stanza of "America" proclaims: "My country . . . sweet land of liberty . . . land where my fathers died, land of the pilgrims' pride . . . of thee I sing."[2]

The precise meaning of such words and phrases, and whether or not they constitute a condensation symbol, depends on the individual who

1. J. G. A. Pocock, *Politics, Language and Time: Essays on Political Thought and History* (New York: Atheneum, 1971), p. 280.
2. Samuel Francis Smith, "America," stanza 1. For other definitions, see David G. Mandelbaum, ed., *Selected Writings of Edward Sapir* (Berkeley: University of California Press, 1949), pp. 565–566; Hadley Cantril, *The Psychology of Social Movements* (New York: John Wiley, 1941), pp. 67–68. A good general discussion of noncognitive symbol systems is Clifford Geertz, "Ideology as a Cultural System," in David E. Apter, ed., *Ideology and Discontent* (New York: Free Press, 1964), pp. 47–76.

uses or hears them. Connotations vary, even for people born in the same country; nor are they constant over time. "Each man is 'necessarily free' to be his own tyrant, inexorably imposing upon himself the peculiar combination of insights associated with his particular combination of experiences."[3] The exact meanings of these terms for a particular individual at a specific time can generally be inferred only from his responses to a given symbol at that time.

However, it is easy to overstress personal differences in meaning. Individual images, like handwriting styles, vary in detail, but the general configuration of images, as of letters, is similar for persons reared within the same culture or subculture. In fact, cultures have been defined as groups of people sharing symbol meanings. "Membership in a people essentially consists in wide complementarity of social communication. . . . A people by this test is a community of predictability from introspection."[4]

Studies of stereotypes as well as opinion surveys have revealed strong similarities in images, evaluations, and emotions evoked by condensation symbols.[5] For instance, the images which the average American or German or Frenchman supplies when asked to describe a Russian or Chinese or Mexican person tend to be very similar among people from each country. At the same time, images diverge from country to country, and their correspondence to actual traits of Russians, Chinese, or Mexicans is often slight. It might be argued that inadequate information forces respondents to adopt the only available connotations, and that they would create their own more accurate mental pictures if they could. But this seems questionable since inaccurate, shared stereotypes abound, even when it is quite easy to verify characteristics. Despite familiarity, the average American has a highly stereotyped and partly inaccurate view of major characteristics shared by Republicans or Democrats, or Jews, or Catholics, or American Indians, or hippies, or Communists.

Verbal condensation symbols are the most potent, versatile, and ef-

3. Kenneth Burke, *Language as Symbolic Action* (Berkeley: University of California Press, 1966), p. 52.

4. Karl W. Deutsch, *Nationalism and Social Communication* (New York: John Wiley, 1953), pp. 71, 86.

5. See, for example, William Buchanan and Hadley Cantril, *How Nations See Each Other* (Urbana: University of Illinois Press, 1953); William Buchanan and Hadley Cantril, "National Stereotypes," in Wilbur Schramm, ed., *The Process and Effects of Mass Communication* (Urbana: University of Illinois Press, 1954), pp. 191–206; Daniel Katz and Kenneth W. Braly, "Verbal Stereotypes and Racial Prejudice," in Guy E. Swanson, T. M. Newcomb, and Eugene L. Hartley, eds., *Readings in Social Psychology* (New York: Holt, 1952).

fective tools available to politicians for swaying mass publics. Politics abounds in such symbols, most of them created by people in public life. "Democracy," "social progress," "self-determination," "socialism," "communism," "capitalism," "imperialism," "colonialism," "exploitation," "repression," "racism," "systemic violence," "freedom fighters," "establishment" — the list is ever-changing, endless.[6] When mass audiences respond strongly and uniformly to the appeals of such symbols, the symbols become Pavlovian cues: the audience reacts automatically to the cue, rather than to the facts of the situation.

The potency and political utility of individual condensation symbols varies, depending on the number of areas to which they can be applied, the intensity of emotional responses that they evoke, and the number of politically important people moved by them. Some condensation symbols have universal appeal, while others stir only a few listeners. Condensation symbols which appeal to only moderately internalized values are much less useful than those which deal with basic values. However, politicians normally use restraint in appealing to the most powerful symbols when lesser symbols will suffice, lest the prime symbols be weakened by overuse.[7] Both potency and distribution of values can change fairly rapidly when societies are in the throes of major political and social changes.

Three characteristics of condensation symbols contribute to their political usefulness. In the first place, the images conjured up by condensation symbols are rich and vivid in descriptive and evaluative dimensions based on direct experiences or indirect learning.[8] If the word "pig" is shouted to a young, radical audience, it probably evokes the picture of a mean-looking uniformed policeman. But that is not all; the image is more variegated and involving. The symbol very likely conjures up visions of gun-toting, club-swinging police units attacking

6. The effect of condensation symbols on the direction of Cold War policies is traced in Wayne Brockriede and Robert L. Scott, *Moments in the Rhetoric of the Cold War* (New York: Random House, 1970). The book analyzes significant speeches paragraph by paragraph to point out how symbol and symbol combinations are used to produce appropriate audience effects.

7. Richard M. Merelman, "Learning and Legitimacy," *American Political Science Review*, 60 (1966), 556; Martin E. Spencer, "Politics and Rhetorics," *Social Research*, 37 (1970), 610.

8. The nature of political images is discussed in Herbert C. Kelman, "Social-Psychological Approaches to the Study of International Relations: Definition of Scope," in Herbert C. Kelman, ed., *International Behavior* (New York: Holt, Rinehart and Winston, 1966), pp. 24–25. The words which embody a condensation symbol may have multiple denotations along with multiple connotations — e.g., "pig" refers to an animal, or to an iron plug, as well as to a person acting in a reprehensible manner.

young protestors. It may bring forth painful mental images of political suppression through exclusion of young protesters from public meetings, imprisonment of protesters, and brutal and unfair treatment at the hands of public officials. All of this may be wrapped in memories of the events of the 1968 Democratic convention in Chicago. In fact, it may amount to a mental replay of that event.

Not only is there a full panoply of connotations for condensation symbols, but there are also series of clashing panoplies. "Pig" used with a different audience may evoke visions of ill-kempt, disorderly, shouting youths assaulting well-behaved police units. Moreover, the same words may have different meanings, each with distinct connotations. This can prove confusing — which may be an asset or a liability, depending on the circumstances. "Democracy" describes a different set of political phenomena when used in a Russian or an American setting, but neither the average Russian nor the average American will be aware that each is using the word to mean different things. Hence when a speaker in the United States labels Russians as a "democratic" people, his audience will most likely think in terms of American connotations and regard Russians as ideological brothers, or the speaker as a fool or a liar.

A second major characteristic of condensation symbols is their capacity to arouse emotions. The word "pig," spoken to young radicals, is very likely to arouse strong negative emotions, possibly blazing hatred. Other words, like "freedom," "homeland," or "Constitution," carry strongly positive emotional valences for many people. Since condensation symbols are meant to be effective mobilizing agents, it does not matter whether the images they convey are literally correct. Obviously a man is not a barnyard animal, nor is the Constitution an unbreakable shield guarding American liberties. What matters is that the symbol evokes a strong response, and this is most likely when it uses pictorial images which stir the listener's emotions.[9]

Condensation symbols supply instant categorizations and evaluations. When one can get publics to refer to the Mylai "massacre" or to the Attica "prison riot" or to "white racism," one is well on the way toward shaping their perceptions and evaluations of these events. Adoption of the label amounts to adoption of its connotations, even though the public's factual knowledge of the events and phenomena may be minimal.[10] When police action against the Black Panther party becomes

9. A. James Gregor, *An Introduction to Metapolitics* (New York: Free Press, 1971), pp. 318–319.

10. Duncan MacRae, Jr., "Scientific Communication, Ethical Argument, and Public Policy," *American Political Science Review*, 65 (1971), 39, calls value-

widely labeled as "genocide," rather than as a "security operation," this changes the political options available to the party as well as to the police.

POLITICAL USES OF CONDENSATION SYMBOLS

What are important political uses of condensation symbols, and what consequences do they entail? Four facets of the subject will be stressed, each involving symbols with a different degree of political potency. The discussion will begin with the general utility of condensation symbols as categorizers and value tags, then turning to their power to rally people to mass movements and their effects in defining political situations, and concluding with a discussion of some of the political disadvantages inherent in the use of condensation symbols. As will be apparent from the discussion, this heuristically useful division is somewhat artificial, since the facets overlap.

Versatile Instant Categorizers and Value Tags

The general utility of condensation symbols springs from the fact that verbal communication must be a form of mental shorthand. Because of the limited time and attention spans of most audiences, it is rarely possible to spell out situations in full detail. If one can use a word or short phrase to elicit fairly predictable mental images from an audience, one can communicate with economy. The fact that each individual may fill the condensation symbol with his own distinct meanings is an asset, rather than a liability, as long as the various meanings produce compatible evaluations in a given group. "The very ambiguities . . . [permit] them, like Rorschach inkblots, to suggest to each person just what he wants to see in them," providing a meaning tailored to each listener's needs.[11] In fact, "The larger and more diverse a political movement's constituency, the more vague and imprecise its unifying symbols and rallying cries are likely to be."[12]

The use of shorthand symbols is particularly valuable in politics because so many situations involved in political dialogue are highly complex and often beyond the listener's ability to judge. If one can com-

laden symbols "secondarily evaluative terms" in contrast to "primarily evaluative terms" like "good" and "bad."

11. Robert E. Lane, *Political Thinking and Consciousness* (Chicago: Markham, 1969), p. 316.

12. Joel D. Aberbach and Jack L. Walker, "The Meaning of Black Power," *American Political Science Review*, 64 (1970), 367.

municate meaningfully with an audience by calling a new welfare program either a "give-away scheme" or an "economic Bill of Rights," one can save the trouble of describing details of the program which the audience would probably not understand. American conservatives have effectively opposed aid to the indigent under the hallowed slogan of "individualism," saving themselves the inconvenience and danger of making their reasons explicit. They have used the symbol of "independence" to fight against unions and the regulation of corporations.[13] Each condensation symbol retrieves a complete mental picture, along with value judgments, from the listener's memory. The communicator, knowing the positive valence carried by "individualism" and "independence," could anticipate that his audience would oppose policies designated as threats to these prized conditions.

A speaker must know which condensation symbols will be effective with his audiences. "George Wallace running for Governor of Alabama, says, 'segregation forever'; George Wallace running for President says, 'law and order.'"[14] Labor leaders addressing their unions may harangue "the bosses." When they speak to the general public, they appeal to "the public interest."[15] Adolf Hitler chose to attack wealthy Germans as "Jewish profiteers" rather than as "dirty capitalists." By guiding public hatred into the channels of anti-Semitism, rather than anti-capitalism, he avoided an alliance with left-wing socialists, whom he also hated.[16] Obviously, a speaker's choice of condensation symbols is limited by the subject matter under discussion and by the basic values of the prevailing culture. Condensation symbols which fail to tap values salient to the audience are ineffective.

Between World War I and the easing of the Cold War in the 1960's, the various condensation symbols referring to communism were extremely potent for most American publics. Martin Spencer claims that their potency resulted from a blending of four dominant value themes of American life: individualism, respect for property, respect for religion, and xenophobia. The connotations of communism which became

13. Ronald D. Rotunda, "The 'Liberal' Label: Roosevelt's Capture of a Symbol," *Public Policy*, 26 (1968), 391–393. For an extensive analysis of the use of condensation symbols in the battle over adoption of Medicare, see Max J. Skidmore, *Medicare and the American Rhetoric of Reconciliation* (University: University of Alabama Press, 1970), esp. pp. 100–107, 116–129, 149–155, 161–167, 175–176.

14. Spencer, "Politics and Rhetorics," pp. 612–613.

15. *Ibid.*

16. Harold D. Lasswell, *Politics: Who Gets What, When and How* (New York: Meridian Books, 1958), p. 43.

embedded in condensation symbols threatened all four simultaneously. Anti-Communist condensation symbols were used to deter programs like social security and public housing, and they fueled McCarthyism and the Cold War.[17]

Another profound value in American life which finds expression in condensation symbols is the preservation of the Constitution and general legal principles. The civil rights movement used such symbols to advantage in its early days by attacking the laws which were being violated by demonstrators as "unconstitutional" while simultaneously defending protest action as in accordance with "the higher law" of human rights.[18] In school desegregation cases, civil rights groups called for southern states to obey the "law of the land." Opponents invoked the slogan of "law and order" as a rhetorical weapon against ghetto riots.

Likewise, Vietnam doves challenged the "constitutional right" of the president to wage an undeclared war and attacked the "legal validity" of the Gulf of Tonkin Resolution in which Congress sanctioned extensive war powers granted to the president.[19] Vietnam hawks similarly appealed to the value of legality; they called the Gulf of Tonkin Resolution a legally binding authorization of presidential action and defended American presence in Vietnam on the basis of the sanctity of SEATO treaties.

On the international scene, Americans tend to respond favorably to policies which are touted as involving "the right of self-determination." When it is claimed that a "threat to freedom in Asia is a threat to freedom in the U.S.," the powerful magic of the word "freedom" is invoked to link the political fate of these continents.[20] When Americans allegedly have made a foreign "commitment," it must be carried out, regardless of costs.

Like many other appeals to "fundamental" American values, the appeal to principles of action according to law reveals a paradox of American political culture. Certain values are highly prized and constantly invoked, and the potency of their invocation can be demonstrated. Nonetheless, the behavior which receives such wide and fervent sanction may be massively violated by a large number of Americans. In fact,

17. Spencer, "Politics and Rhetorics," p. 612.
18. *Ibid.*, p. 601; Merelman, "Learning and Legitimacy," p. 553.
19. Spencer, "Politics and Rhetorics," p. 602.
20. Charles E. Osgood, "Conservative Words and Radical Sentences in the Semantics of International Politics," in Gilbert Abcarian and John W. Soule, eds., *Social Psychology and Political Behavior: Problems and Prospects* (Columbus: Charles E. Merrill, 1971), p. 106.

those who most fervently profess a public value may be the first ones to abandon it in deed, if this is required to protect their private interests.

For most political situations, positive and negative value tags abound. "Just as the same odor may be called an *aroma* or a *stench*, depending upon how one wants the listener to feel about it, so may the same guerillas be called *freedom-fighters*, *rebels*, or *terrorists*, depending upon how one wishes the listener to feel about them." [21] Once the tag has been attached to a concept, it tends to be perpetuated and reinforced because of the desire for cognitive consonance. Henceforth, the object which has received negative tags will receive further negative evaluations, and the positively tagged one will accumulate more positive tags.

Categorizing may have profound consequences when it involves matters for which people are prepared to fight and die. "Those whose acts are named 'communistic' must be killed by those whose acts are named 'democratic.' What is a 'communist,' or a 'democrat'? Often, indeed, whoever we name so. What do these names 'really' mean? Few know. They are simply god and devil terms, and as we all know, devils must be 'driven out' of the community, as of the self, if law and order are to prevail." [22]

Not only may condensation symbols incite people to violent actions, but they also may sanctify otherwise repulsive deeds. "We punish, enslave, torture, and kill in the name of principles of the socio-political order . . . if we loot a neighboring state, it is to uphold the 'honor' of our country, or to get 'living space for a superior race' . . . if we torture and burn a heretic, it is to uphold the faith; if we jail political enemies, it is to rid the community of 'enemies within.'" [23] Wars may be fought for material things such as food, clothing, and shelter, or territory, or access routes. "But as we plunge into battle, we cannot fight long and hard unless we fight in the name of some great principle of social order, for it is such names which give our relationship the glory and radiance we need to stave off the pressing horrors of decay and death." [24] During its bleakest hours, the American Revolution was re-

21. *Ibid.*; also see Felix S. Cohen, "The Reconstruction of Hidden Value Judgments: Word Choices as Value Indicators," p. 552; Quincy Wright, "Symbols of Nationalism and Internationalism," p. 391; both in Lyman Bryson, ed., *Symbols and Values: An Initial Study* (New York: Harper, 1954).

22. Hugh Dalziel Duncan, *Symbols in Society* (New York: Oxford University Press, 1968), pp. 23–24.

23. *Ibid.*, p. 66.

24. *Ibid.*, p. 24; also Deutsch, *Nationalism and Social Communication*, p. 90.

vived by the brilliant words of Thomas Paine, rather than by any brilliant military strategy.

However, there are limits to categorizing and value-tagging, especially in a democratic society where blatant deceptions are apt to be questioned. When there is reason to suspect that the application of inappropriate condensation symbols will be successfully challenged in a given situation, they may not be applied. In fact, the action to be justified by the symbol may be abandoned for lack of a good rationalizing rhetoric or because potent condensation symbols can be marshaled against it. "Groups may hesitate to violate laws in America, not because of strong commitments to legality, but because of the weight of public opinion that may be mobilized against them by the use of legal rhetoric." [25]

The Pied Piper Phenomenon

Many aspects of social action depend on the ability of political leaders to rally masses of people around them. There are three political organizing efforts in which the use of condensation symbols to "create and sustain social integration" is particularly significant: the efforts of established governmental powers to retain the allegiance of people to their country; the efforts of political subgroups within the country, such as political parties and interest groups, to gain a following; and the efforts of political dissidents to instigate a revolution.[26]

Through the processes of political socialization, the average individual acquires lifelong, almost automatic political loyalties to the values of the system which claims his political allegiance. Political elites, "by the use of sanctioned words and gestures," can elicit "blood, work, taxes, applause, from the masses. When the political order works smoothly, the masses venerate the symbols." [27] Expert manipulation of the nation's condensation symbols is "among the major weapons in any ruler's arsenal of power. It is on his skill in the manipulation of such symbols that the success or failure of the political leader, more often than not, depends. This skill indeed is one of the central charismatic qualities that make for mass leadership or predominance." [28]

The values embodied in condensation symbols used for basic political socialization tend to be quite general. They relate to the greatness,

25. Spencer, "Politics and Rhetorics," p. 604.
26. Duncan, Symbols in Society, p. 21.
27. Lasswell, Politics, p. 31.
28. Ithiel de Sola Pool, Symbols of Democracy (Stanford: Stanford University Press, 1952), p. iv.

justice, or beauty of one's particular country and nation, the propriety of its ideology, and the merits of its God-given destiny and way of life. Though applied to a particular country, they generally are basic social values shared by people in many different polities. They sustain in citizens a willingness to support the body politic, even when this involves considerable sacrifice.

The kinds of basic symbols which stir and invigorate political allegiance for the established order abound in the inaugural oratory of American presidents. "Inaugural oratory has invariably contained references to the deity, and usually to words like 'freedom,' 'liberty,' 'independence,' 'economy,' 'self-government.' . . . Such expressions as 'our fathers, our fore-fathers, the framers, the founders, our sages, heroes' were seldom left out. . . . Usually there were self-adulatory words like 'intelligence of our people, our righteous people, our great nation.'" [29]

Even the style of major public addresses fulfills a function closely akin to a favorable condensation symbol.[30] It conveys the meaning of authority and compulsion to unite behind the speaker and the majesty of his office. For instance, President Johnson opened his third State of the Union message in hallowed, hortatory style with: "I come before you to report on the State of the Union for the third time." As Lee Mc-Donald points out, in everyday language the president might have said, "This is the third time I have been here to talk to you about some of the problems some of the people in the federal government have been working on." Johnson's opening phrase, "I come before you," "suggests the formality and dignity of a state occasion. The phrase registers a sense of eventfulness as in 'I come bearing gifts.' One seems to see a tired but elated warrior dismounting from his steed among cheers from the multitude, having ridden at breakneck speed from a neighboring kingdom." The object of this kind of speech is "to renew the authority of the speaker and to invigorate the sense of community among the auditors." [31]

Such symbolism is not confined to the American scene. "No historian questions that symbols of nationalism have been used effectively by leaders in building and sustaining modern states and shaping their policies and fighting their wars." In fact, "political analysis indicates that

29. Lasswell, *Politics*, p. 35
30. For a discussion of language styles, see ch. 2, above. Also see Murray Edelman, *The Symbolic Uses of Politics* (Urbana: University of Illinois Press, 1964), pp. 134–138.
31. Lee C. McDonald, "Myth, Politics and Political Science," *Western Political Quarterly*, 22 (1969), 143.

today the symbols of nationalism are far more effective in inducing political cohesion and action than those of internationalism." [32]

Though the precise meanings of these symbols differ for individuals and change over time, their emotional content is shared and "induces people to unite in groups and in movements for common purposes," [33] permitting the principle of "convergent selectivity" to operate.[34] People share overall evaluations of individuals or measures, though the reasons for the choice may vary widely and may even be contradictory; thus mass support for men and measures can be secured from populations whose interests and outlooks diverge widely. The potency of condensation symbols tends to be increased through group interaction. As Murray Edelman has observed: "A mutual cuing within a group of evocative connotations may establish an aura around a sign, so that intensity is lent to the response. . . . The word is not in itself the cause; but it can evoke everything about the group situation that lends emotion to its political interests, abstracting, reifying, and magnifying." [35]

Just as condensation symbols are used to create and maintain emotional commitment to the nation, so they are used to inspire allegiance for less inclusive organizations within the confines of the state. These organizations may either try to appropriate the symbols dominant in the society and used by established authorities, or they may explicitly oppose these symbols and attempt to bring forth a new political rhetoric.

In the United States, the Republican and Democratic parties largely appeal to established symbols including free enterprise, individual rights, and the public welfare. Dissident movements, like the Black Panther party or Students for a Democratic Society, appeal to an unestablished creed, such as opposition to the capitalist system and the right of the downtrodden to use violence to gain their objectives. In the process they may "assign different meanings to familiar words and coin new words. The meaning of words like 'deviant,' 'criminal,' 'violent,' varies according to the group which provides the labelling." [36] The individuals and actions to which these labels are attached vary as well.

32. Wright, "Symbols of Nationalism," p. 398.

33. *Ibid.*, p. 384.

34. William Stephenson, *The Play Theory of Mass Communication* (Chicago: University of Chicago Press, 1967), ch. 1; Herbert Blumer, "The Crowd, the Public, and the Mass," in Schramm, *Process and Effects*, pp. 363–379.

35. Edelman, *Symbolic Uses of Politics*, p. 116.

36. Terry Nardin, "Language and Political Violence," *Peace Research Review*, 4 (1971), 58.

The precise social dynamics by which new condensation symbols are created and accepted remains unclear. "Exactly how, in politics, individuals and groups are labelled by their political adversaries, how such labelling affects the manner in which they are treated, and how such treatment in turn helps to shape their group consciousness, images of their adversaries, and political actions in general has not been systematically investigated." [37]

One of the few efforts to trace the genesis of a political symbol is Ronald Rotunda's story about the fight for the tag "liberal" during the administration of Franklin Roosevelt. The term had originally been used by English Tories as a derogatory label to identify the Whigs with "un-English" continental revolutionaries. But the Whigs had adopted it proudly, because the adjective "liberal" had laudatory connotations for most Englishmen. Whig sentiments turned out to be correct. In the United States, Republicans and Democrats both tried to appropriate the symbol in the late 1920s and early 1930s because, as with the British public, it carried favorable connotations for Americans.[38] Herbert Hoover insisted that he was a "true liberal" and that Roosevelt was a communist, socialist, fascist, or other kind of totalitarian.

Roosevelt believed that he needed a well-established condensation symbol to lend dignity and acceptability to the new social welfare and economic regulation programs which he planned to institute. The "socialist" tag was too entwined with communism; emphasis on "democratic" would have made it more difficult to attract much-needed Republican support; "progressive" was too closely associated with Theodore Roosevelt and Robert La Follette. The term "New Deal," though attractive, had no established meaning of its own, so it could not counteract conservative symbols and lure Republicans to the Roosevelt fold. "By associating his policies with a word such as 'liberal,' instead of 'Democratic,' a Republican could more easily justify his vote for FDR because he could mentally say to himself: 'I am for Roosevelt not because he is a Democrat but because he is a liberal.'" [39]

Hoover fought back in the 1932 and 1936 elections. He called the New Deal "false liberalism" and warned that its slogans "have been used mostly for camouflage and for political assassination." [40] But after 1936 the liberal-conservative dichotomy stressed by Roosevelt began to

37. *Ibid.*, p. 62.
38. Rotunda, "'Liberal' Label," p. 378.
39. *Ibid.*, p. 399.
40. *Ibid.*

stick in the public mind, and the Republicans lost the label. The Republicans had ceased to fight strongly for the symbol after Roosevelt's court-packing plan had discredited New Deal liberalism and the word "liberal" had become tarnished. Like most students of condensation symbols, Rotunda did not investigate how instrumental the "liberal" label was in making Roosevelt's program acceptable to the public. Hence we know what political leaders thought about its importance, but have no proof of its actual effects.

Although there is little proof that good slogans and condensation symbols are important factors in determining which movements will attract followers, most practitioners of the political art firmly believe in the presuasive powers of well-designed slogans.[41] Much of the art of political campaigning is based on the assumption that capture of the right symbol may clinch victory. "New Deals," "Fair Deals," "Square Deals," "New Frontiers," and "the Great Society" all were designed to make a vote for the bearer of the symbol irresistible.

One of the most dramatic recent efforts to concoct powerful condensation symbols to organize a political movement involves the attempt to politicize black Americans. It had been clear to black leaders for a long time that their movement for equality in American society needed new symbols — symbols which would break with the "Negro" stereotype with its connotations of an inferior individual, lazy, stupid, and willing to be kicked around. The slogan which emerged to fill these needs, "Black Power," developed a rhetorical magic which spoke to blacks' condition "in a way that 'freedom now' and non-violent 'we shall overcome' no longer did." [42] "For people who had been crushed so long by white power and who had been taught that black was degrading, it had a ready appeal." [43]

The slogan had been used off and on for several years by such black leaders as Richard Wright, James Baldwin, Lerone Bennett, Jr., and Adam Clayton Powell. However, it had never caught on until it was presented in a dramatic setting to an aroused audience which had been conditioned to defy established authority. During a huge mass meeting in a city park in Greenwood, Mississippi, in the turbulent summer of 1964, Stokely Carmichael, a charismatic black leader, mounted the platform. "After arousing the audience with a powerful attack on Missis-

41. Harold D. Lasswell, Nathan Leites et al., *The Language of Politics: Studies in Quantitative Semantics* (Cambridge: MIT Press, 1965), p. 15.

42. Robert L. Scott and Wayne Brockriede, *The Rhetoric of Black Power* (New York: Harper and Row, 1969), p. 80.

43. Martin Luther King, *Where Do We Go from Here, Chaos or Community?* (New York: Harper and Row, 1967), p. 29–32.

sippi justice, he proclaimed: 'What we need is Black Power.' Willie
Ricks, the fiery orator of SNCC, leaped to the platform and shouted,
'What do you want?' The crowd roared, 'Black Power.' Again and again
Ricks cried, 'What do you want?' and the response 'Black Power,' grew
louder and louder, until it reached fever pitch." [44]

Moderate black leaders like Martin Luther King conceded that it was
a powerful slogan, but expressed fears that some of its connotations
might hurt the black cause by dividing black from black and black
from white. As King expressed it: "It was my contention that a leader
has to be concerned about the problem of semantics. . . . While the
concept of legitimate Black Power might be denotatively sound, the slogan 'Black Power' carried the wrong connotations. I mentioned the implications of violence that the press had already attached to the
phrase. And I went on to say that some of the rash statements on the
part of a few marchers only reinforced this impression." In King's eyes,
it was a slogan which would "confuse our allies, isolate the Negro community and give many prejudiced whites . . . a ready excuse for self-
justification. . . . The words 'black' and 'power' together give the impression that we are talking about black domination rather than black
equality." He suggested the slogan "Black Consciousness" or "Black
Equality" as less vulnerable and more accurate in describing the goals
of the black community. [45]

While the leaders of many black organizations agreed with the sentiments expressed by King, the leadership of SNCC and CORE did not.
Power was the name of the game. Stokely Carmichael argued that all
ethnic minorities had gone after power, even though they had not used
it for a slogan. Black leaders had a right to insist that the definition
of black power be left up to them. "Now I say 'black power' and someone says, 'you mean violence.' . . . The first need of a free people is
to be able to define their own terms and have the terms recognized by
their oppressors. We must define what we are and move from our definitions and tell them [whites] to recognize what we say we are." To
Carmichael, "the power to define is the most important power that we
have. He is master who can define." [46]

Use of the Black Power slogan was supplemented by verbal efforts to
build up self-respect and determination among blacks. Martin Luther

44. *Ibid.*
45. *Ibid.*
46. Stokely Carmichael, speech at Morgan College, January 16, 1967, quoted in
Haig A. and Hamida Bosmajian, *The Rhetoric of the Civil Rights Movement*
(New York: Random House, 1969), pp. 114–115.

King admonished his followers that "the Negro must boldly throw off the manacles of self-abnegation and say to himself and to the world, 'I am somebody. I am a person. I am a man with dignity and honor. I have a rich and noble history . . . I'm black and I'm beautiful,' and this self-affirmation is the black man's need, made compelling by the white man's crimes against him." [47] At the same time, the use of disrespectful names for whites helped to break down the fear of whites which presumably retarded black political organization. Terms like "honkey," "whitey," or "the man," uttered with an appropriately derisive intonation, lowered the whites to the same level of impotence and contempt that had accompanied use of the word "nigger" by many whites.

A graphic, gripping style can serve as a condensation symbol to whip up support through the powerful images and emotions which it stirs. Martin Luther King could arouse his listeners to unite in angry compassion behind him when he painted the plight of southern blacks in simple, bold word pictures. "Negroes with the pangs of hunger and anguish of thirst were denied access to the average lunch counter . . . Negroes, burdened with the fatigue of travel, were still barred from the motels of the highways and the hotels of the cities. . . . But things are different now. In assault after assault, we caused the sagging walls of segregation to come tumbling down." [48]

When a movement lacks condensation symbols which are effective enough to rally a viable following, it may be doomed to failure. The fate of the New Left has been cited as a case in point. "It is significant that this generation of dissenters has failed to produce a literature or even a polemic that is likely to endure. . . . The same phrases – 'up against the wall,' 'get the pigs,' 'tell it like it is' – are endlessly repeated, less for their intrinsic eloquence than for their emotive and symbolic value. . . . Even the most outrageous obscenities lose their impact when they are used *ad nauseam*." The only widely attractive slogan of the New Left is "Power to the People," although it has lost some of its appeal because it was made so indisputably clear that this meant power to leftist radicals only. It has been argued that lack of an effective rhetoric forced the New Left to substitute the body rhetoric of violence in an effort to accomplish its goals and hold the movement together. [49]

47. Quoted in Scott and Brockriede, *Rhetoric of Black Power*, pp. 155–156.
48. *Ibid.*, p. 147.
49. *Time*, May 18, 1970.

In the course of power struggles within an established system, the contending parties usually appeal to many of the same condensation symbols. Things are different in a revolutionary situation; revolutionaries must detach people from the established symbols and substitute other symbols for them. "Revolutionary propaganda selects symbols which are calculated to detach the affections of the masses from the existing symbols of authority to attach these affections to challenging symbols, and to direct hostilities toward existing symbols of authority . . . the great revolutions are in defiance of emotions which have been directed to nurses, teachers, guardians and parents along 'accredited' channels of expressions. Revolutions are ruptures of conscience." [50] The precise dynamics of the process of symbol shift have not been investigated. The gradual build-up of dissatisfaction with old symbols and those who profess them, the rise of new leaders outside of the established power structure and eager to displace it, and the timing of verbal assaults with social developments harmful to the prestige of the old order all seem to be significant factors.

Revolutions entail major shifts in condensation symbols. "From the 'divine right of kings,' to the 'rights of man,' from the 'rights of man,' to the 'proletarian dictatorship'; these have been the principal vocabulary changes in the political history of the modern world. . . . In each case, a language of protest, long a utopian hope, became the language of an established order, an ideology." [51] Upheavals in power and social relationships are sometimes preceded by a victory of condensation symbols. The old leadership capitulates to the new slogans and adopts them long before the actual turnover in power.

When consensus breaks down, conflicting condensation symbols enhance the polarization of political forces. Revolutions "transform the pluralistic universe of social symbols into the uncompromising alternatives of total-friend, total-adversary relationships . . . there exist only the monopolistic owners of the social or religious verities and the ignorant and stubborn opponents to the truth that makes historical men free." [52] The stirring slogans of the French Revolution — Liberty, Equality, Fraternity — both thrilled and chilled the hearts of many Frenchmen. Lenin's passionate appeals to the working masses of Russia sounded like vile blasphemies to the country's old elites. Thus the ode to the new order is forever the dirge of the old.

50. Lasswell, *Politics*, p. 42.
51. *Ibid.*, pp. 113–115.
52. Albert Salomon, quoted in Wright, "Symbols of Nationalism," p. 401.

The Power of Naming

This book has repeatedly discussed how verbal conceptualizations define political reality and shape political preferences and actions. "The terms in which we name or speak of anything do more than designate it; they place it in a class of objects, thereby suggest with what it is to be judged and compared, and define the perspective from which it will be viewed and evaluated . . . language is . . . the key to the universe of speaker and audience . . . this function of language is no ephemeral influence, but the central factor in social relations and actions." [53]

Conceptualizations expressed in the form of condensation symbols are particularly effective for mass political indoctrination. The reasons have already been discussed. Through appropriate condensation symbols "those in power create and control the images, or names, that will legitimize their power . . . whoever creates or controls these names controls our lives." [54] When Mussolini labelled the Mediterranean as *mare nostrum,* he paved the way for the acceptance of expansionism as an unquestionable right of the Italians. Categorizing access to West Berlin or control over the off-shore islands of Communist China and Formosa as issues of "freedom versus communism" turned narrow territorial disputes, which could have been compromised, into nonnegotiable conflicts.[55] When issues are verbally escalated to become matters of principle, contending parties may be forced by public pressure or their own sense of honor to refuse to yield.

One aspect of naming which has attracted a good deal of attention in political dialogue is the function performed by euphemisms. The dictionary defines euphemism as "the use of an auspicious word for an inauspicious one." In politics, this involves an attempt to control audience reactions by avoiding words and verbal images with negative connotations and substituting for them words with neutral or positive connotations. Wars have called forth a good deal of euphemistic language to make it easier for the participants to accept their tasks in battle and on the home front. Much military jargon, formal as well as informal, is designed to deemphasize the fact that human beings are deliberately killed. "Targets" are hit, prisoners are "wasted," and there are "casualties," but not "dead" and "wounded." In the Vietnam war many American soldiers referred to South Vietnamese only as "dinks."

53. Edelman, *Symbolic Uses of Politics,* p. 131.
54. Duncan, *Symbols in Society,* p. 33.
55. K. J. Holsti, *International Politics: A Framework for Analysis,* 2d ed. (Englewood Cliffs, N.J.: Prentice-Hall, 1972), p. 198, calls this "issue escalation."

"Psychologically and morally . . . it is much easier to kill a 'dink' than it is to shoot a 'Vietnamese.'" Observers of the war believed that the "dink syndrome" played a part in the casual killing of many civilians in Vietnam.[56]

The testimony of Lieutenant William W. Calley, on trial for killing civilians in Vietnam, clearly reveals how depersonalized events can become. "I was ordered to go in there and destroy the enemy. That was my job on that day. That was the mission I was given. I did not sit down and think in terms of men, women and children. They were all classified the same, and that was the classification that we dealt with, just as enemy soldiers." The "enemy," as Calley reified it, was "communism." "Nobody in the military system ever described them as anything other than communism. They didn't give it a race, they didn't give it a sex, they didn't give it an age. . . . That was my enemy out there."[57] By verbal classification, the "enemy" had been deprived of humanity.

Deterrent theorists, who deal with the horrible possibility of nuclear war, often feel compelled to cloak their speculations about death and destruction in euphemisms. Herman Kahn, a master of this kind of verbal sorcery, "acknowledges that 'destruction is likely to be greatly intensified at the upper end of the escalation ladder.'"[58] This is a restrained way of saying that if a limited war gets out of hand, it may lead to death for millions and catastrophe for whole societies. Kahn also talks about "sanitary campaigns" in which an occasional missile base may be "taken out," making war sound like a garbage removal operation. "Nuclear stalemate" conveys an image of static deadlock, threatening neither side; "nuclear umbrella" makes the public feel sheltered, despite the fact that there is presently no defense against nuclear attack.[59] A touch of celestial nobility is bestowed upon intercontinental ballistic missiles when they are named Thor, Atlas, Jupiter, or Zeus.[60]

"Pacification" as used during the Vietnam war signified anything

56. *Newsweek*, Dec. 1, 1969, p. 37. Even aside from war, most Americans have a low tolerance for death symbols. Euphemistically, we talk about people "passing away," "expiring," "going to eternal rest," and humorously "kicking the bucket," or going to "Davy Jones's locker."

57. Quoted in Peter L. Berger, "Languages of Murder," *World View*, 15 (1972), 10.

58. Quoted in Philip Green, *Deadly Logic: The Theory of Nuclear Deterrence* (Columbus: Ohio State University Press, 1966), p. 223.

59. Jerome D. Frank, *Sanity and Survival: Psychological Aspects of War and Peace* (New York: Random House, 1967), p. 29.

60. Osgood, "Conservative Words and Radical Sentences," p. 107.

from fortifying villages to burning them to the ground. Primitive junks and sampans became "water-borne logistic craft" when they were marked for destruction.[61] Air raids sounded more innocuous and defensible when they were called "protective reaction strikes," and an invasion of Cambodia was made more respectable by labeling it an "incursion."

Euphemisms are not the sole preserve of the military and foreign policy makers. Attorney General John Mitchell reportedly asked the Ways and Means Committee of the House of Representatives to talk about increased "quick entry rights" for federal agents, rather than more "no-knock authority." The attorney general felt that the police authority to enter a suspect's quarters forcibly, without warning, after warrants had been obtained, would be more palatable with the new terminology.[62] For the sake of an improved image, prisons have been dubbed "correctional facilities," theft and vandalism on college campuses have been called "ripping off," "liberating," and "trashing," and pilferage in business establishments becomes respectable as "inventory leakage." [63]

On the social front, "depressions" sound less serious when they are called "recession." "Poverty," by U.S. Census bureau magic, has been transformed into the more affluent sounding "low-income level." "Poor children have disappeared, if not from the slums, then at least from the language. First they become 'deprived,' then 'disadvantaged,' and finally 'culturally disadvantaged,' as though they lacked nothing more serious than a free pass to Lincoln Center." [64] Old people now are called "senior citizens," and "beautiful people" may designate ugly people with money. George Orwell's age of doublethink and doublespeak is already with us.[65]

The Disadvantages of Condensation Symbols

A number of serious disadvantages spring from the use of euphemisms and other condensation symbols. By oversimplifying or blurring complex situations, by overstressing some aspects at the expense of others, by arousing emotions and bypassing reason, or by calming

61. *Ibid.*, p. 108.

62. *New York Times*, July 21, 1970.

63. Grace Hechinger, "The Insidious Pollution of Language," *Wall Street Journal*, Oct. 27, 1971.

64. *Ibid.*

65. George Orwell, "Politics in the English Language," in Maurice Stein et al., eds., *Identity and Anxiety* (Glencoe, Ill.: Free Press, 1960), pp. 308–319. Also see George Orwell, *Animal Farm* (New York: Harcourt, Brace, 1946).

needed anxiety and anger, they interfere with the perception of reality. To particularize the indictment into five major counts: first, condensation symbols lull people into a false and often paralyzing sense of security by making harmful conditions seem innocuous. "The real danger is that word pollution makes bureaucratic bungling seem harmless, renders anti-social behavior acceptable, gives so benign an image of poverty and social injustice as to lull people into believing that there is nothing to worry about, and gives war an antiseptic look." [66] Dangerous situations are consequently ignored, except for linguistic manipulation of the danger image.

Second, condensation symbols lead to distorted, oversimplified perception of reality. When poverty and crime are blamed on "systemic violence," people mistakenly believe that a cause has been identified and a remedy will follow. But the term is largely meaningless — it fails to define what is meant by "system" and by "violence." Responsibility for remedial action is easily evaded when blame is placed on such depersonalized concepts as "the system," "the establishment," "City Hall," or the "military-industrial complex." [67] Likewise, when politicians refer to "the national interest" which must be protected by a particular foreign policy, it makes their listeners conceive of the entire nation as a monolithic interest group whose welfare is at stake. The symbol hides the fact that there are many diverse interests within the nation, along with diverse opinions about the nature of policies that would be highly beneficial for most groups. Appeals to the "national interest" make people respond to the fiction of a unanimous will which cannot be defied, rather than the reality of particularized interest groups peddling their version of salvation.

A third objection concerns the fact that the ambiguity of condensation symbols can lead to serious misunderstandings among social groups. The meaning which the user intended or which the audience will put on his words is often uncertain. Since rousing terms are involved, the resulting misunderstandings may be extremely serious. For instance, the meaning of the phrase "law and order" during the 1968 presidential campaign was totally unclear. Middle America seemed to love the phrase. "The two surest-fire applause lines in any candidate's speech were always applause for 'law and order' at home and peace

66. Hechinger, "Insidious Pollution of Language." Also see Joyce O. Hertzler, *A Sociology of Language* (New York: Random House, 1965), pp. 276ff.

67. Ernest W. Lefever, "Wreckless Rhetoric and Foreign Policy," *World View*, 11 (1970), 9–10. Also see Jeremy J. Stone, *Strategic Persuasion: Arms Limitation through Dialogue* (New York: Columbia University Press, 1967), p. 41.

in Vietnam." [68] One could interpret this as a yearning for reduced crime and increased safety of city streets. But liberals did not interpret it that way; to them, appeals to law and order were slaps at the civil liberties of minorities. The crowds' applause was an accolade for bigotry, demonstrating the incorrigible prejudices of American society. "The phrase 'law and order' had descended through American politics wrapped in the rhetoric of the right; it smacked of nightriders, vigilantes, of union-busting, of the witch hunts and red hunts of A. Mitchell Palmer." [69] Liberals claimed that it was a code word for racism and meant that the users wanted to club blacks into submission. It was a justifying slogan for repression. To talk about law and order in public "was tantamount to indiscriminate support of police brutality, and the beating of innocents while defending the sheriffs of Alabama and Mississippi, the FBI and the House Un-American Activities Committee all at once." [70] Hence "law and order" became a highly divisive condensation symbol which further split an already badly divided American society.

Similar ambiguities plague the use of the "violence" label on the American scene. If a liberal politician tagged police beating of student demonstrators as "violence," 44 percent of his male audience would be apt to consider this a distortion of the situation.[71] To them, use of force by the police would not constitute violence. In the sample of males from which these figures are taken, shooting of looters by police was called "violence" by only 23 percent of white union members, compared to 59 percent of blacks in the sample. College students and white union members had diametrically opposed views on the type of action to which the tag "violence" could be properly affixed. Such ambiguities in the meaning of widely used condensation symbols make it very difficult for various population groups to understand each other. They spread feelings of mutual deception, distrust, and wide and unabridgeable disparities in basic values.[72]

The ambiguities of condensation symbols can also poison interna-

68. Theodore White, *The Making of the President, 1968* (New York: Atheneum, 1969), p. 220.
69. *Ibid.*
70. *Ibid.*
71. Institute for Social Research, University of Michigan, *ISR Newsletter,* Spring, 1971 (Ann Arbor: University of Michigan Press, 1971), p. 5. Data come from a study of an all-male sample composed of 63 college students, 303 blacks, and 279 white union members.
72. Other surveys have shown a wide disparity between connotations of "justice" as supplied by white and black populations.

tional relations. A comparative study of the meaning of "socialism" and "capitalism" to people in the United States and in various European countries showed that, in Europe, "socialism" had generally favorable connotations and "capitalism" was viewed unfavorably. The reverse was true in the United States. However, what Americans called "capitalism" closely resembled in its essential features what Europeans called "socialism." The "socialism" of the Europeans was quite different from the Communistic world order which Americans had in mind when they spoke of "socialism." Accordingly, the American habit of extolling the virtues of "capitalism" and denouncing the evils of "socialism" set the stage for major misunderstandings.[73]

In international relations, the word "aggression" has been a widely used pejorative condensation symbol. Countries called "aggressors" and actions labelled as "aggression" have called forth fear, hate, and condemnation, yet no one has ever been able to define the concept to the satisfaction of political experts. Attempts to define what constitutes "aggression" date back to the Congress of Vienna of 1815. In 1952, the UN General Assembly set up a fifteen-nation special committee to define aggression; it has worked without success ever since.[74] Meanwhile, the term, used as a verbal weapon to damage national reputations, continues to spread confusion about the sequence and nature of the international events which have been labeled "aggression."

Serious ambiguities may arise because the original circumstances which gave rise to a symbol have changed, yet the connotations of the symbol remain the same. "Hawks" and "doves," when originally identified during the Vietnam war, differentiated proponents of stepped-up war from those who wished to maintain or reduce the level of military activity. As policy options changed away from the possibility of escalation to various forms of withdrawal, the meaning of the terms became murky; labeling people as hawks or doves produced a confusing array of political characterizations of the same individuals. The commonality of meaning has been similarly eroded for such terms as isolationist and interventionist, liberal and conservative, containment and liberation.[75]

73. Ralph White, quoted in Osgood, "Conservative Words and Radical Sentences," p. 109.

74. These efforts are discussed in Benjamin B. Ferencz, "Defining Aggression: Where It Stands and It's Going," *American Journal of International Law*, 66 (1972) 491–508. Also see Julius Stone, *Aggression and World Order* (Berkeley: University of California Press, 1958).

75. Cynthia Enloe and Mostafa Rejai, "The New Style in U.S. Foreign Policy," *World View*, 13 (1970), 5–8.

Fourth, condensation symbols may subject people to the magnetism of powerful, emotion-laden cues which they dare not question or defy. The symbols become "symbolic sanctions" which command or prohibit certain behaviors; not to conform is to label oneself a social deviate or outcast, or to forego the rewards of a highly favorable designation.[76] Use of "condensation symbols can become a hazard to rational action because it can prevent systematic analysis of one's situation and interests . . . men support or oppose as a conditioned response whatever is accepted in their group . . . words then are no longer descriptive but purely evocative."[77]

When controversies over race relations, or free enterprise, or dealings with other powers or political movements become tagged with the concepts of liberty and equality on one side, or social disorder and disintegration on the other, people may be effectively deprived of their right to choose sides. One cannot readily side with evil or align against virtue without becoming sullied in the process. If it is "patriotic" to fight in a war and "traitorous" to refuse to fight, the average person prefers risking his life to risking his reputation. The decision becomes a question of adhering to or rejecting the mores of one's community, rather than a question of weighing a situation on its merits.

A fifth and final disadvantage of condensation symbols which has received wide public attention in recent years is their power to inflame the public dialogue. Reasoned discussion suffers when tempers flare, and cooperation and widely acceptable decisions are difficult to obtain under those circumstances. In fact, the epithets and vulgarisms which totalitarian powers use to denounce their enemies are often cited as proof of inability to reach decisions through democratic dialogue.[78]

On the American domestic scene, the use of abusive condensation symbols has increased by leaps and bounds in recent years. Political leaders have begun to worry seriously and publicly about the effects of

76. Roger Brown and Don E. Dulany, "A Stimulus-Response Analysis of Language and Meaning," in Paul A. Henley, ed., *Language, Thought and Culture* (Ann Arbor: Ann Arbor Paperbacks, 1965), pp. 51–54; Merelman, "Learning and Legitimacy," p. 555.

77. Edelman, *Symbolic Uses of Politics*, p. 125; also see Murray Edelman, "Escalation and Ritualization of Political Conflict," *American Behavioral Scientist*, 13 (1969), 232.

78. Holsti, *International Politics*, p. 202. Western powers may accomplish many of the same effects in a subtler way. Instead of calling a foreign diplomat a liar, they may describe his actions in a manner which clearly implies that he has lied. The impact of inflammatory language is discussed in John Waite Bowers, "Some Correlates of Language Intensity," *Quarterly Journal of Speech*, 50 (1964), 415–420.

verbal excesses on such democratic essentials as respect for the opposition and willingness to listen to all viewpoints. Political dialogue "continues to be poisoned by inflammatory rhetoric and impassioned code words that confuse the issue, distort the options . . . and erode the President's capacity to act effectively. . . ."[79] Demonstrators have been warned by a presidential fact-finding commission that "the use of obscenities and derogatory terms such as 'pigs' and 'honkies' during a demonstration may trigger a violent if unjustifiable response" and escalate tensions.[80]

The disadvantages of condensation symbols should not obscure their advantages as tools of the political trade. They are an essential form of political communication in a complex, time-pressured world. Like any tool, they can be used for both good and ill; producers and consumers of condensation symbols must be aware of this. The choice is not between employing or avoiding symbols, but between accepting indiscriminate uses or insisting on careful, ethical language choices.

INFERENCES DRAWN FROM CONDENSATION SYMBOLS

Since condensation symbols are verbal stimuli which evoke multifaceted deeply involving images, study of their uses and effects sheds light on the distribution and potency of political values. A few examples will indicate the types of inferences made particularly accessible through a study of condensation symbols. The discussion will be brief, because examples of inference-making presented in different contexts in previous chapters have already illustrated the usefulness of condensation symbols for certain types of inferences.[81]

Inferences about Values and Value Changes

In any community, political descriptions, discussions, and arguments are rich in a number of condensation symbols which relate the subject under discussion to the value structure of the community. By studying the symbols and symbol evaluations used in particular situations, or during certain periods, one can discern major values and concerns. This knowledge is essential for inferring the character of the community and predicting its likely responses to political stimuli. The fact that most symbols involving political dissent, such as "civil disobedience" or "non-

79. Lefever, "Rhetoric," p. 9.
80. U.S. Government, *The Report of the President's Commission on Campus Unrest* (Washington, D.C.: U.S. Government Printing Office, 1970), p. 464.
81. In particular, see chs. 1 and 6, above.

violence," carry positive connotations for many contemporary American publics permits inferences about changes in attitudes toward authority, deviations from established norms of behavior, and conceptions of individual rights. Concerns about "repression," "privacy," and "alienation" reveal perceptions of government as an oppressive force from which the individual must be protected.[82] Society-wide approval for many terms denoting social welfare goals indicates that these have become consensual values.

Comparisons of communities based on differences in responses to the same condensation symbols permit inferences about differences in characteristics and action potential. If the mass media abound in positive references to peaceful coexistence, disarmament, disengagement, and international cooperation in one country at a particular time, and in negative references to these symbols in another country at the same time, one may be able to draw accurate inferences about the political circumstances responsible for the differences. Use of phrases such as "cult of the individual" or "collective leadership" or "revisionism" on the one hand, and "counterculture," "Establishment," or "women's lib" on the other would permit inferences about the cultural origins of the speaker. A reference to the war of 1861–65 in the United States as the "Rebellion of the Southern States," the "Civil War," the "War between the States," or the "War to Repel Yankee Aggression" would tell much about the intellectual sources on which the speaker had relied.[83]

Joseph Zikmund undertook an interesting comparative analysis of national anthems on the assumption that anthems, because of their prominence in national life, reflect the nation's basic major ideals. The analysis showed that ". . . the most common symbolic themes seem to be martial, either in victory or independence, in defense against the foreign enemy or in just plain sabre-rattling. The call to arms and military glory in the name of the homeland far outweighs the call for peace."[84] However, most militaristic references were to past glories rather than future battles, giving the impression that nations considered the military struggle as a thing of the past. Nor was the martial emphasis universal. A number of countries, particularly in Asia, lack martial motives in their national anthems. Indonesia is a notable exception. Moreover,

82. Ithiel de Sola Pool, "The Language of Politics: 1971," APSA paper (1971), pp. 16–17.

83. Frank, Sanity and Survival, pp. 29–30. Pool, "The Language of Politics: 1971," contains a list of new condensation symbols which have developed since 1950.

84. Joseph Zikmund II, "National Anthems as Political Symbols," Australian Journal of Political History, 15 (1969), 75.

a number of countries have changed their national anthems away from themes of military glory to themes of more peaceful endeavors.

While interesting, inferences about the prevalence of militaristic attitudes drawn from national anthems seem of questionable validity as indicators of current national values. Anthems constitute a tiny fragment of verbal behavior in any society and are stylized and rigid. Once adopted, they are not readily altered to reflect changes in national values, or even new oratory styles. Studies which judge the conflict potential of a society by the diversity and nature of conflict symbols appearing in newspaper editorials over a prolonged period seem to be on more solid scientific ground.[85]

It may be as profitable to identify missing symbols as to trace those which are widely represented in the community's verbal behavior. Thus Quincy Wright, in his studies of symbols of nationalism and internationalism, discovered that symbols of internationalism were rarely linked with symbols of personal allegiance. The theme of love of country, love of people, and love of flag was perennial, but there were few references to love of any international body, love of world community, or love of international law.[86] The World Attention Surveys, which measured the frequency of appearance of various condensation symbols in the editorials of prestige newspapers throughout the world, found that fewer than one-third of the symbols involved international themes.[87] This type of information, corroborated by other data, leads to the inference that internationalism is a comparatively minor value for most people. The inference that internationalism is deemphasized, in turn, permits a number of subsidiary inferences.

Change in the nature, meaning, and valence of condensation symbols may permit important inferences about the pace and direction of social change in political systems. Ithiel de Sola Pool has noted the constancy of political symbols between 1890 and 1950 in five countries whose elite newspapers were studied. Basic symbols were constant for Britain, France, Germany, and the United States; major symbol changes occurred only in the Soviet Union.[88] By contrast, there has been almost exponential growth of new symbols in the five countries since then, mostly coined by left-wing intellectuals to stress the rights

85. See, e.g., Ithiel de Sola Pool, The "Prestige" Papers: A Survey of Their Editorials (Stanford: Stanford University Press, 1952).

86. Wright, "Symbols of Nationalism," p. 389.

87. Pool, The "Prestige" Papers; Ithiel de Sola Pool, Symbols of Internationalism (Stanford: Stanford University Press, 1951), p. 34ff.

88. Pool, "The Language of Politics: 1971," p. 5. On the gradual obsolescence of symbols, see Merelman, Learning and Legitimacy, p. 554.

of individual deviance. Even life styles, like "hippie" and "beatnik," have become political terms.[89]

Changes in May Day slogans in the Soviet Union have been studied to infer basic changes in the country's foreign policy from 1919 to 1943.[90] Universal revolutionary slogans prevailed in the early years. Later, slogans became more nationalistic and focused on domestic matters; references to enemies of the Revolution dropped.[91] These changes permitted inferences that the Russian belief in the imminence of world revolution was being replaced by concentration on internal policies. The analysts concluded that "the history of the Soviet Union could easily be written in terms of changing slogans."[92]

The disappearance of symbols may also be instructive. The phrase "victory of the free world" was born with the Cold War and served as a powerful evocative symbol. Now, when the Cold War seems to be yielding to friendlier interaction climates, a gradual depreciation of the symbol has begun; it may well drop entirely from use. Other symbols such as the "white man's burden," the "divine right of kings," or "redemption of the Holy Places from the infidels" have long since passed into historical limbo. Their demise marks the disappearance of the concepts for which they stood as powerful political motivating forces.

Some symbols remain active, but with content changed to reflect social developments. The symbol of "equality" in the context of American history is a good example. To the black man, the cry for "equality" at first meant equality in subordination, then separate-but-equal facilities, and now desegregation and equal opportunities. By tracing meaning changes in the symbol, one can infer value changes among large segments of the American public.

Inferences about Characteristics of the Symbol User

Besides inferences based on the distribution and uses of symbols within a society, one can make inferences about the characteristics of symbol users. "The words a group employs and on which it relies to evoke a response can often be taken as an index of group norms and conceptual frameworks."[93] Patriotic and veterans' organizations use

89. Pool, "The Language of Politics: 1971," p. 19.
90. S. Yacobson and Harold D. Lasswell, "Trend: May Day Slogans in Soviet Russia, 1918–1943," in Harold Lasswell, Nathan Leites et al., *Language of Politics*, 232–297.
91. *Ibid.*, pp. 244ff.
92. *Ibid.*, p. 284.
93. Edelman, *Symbolic Uses of Politics*, p. 121.

the older, more conservative term "freedom," whereas civil liberties groups use the newer, more radical term "liberty." "The terms 'social welfare' and 'charity,' similarly serve as indexes to sub-cultures and to differences in norms. . . ."[94] Users of "social welfare" are more apt to be on the left of the political spectrum, while users of the term "charity" are often on the right.

Certain national epithets are inherently prejudicial. Communicators who use terms like "nigger," "Jap," "Wop," "Kraut," or "Frog" exhibit disdain for the group labeled with the distasteful name.[95] As discussed previously, during World War II groups with Communist leanings were detected by scrutinizing their use of condensation symbols. When communications within a group were rich in symbols such as "bourgeois," "class struggle," "collectivism," "exploitation," "proletariat," "revolution," and the like, it was inferred that the members were sympathetic to Communist movements.[96]

Condensation symbols may reveal how communicators conceptualize politics. People who speak of the "military-industrial complex," or "American imperialism," obviously subscribe explicitly or implicitly to distinct theories about political power. A speaker who states that "campus leftists today stepped up their efforts to provoke confrontation with university officials" apparently believes that left-wing movements exist and have tried previously to provoke confrontation.[97]

Similarly, the slogans of the Black Power movement indicate the change in blacks' outlooks on society. Joel Aberbach and Jack Walker have stated, "Nothing better symbolized the changing mood and style of black protest in America than recent changes in the movement's dominant symbols. Demonstrators who once shouted 'freedom' as their rallying cry now were shouting 'black power' . . . a much more provocative and challenging slogan. The old symbols of middle class respectability had become meaningless. Instead they have been replaced by vigorous slogans which indicate the desire to participate in the political struggle for power."[98]

Aberbach and Walker also tested the meaning of the "Black Power" slogan for people in the Detroit area; they hoped to infer a respondent's social self-image from the meaning assigned to the slogan. The definition which the individual chooses for a condensation symbol "may tell

94. *Ibid.*, p. 122.
95. Cohen, "Reconstruction of Hidden Value Judgments," p. 547.
96. Lasswell, Leites et al., *Language of Politics*, p. 226–227.
97. Nardin, "Language and Political Violence," p. 56.
98. Aberbach and Walker, "Meaning of Black Power," p. 367.

us a great deal about how he defines himself politically in a society torn by racial strife." [99] An individual may see the slogan as a call to blacks to organize and build a sense of community; he may see it as a pressure group tactic; or he may see it as a call for revolution and subversion.

On a table which specified eight meanings plus a "don't know" category, 22.6 percent of the blacks indicated that the slogan meant racial unity to them, 22.3 percent said it meant nothing to them, and 19.6 percent indicated that it meant a fair share for black people. None of the other possible answers received as much as 10 percent of the responses. Among whites, 38.6 percent thought it meant blacks ruling whites, 11.9 percent thought it meant trouble, rioting and disorder, and 11.7 percent had other negative, imprecise comments. The rest of the responses were scattered.[100] "In most cases reactions are intense and interpretations of the idea's meaning are related to an individual's basic orientation towards social and political problems. Whites have an overwhelmingly negative reaction to 'Black Power.' The slogan is seen by most whites as an illegitimate revengeful challenge." Among blacks, however, over 40 percent of the people questioned considered the term either as a call for fair and equal treatment, or as an appeal for racial solidarity.[101] The meanings assigned to the term indicated that the respondents differed substantially in their political conceptualizations and permitted inferences about their orientations and reactions.

The same type of analysis could be used for data on the different meanings of the term "violence." Other studies have investigated differential meanings of such terms as "justice" and "equality." [102] These, too, can be used for inferences about the political attitudes of respondents.

Semantic differential analysis of individual reactions to the names of political candidates has yielded interesting insights into political attitudes when these names are condensation symbols. Reactions to the concept "Eugene McCarthy" were examined for the qualities which the respondent projected on the symbol. The analysts argued that the qualities which an individual would see in the candidate would correlate with his psychic needs, as expressed in personality tests.[103] Since

99. *Ibid.*, p. 368.

100. *Ibid.*, p. 386.

101. *Ibid.*, p. 387.

102. See, for example, Richard M. Johnson, "The Social Climate for Race and Poverty Measures," APSA paper (1970).

103. Stephen R. Brown and John D. Ellithorp, "Emotional Experiences in Political Groups: The Case of the McCarthy Phenomenon," *American Political Science Review*, 64 (1970), 364.

a dependent respondent would project the candidate as a father figure, one might then infer dependence from a father-figure projection.

The use of certain adjectives and verbs can turn a speaker's phrases into condensation symbols which reveal basic political attitudes. What a person calls "foreign" and "strange" can reveal much about his background. Using an adjective which is correct but not relevant in a particular context may indicate prejudice. When a racial or religious or national identification is gratuitously combined with a discussion of a criminal act, prejudice on the part of the user may be inferred. The speaker who talks about a black or white or Jewish or Catholic murderer, when these are not relevant aspects of the crime, is using the defining term to condense negative feelings against a racial or religious group.[104]

The type of terminology used by the House Appropriations Committee has led to inferences about the committee's attitude toward the process of budget cutting. The committee speaks of budgets as being filled with fat, grease, pork water, waste tissue, soft spots, and similar unappetizing components. These are cut, carved, sliced, pruned, whittled, squeezed, wrung, trimmed, slashed, and similarly mutilated. The operations are performed with a knife, blade, meat axe, hatchet, or fine-tooth comb. Budgets are hailed for being "cut to the bone." [105] A person's attitude toward war may be gauged by whether he uses the word "murder" or "killing" to describe events on the battlefield. In tense social conditions, people fight, battle, struggle, and wipe out the opposition. There may even be some significance in the fact that Britishers stand for election, while Americans run for office.[106]

SUMMARY

Condensation symbols are verbal stimuli which carry little independent information but which activate a wide variety of similar perceptions and connotations in their listeners. These perceptions and connotations usually involve fundamental social values and are fraught with emotions; once these emotions have been stirred, particularly in a mass setting where the sense of sharing intensifies feelings, it becomes com-

104. Cohen, "Reconstruction of Hidden Value Judgments," p. 547.
105. Richard F. Fenno, Jr., "The Appropriations Committee as a Political System," *American Political Science Review*, 56 (1962), 312.
106. Also see Karin Dovring, *Road of Propaganda: The Semantics of Biased Communications* (New York: Philosophical Library, 1959), p. 120; Martin Landau, "On the Use of Metaphor in Political Analysis," *Social Research*, 28 (1961), 331–353.

paratively easy to induce mass actions. The symbols may become Pav-lovian cues which political leaders can use to elicit instant, powerful, and fairly predictable mass responses. Arousing emotionally based mass support is the most portentious political function performed with the aid of condensation symbols.

The effects of a particular condensation symbol on a specific audi-ence will vary, depending on the perceptions stored in the memories of audience members. Some symbols, like those that appeal to basic group allegiances, will arouse responses from a wide range of audiences. Others, like the slogans of minor political movements, will have mean-ing and power for only a small circle of followers. Symbols like "com-munism," which simultaneously tap basic concerns such as patriotism, home and job security, and basic moral and religious values, are po-tentially most powerful. Since political cultures abound in God and Devil symbols, politicians rarely lack the cues to engender favorable or unfavorable situation appraisals in their audiences. But when it be-comes impossible to find the right symbols or to attach them believably to a situation, the actions to be justified with the aid of condensation symbols may have to be abandoned.

Condensation symbols are a highly economical form of political com-munication because one short word or phrase can activate large amounts of information stored in the listeners' memories. Use of the stimulus word or phrase spares the speaker the often arduous task of conveying new ideas to mass audiences through a careful, detailed ac-count which must be designed to be widely understood and to evoke predictable responses.

Political leaders employ condensation symbols to gain and sustain mass followings for their nation, their party, their faction, or their so-cial group by linking themselves and their policies and ideologies to values already prized by their actual and potential followers. In fact, without condensation symbols most social groups, large or small, would not be able to produce the feelings of mutuality which are needed for group cohesion and action. Social movements which seek to generate strong ties among their followers may take painstaking care to create effective condensation symbols; without such symbols, the movement may fail or grow at an unduly slow pace.

It is particularly crucial, as well as extremely difficult, for revolu-tionary forces to devise appropriate condensation symbols. Revolution-aries must first destroy the appeal of existing positive value symbols by linking them to negative condensation symbols; then they must gain approval for new values by creating new condensation symbols for them, or by linking them to previously accepted symbols in a novel way. If the symbolic underpinnings of the established system have been profoundly internalized by the population, detaching old allegiances and transferring them to new political forces is a formidable task.

Political categorization is another vital function which politicians perform readily with the aid of condensation symbols. When gasoline rationing has been indelibly labeled as "un-American," it becomes a policy which must be judged primarily on its ideological suitability for the American people, rather than on its economic merits. Moreover, it has been marked as "bad" in the eyes of the multitudes for whom anything which is not "American" is inferior.

Linking a favorable or unfavorable condensation symbol to a person or idea enables a communicator to transfer the established category and evaluation of the condensation symbol to the person or idea. The speaker can indicate appropriate and inappropriate parameters for appraising the factors under examination. Mass audiences tend to accept the categorization because it is easier to apply the preformed evaluation inherent in the symbol than to make an independent evaluation. In this manner, the political universe can be readily ordered for mass publics who only need to be furnished with the appropriate verbal tags to decide what is good and bad in their world.

The ready acceptability of condensation symbols makes it tempting to use them to blur reality, to provide simplistic explanations, to create or calm fears when such action is not warranted and, generally, to immobilize the capacities for critical thinking of the individuals who make up mass publics. Some of the vilest deeds of personal violence known to man have been made acceptable and even praiseworthy simply by tagging them with positive condensation symbols.

Analysis of the condensation symbols which politicians use for particular audiences, and of the responses evoked, may lead to valuable inferences about the norms, concerns, and value structures of individuals and groups. The fact that symbols relating to civil disobedience and nonviolent dissent elicit supportive responses from many American audiences today permits inferences about current perceptions of the relation of the individual to society. Absence of references to symbols of internationalism in the political dialogue of major world powers has led to inferences about the comparative importance of nationalistic and cosmopolitan orientations. The use of particular symbols also permits inferences about how the symbol user conceptualizes the political process, and whom he views as enemies and friends. Condensation symbols may even provide clues to psychological needs of communicators and their audiences. If terminology of reassurance and strong leadership abounds, one can infer that the communication situation reflects deep-seated feelings of insecurity which exist or are presumed to exist among the communicators.

Epilogue

What knowledge about the role of verbal behavior in politics is now available to social scientists? What has been learned from systematic studies of verbal behavior? What sparsely explored and unchartered areas of knowledge are beckoning as the next targets for research?

Four major areas of the field of political linguistics have been charted in this book. First were the dilemmas and difficulties which confront political communicators when they encode messages designed to elicit desired responses from their audiences. Failure to select the right message or to encode it properly may impair the quality of political interaction, sometimes entailing political impotence or even disaster.

Yet, despite these possibly awesome consequences, the encoding and decoding process has remained largely an art. In most political encounters it is heavily based on intuitive abilities, rather than on scientifically derived rules and skills. Studies of the general principles of persuasion and of verbal aspects of group dynamics are among the all-too-scant pioneering efforts in this area; a few studies of the substance and manner of conceptualizations of political messages by political leaders and by the mass media have also been made.

Second, this book has considered some of the major effects of political messages. These message effects run the gamut from conveying politically relevant information which changes the body of available political knowledge, to using words as surrogates for action so that new power configurations are called into existence by such verbal means as promises or threats.

Solid proof remains the weak point of studies which trace and analyze verbal behavior's effects. Most political situations involve a combination of diverse verbal and non-verbal stimuli which makes it difficult to isolate the effects produced by a particular stimulus. It is rarely possible to find essentially similar political incidents in which nonverbal factors are constant and only the verbal factors vary. Hence the effects of variations in verbal stimuli can seldom be determined precisely. Laboratory and experimental studies provide some confirmation for hypotheses about effects of various verbal formulations, but findings from these artificially simplified situations may not apply to the far more complex reality of natural settings.

Third, this book has examined the possibilities of gaining political knowledge through inferences based on verbal output. What is actually verbalized may be but the tip of an iceberg of information which can be probed more deeply through inferential reasoning. Messages often carry rich inferential clues about the communicator's personality and life situation, about the actual and assumed characteristics of the audience, and about the situational context which molded the message.

The problem of proof is somewhat less acute here than in cause-and-effect linkages. The accuracy of many types of inferences can be checked if there are clues about the inferred event. Yet major problems remain in perfecting the inferential process so that we can identify indicators which will make accurate predictions possible. Hunches and intuition must be at least partly supplanted by testable theories and unambiguous rules.

Fourth, we have explored various approaches to analysis and measurement of verbal behavior, describing the main tools available to the verbal behavior researcher and calling attention to grave problems which must be solved before verbal behavior research can reach its fullest potential. The most serious deterrents to massive verbal behavior studies have been the drudgery of the process and the difficulty of eliminating subjectiveness in coding. The availability of computer programs for examining large amounts of verbal data promises a satisfactory resolution of such technological problems. While optimism certainly seems warranted, the current slow progress in methodological improvements engenders a sense of caution.

Beyond the technical problems of coding large bodies of verbal data, the problems of creating a theoretically adequate foundation for guiding measurement and analysis continue to loom large. The ability to measure with precision is of limited value when there are unresolved doubts about the aspects of verbal behavior that should be measured in order to gain greatest insight into a particular problem.

In exploring these major facets of political linguistics, a wide range of verbal behavior studies has been examined. The reader has been presented with a panoramic view of the major advances which social scientists have made thus far, and he has been exposed to the frustrations which have plagued them. The studies reported in the book have provided examples of many theories which have been offered to explain and predict certain types of verbal behavior or to draw inferences from specific verbal output. The various theories based on mirror models are examples. At the micro-level, mirror-model theorists explain how verbal behavior reflects psychological states and perceptions of the individual communicator; at the macro-level, they have shown how verbal behavior of entire societies, as reflected in their literature and the mass media, mirrors the values of these societies.

A number of studies described in the book illustrate that such theories are helpful in explaining and predicting verbal output, but these studies also reveal that these and other theories of verbal behavior require a great deal of amplification and refinement to account for the many exceptions to the gross theory. Some of these refinements are now emerging — such as the theories of cognitive consistency and of games, which delineate some circumstances under which expressed perceptions are unlikely to mirror the objective realities of a given situation. But a great deal of groundwork remains to be done in developing new theories, in refining existing theories, and in testing promising theoretical formulations empirically.

Since the advent of the computer has refocused attention on quantitative studies it seems especially urgent to reexamine the theories which underlie quantitative verbal analyses. In particular, assumptions about the consequences of frequency and infrequency, and of high and low intensity of verbal mention need to be tested. To count the appearances of a specified verbal behavior is wasteful if we lack empirically tested theories which confirm that this does, indeed, matter. It is not unduly difficult to devise the necessary tests. A simple questionnaire, following exposure to a political speech in laboratory or natural settings, could test whether frequency of mention of topics has the hypothesized effects on audiences. Likewise, one could test the relationship between frequency of mention of policies and subsequent action involving these policies. Further analyses could ascertain whether there is a fatigue or redundancy factor which makes interest and significance curves slow down or slump after an optimum frequency has been reached. These analyses could determine whether the impact of novelty outweighs the effects of frequency and, if so, whether this is usual or happens only when certain other contingencies have been met.

In his survey and analysis of research on the effects of the mass media, Joseph Klapper concluded with a word of advice which seems applicable to verbal behavior research in general. The most fruitful approach to research appears to be "neither the path of abstract theorizing nor the path . . . of seeking simple and direct effects of which mass communication is the sole and sufficient cause." Rather, there is far "greater hope in the new approach which begins with the existing phenomenon — an observed change of opinion, for example — and which attempts to assess the roles of the several influences which produced it." This can be done through field studies or through "logically related controlled experiments in which the multifarious extramedia factors being investigated are built into the research design. These are the paths which . . . have brought us to the point of tentative generalization and which seem likely to lead further toward the still distant goal of empirically documented theory."[1] These paths also seem most promising for discovering the forces which shape various types of verbal behaviors, and for assaying their effects.[2]

The potential societal benefits from verbal behavior research seem significant enough to warrant substantial commitments of thought, energy, and financial resources. Two kinds of interrelated harvests beckon the researcher: greater knowledge and understanding of past and present social settings, and the possibility of increased power to guide political forces into desired directions. The possibilities are vast and varied in both areas because of the abundance of verbal data concerning human affairs, and because of the countless occasions when political actors use verbal behavior in efforts to control their environment.

When we talk about social engineering, we enter a realm laced with fears about the potential dangers of abuse. What will happen to cherished freedoms if demagogues can learn to pull verbal strings which make audiences respond like puppets? The answer is that knowledge about successful verbal manipulation encompasses knowledge to recognize manipulation when it occurs. This should confer the ability to

1. Joseph T. Klapper, *The Effects of Mass Communication* (New York: Free Press, 1960), p. 257.

2. Some examples are studies of verbal behavior in Congress, such as Paul Lutzker, "The Behavior of Congressmen in a Committee Setting: A Research Report," *Journal of Politics*, 31 (1969), 140–166, and D. A. Strickland, "On Ambiguity in Political Rhetoric: Defeat of the Rat Control Bill in the House of Representatives, July, 1967," *Canadian Journal of Political Science*, 2 (1969), 338–344; studies of persuasive appeals and the inferences which may be drawn from them, such as Robert K. Merton, *Mass Persuasion: The Social Psychology of a War Bond Drive* (New York: Harper, 1946) and Alexander L. George, *Propaganda Analysis* (White Plains, N.Y.: Row, Peterson, 1959); studies of verbalized perceptions of political elites, such as Ole R. Holsti, "Individual Differences in 'Definition of the Situation,'" *Journal of Conflict Resolution*, 14 (1970), 303–310, and Robert D. Putnam, *The Beliefs of Politicians: Ideology, Conflict, and Democracy in Britain and Italy* (New Haven: Yale University Press, 1973); studies of conceptualizations of U.S. foreign policies, such as Graham T. Allison, "Conceptual Models and the Cuban Missile Crisis," *American Political Science Review*, 63 (1969), 689–718, and Susan Welch, "The American Press and Indochina, 1950–56," in Richard L. Merritt, ed., *Communication in International Politics* (Urbana: University of Illinois Press, 1972), pp. 207–231; and studies of international conflict perception, such as Doris A. Graber, "Perceptions of Middle East Conflict in the UN, 1953–65," *Journal of Conflict Resolution*, 13 (1969), 454–484 and Allen S. Whiting, *China Crosses the Yalu: The Decision to Enter the Korean War* (New York: Macmillan, 1960).

counteract manipulation on those who do not wish to respond in the manner desired by the communicator.

While possible abuses of communicative power are frightening, the lack of know-how in controlling verbal stimuli and their responses is at least as frightening. It is devastating to contemplate that one may muff an important political decision or convey misleading impressions through inept use of conceptualizations and words. It is terrifying to ponder that imprecise verbal formulations which convey a threat or reassurance may lead to war. As long as verbal formulations are man's chief instrument for controlling his social systems, it seems imperative to supply him with an instrument of maximum precision.

Perfection of verbal tools has the added advantage of conferring powers on actors and entities who lack the material resources by which political power is ordinarily gauged. Small and weak nations can compete on comparatively equal terms with their stronger colleagues in the debating forums of the world. The right ideas and words can sometimes make the Goliath forces of political machines succumb to the onslaughts of reforming Davids.

Not only are verbal resources cheaply and readily available to nearly all political entities, but they also lend themselves to a much greater variety of maneuvers than do most physical resources. What one can do with weapons, or fortifications, or agricultural products, or mineral resources is rigidly limited, but word power can conjure up a nearly limitless array of images to serve political purposes. What one chooses to emphasize, how one chooses to present it, and the context into which one decides to place it are matters of wide discretion. Likewise, it is possible to modify verbal choices far more readily than it is possible to alter the allocation of other resources.

Successful social engineering through control of verbal behavior requires not only knowledge of and control over particular cause-and-effect linkages, but also an understanding of the general dimensions of a socially healthy verbal environment. If one seeks to defuse explosive political situations, like the perennial conflict in the Middle East, or racial and ethnic tensions in various parts of the world, one needs to know the verbal factors which increase or decrease tensions. However, it is not at all clear whether a low-tension environment helps or hinders sound social development, and whether there are optimum levels for expressed consensus and dissent. If there are certain verbal requirements for a socially healthy environment, and if certain verbal behaviors indicate social pathology, then it may be possible to monitor the society for signs of pathology. This would be the first step toward developing a curative process, or toward arresting social ills.

The field of applied political linguistics holds promise, then, for improving the quality of political life. To perfect social tools which grant us greater control over our political destinies is a socially desirable goal, notwithstanding the fact that these tools may be used by people whom we detest for purposes which we abhor.

The remaining pages suggest a few intriguing, feasible, and socially productive research projects. Some call for cumulation of existing types of studies, others for new approaches. I am proposing them to attract other scholars to an area of scholarship whose challenges have remained largely unmet since they were first outlined by the pioneering verbal behavior studies of Harold Lasswell and his co-investigators.

In the study of words as social indicators, the validation of results of past social indicator studies is high on the list of urgent research tasks. We need to investigate the extent to which various mass media really reflect the major concerns of elements within a society. Much political action is premised on the assumption that the mass media are an accurate mirror; moreover, verbal data reported in the mass media often are the only readily available source for political information and decision-making. Thus it is extremely important to learn what political indicators can be gathered from this source.

Validating mass media data will require analyses of media content, coupled with other studies of nonmedia indicators which measure social concerns. The content analysis findings could be compared with survey research probes into societal concerns, with studies of the foci of governmental activity and expenditures, and with analyses of the directions of private and public research.

Likewise, complementary data should be analyzed to test the accuracy with which spontaneously produced verbal data reflect changing attitudes toward such societally significant matters as income and welfare, race and sex roles, respect for established authorities and laws, or violence and nonviolence. Race, income, welfare, and sex attitudes might also be reflected in data on occupational choices open to various groups, in patterns in the use of housing and educational facilities, and in data on the availability of credit. Verbal data on respect for established authority and on attitudes toward violence could be confirmed by analyzing social acceptance of individual dissidents and perpetrators of violence. They could be validated through police statistics on certain types of law infractions, and through indexes of the sales appeals of certain types of publications.

Historical data offer a rich lode of information which can be mined to test and develop theories about significant verbal behaviors of political elites. Verbal records left by major politicians can be examined for evidence of their operational codes, their justifications for actions, and their personality characteristics and aspirations. Politicians' predictions and promises can be checked against the actual historical record. If predictions turn out to be incorrect, the source of error may be readily apparent from a comparison of predicted and actual results.

Assuming that it is possible through scientific analysis to eliminate many of the errors which have plagued intuitive predictions, it may be possible to develop reasonably accurate scales for predicting future conduct from past verbal behavior. These scales could be used in the selection of political leaders. Accurate rankings of qualities and outlooks reflected in verbal behavior would permit voters to choose candidates for office far more intelligently; changes in the political philosophies and reality perspectives of incumbents might be detectable through a continuous analysis of their verbal output long before these become apparent in actual policy decisions. By keeping a president's or a legislator's verbal output under constant scrutiny and checking predictions against actions, it may be possible to develop verbal measurement instruments to appraise the developing political scene.

Far more attention needs to be paid to conflicting conceptualizations by political elites, and to their effects. What are the differences in conceptualizations of the Common Market, the long-range aims of Communist powers, or the Middle East situation? How do various European countries view these matters, and how do their views differ from those prevalent in the United States and in Asia? How do various social and ethnic groups conceptualize "equality," "discrimination," "poverty level," "violence," and similar concepts? Many harmful misunderstandings have arisen because political actors erred in assuming conceptualizations or failed to comprehend the nature and consequences of the differences. Precious verbal clues were ignored, even though they were obvious or could have been discovered by research.

When the divergence of conceptualizations seems socially harmful, it may be profitable to investigate how such a divergence can be avoided or mitigated. What role does verbalization play in the acceptance of competing conceptualizations? When different definitions and explanations are available, what part do substance, interpretation, verbal form, author, or transmittor characteristics and similar factors play in gaining acceptance for one version and rejection of the other?

It is generally assumed that most political conceptualizations expressed by political elites are accepted by their followers, although recent public opinion studies have cast doubts on the accuracy of this assumption. Many more studies are needed to establish the degree to which verbalized perceptions of elites are shared by their audiences. We also need to test more fully the extent to which the elites' verbalized descriptions of past, present, and future reality and their verbalized explanations of causality and interrelationships become the conceptual settings into which political contests are actually cast.

If the verbalized descriptions do, indeed, become the settings, we need to know how confining these settings are, how much distortion they impose on the interpretation of incoming information, and how severely they restrict the options which politicians and their followers are willing to consider. Again, historical data may be extremely useful in developing and testing relevant hypotheses.

If verbal behavior turns out to be a major cause of past faulty decisions, it may be possible to learn from history and develop better verbal techniques for the future. For instance, if the record shows that decision-making sessions of a government ministry explore only a narrow range of options if the chief minister expresses his views first, it may be possible to demonstrate that a change in speaking order or in the array of speakers produces a more desirable range of options.

To make effective verbal steering possible, a great deal of research needs to be done to establish the effects which particular verbalizations and forms of verbal transmission have on the conduct of politics. The effects of particular verbal behaviors have often been alleged but rarely confirmed outside of the laboratory. We need more proof that what is said by political actors at different levels of the political system and how it is verbally formulated and transmitted do, in fact, influence political outcomes. We need to know how regularly certain effects occur, and what deviations are produced by specific intervening variables. We must test whether rules vary at particular levels of government and the extent to which they are affected by major and minor differences in political culture.

To get this proof, we need more long-range and comparative studies. It would be instructive to hypothesize the effects which certain types of verbal behavior — a formal executive message, for instance — have within a given legislative body, and then to test the hypothesis by checking cause-and-effect linkages through a series of similar or dissimilar legislative sessions. The same project could be designed for comparative research by comparing cause-and-effect linkages in several bodies (such as a number of state legislatures), or at different levels of the political system (such as Congress, a state legislature, and a city council). There could be controls for major intervening variables, such as party distribution within the legislative body, length and continuity of legislative terms, and variations in constitutional and actual powers. Preliminary simulations or experiments might also help, to simplify highly complex natural settings so that a few salient aspects of verbal behavior can be examined free from distracting extraneous variables.

A series of case studies of verbal behavior in various political situations would provide us with norms for judging what types of behavior can normally be expected at various levels and what behaviors are socially sanctioned in various communities. Such knowledge is extremely important for politicians and their publics who now are groping uncertainly for standards of conduct and standards of evaluation. Where does legitimate persuasion end and demagoguery begin? What is "relevant," "appropriate," "constructive" verbal behavior?

Case studies could shed light on the verbal and situational factors contributing to the charisma which permits some political leaders to become Pied Pipers. Laying bare the elements of charisma might enable other politicians to incorporate these elements into their leadership styles, and thereby enhance their capacity to inspire support from their own followers.

Case studies could clarify the genesis and use of various condensation symbols and their relation to the success and failure of political movements. They might explain the phenomenon of planned and unplanned symbol shift by which societies move from support for one set of verbally expressed values to support for another. A series of studies describing changing condensation symbols, as political leaders move their people from a mood of peace to a mood of war, or from a system of capitalism to one of state socialism, could tell us much about the general features of a symbol shift. The isolated case studies produced thus far are interesting, but they are insufficient to develop the general theories which are so sorely needed.

Since so many of verbal behavior's effects depend on verbal interactions, a great deal more attention needs to be paid to the shuttling of verbal stimuli and responses. This is one area in which theories, already developed in laboratory settings, are waiting to be tested in the field. Game theory especially may prove quite helpful in analyzing verbal interactions if the emphasis is directed toward mixed-motive, multi-value rather than zero-sum, uni-value games. Again, historical situations should not be overlooked as a rich source of data for hypothesis-testing. There it would be possible to verify the conformance of theoretically derived solutions with the actual events.

Series of case studies testing the same hypotheses are apt to be far more productive than a number of isolated, disparate investigations. To produce a series of parallel case studies in verbal behavior, far more cooperation is needed within the scholarly community. The massive social problems faced by modern society can no longer be tackled by individual scholars with limited resources. We need concerted, cooperative attacks on debilitating social ignorance and impotence. The field of verbal behavior studies may be one major front in the battle for control of societal forces.

Bibliographical Essay

This bibliographical essay provides a brief guide to the sources likely to prove most helpful to a reader who is beginning to delve more selectively and deeply into various aspects of verbal behavior in political contexts. The essay is arranged by topics which roughly correspond to the chapter divisions of the book. It takes into consideration the relevant literature on verbal behavior and politics in the social sciences and humanities. It does not pretend to be exhaustive on any topic; rather, it points to a limited number of representative studies, many with extensive bibliographies of their own, which provide a good starting point for gaining additional insights into the subject areas encompassed in this book.

The essay includes works which are not cited in the footnotes because there was no direct reference to them in the text, or because they deal with subject matter peripheral to this study. To keep the bibliographical information from appearing too overwhelming, many references cited in the footnotes have been excluded from this essay. Therefore, the reader should use this essay as a starting point for further investigations and then turn to the footnotes for additional materials. The wealth of information in the sources mentioned in the essay and the footnotes, and the bibliographies in these sources, should keep the reader's inquiry moving forward in high gear.

GENERAL INTRODUCTIONS TO VERBAL BEHAVIOR STUDIES AND PROBLEMS OF ENCODING AND DECODING

The reader interested in a general overview of the literature about verbal behavior should begin with one of several wide-ranging collections of essays, such as Floyd W. Matson and Ashley Montagu, eds., *The Human Dialogue* (New York: Free Press, 1967), or Alfred G. Smith, ed., *Communication and Culture: Readings in the Codes of Human Interaction* (New York: Holt, Rinehart and Winston, 1966). For the reader who is particularly interested in communications principles and theories, good introductions are Wilbur Schramm and Donald F. Roberts, eds., *The Process and Effects of Mass Communication*, rev. ed. (Urbana: University of Illinois Press, 1971), and Ithiel de Sola Pool, Wilbur Schramm et al., *Handbook of Communication* (Chicago: Rand McNally, 1973). For a more thorough analysis and a plea to social scientists to include linguistic analysis in their research approaches, the reader should consult Dell Hymes, *Foundations in Sociolinguistics: An Ethnographic Approach* (Philadelphia: University of Pennsylvania Press, 1974).

General works which take a more uniform, often discipline-linked approach to man's use of language to order his environment include Joyce O.

Hertzler, *A Sociology of Language* (New York: Random House, 1965), Alfred R. Lindesmith and Anselm L. Strauss, *Social Psychology*, 3rd ed. (New York: Holt, Rinehart and Winston, 1968), and, particularly, George N. Gordon, *The Languages of Communication: A Logical and Psychological Examination* (New York: Hastings House, 1969). Gordon's book stresses psychological aspects which make it difficult to encode messages to elicit the desired meanings, and it contains an excellent chapter on "Why Communications Fail." A brief overview of sociolinguistics is presented in "Sociolinguistics" by Allen D. Grimshaw, in the above-mentioned *Handbook of Communication* by Ithiel de Sola Pool, Wilbur Schramm et al.

For the reader who prefers a more strictly psychologically oriented approach to the nature and functions of language, including its abnormal aspects, Julius Laffal, *Pathological and Normal Language* (New York: Atherton, 1965), is a good source. Adherents to the psychological approach of B. F. Skinner will find his *Verbal Behavior* (New York: Appleton, Century, Crofts, 1957) indispensable. A provocative sociological perspective on language learning, which stresses class-based differences, is Basil Bernstein, *Class, Codes and Control*, 2 vols. (London: Routledge and Kegan Paul, 1971). Volume 1 presents Bernstein's theories, and volume 2 contains a series of applications. The way in which psychological factors in perception enter into encoding and decoding processes is described and analyzed in technical terms by Abraham Moles in *Information Theory and Esthetic Perception* (Urbana: University of Illinois Press, 1968).

A strong emphasis on myth and symbolism characterizes Kenneth Burke, *Language as Symbolic Action* (Berkeley: University of California Press, 1966), Ernst Cassirer, *Language and Myth* (New York: Harper, 1946), Murray Edelman, *The Symbolic Uses of Politics* (Urbana: University of Illinois Press, 1964), Alfred North Whitehead, *Symbolism: Its Meaning and Effect* (New York: Macmillan, 1958), Charles W. Morris, *Signs, Language and Behavior* (New York: George Braziller, 1955), and, with a strong anthropological perspective, Claude Levi-Strauss, *Structural Anthropology* (Garden City: Doubleday, 1967). Among these examinations of myths and symbols, Edelman's study is by far the best introduction to the use of verbal symbols by politicians to manipulate publics. A brief discussion of myth as a recurrent element in the language of politicians is Lee C. McDonald's "Myth, Politics and Political Science," in *Western Political Quarterly*, 22 (1969), 141–150.

The controversy between linguistic instrumentalists (who view language as a mere tool for expressing experiences) and linguistic determinists (who believe that language determines what can be experienced by the individual) is well outlined by Hansfried Kellner in "On the Sociolinguistic Perspective of the Communicative Situation," *Social Research*, 37 (1970), 71–87. Further insight into this complex topic can be gained from the writings of two of the chief proponents of linguistic determinism: Benjamin Lee Whorf, *Language, Thought and Reality: Selected Writings of Benjamin Lee Whorf*, ed.

John B. Carroll (Cambridge: MIT Press, 1956), and Edward Sapir, *Culture, Language and Personality: Selected Essays*, ed. David G. Mandelbaum (Berkeley: University of California Press, 1962). Critiques of linguistic determinism are presented in Harry Hoijer, ed., *Language in Culture* (Chicago: University of Chicago Press, 1954), and Dell Hymes, ed., *Language in Culture and Society: A Reader in Linguistics and Anthropology* (New York: Harper and Row, 1964). Deterministic linguistic theories have been tested by Edmund S. Glenn in his UN transcript work, in which he attempts to discover language-based conceptual differences. See his "Meaning and Behavior: Communication and Culture," *Journal of Communication*, 16 (1966), 248–272.

The connection between linguistics and philosophy and current trends of research in philosophical aspects of language are set forth with a fair amount of technical detail and good bibliographical information in a collection of essays edited by Jerry A. Fodor and Jerrold J. Katz, *The Structure of Language: Readings in the Philosophy of Language* (Englewood Cliffs, N.J.: Prentice-Hall, 1964). For the reader with no background in linguistics, a better introduction to the study of the political ramifications of philosophical studies of language is Hanna Fenichel Pitkin, *Wittengenstein and Justice: On the Significance of Ludwig Wittgenstein for Social and Political Thought* (Berkeley: University of California Press, 1972). Besides its thorough analysis of the work of Wittgenstein (note particularly his *Philosophical Investigations*, trans. G. E. M. Anscombe, 3rd ed. [New York: Macmillan, 1968], and *Tractatus Logico-Philosophicus*, trans. D. F. Pears and B. F. McGuinness [New York: Humanities Press, 1966]), the book contains brief sketches of relevant writings by Noam Chomsky (note his *Syntactic Structures* [The Hague: Mouton, 1957], *Cartesian Linguistics* [New York: Harper and Row, 1966], and *Language and Mind* [New York: Harcourt, Brace and World, 1972]), Maurice Merleau-Ponty (note his *In Praise of Philosophy*, trans. John Wild and James M. Edie [Evanston: Northwestern University Press, 1963]), J. L. Austin (*How to Do Things with Words*, ed. J. O. Urmson, [New York: Oxford University Press, 1965]) and Stanley Cavell (*Must We Mean What We Say?* [New York: Charles Scribner's, 1969]). A brief introduction to major trends of thoughts about ordinary language philosophy is Vere C. Chappel, ed., *Ordinary Language* (Englewood Cliffs, N.J.: Prentice-Hall, 1964).

J. G. A. Pocock's *Politics, Language and Time* (New York: Atheneum, 1971) is representative of works dealing with the history of changing meanings and usages of political language in different governmental systems, and the effects which these variations have on the formulation of political questions and on their possible answers. In the same vein, A. James Gregor's *An Introduction to Metapolitics* (New York: Free Press, 1971), subtitled "A Brief Inquiry into the Conceptual Language of Political Science," sets forth obstacles to political research and understanding among political scientists which result from the use of imprecise, ill-defined language. Gregor claims that much that passes for substantive political dispute is merely a matter of imprecise language and failure to agree on the meanings of terms like "truth," or "power," or "representative government." William E. Connolly argues similarly in *The Terms of Political Discourse* (Lexington, Mass.: D. C. Heath, 1974) that social scientists and politicians must commit themselves to particular definitions of political concepts. He focuses on appropriate meanings of the concepts "interest," "power," and "freedom." A briefer discussion of the distinctions between "power," "influence," and "authority" is David V. J. Bell, *Power, Influence, and Authority: An Essay in Political Linguistics* (New York: Oxford University Press, 1975). A concurring view, presented in an article-length essay, is available in Duncan MacRae, Jr., "Scientific Communication, Ethical Argument, and Public Policy," *American Political Science Review*, 65 (1971), 38–50.

General rules for encoding messages so that they will convey desired meanings, as well as rules for decoding messages and spotting lies, are presented in Robert Jervis, *The Logic of Images in International Relations* (Princeton: Princeton University Press, 1970). His discussion is relevant for domestic as well as international politics. The more general works on political rhetoric cited on pp. 351–353 below should also be consulted. Rules for coping with language strategies during the decoding process are explained in Erving Goffman, *Strategic Interaction* (Philadelphia: University of Pennsylvania Press, 1970). For readers concerned with encoding and decoding problems within large bureaucratic structures, there are several helpful chapters in James March and Herbert Simon, *Organizations* (New York: John Wiley, 1958).

A number of books and articles focus on problems of encoding and decoding which plague communications among peoples of different cultures and nationalities. A good general introduction is Arthur S. Hoffman, ed., *International Communication and the New Diplomacy* (Bloomington: Indiana University Press, 1968). Among the essays in the book, one by Bryant Wedge on "Communication and Comprehensive Diplomacy" is particularly valuable for its brief case studies and introduction to a systematic approach to decoding in an international setting. Where encoding involves propaganda messages directed toward people from a different culture, its success hinges on awareness of cultural requirements. Some of the problems encountered by encoders are set forth in Karin Dovring, *Road of Propaganda: The Semantics of Biased Communication* (New York: Philosophical Library, 1959). Culture-based divergencies in decoding the meanings of international commitments are explored in Franklin B. Weinstein, "The Concept of Commitment in International Relations," *Journal of Conflict Resolution*, 13 (1960), 39–56, and in Glen H. Fisher, *Public Diplomacy and the Behavioral Sciences* (Bloomington: Indiana University Press, 1972).

When hostile, suspicious countries are trying to communicate their respective intentions to each other, encoding and decoding face unusually serious difficulties. A case study of such a situation is detailed in Allen S. Whiting,

China Crosses the Yalu: The Decision to Enter the Korean War (New York: Macmillan, 1960). The tragic consequences which may spring from stereotypic encoding of images of the enemy and from faulty decoding are outlined in such works as Ralph K. White, *Nobody Wanted War: Misperceptions in Vietnam and Other Wars* (Garden City: Doubleday, 1968); Herman Kahn, *On Escalation: Metaphors and Scenarios* (New York: Praeger, 1965); and Jeremy J. Stone, *Strategic Persuasion: Arms Limitations through Dialogue* (New York: Columbia University Press, 1967).

STUDIES OF FUNCTIONS, EFFECTS, AND INFERENCES

Language performs many functions in the conduct of politics and has a wide variety of intended and unintended effects. A single message usually performs several functions simultaneously, with multiple effects. Therefore most of the studies identified below as focusing on particular types of language effects illustrate a much broader range of functions and effects than a particular categorization implies.

A good starting point for studying the effects of verbal behavior on politics is a pioneering collection of essays edited by Harold D. Lasswell, Nathan Leites et al., *The Language of Politics: Studies in Quantitative Semantics* (Cambridge: MIT Press, 1965). The collection was one of the first attempts to present a series of scientific, content analysis–based studies of the implications for politics springing from particular verbal choices and language styles. The essays provide data concerning numerous language functions such as attention arousal, definitions of the situation, creation of policy-relevant moods, and use of language as a stimulus to action. Several articles in Ithiel de Sola Pool, Wilbur Schramm et al., *Handbook of Communication* (Chicago: Rand McNally, 1973), also focus on the effects of verbal output, particularly the essays by William McGuire, Everett M. Rogers and David O. Sears, and Richard E. Whitney.

More limited in scope are two of my articles which analyze verbal behavior in the UN General Assembly. They are: "Conflict Images: An Assessment of the Middle East Debates in the United Nations," *Journal of Politics*, 32 (1970), 339–378, and "Perceptions of Middle East Conflict in the UN, 1953–1965," *Journal of Conflict Resolution*, 13 (1969), 454–484. The articles analyze the conceptual structure and manner of verbalization employed in these debates, outline likely effects, and use debating patterns to draw inferences about political alignments and perceptions within the UN. The roles of common languages and shared perceptions and ability to communicate in creating and sustaining nationalism are perceptively analyzed in Karl W. Deutsch, *Nationalism and Social Communication* (New York: John Wiley, 1953), and in Alan P. Liu, *Communication and National Integration in Communist China* (Berkeley: University of California Press, 1971). Words as clues to perceptions and indexes to political realities perceived by a variety of political actors are examined in Nazli Choucri, "The Perceptual

Base of Non-Alignment," *Journal of Conflict Resolution*, 13 (1969), 57–74. The article discusses the conceptualizations of nonalignment expressed by several Third World leaders.

The effects of mass media discussion, the use of particular political value symbols, and the inferences about social structures which may be drawn from newspaper content have been studied extensively by Harold Lasswell and his co-workers. The results of one massive research project have been published in several brief volumes known as the RADIR Studies or Hoover Institute Studies. The basic study is a small book by Harold Lasswell, Daniel Lerner, and Ithiel de Sola Pool, *The Comparative Study of Symbols* (Stanford: Stanford University Press, 1952), which describes and interprets the use of terms of political ideology in the editorials of prestige newspapers in Great Britain, France, Russia, Germany, and the United States over a sixty-year period. The study presents several hypotheses about the use and effects of political symbols in different political systems. It forms part of the literature employing a mirror theory of the mass media. Mirror theorists contend that the changing values and concerns expressed in the mass media mirror the changing values and concerns and symbolic behavior patterns of the society served by the media in question. Other volumes in this series include *Symbols of Democracy, Symbols of Internationalism,* and *The Prestige Papers*, all by Ithiel de Sola Pool. The studies were published by Stanford University Press in 1951 and 1952 and have been reissued. They remain important both as pioneering efforts in content analysis techniques, and as studies of changing political symbols.

A number of studies describe political realities which are verbally created by significant political actors or which result from a combination of mass media images with direct observations and third-person reports. Some of these studies deal generally with verbal image creation; others focus on a particular event or a specific type of image, or on realities created by particular political actors.

Among general studies, Kenneth Boulding's *The Image: Knowledge in Life and Society* (Ann Arbor: University of Michigan Press, 1956) is instructive. A general work with a psychological orientation is Joseph de Rivera, *The Psychological Dimension of Foreign Policy* (Columbus, Ohio: Charles E. Merrill, 1968). It sets forth a number of psychological aspects of the verbal construction of political reality. The purposive creation of verbal reality to obtain predetermined political effects is described generally by Robert Jervis in *The Logic of Images in International Relations* (Princeton: Princeton University Press, 1970). A somewhat different approach is taken by historian Daniel J. Boorstin, who calls attention to the fact that many political events are created by the mass media and political promoters merely to provide a basis for a verbal image which can be publicized for purposes of interest to the image's creator. His book is *The Image: A Guide to Pseudo-Events in America* (New York: Harper, 1964).

Turning to more specialized studies, the effects which verbal formulations (such as the declaration of an undefined "vital stake in China") can have on political thinking and policy formulation are illustrated by Marilyn Blatt Young in *The Rhetoric of Empire: American China Policy, 1895–1901* (Cambridge: Harvard University Press, 1968). How different verbal emphases on aspects of the same political situation can create quite diverse realities is delineated by Oran R. Young in *The Politics of Force: Bargaining during International Crises* (Princeton: Princeton University Press, 1968). Young depicts the various reality images presented by opposing sides in the Berlin, Taiwan, and Cuban missile crises since World War II. A brief appraisal of the potential impact of differential verbalizations of the same situation is also presented in Charles E. Osgood, "Conservative Words and Radical Sentences in the Semantics of International Politics," in Gilbert Abcarian and John W. Soule, eds., *Social Psychology and Political Behavior: Problems and Prospects* (Columbus, Ohio: Charles E. Merrill, 1971). A small book by Thomas Franck and Edward Weisband, *Word Politics: Verbal Strategy among the Super Powers* (New York: Oxford University Press, 1972), provides an astute analysis of the effects which spring from various types of public definitions of foreign policy situations.

Faulty conceptualizations of the elements of international conflict may spell disaster. The effects of becoming imprisoned in misleading reality sleeves are examined in such works as Philip Green's *Deadly Logic: The Theory of Nuclear Deterrence* (Columbus: Ohio State University Press, 1966) and Ralph K. White's *Nobody Wanted War: Misperceptions in Vietnam and Other Wars* (Garden City: Doubleday, 1968). The effects of verbal characterizations of "the enemy" on political transactions with opponents are also detailed in a series of case studies presented in David J. Finlay, Ole R. Holsti, and Richard R. Fagen, eds., *Enemies in Politics* (Chicago: Rand McNally, 1967). Cases involve Cuba, Ghana, and the United States.

In *How Nations See Each Other* (Urbana: University of Illinois Press, 1953), William Buchanan and Hadley Cantril demonstrate the stereotypical reality sleeves in various nations which make their people see foreigners in an unfavorable light. The consequences of such stereotyping on subsequent interpretations of communications have been explored by Bryant Wedge, who examined the image of the United States as foreigners see it. Some of his findings are contained in "Nationality and Social Perception," *Journal of Communication*, 16 (1966), 273–282.

One of the most common and publicized forms of political reality creation occurs during political discourse designed to win support for men and measures. Books analyzing the art of campaigning which contain extensive bibliographies include Harold Mendelsohn and Irving Crespi, *Polls, Television, and the New Politics* (Scranton: Chandler Publishing Company, 1970), and Dan Nimmo, *The Political Persuaders: The Techniques of Modern Election Campaigns* (Englewood Cliffs, N.J.: Prentice-Hall, 1970). Other works dealing with the images of political leaders in office and aspiring to office, and with the images of policies, will be discussed in the sections on political elites and on public assemblies.

An important aspect of political reality creation is the formulation of cause-and-effect sequences through explicit, often unsupported claims about the connection between events, or through analogies. Kenneth W. Grundy, in "African Explanations of Underdevelopment: The Theoretical Basis for Political Action," *Review of Politics*, 28 (1966), 62–75, examines various explanations current in African countries regarding the causes of economic and political underdevelopment. He shows how policies to cope with underdevelopment have been widely influenced by the prevailing verbalizations about the causes of underdevelopment.

The role of conceptual linkages in determining foreign policy decisions is discussed in James N. Rosenau, "Foreign Policy as Adaptive Behavior: Some Preliminary Notes for a Theoretical Model," *Comparative Politics*, 2 (1970), 365–387. The conceptual linkages which various American administrations provided for the events of the Vietnam war and American policies necessitated by these events are cited in considerable detail in F. M. Kail, *What Washington Said: Administration Rhetoric and the Vietnam War, 1949–1969* (New York: Harper and Row, 1973). John G. Stoessinger's *Nations in Darkness: China, Russia, America* (New York: Random House, 1971) contains examples of conceptual linkages made by foreign policy leaders. Dealing with conceptual linkages on the domestic level, particularly as they pertain to creating legitimacy images for government, is Richard M. Merelman's article on "Learning and Legitimacy," *American Political Science Review*, 60 (1966), 548–561.

When public figures express their views about political reality or publicly commit themselves to a cause of action, they set in motion psychological and political pressures which push them toward keeping their word. In this manner, verbal commitments become potent forces for political action. A number of general studies by psychologists explain the commitment process and its conseqences on attitudes and behavior. They include Leon Festinger's pioneering work, *A Theory of Cognitive Dissonance* (Evanston: Row, Peterson, 1957); Arthur R. Cohen, *Attitude Change and Social Influence* (New York: Basic Books, 1964); Jack W. Brehm and Arthur Cohen, *Explorations in Cognitive Dissonance* (New York: John Wiley, 1962); and Charles A. Kiesler, *The Psychology of Commitment* (New York: Academic Press, 1971). The relationship between expressed attitudes and overt behavioral responses is examined in Allan W. Wicker, "Attitudes Versus Actions: The Relationship of Verbal and Overt Behavioral Responses to Attitude Objects," *Journal of Social Issues*, 25 (1969), 41–78.

How diplomats can use the commitment process to their own advantage by making commitments or eliciting them from others is explained in Jervis's *Logic of Images in International Relations*, and in a book by Thomas C. Schelling, *Arms and Influence* (New Haven: Yale University Press, 1966). The effects of verbal commitments on international relations are perceptively analyzed in Franklin B. Weinstein, "The Concept of Commitment in International Relations," *Journal of Conflict Resolution*, 13 (1969), 75–101, and in Nazli Choucri and Robert C. North, "The Determinants of International Violence," *Peace Research Society Papers*, 12 (1969), 33–63. A somewhat more general, albeit brief discussion of how definitions of political situations turn into commitments to particular realities is contained in Charles E. Osgood's "Conservative Words and Radical Sentences in the Semantics of International Politics," in Abcarian and Soule, eds., *Social Psychology and Political Behavior*.

Examples of articles dealing with verbal behavior which serves as a surrogate for action are Keijo Korhonen, "Disarmament Talks as an Instrument of International Politics," *Cooperation and Conflict*, 5 (1970), 152–167, and an essay on the uses of blame by Helge Hveem, " 'Blame' as International Behavior," *Journal of Peace Research*, 4 (1970), 49–67.

The problems which arise when one wants to draw inferences from verbal behavior are discussed in many of the general works cited earlier. Among specialized studies dealing with inferential processes in political situations, the most detailed and helpful is Alexander L. George's *Propaganda Analysis* (White Plains: Row, Peterson, 1959). The book describes methods which the FCC developed during World War II to make inferences about events inside Germany on the basis of monitored radio and press communications. Various aspects of inference-making are also dealt with in a very useful collection of essays in Part II of George Gerbner, ed., *The Analysis of Communication Content* (New York: John Wiley, 1969). A brief discussion of some of the more mundane problems of inference-making which face content analysts can be found in Charles E. Osgood, "The Representational Model and Relevant Research Methods," in Ithiel de Sola Pool, ed., *Trends in Content Analysis* (Urbana: University of Illinois Press, 1959). Examples of specific ways in which inferences may be drawn from verbal behavior in international relations are presented in Jervis's *Logic of Images in International Relations*.

Political scientists at Stanford University under the direction of Robert C. North have investigated the communications of major political actors who participated in the decisions which led to World War I. Parts of this massive study, which made extensive use of content analysis, are directed toward inferring motivations and reasoning processes of foreign policy leaders from their verbal output. Representative articles are Dina A. Zinnes, "The Expression and Perception of Hostility in Prewar Crisis, 1914," and Ole R. Holsti, Robert C. North, and Richard A. Brody, "Perception and Action in the 1914 Crisis," both in J. David Singer, ed., *Quantitative International Politics: Insights and Evidence* (New York: Free Press, 1968). Others are Ole R. Holsti and Robert C. North, "Perceptions of Hostility and Economic Variables," in Richard L. Merritt and Stein Rokkan, eds., *Comparing Nations: The Use of Quantitative Data in Cross-National Research* (New Haven: Yale University Press, 1966), and Dina A. Zinnes, Robert C. North, and Howard E. Koch,

Jr., "Capability, Threat, and the Outbreak of War," in James N. Rosenau, ed., *International Politics and Foreign Policy* (New York: Free Press, 1969). A related, more recent study is Kjell Goldmann, "East-West Tension in Europe, 1946–1970: A Conceptual Analysis and a Quantitative Description," *World Politics*, 26 (1973), 106–125. A critical appraisal of these types of studies is made by Ole Holsti in "The Values of International Tension Measurement," *Journal of Conflict Resolution*, 7 (1963), 608–617.

A more impressionistic attempt to infer goals and motivations of political leaders from their verbal communications and mass media output is contained in Allen S. Whiting, *China Crosses the Yalu: The Decision to Enter the Korean War* (New York: Macmillan, 1960). An interesting theory about inferences to be drawn from Chairman Mao's pronouncements and leadership behavior before, during, and after the Great Leap Forward is presented in Paul J. Hiniker, *Ideological Polarization in Mao's China* (forthcoming).

Other studies which seek to draw inferences about the personalities and attitudes of political leaders from their verbal output include James D. Barber, "Adult Identity and Presidential Style," *Daedalus*, 97 (1968), 938–968; Richard E. Donley and David G. Winter, "Measuring the Motives of Public Officials at a Distance: An Exploratory Study of American Presidents," *Behavioral Science*, 15 (1970), 227–236; and Ole R. Holsti, "Cognitive Dynamics and Images of the Enemy," in David J. Finlay, Ole R. Holsti, and Richard R. Fagen, eds., *Enemies in Politics* (Chicago: Rand McNally, 1967). Others are William Eckhardt and Ralph K. White, "A Test of the Mirror-Image Hypothesis: Kennedy and Khrushchev," *Journal of Conflict Resolution*, 11 (1967), 325–332, and Nathan Leites, Elsa Bernaut, and Raymond L. Garthoff, "Politburo Images of Stalin," *World Politics*, 3 (1951), 317–339. Jum C. Nunnally, "Individual Differences in Word Usage," in Sheldon Rosenberg, ed., *Directions in Psycholinguistics* (New York: Macmillan, 1965), discusses inferences about the psychological make-up of message-senders which can be drawn from use of particular words. The motives and perceptions of clients of public agencies have been inferred from the conceptualizations contained in their correspondence with these agencies. How this can be done is reported by Elihu Katz, Michael Gurevitch, Brenda Danet, and Tsiyona Peled in "Petitions and Prayers: A Method for the Content Analysis of Persuasive Appeals," *Social Forces*, 47 (1969), 447–463.

The images contained in popular literature may yield inferential clues about the audiences for which the literature has been prepared. Inferences to be drawn from achievement motivation found in the literature of various nations are discussed by David C. McClelland in *The Achieving Society* (Princeton: Van Nostrand, 1961). A brief description of McClelland's methods is provided by Richard deCharms and Gerald H. Moeller in "Values Expressed in American Children's Readers: 1900–1950," *Journal of Abnormal and Social Psychology*, 64 (1962), 136–142. Several studies attempt to infer national character traits from literary output. Examples include Hans Sebald, "Studying National Character through Comparative Content Analysis," *So-*

cial Forces, 40 (1962), 318–322, and Herbert S. Lewin, "Hitler Youth and the Boy Scouts of America: A Comparison of Aims," *Human Relations*, 1 (1947), 206–227. The published opinions and rulings of U.S. Supreme Court judges have been used to infer their judicial philosophies and to predict their likely decisions. An example is Glendon Schubert, "Jackson's Judicial Philosophy: An Exploration in Value Analysis," *American Political Science Review*, 59 (1965), 940–963.

Comparison of messages from various sources may permit inferences about similarities and differences among message-senders. Comparative techniques have frequently been used for propaganda analysis. Examples are Bernard Berelson and Sebastian de Grazia, "Detecting Collaboration in Propaganda," *Public Opinion Quarterly*, 11 (1947), 244–253; Harold D. Lasswell, Nathan Leites et al., "Propaganda Detection and the Courts," in Harold D. Lasswell and Nathan Leites, eds., *The Language of Politics: Studies in Quantitative Semantics* (Cambridge: MIT Press, 1965) and Ralph K. White, "Hitler, Roosevelt and the Nature of War Propaganda," *Journal of Abnormal and Social Psychology*, 44 (1949), 157–174.

Message comparisons have also been useful for assessing cohesion and conflict within the Communist system. Details are presented in P. Terry Hopman, "International Conflict and Cohesion in the Communist System," *International Studies Quarterly*, 11 (1967), 212–236, and two studies by Ole Holsti, "East-West Conflict and Sino-Soviet Relations," *Journal of Applied Behavioral Science*, 1 (1965), 115–130, and "External Conflict and Internal Consensus: The Sino-Soviet Case," in Philip J. Stone, Dexter C. Dunphy, Marshall S. Smith, and Daniel M. Ogilvie, *The General Inquirer: A Computer Approach to Content Analysis* (Cambridge: MIT Press, 1966).

Comparisons of stylistic features of verbal output may lead to inferences about authorship. Well-known examples are Milton Rokeach, Robert Homant, and Louis Penner, "A Value Analysis of the Disputed Federalist Papers," *Journal of Personality and Social Psychology*, 16 (1970), 245–250, and F. Mosteller and D. W. Wallace, *Inference and Disputed Authorship: The Federalist* (Reading, Mass.: Addison-Wesley, 1964). Both studies agreed on the identity of the author of the disputed papers. Changing images of political leaders in the literature of a nation may permit inferences about changing political perceptions. For an astute analysis of the possibilities and pitfalls of inference-making in this area, see Bernth Lindfors, "The African Politician's Changing Image in African Literature in English," *Journal of Developing Areas*, 4 (1969), 13–28.

LITERATURE ON VERBAL MEASUREMENT TECHNIQUES

In recent years, there has been a steady flow of books which survey and describe research techniques in human communication. A typical example is Philip Emmert and William D. Brooks, eds., *Methods of Research in Communication* (Boston: Houghton Mifflin, 1970). The book contains a chapter on content analysis by John Waite Bowers, a chapter on interaction analysis by Edmund J. Amidon, and a chapter on semantic differentiation by Donald K. Darnell. There are also chapters on stylistic analysis by Mervin D. Lynch, Q-sort technique by William D. Brooks, and kinesics by Larry L. Barker and Nancy B. Collins.

Turning to studies which concentrate on content analysis, the reader should find a small volume by Ole R. Holsti extremely useful. *Content Analysis for the Social Sciences and Humanities* (Reading, Mass.: Addison-Wesley, 1969) combines a broad discussion of the nature and limitations of content analysis with a wide range of examples and explicit instructions on conducting content analyses. The content analysis–based studies discussed in the book permit an appraisal of the method's usefulness and strategies. A somewhat briefer exposition is contained in Holsti's "Content Analysis" chapter in Gardner Lindzey and Elliot Aronson, eds., *The Handbook of Social Psychology*, 2nd ed. (Reading, Mass.: Addison-Wesley, 1968), II. Older, but still valuable as a brief examination of content analysis techniques, is Bernard Berelson's chapter on "Content Analysis" in Gardner Lindzey, ed., *Handbook of Social Psychology* (Cambridge: Addison-Wesley, 1954), I.

Various problems face content analysts, depending on the nature of verbal behavior which they are examining and the purposes of the analysis. These problems are explored by experts in George Gerbner, ed., *The Analysis of Communication Content* (New York: John Wiley, 1969). Part One of the book provides a general analysis of the elements which must be examined when one wishes to discern message content. Klaus Krippendorff's essay on "Models of Messages: Three Prototypes" should not be missed. Similar to the Gerbner volume, but older and less inclusive, is Ithiel de Sola Pool, ed., *Trends in Content Analysis* (Urbana: University of Illinois Press, 1959).

Despite its age, one of the best descriptions of political content analysis, presented as part of a major analysis project, is Harold D. Lasswell, Daniel Lerner, and Ithiel de Sola Pool, *Comparative Study of Symbols* (Stanford: Stanford University Press, 1952). This opening volume of the Hoover Institute Studies presents the rationale for and limitations of content analysis as they emerged from a study of elite editorials from five countries published over a sixty-year span. A later study provides additional information as well as several case studies illuminating the uses of content analysis for political communications research: Harold D. Lasswell, Nathan Leites et al., *The Language of Politics: Studies in Quantitative Semantics* (Cambridge: MIT Press, 1965). Linguistic, methodological, substantive, and technological developments which are making content analysis an increasingly useful research technique are discussed in Robert E. Mitchell, "The Use of Content Analysis for Exploratory Studies," *Public Opinion Quarterly*, 31 (1967), 230–241.

A number of books and articles discuss the uses of content analysis in social science subfields. Ithiel de Sola Pool presents an excellent overview of content analysis as a method for gathering political intelligence in his "Content Analysis and the Intelligence Function," in Arnold Rogow, ed., *Politics, Personality and Social Science in the Twentieth Century* (Chicago: University of Chicago Press, 1969). The usefulness of content analysis for foreign policy analysis is scrutinized by Gilbert R. Winham in "Quantitative Methods in Foreign Policy Analysis," *Canadian Journal of Political Science*, 2 (1969), 187–199. Content analysis as a way to study various aspects of propaganda is discussed extensively in Alexander L. George, *Propaganda Analysis* (White Plains: Row, Peterson, 1959), in Lasswell and Leites's above-mentioned *Language of Politics*, and in Robert K. Merton, *Mass Persuasion: The Social Psychology of a War Bond Drive* (New York: Harper, 1946). Unlike the others, Merton's book focuses on the nature of the persuasive appeals, rather than on inferences to be drawn from the propaganda.

When the content analyst deals with verbal materials emanating from or disseminated to a foreign culture, he must be sensitive to cultural factors which are reflected in the output. The nature of these factors is scrutinized in a series of articles by Edmund S. Glenn; representative is "Meaning and Behavior: Communication and Culture," *Journal of Communication*, 16 (1966), 248–272. A more general philosophical introduction to the cultural relativity of political concepts, which will aid in detecting culture-related differences, is a small book by T. D. Weldon, *The Vocabulary of Politics* (Baltimore: Penguin Books, 1960). For rules on deciphering the content of messages originating from Communist elites, the reader should consult William E. Griffith, "On Esoteric Communications," *Studies in Comparative Communism*, 3 (1970), 47–54. Other works which wrestle with the problem of analyzing verbal output from Communist societies are Alex Inkeles, *Public Opinion in Soviet Russia: A Study in Mass Persuasion* (Cambridge: Harvard University Press, 1958), and Gayle F. Durham Hollander, *Soviet Political Indoctrination* (New York: Praeger, 1972).

The opportunities for undertaking research projects that involve massive amounts of content analysis have expanded greatly with the development of computer routines for content analysis. One of the most thorough introductions to the principles underlying computerized content analysis is Part One of Phillip J. Stone, Dexter C. Dunphy, Marshall S. Smith, and Daniel M. Ogilvie, *The General Inquirer: A Computer Approach to Content Analysis* (Cambridge: MIT Press, 1966). Part Two contains a series of applications, including three political science case studies. Another good general source for gaining insight into computer-based content analysis is Part Four of George Gerbner, ed., *The Analysis of Communication Content* (New York: John Wiley, 1969), "Computer Techniques in Content Analysis and Computational Linguistics."

While quantifiers are joyous about having the computer available as an ever-willing servant to count verbal structures and their components, some social scientists raise serious questions about the usefulness of such studies. Not many of these negative appraisals have found their way into the literature, probably because the supporters of quantitative methods have hitherto been careful in detailing the limitations of their research methods. Criticism of quantification is contained in Robert Jervis, "The Costs of the Scientific Study of Politics: An Examination of the Stanford Content Analysis Studies," *International Studies Quarterly*, 11 (1967), 367–392. Methodological shortcomings in quantitative content analysis are also pointed out by Morris Janowitz in "Content Analysis and the Study of the 'Symbolic Environment,'" in Arnold Rogow, ed., *Politics, Personality, and Social Science in the Twentieth Century* (Chicago: University of Chicago Press, 1969), and in Lasswell, Leites et al., eds., *The Language of Politics*. The particular merits of qualitative content analysis are set forth in Alexander George, "Quantitative and Qualitative Approaches to Content Analysis," in Pool, ed., *Trends in Content Analysis*, and, less supportively, in John E. Mueller, "The Use of Content Analysis in International Relations," in George Gerbner, ed., *The Analysis of Communication Content* (New York: John Wiley, 1969).

While the focus in content analysis studies varies widely, depending on the needs of the researcher, interest in certain content features has been widespread. Standard methods, many labeled with specific names, have been developed to assess these content features. An example is value analysis, developed by Ralph K. White and described in *Value Analysis: The Nature and Use of the Method* (Glen Gardner: Libertarian Press, 1951). Value analysis searches for social values expressed in content. Another special technique is evaluative assertion analysis, which searches for the evaluation placed on social concepts. It is described by Charles E. Osgood, Sol Saporta, and Jum C. Nunnally in "Evaluative Assertion Analysis," *Litera*, 3 (1956), 47–102. More familiar to social scientists is achievement motivation analysis, explained by David McClelland in *The Achieving Society* (Princeton: Van Nostrand, 1961); it provides a method for examining achievement motivation expressed in literary works.

Reactions to verbal stimuli can be measured and compared through semantic differential techniques developed and described by Charles E. Osgood, George G. Suci, and Percy H. Tannenbaum in *The Measurement of Meaning* (Urbana: University of Illinois Press, 1957). A brief exposition of the technique is found in Donald K. Darnell's chapter "Semantic Differentiation," in Philip Emmert and William D. Brooks, ed., *Methods of Research in Communication* (Boston: Houghton Mifflin, 1970). Applications are presented in James G. Snider and Charles E. Osgood, eds., *Semantic Differential Technique: A Source Book* (Chicago: Aldine, 1969). For a discussion of cross-cultural uses of the semantic differential techniques, see Charles E. Osgood, William H. May, and Murray S. Miron, *Cross-Cultural Universals of Affective Meaning* (Urbana: University of Illinois Press, 1975). Q-methodology is another measure for gauging reactions to verbal stimuli; it is described in William Stephenson, *The Study of Behavior: Q Technique and Its Methodology* (Chicago: University of Chicago Press, 1953). A briefer description is contained in William Stephenson, "Application of Q-Method to the Measurement of Public Opinion," *Psychological Record*, 14 (1964), 265–273. Measurements have also been devised for body language; Ray L. Birdwhistell's essays on *Kinesics and Context: Essays on Body Motion Communication* (Phiadelphia: University of Pennsylvania Press, 1970) are a delightful exposition. A brief overview is presented in Randall P. Harrison's essay "Nonverbal Communication," in Ithiel de Sola Pool, Wilbur Schramm et al., *Handbook of Communication* (Chicago: Rand McNally, 1973).

Aspects of verbal interactions have been studied carefully by a number of social scientists concerned with small groups. One of the most widely used techniques for this type of analysis is described by Robert F. Bales in *Interaction Process Analysis* (Reading, Mass.: Addison-Wesley, 1950), and, quite briefly, in his chapter on "How People Interact in Conferences," in Alfred G. Smith, ed., *Communication and Culture: Readings in the Codes of Human Interaction* (New York: Holt, Rinehart and Winston, 1966), pp. 94–102. A brief sketch of Bales's method is also available in Thomas W. Madron, *Small Group Methods and the Study of Politics* (Evanston: Northwestern University Press, 1969). Sign process analysis for gauging group interaction is described in Theodore M. Mills, *Group Transformation: An Analysis of a Learning Group* (Englewood Cliffs, N.J.: Prentice-Hall, 1964). A valuable general overview of research methods for analyzing group interactions is Karl E. Weick, "Systematic Observational Methods," in Gardner Lindzey and Elliot Aronson, eds., *The Handbook of Social Psychology*, 2nd ed. (Reading, Mass.: Addison-Wesley, 1968), II. Most of the works dealing with small groups which are listed below in the section on public assemblies and small bargaining groups also contain reports on research methods for analyzing verbal interactions in small groups.

STUDIES OF MASS MEDIA CONTENT AND ITS EFFECTS

The mass media's verbal output has been appraised from different vantage points. These include the study of media output as a reflection of a particular society's values, the study of the political reality presented to masses and elites by the media, and studies of the effects of media presentations on the course of political events in general and on the perceptions of individuals in particular. Studies dealing with content are on firmer scientific grounds than studies dealing with media effects; in the latter, it is difficult to establish causal relationships in a setting with a large number of interacting variables which cannot be examined in isolation.

The most extensive examples of investigations of social systems through their mass media symbolism are contained in the Hoover Institute Studies. These works present the findings of symbol analyses of the editorials in one elite newspaper in Great Britain, France, Russia, Germany, and the United

States over the 1890–1949 period. Separate studies by Ithiel de Sola Pool, published by Stanford University Press in 1951 and 1952, deal respectively with *Symbols of Democracy*, *Symbols of Internationalism*, and, more generally, with the variety of political symbols appearing in *The Prestige Papers*. A general introduction to the series, written jointly by Harold Lasswell, Daniel Lerner, and Ithiel de Sola Pool, deals with *The Comparative Study of Symbols*. A later study which compares press images of politics in the *New York Times* and the *Times of India* from 1950 to 1958 is Satish K. Arora and Harold D. Lasswell, *Political Communication: The Public Language of Political Elites in India and the United States* (New York: Holt, Rinehart and Winston, 1968).

Investigations of media output as a mirror of the society whose stories the media are telling are Karl W. Deutsch et al., *Political Community and the North Atlantic Area* (Princeton: Princeton University Press, 1957) and *France, Germany and the Western Alliance* (New York: Scribner's, 1967); also Peter A. Toma, "Sociometric Measurements of the Sino-Soviet Conflict: Peaceful and Nonpeaceful Revolutions," *Journal of Politics*, 30 (1968), 732–748. A long-term research project to study cultural indicators culled from prime-time network television dramas has been under way at the University of Pennsylvania's Annenberg School of Communications under the direction of George Gerbner and Larry Gross. Progress reports and papers have made some of the information available. For interesting case studies which reflect mirror theories, the reader should check Ernst F. Mueller, "Attitudes toward Westbound Refugees in the East German Press," *Journal of Conflict Resolution*, 14 (1970), 311–333, and G. Cleveland Wilhoit, "Political Symbol Shifts in Crisis News," *Midwest Journal of Political Science*, 13 (1969), 313–319. Warnings about the accuracy of inferences drawn about society from its mass media are voiced in the general works on content analysis cited earlier, particularly the work of Berelson and Holsti, and in Alexander L. George, *Propaganda Analysis* (White Plains: Row, Peterson, 1959). George points out that governmental communications strategies may dictate the image of reality which mass media are able to offer.

The mass media present readers with pictures of the world which are difficult to verify, especially when the events described are taking place in far-off places. Several studies have therefore examined the coverage of foreign news, with particular emphasis on the distortions which commonly occur. An invaluable introduction to these types of studies is provided by two lengthy articles in *Journal of Peace Research*, 2 (1965), 39–91, which examine the factors that shape foreign news reporting and lead to systematic distortions. They are Johan Galtung and Mari Holmboe Ruge's "The Structure of Foreign News," and Einar Östgaard's "Factors Influencing the Flow of News." The images which spring from foreign news coverage are discussed in a book-length study by Bernard C. Cohen, *The Press and Foreign Policy* (Princeton: Princeton University Press, 1963), and in a brief article by Øystein Sande, "The Perception of Foreign News," *Journal of*

Peace Research, 3–4 (1971), 221–237. Two examples of coverage of specific foreign events are Susan Welch, "The American Press and Indochina, 1950–56," in Richard L. Merritt, ed., *Communication in International Politics* (Urbana: University of Illinois Press, 1972), which covers the early phases of the Vietnam war, and John D. Cozean, "Profile of U.S. Press Coverage on Cuba: Was the Bay of Pigs Necessary?" *Journal of International and Comparative Studies*, 5 (1972), 18–53, which deals with the effects of mass media coverage of U.S.-Cuban relations.

Analysis of mass media coverage of domestic events is less frequent, except for a few special topics such as elections, the description of violent events, and the portrayal of specific population subgroups. An excellent series of case studies showing mass media structuring of political reality in Great Britain is presented by Colin Seymour-Ure in *The Political Impact of Mass Media* (Beverly Hills: Sage, 1974). Further light on how this type of structuring of reality affects the conduct of politics is shed by an article by Maxwell E. McCombs and Donald L. Shaw entitled "The Agenda-Setting Function of Mass Media," *Public Opinion Quarterly*, 36 (1972), 176–187.

The effects of mass media in conveying information essential for mass publics form the theme of a number of studies. Ithiel de Sola Pool briefly discusses public information about modernization in "The Mass Media and Politics in the Modernization Process," in Lucian W. Pye, ed., *Communications and Political Development* (Princeton: Princeton University Press, 1963). "Communication and Development" is also the subject and title of an essay by Frederick W. Frey in Ithiel de Sola Pool, Wilbur Schramm et al., *Handbook of Communication* (Chicago: Rand McNally, 1973). The media's accuracy in covering judicial decisions has been scrutinized in Chester A. Newland, "Press Coverage of the United States Supreme Court," *Western Political Quarterly*, 17 (1964), 15–36, and David L. Grey, *The Supreme Court and the News Media* (Evanston: Northwestern University Press, 1968). How media-created, widely publicized reality can narrow the freedom of political decision-makers is discussed in Karl W. Deutsch, "Mass Communication and the Loss of Freedom in National Decision-Making," *Journal of Conflict Resolution*, 1 (1957), 200–211.

Turning to more specialized political realities: the effects of the mass media in conveying political information about elections and in influencing decisions are discussed in many studies. Representative examples include Bernard Berelson, Paul E. Lazarsfeld, and William N. McPhee, *Voting: A Study of Opinion Formation in a Presidential Campaign* (Chicago: University of Chicago Press, 1964); Jay G. Blumler and Denis McQuail, *Television in Politics: Its Uses and Influences* (London: Faber and Faber, 1968); a series of essays in Eugene Burdick and Arthur J. Brodbeck, eds., *American Voting Behavior* (Glencoe: Free Press, 1959); Angus Campbell et al., eds., *Elections and the Political Order* (New York: Wiley, 1967); and Sidney Kraus, ed., *The Great Debates* (Gloucester: Peter Smith, 1968). Also see my "The Press as Opinion Resource during the 1968 Presidential Campaign,"

Public Opinion Quarterly, 35 (1971), 168–182, and "Press Coverage and Voter Reaction in the 1968 Presidential Election," *Political Science Quarterly*, 87 (1974), 68–100.

There is an extensive literature on the effect of media-depicted violence on attitudes and actions of the audience. Many studies and viewpoints are summarized in Robert K. Baker and Sandra J. Ball, *Violence and the Media: A Staff Report to the National Commission on the Causes and Prevention of Violence* (Washington: U.S. Government Printing Office, 1969). In recent years, researchers have also focused on media coverage's effects on the behavior and attitudes of distinct population groups, particularly American blacks. Two representative studies are Philip Meyer, "Aftermath of Martyrdom: Negro Militancy and Martin Luther King," *Public Opinion Quarterly*, 33 (1969), 160–173, and Paula B. Johnson, David O. Sears, and John B. McConahay, "Black Invisibility, the Press, and the Los Angeles Riot," *American Journal of Sociology*, 76 (1971), 698–721.

The most comprehensive review of various media effects on audiences (tested through empirical studies prior to 1960) is Joseph T. Klapper, *The Effects of Mass Communication* (New York: Free Press, 1960). Though out of date, the book still covers most significant areas of concern about the effects of mass media.

Deliberate media bias and its consequences have led to a number of studies, many of them controversial because of alleged research and researcher biases. Examples of mass media stereotyping of political figures to accord with the biases of a particular medium are recorded in John C. Merrill, "How *Time* Stereotyped Three U.S. Presidents," *Journalism Quarterly*, 42 (1965), 563–570. A more general discussion of role stereotypes is Lionel S. Lewis, "Political Heros: 1936 and 1960," *Journalism Quarterly*, 42 (1965), 116–118. Highly biased studies of bias are Edith Efron, *The News Twisters* (Los Angeles: Nash Publications, 1972), which deals with news coverage of President Nixon, and Robert Cirino, *Don't Blame the People: How the News Media Use Bias, Distortion and Censorship to Manipulate Public Opinion* (Los Angeles: Diversity Press, 1971), which complains about lack of coverage of socially significant stories.

Several studies have compared the reporting of verbal events, such as public speeches, with the original event; substantial differences become apparent. Examples are Robert L. Scott and Wayne Brockriede, *The Rhetoric of Black Power* (New York: Harper and Row, 1969), and Raymond F. Smith, "On the Structure of Foreign News," *Journal of Peace Research*, 6 (1969), 23–36, which compared official documents concerning the Sino-Indian border conflict of 1962 with coverage in the *New York Times*. Studies focusing on mass media personnel to explain the nature of the political reality which flows from reporters' pens include Dan P. Nimmo, *Newsgathering in Washington: A Study of Political Communication* (New York: Atherton Press, 1964), and William L. Rivers, *The Opinion Makers: The Washington Press Corps* (Boston: Beacon Press, 1965).

STUDIES OF ELITE VERBALIZATIONS AND POLITICAL RHETORIC

In politics, the bulk of recorded verbal behavior comes from the mouths of elites; therefore many of the studies cited earlier present examples of elite verbal behavior. Such studies draw conclusions about the importance of this behavior, frequently without acknowledging that the elite nature of the source is an important intervening variable. This section identifies published studies in which the special qualities of elite articulations are clearly acknowledged. However, other studies, particularly those mentioned in the section on functions, effects, and inferences, should also be consulted.

The nature and effects of elite conceptualizations of major policies — in this case, nonalignment — are carefully analyzed in Nazli Choucri, "The Perceptual Base of Non-Alignment," *Journal of Conflict Resolution*, 13 (1969), 57–74. For greater theoretical depth and more detailed analysis, the author's doctoral dissertation, "The Perceptual Base of Nonalignment" (Stanford, 1967), should be examined. The effects which ensue from particular conceptualizations of specific foreign policy crises are traced by Thomas Franck and Edward Weisband in *Word Politics: Verbal Strategy among the Super Powers* (New York: Oxford University Press, 1972). The book compares the conceptualizations developed by American foreign policy elites vis-à-vis Guatemala, Cuba, and the Dominican Republic with the conceptualizations which Soviet foreign policy leaders developed vis-à-vis Hungary and Czechoslovakia. Other valuable studies of elite conceptualizations of foreign policy situations are John G. Stoessinger, *Nations in Darkness: China, Russia, America* (New York: Random House, 1971); Ralph K. White, *Nobody Wanted War: Misperceptions in Vietnam and Other Wars* (Garden City: Doubleday, 1968); and D. M. Lampton, "The U.S. Image of Peking in Three International Crises," *Western Political Quarterly*, 26 (1973), 28–50.

Several scholars have analyzed the official pronouncements of major public figures to relate the values and conceptualizations contained in them to public values and conceptualizations. Representative articles are by Marshall S. Smith with Philip Stone and Evelyn N. Glenn, "A Content Analysis of Twenty Presidential Nomination Acceptance Speeches," in Philip J. Stone, Dexter C. Dunphy, Marshall S. Smith, and Daniel M. Ogilvie, *The General Inquirer: A Computer Approach to Content Analysis* (Cambridge: MIT Press, 1966), and James W. Prothro, "Verbal Shifts in the American Presidency: A Content Analysis," *American Political Science Review*, 50 (1965), 726–739.

Attitude expressions of various political elites below the top leadership level have also been studied and searched for clues to the political behavior of these elites. See, for example, Robert C. Angell, Vera S. Dunham, and J. David Singer, "Social Values and Foreign Policy Attitudes of Soviet and American Elites," *Journal of Conflict Resolution*, 8 (1964), 33–491, which contains a series of separate essays dealing with the topic. Graham T. Allison places special emphasis on elite conceptual models in "Conceptual Models and the Cuban Missile Crisis," *American Political Science Review*, 63 (1969), 589–718.

The significance of the expressed role conceptions of political elites is detailed in K. J. Holsti, "National Role Conceptions in the Study of Foreign Policy," *International Studies Quarterly*, 14 (1970), 233–309, and in two studies which emphasize the concept of "operational code." They are Alexander George, "The 'Operational Code': A Neglected Approach to the Study of Political Leaders and Decision-Making," *International Studies Quarterly*, 13 (1969), 190–222, and David S. McLellan, "The 'Operational Code' Approach to the Study of Political Leaders: Dean Acheson's Philosophical and Instrumental Beliefs," *Canadian Journal of Political Science*, 4 (1971), 52–75.

Verbalized elite perceptions about political values, problems, and policies are carefully detailed and analyzed in Robert D. Putnam, *The Beliefs of Politicians: Ideology, Conflict and Democracy in Britain and Italy* (New Haven: Yale University Press, 1973). A briefer version by the same author is "Studying Elite Political Culture: The Case of 'Ideology,'" *American Political Science Review*, 65 (1971), 651–681. Also helpful is Ole R. Holsti, "Individual Differences in 'Definition of the Situation,'" *Journal of Conflict Resolution*, 14 (1970), 303–310.

Examinations of the perceptions of political leaders and their role conceptions, as expressed in verbal output, often allude to psychological traits of leaders which may explain these perceptions or which may be inferred from them. Several studies which concentrate on these psychological aspects are cited on p. 341 above.

When politicians express their appraisal of political realities and appeal to certain principles and values, it is always difficult to determine where exposition of their genuine perceptions ends and political advocacy begins. Where the verbal behavior under study consists primarily of public addresses by political leaders who seek to win support for particular men and policies, it is usually more fruitful to study the addresses for the nature of the appeals, rather than as a source of the speakers' political beliefs. However, as the literature on verbal commitment discussed earlier illustrates, rhetorical utterances may become guidelines for policy because the speaker feels publicly committed to the expressed analysis and course of action. Moreover, the widespread view that political rhetoric generally bears little relation to subsequent public action may be overly cynical. Studies which examine the values expressed in the public addresses of American presidents indicate a fairly good correspondence between words and actions. A representative example is Randall B. Ripley, *Kennedy and Congress* (Morristown: General Learning Press, 1972). A careful, perceptive analysis by Gerald M. Pomper, *Elections in America: Control and Influence in Democratic Politics* (New York: Dodd, Mead, 1968), demonstrates that party platforms are more credible than political folklore indicates. The book examines the extent to which commitments expressed in platforms are carried out in subsequent political actions.

Most studies dealing with particular elections or with the history of policies and legislative measures contain a few descriptions, and occasionally brief analyses, of the verbal conceptualizations which were used to describe the contest and gain supporters and opponents in the process. Other studies concentrate on the rhetorical aspects of the situation. Examples of the latter type are two books by Wayne Brockriede and Robert L. Scott, *Moments in the Rhetoric of the Cold War* (New York: Random House, 1970) and *The Rhetoric of Black Power* (New York: Harper and Row, 1969), and a volume by F. M. Kail, *What Washington Said: Administration Rhetoric and the Vietnam War, 1949–1969* (New York: Harper and Row, 1973). Two more analytical books are Max J. Skidmore, *Medicare and the American Rhetoric of Reconciliation* (University: University of Alabama Press, 1970), and Marilyn Blatt Young, *The Rhetoric of Empire: American China Policy, 1895–1901* (Cambridge: Harvard University Press, 1968). An interesting, briefer analysis of verbal strategies of legislative leaders is D. A. Strickland, "On Ambiguity in Political Rhetoric: Defeat of the Rat Control Bill in the House of Representatives, July 1967," *Canadian Journal of Political Science,* 2 (1969), 338–344.

The arguments used by President Johnson to win support for his Vietnam policies are scrutinized in Walter Bunge, Robert V. Hudson, and Chung Woo Suh, "Johnson's Information Strategy for Vietnam: An Evaluation," *Journalism Quarterly,* 45 (1968), 419–425. A more general view of the verbal battles over Vietnam is presented by Stephen A. Garrett in "The Relevance of Great Debates: An Analysis of the Discussion over Vietnam," *Journal of Politics,* 33 (1971), 478–508. Garrett examines the intellectual level of elite appraisals of the Vietnam war.

Turning to more generalized discussions of political rhetoric, a timeless classic remains Aristotle's *Rhetoric.* It has been reprinted, among other places, in *The Works of Aristotle* (Chicago: Encyclopaedia Britannica, 1962), II. Good discussions of the basic themes which underlie most political rhetoric are contained in Murray Edelman's two books, *The Symbolic Uses of Politics* (Urbana: University of Illinois Press, 1964) and *Politics as Symbolic Action: Mass Arousal and Quiescence* (Chicago: Markham, 1971), and in Kenneth Burke, *Language as Symbolic Action* (Berkeley: University of California Press, 1966). A more sociological perspective is taken in Hugh Dalziel Duncan, *Communication and Social Order* (New York: Bedminster Press, 1962). Also useful for general insights on political rhetoric are Michael A. Weinstein, "Political and Moral Consciousness," *Midwest Journal of Political Science,* 14 (1970), 185–215, and Les Cleveland, "Symbols and Politics: Mass Communication and the Public Drama," *Politics,* 4 (1969), 186–196. The audience's influence on shaping the verbal output of public figures is analyzed in a study by Raymond A. Bauer, "The Communicator and the Audience," *Journal of Conflict Resolution,* 2 (1958), 67–77.

Tactics used by political leaders, particularly in the field of foreign policy, to manipulate political images are described and analyzed in detail in Robert Jervis, *The Logic of Images in International Relations* (Princeton: Princeton University Press, 1970). A much briefer treatment is Kjell Goldmann, "International Norms and Governmental Behavior," *Cooperation and Conflict*, 4 (1969), 162–204.

A perceptive analysis of the political rhetoric of individual charismatic leaders can be found in Stanley and Inge Hoffman, "The Will to Grandeur: de Gaulle as Political Artist," and David E. Apter, "Nkrumah, Charisma and the Coup," both in Dankwart A. Rustow, ed., *Philosophers and Kings: Studies in Leadership* (New York, George Braziller, 1970). Against the background of these essays, an article by David Manning White is particularly instructive. In "Power and Intention," *American Political Science Review*, 65 (1971), 749–759, White warns that political leaders cannot fully control the impact and interpretation of their utterances.

Interesting comparisons of rhetoric common in totalitarian and non-totalitarian societies are presented in Harold D. Lasswell, Nathan Leites et al., eds., *The Language of Politics: Studies in Quantitative Semantics* (Cambridge: MIT Press, 1965). The essays in this collection illustrate various conceptions of language strategy. How such language strategies can be studied through the use of game-theoretical principles is described in Vincent Lemieux, "Le Jeu de la Communication Politique," *Canadian Journal of Political Science*, 3 (1970), 359–375.

REPORTS ON VERBAL BEHAVIOR IN PUBLIC ASSEMBLIES AND SMALL BARGAINING GROUPS

Since the cast of players in public assemblies and in the kinds of small bargaining groups discussed in this book belong to the guild labeled "political elites," the literature cited in the previous section should be consulted along with the more specialized literature in this section. Studies of verbal behavior in public legislative assemblies have been comparatively scant. There are numerous books covering the rules for debating in the assemblies of the world, along with voluminous records of actual public debates. Scholars interested in the legislative fate of particular measures have culled tiny slices of the debating process to illustrate legislative reactions to these measures. However, there has been very little serious general analysis of the debating process and other verbal behaviors in large public assemblies. There is virtually no literature covering verbal activities in informal public assemblies such as public meetings, party gatherings, or large demonstrations. The picture is different for verbal behavior studies in small groups. Thanks largely to the efforts of sociologists interested in group interaction processes, and some labor economists specializing in collective bargaining studies, a considerable literature exists on this topic. Much of it is directly relevant to understanding the bargaining process in small political groups.

Some general works which deal with various legislatures devote limited attention to verbal behavior within these bodies. Examples are Donald R. Matthews, *U.S. Senators and Their World* (Chapel Hill: University of North Carolina Press, 1960); Bertram M. Gross, *The Legislative Struggle* (New York: McGraw-Hill, 1953); Anthony Barker and Michael Rush, *The Member of Parliament and His Information* (London: George Allen and Unwin, 1970); and Peter G. Richards, *Parliament and Foreign Affairs* (Toronto: University of Toronto Press, 1967).

Several articles and books which focus mostly on passage of particular measures pay substantial attention to the debating process as such. These include D. A. Strickland, "On Ambiguity in Political Rhetoric: Defeat of the Rat Control Bill in the House of Representatives, July 1967," *Canadian Journal of Political Science*, 2 (1969), 338–344, and a study of Senate debating behavior by Robert G. Lehnen, "Behavior on the Senate Floor: An Analysis of Debate in the U.S. Senate," *Midwest Journal of Political Science*, 11 (1969), 505–521. Verbal tactics used to gain passage for the 1965 Education Act are detailed in Eugene Eidenberg and Roy D. Morey, *An Act of Congress: The Legislative Process and the Making of Education Policy* (New York: Norton, 1969). Similarly, the verbal tactics which led to the adoption of Medicare legislation are set forth in Max J. Skidmore, *Medicare and the American Rhetoric of Reconciliation* (University: University of Alabama Press, 1970).

Debate in the French Parliament centering around the selection of a new chief executive is analyzed in Constantin Melnik and Nathan Leites, *The House without Windows: France Selects a President* (Evanston: Row, Peterson, 1958). An even tighter focus on debate aspects in the British House of Commons is V. Herman, "Adjournment Debates in the House of Commons," *Parliamentary Affairs*, 26 (1972–73), 92–104. Herman analyzes the functions performed by adjournment debates during the 1966–67 sessions.

Two works which deal with special aspects of verbal behavior in public assemblies are Gerhard Loewenberg, "The Influence of Parliamentary Behavior on Regime Stability," *Comparative Politics*, 3 (1971), 177–200, which deals with the significance of consensus building through the process of public debate, and Bernard C. Cohen, *The Political Process and Foreign Policy: The Making of the Japanese Peace Settlement* (Princeton: Princeton University Press, 1957), which examines the process of consensus-building for a pending treaty, with particular emphasis on securing legislative consensus.

Verbal behavior in congressional committees and hearings is described and analyzed in Michael W. Kirst, *Government without Passing Laws: Congress' Nonstatutory Techniques for Appropriations Control* (Chapel Hill: University of North Carolina Press, 1969); Richard F. Fenno, Jr., *The Power of the Purse: Appropriations Politics in Congress* (Boston: Little, Brown, 1966); and, also by Fenno, "The House of Representatives and Federal Aid to Education," in Robert L. Peabody and Nelson Polsby, eds., *New Perspec-*

tives on the House of Representatives (Chicago: Rand McNally, 1962). See also Ralph K. Huitt, "The Congressional Committee: A Case Study," *American Political Science Review*, 48 (1954), 340–365.

Verbal behavior in the United Nations has been examined from several different perspectives. Examples include my two articles, "Conflict Images: An Assessment of the Middle East Debates in the United Nations," *Journal of Politics*, 32 (1970), 339–378, and "Perceptions of Middle East Conflict in the UN, 1953–65," *Journal of Conflict Resolution*, 13 (1969), 454–484; also R. L. Friedheim, J. B. Kadane, and J. K. Gamble, Jr., "Quantitative Content Analysis of the United Nations Seabed Debate: Methodology and a Continental Shelf Case Study," *International Organization*, 24 (1970), 479–502. Some studies which deal with particular issues handled by the United Nations also pay fleeting attention to debate tone and content. The importance of formal as well as informal verbal encounters of members of public assemblies, such as the United Nations, is described in Chadwick F. Alger, "Non-Resolution Consequences of the United Nations and Their Effect on International Conflict," *Journal of Conflict Resolution*, 5 (1961), 128–145.

While scholars have shied away from investigating verbal behavior in large public assemblies, they have delved with considerable zeal into the intricacies of negotiating sessions at small and large international conferences. General views of the bargaining process at the international level in various political settings are presented in Fred Charles Iklé, *How Nations Negotiate* (New York: Praeger, 1964); Arthur Lall, *Modern International Negotiation: Principles and Practice* (New York: Columbia University Press, 1966); and Johan Kaufmann, *Conference Diplomacy* (Dobbs Ferry: Oceana, 1968). Shorter discussions are Jack Sawyer and Harold Guetzkow, "Bargaining and Negotiations in International Relations," in Herbert Kelman, ed., *International Behavior* (New York: Holt, Rinehart and Winston, 1965); George Kent, "Determinants of Bargaining Outcomes," *Peace Research Society Papers*, 11 (1969), 23–42; and David H. Davis, "Consensus or Conflict: Alternative Strategies for the Bureaucratic Bargainer," *Public Choice*, 13 (1972), 21–29. A more general discussion of communications variables in political decision-making involving separate political entities is contained in Michael Haas's essay on "Communication Factors in Decision Making," *Peace Research Society Papers*, 12 (1969), 65–86.

Among studies which carefully analyze the elements of the bargaining process with a game-theoretical perspective are Thomas C. Schelling, *The Strategy of Conflict* (London: Oxford University Press, 1968), and, by the same author, *Arms and Influence* (New Haven: Yale University Press, 1966). Another good source is Anatol Rapoport, *Fights, Games and Debates* (Ann Arbor: University of Michigan Press, 1960). The relevance of the initial power position of the parties in international conflicts to the outcome of their negotiations is examined in Coral Bell, *Negotiation from Strength* (New York: Knopf, 1963).

Several studies examine bargaining behavior within a particular setting. Two examples are by Lloyd Jensen: "Soviet-American Bargaining Behavior in the Postwar Disarmament Negotiations," *Journal of Conflict Resolution*, 7 (1963), 522–541, and "Approach-Avoidance Bargaining in the Test Ban Negotiations," *International Studies Quarterly*, 12 (1968), 152–160. Verbal structuring of a situation for greatest success in bargaining is also explored in Jeremy J. Stone, *Strategic Persuasion: Arms Limitations through Dialogue* (New York: Columbia University Press, 1967).

The various verbal phases by which nations seek to maximize political gain and minimize losses during times of international crisis are described and illustrated in Oran R. Young, *The Politics of Force: Bargaining during International Crises* (Princeton: Princeton University Press, 1968). Illustrations include the Berlin crises of 1948–49 and 1961, the Taiwan Strait crisis of 1958, and the Cuban missile crisis of 1962. Young has also written a book on the role of the mediator in the bargaining process in international disputes, *The Intermediaries: Third Parties in International Crises* (Princeton: Princeton University Press, 1967). The propaganda aspects of international negotiations are detailed in Joseph L. Nogee, "Propaganda and Negotiation: The Case of the Ten-Nation Disarmament Committee," *Journal of Conflict Resolution*, 7 (1963), 510–521. A study which carefully delineates interaction patterns in international conferences is Diane S. Clemens, "The Structure of Negotiations: Dynamics and Interaction Patterns of the Crimean Conference," *Peace Research Society Papers*, 11 (1969), 57–65.

While airing of disparate viewpoints presents an opportunity for increasing understanding among negotiating parties and possibly reaching mutually satisfactory accommodations, adverse consequence may ensue as well. The disadvantages which may spring from a public airing of conflicts are highlighted in David Carlton, "Great Britain and the Coolidge Naval Disarmament Conference of 1927," *Political Science Quarterly*, 83 (1968), 573–598.

Most principles and techniques which are useful for negotiations in an international setting are also valid for various situations in domestic politics. Nonetheless, there are differences which spring from the uniqueness of the setting. The reader may find it useful to discover some of these differences by comparing the elements of negotiations in a domestic labor dispute with the elements affecting negotiations in international disputes. Useful works for such comparisons are Ann Douglas, *Industrial Peacemaking* (New York: Columbia University Press, 1962), and Carl Stevens, *Strategy and Collective Bargaining Negotiation* (New York: McGraw-Hill, 1963).

Additional insights into the bargaining process can be gleaned from a brief review of literature on principles of persuasion. Helpful studies include Carl I. Hovland, Irving L. Janis, and Harold H. Kelley, *Communications and Persuasion: Psychological Studies of Opinion Change* (New Haven: Yale University Press, 1953); Winston L. Brembeck and William S. Howell, *Persua-*

sion: A Means of Social Control (New York: Prentice-Hall, 1952); and Gary Cronkhite, *Persuasion: Speech and Behavioral Change* (Indianapolis: Bobbs-Merrill, 1969). An interesting study of the effectiveness of persuasion is Harvey London, Philip Meldman, and A. Van C. Lanckton, "The Jury Method: How the Persuader Persuades," *Public Opinion Quarterly*, 34 (1970), 171–183. Among students of persuasion in group settings, it is a disputed issue whether or not threats, deceptions, and lies are sound bargaining tactics. The issue is debated in George Kent, *The Effects of Threats* (Columbus: Ohio State University Press, 1967); Coral Bell, *Negotiation from Strength* (New York: Knopf, 1963); Herman Kahn, *On Escalation: Metaphors and Scenarios* (New York: Praeger, 1965); and Robert Jervis, *The Logic of Images in International Relations* (Princeton: Princeton University Press, 1970).

As mentioned earlier, verbal interactions in small bargaining groups have been studied extensively in both natural and experimental settings. Several general works by sociologists and political scientists present much of the relevant research. The reader is directed to Gerald M. Phillips, *Communications and the Small Group* (New York: Bobbs-Merrill, 1966); A. Paul Hare, Edgar F. Borgatta, and Robert F. Bales, eds., *Small Groups: Studies in Social Interaction* (New York: Knopf, 1965); Thomas W. Madron, *Small Group Methods and the Study of Politics* (Evanston: Northwestern University Press, 1969); and Robert T. Golembiewski, *The Small Group: An Analysis of Research Concepts and Operations* (Chicago: University of Chicago Press, 1962). An early work which has been updated through several editions is Dorwin Cartwright and Alvin F. Zander, *Group Dynamics: Research and Theory*, 3rd ed. (New York: Harper and Row, 1968). The reader should also consult the above section on verbal measurement techniques for a list of books which emphasize research techniques for examining small group verbal interactions.

Analyses of verbal interactions in congressional committees are particularly interesting for the student of verbal behavior in political settings. Recommended readings on this topic include: Paul Lutzker, "The Behavior of Congressmen in a Committee Setting: A Research Report," *Journal of Politics*, 31 (1969), 140–166; Richard F. Fenno, Jr., "The Appropriations Committee as a Political System," *American Political Science Review*, 56 (1962), 310–324; Seymour Scher, "Congressional Committee Members as Independent Agency Overseers: A Case Study," *American Political Science Review*, 54 (1960), 911–920; and Ralph K. Huitt, "The Congressional Committee: A Case Study," *American Political Science Review*, 48 (1954), 340–365.

Small group decision-making which is responsible for shaping foreign policy has been a recent focus of scholarly attention, often in an effort to devise methods for improving this dangerously imperfect process. A valuable study of the shortcomings of verbal aspects of decision-making at top levels in the American government is Alexander L. George, "The Case for Multiple Advocacy in Making Foreign Policy," *American Political Science Review*, 64 (1972), 751–785. For greater impact, it should be read along with Alexander L. George, David K. Hall, and William E. Simons, *The Limits of Coercive Diplomacy: Laos, Cuba, Vietnam* (Boston: Little, Brown, 1971). The pitfalls of the phenomenon of "group-think" which arise from psychological constraints imposed by interpersonal relations and communications among foreign policy makers are examined in Irving L. Janis, *Victims of Groupthink: A Psychological Study of Foreign-Policy Decisions and Fiascoes* (Boston: Houghton Mifflin, 1972).

A series of experiments arranged to solve international conflicts through control of verbal behavior during gatherings of political leaders has been carefully described and analyzed by John Burton, Leonard Doob, and their associates. Examples of Burton's work are *Conflict and Communication* (New York: Free Press, 1969) and "Resolution of Conflict," *International Studies Quarterly*, 16 (1972), 5–30. Critical comments by Jean-Pierre Cot (pp. 31–40) and Laura Nader (pp. 53–58) are appended to the latter. The work of Doob and his associates is discussed in *Resolving Conflict in Africa: The Fermeda Workshop* (New Haven: Yale University Press, 1970). Application of the controlled communications technique to a domestic conflict setting forms the subject of an article by Robert R. Blake, Jane S. Mouton, and Richard L. Sloma on "The Union-Management Intergroup Laboratory," *Journal of Applied Behavioral Science*, 1 (1965), 26–57. A critical appraisal of the Burton and Doob experiments is presented by Herbert C. Kelman, "The Problem-Solving Workshop in Conflict Resolution," in Richard L. Merritt, ed., *Communication in International Politics* (Urbana: University of Illinois Press, 1972), and Ronald J. Yalem, "Controlled Communication and Conflict Resolution," *Journal of Peace Research*, 3–4 (1971), 263–272.

Cultural norms which develop within a group and provide limits within which the bargaining process must move are delineated in James D. Barber, *Power in Committees: An Experiment in the Governmental Process* (Chicago: Rand McNally, 1966); Erving Goffman, *Strategic Interaction* (Philadelphia: University of Pennsylvania Press, 1970); and Eric Berne, *The Structure and Dynamics of Organizations and Groups* (Philadelphia: Lippincott, 1963). An interesting example of cultural differences in group norms, as they emerge in group interactions, is Brenda Danet, "The Language of Persuasion in Bureaucracy: 'Modern' and 'Traditional' Appeals to Israel Customs Authorities," *American Sociological Review*, 36 (1971), 847–859.

Works on Condensation Symbols

A good general introduction to the use of verbal symbols, including condensation symbols, is provided in Hugh Dalziel Duncan, *Symbols in Society* (New York: Oxford University Press, 1968), and Kenneth Burke, *Language as Symbolic Action* (Berkeley: University of California Press, 1966). Other helpful guides to the subject are A. James Gregor, *An Introduction to Metapolitics* (New York: Free Press, 1971), a series of essays in Lyman Bryson et al., eds., *Symbols and Values: An Initial Study* (New York: Harper, 1954), and Clifford Geertz, "Ideology as a Cultural System," in David E. Apter, ed., *Ideology and Discontent* (New York: Free Press, 1964). The reader should consult the introductory section of this essay for additional general sources on symbolism and myths.

A number of scholars have been interested in the varied meanings which specific condensation symbols have for different population groups. Examples of such studies are Joel D. Aberbach and Jack L. Walker, "The Meaning of Black Power," *American Political Science Review*, 64 (1970), 367–388, and Terry Nardin, "Language and Political Violence," *Peace Research Review*, 4 (1971), 52–63. A more general treatment is Martin E. Spencer's "Politics and Rhetorics," *Social Research*, 37 (1970), 597–623. Despite cultural variances among population groups, many images which are evoked by condensation symbols are widely shared because they are based on stereotypes. Numerous examples are presented in William Buchanan and Hadley Cantril, *How Nations See Each Other* (Urbana: University of Illinois Press, 1953), which shows that stereotypical images of foreign nationals can become condensation symbols whose meanings are shared nationwide. Other examples of condensation symbols whose meanings are closely linked to verbal stereotypes can be found in Kenneth E. Boulding, "National Images and International Systems," *Journal of Conflict Resolution*, 3 (1959), 120–131, and in Daniel Katz and Kenneth W. Braly, "Verbal Stereotypes and Racial Prejudice," in Guy E. Swanson, T. M. Newcomb, and Eugene L. Hartley, eds., *Readings in Social Psychology* (New York: Holt, 1952).

Condensation symbols need not necessarily take the form of single words or brief slogans. Murray Edelman, *The Symbolic Uses of Politics* (Urbana: University of Illinois Press, 1964), explains how language styles and various physical settings can serve as condensation symbols. Likewise, the use of myth and metaphor can become a form of condensation symbol, as described in Lee C. McDonald, "Myth, Politics and Political Science," *Western Political Quarterly*, 22 (1969), 141–150. The names of candidates for political office may also become positive or negative condensation symbols. An interesting explanation of voter reactions to such name symbols is given in Stephen R. Brown and John D. Ellithorp, "Emotional Experiences in Political Groups: The Case of the McCarthy Phenomenon," *American Political Science Review*, 64 (1970), 349–366.

Although condensation symbols can take many verbal forms, they have been studied most frequently in the form of so-called key words. Content analysts have combed verbal output for the presence or absence of these key words. From their findings they have drawn conclusions about value structures and the nature of political appeals in various societies and political situations. Many of the political symbols analyzed in the Hoover Institute Studies are condensation symbols, making these studies a productive source for examining the nature and uses of condensation symbols. The student of condensation symbols should therefore consult Ithiel de Sola Pool's *Symbols of Democracy* and *Symbols of Internationalism*, as well as *The Prestige Papers: A Survey of their Editorials*, all published by Stanford University Press in 1951 and 1952.

Additional examples of the nature and uses of condensation symbols can be found in Harold D. Lasswell, Nathan Leites et al., eds., *The Language of Politics: Studies in Quantitative Semantics* (Cambridge: MIT Press, 1965); Charles E. Osgood, "Conservative Words and Radical Sentences in the Semantics of International Politics," in Gilbert Abcarian and John W. Soule, eds., *Social Psychology and Political Behavior: Problems and Prospects* (Columbus: Charles E. Merrill, 1971); and Quincy Wright, "Symbols of Nationalism and Internationalism," in Lyman Bryson et al., eds., *Symbols and Values: An Initial Study* (New York: Harper, 1954).

Guidelines for inferring value structures and other political information from the use of condensation symbols are provided by Felix S. Cohen, "The Reconstruction of Hidden Value Judgments: Word Choices as Value Indicators," in the Bryson collection just cited, and in Martin Landau, "On the Use of Metaphor in Political Analysis," *Social Research*, 28 (1961), 331–353. Insights into the political significance of condensation symbols would be improved if scholars would trace the genesis and subsequent development of a number of such symbols, but there are few such histories. Two brief examples are Ronald D. Rotunda, "The 'Liberal' Label: Roosevelt's Capture of a Symbol," *Public Policy*, 26 (1968), 377–408, and W. Paul Adams, "Republicanism in Political Rhetoric before 1776," *Political Science Quarterly*, 85 (1970), 397–421. More general chronicles from which the reader can deduce how condensation symbols developed in connection with the civil rights movement are Robert L. Scott and Wayne Brockriede, *The Rhetoric of Black Power* (New York: Harper and Row, 1969), and Haig A. and Hamida Bosmajian, *The Rhetoric of the Civil Rights Movement* (New York: Random House, 1969).

A general discussion of the various types of condensation symbols available for political argument is presented in Martin E. Spencer, "Politics and Rhetorics," *Social Research*, 37 (1970), 597–623. Other studies which provide information on using condensation symbols to manipulate politics are Harold D. Lasswell, *Politics: Who Gets What, When and How* (New York: Meridian, 1958), and two shorter presentations: Murray Edelman, "Escalation and Ritualization of Political Conflict," *American Behavioral Scientist*, 13 (1969), 231–246, and Richard M. Merelman, "Learning and Legitimacy," *American Political Science Review*, 60 (1966), 548–561.

Among the condensation symbols which political actors use to elicit controlled responses from their audiences are euphemisms: symbols or phrases designed to diminish the impact of symbols with negative connotations. Insight into the uses of euphemisms is provided by George Orwell in *Animal Farm* (New York: Harcourt, Brace, 1946). A more analytical essay by the same author is "Politics in the English Language," in Maurice Stein et al., eds., *Identity and Anxiety* (Glencoe: Free Press, 1960). For a condemnation of euphemisms which hide the horrors of war, see Philip Green, *Deadly Logic: The Theory of Nuclear Deterrence* (Columbus: Ohio State University Press, 1966).

Several studies analyze the role which condensation symbols play during legislative battles; the studies in the previous section which deal with the enactment of legislation provide examples. Similarly, in the section on elite verbalizations and political rhetoric, the works dealing with the political rhetoric designed to sell candidates or to justify policies or legislative proposals are relevant. The symbolic aspects of war and the use of condensation symbols before, during, and after wars are discussed in Jerome D. Frank, *Sanity and Survival: Psychological Aspects of War and Peace* (New York: Random House, 1967). Condensation symbols in national anthems have been compared and analyzed in Joseph Zikmund II, "National Anthems as Political Symbols," *Australian Journal of Political History*, 15 (1969), 73–80.

How condensation symbols can be used to advance the cause of social movements is described in Hadley Cantril, *The Psychology of Social Movements* (New York: Wiley, 1941), as well as in a number of historical accounts which trace the rise and demise of such movements. Books dealing with the French Revolution of 1789 and the Russian Revolution of 1917, as well as with the European and American liberation movements of the early nineteenth century, are particularly instructive.

Author Index

Burton, John W., 254, 261, 265–269, 273, 358
Butt, Ronald, 240

Campbell, Angus, 242, 348
Campbell, James H., 116
Cantril, Hadley, 46, 106, 182, 289–290, 338, 359, 361
Carlton, David, 245, 356
Carmichael, Stokely, 302
Carroll, John B., 11, 334
Carroll, Lewis, 92
Cartwright, Dorwin P., 97, 357
Cassirer, Ernst, 9, 333
Cater, Douglas, 141
Cavell, Stanley, 334
Chappell, Vere C., ix, 334
de Charms, Richard, 74, 95, 119, 341
Chomsky, Noam, 14, 334
Choucri, Nazli, 13, 179–180, 191, 193, 336–337, 340, 350
Cirino, Robert, 349
Clemens, Diane S., 227, 356
Cleveland, Les, 184–186, 352
Cohen, Arthur R., 55–56, 339
Cohen, Bernard C., 136, 141, 144, 148, 224, 233, 237, 240, 347, 354
Cohen, Felix S., 296, 316, 318, 360
Cohen, Michael D., 229, 284
Collins, Nancy B., 116, 343
Connolly, James Evartz, 157
Connolly, William E., 335
Converse, Philip E., 242
Cooper, Chester L., 35, 237
Cot, Jean Pierre, 358
Cozean, John D., 150, 159, 348
Crespi, Irving, 64, 338
Cronkhite, Gary, 281–282, 357
Cyert, Richard, 274

Danet, Brenda, 30, 84, 259, 282, 341, 358
Daniel, Jack L., 281
Darnell, Donald K., 121–122, 343, 345
Davis, David H., 355
Davison, W. Phillips, 26
Deutsch, Karl W., xi, xiii, 28, 106, 137, 158, 168–170, 290, 336, 347–348
Deutsch, Morton, 39, 255, 284, 296

Dexter, Lewis A., 142
Donley, Richard E., 87, 208, 341
Donohue, George A., 153
Doob, Leonard W., 265, 268, 358
Douglas, Ann, 270, 275, 280–281, 356
Dovring, Karin, 30, 76, 81, 318, 335
Dulaney, William L., 109
Dulany, Don E., 311
Duncan, Hugh Dalziel, 6–7, 19, 23, 63, 68, 101, 221, 281, 296–297, 305, 352, 358
Dunham, Vera S., 181, 350
Dunn, Delmer D., 148
Dunphy, Dexter C., 81, 99, 143, 181, 342, 344, 350

Eckhardt, William, 95, 118, 341
Edelman, Murray, 65, 102, 177, 184, 188, 238, 258, 298–299, 305, 311, 315–316, 333, 352, 359–360
Edie, James M., 334
Edinger, Lewis J., 169–170
Efron, Edith, 349
Eidenberg, Eugene, 215, 236, 243, 354
Eliot, T. S., 92
Ellithorp, John D., 317, 359
Emerson, Rupert, xii
Emmert, Philip, 92, 113, 115, 117, 120–121, 123, 342, 345
Enloe, Cynthia, 310
Eulau, Heinz, 197, 229

Fadner, Raymond, 123
Fagen, Richard R., xii, 54, 88, 99, 197, 229, 338, 341
Feis, Herbert, 228
Fendrich, James M., 56, 70, 125
Fenno, Richard F., Jr., 217, 219, 221–222, 232, 242, 318, 354, 357
Ferencz, Benjamin B., 310
Ferguson, LeRoy, 197
Festinger, Leon, 53, 73, 97, 263, 339
Fink, C. F., 251
Finkelstein, Louis, 12, 37
Finlay, David J., 54, 88, 197, 229, 338, 341
Fisher, Glen H., 335
Fisher, Ronald J., 265
Fodor, Jerry A., 334
Foster, H. Schuyler, 159

Subject Index